D1799978

Operational Research for Emergency Planning in
Healthcare: Volume 2

The OR Essentials series
Series editor: **Simon JE Taylor**, Brunel University, UK

The *OR Essentials* series presents a unique cross-section of high quality research work fundamental to understanding contemporary issues and research across a range of Operational Research (OR) topics. It brings together some of the best research papers from the highly respected journals of the Operational Research Society, also published by Palgrave Macmillan.

OR deals with the use of advanced analytical methods to support better decision making. As a multidisciplinary field, it has strong links to management science, decision science, computer science and has practical applications in areas such as engineering, manufacturing, commerce, healthcare and defence.

OR has long-standing historical roots. However, as a modern discipline its origins lie in the years immediately before World War II when mathematical techniques were developed to address urgent defence problems. Now it is commonplace and a key discipline taught in universities across the world, at undergraduate and postgraduate levels. There are several international societies dedicated to the advancement of OR (e.g. the Operational Research Society and INFORMS – The Institute for Operations Research and the Management Sciences) and there are many high quality peer-reviewed journals dedicated to the topic.

The *OR Essentials* books are a vital reference tool for students, academics, and industry practitioners, providing easy access to top research papers on cutting-edge topics within the field of Operational Research.

*Titles include*:

Navonil Mustafee (*editor*)
OPERATIONAL RESEARCH FOR EMERGENCY
PLANNING IN HEALTHCARE: VOLUME 2

Simon JE Taylor (*editor*)
AGENT-BASED MODELLING AND SIMULATION

Roger A Forder (*editor*)
OR, DEFENCE AND SECURITY

Mike Wright (*editor*)
OPERATIONAL RESEARCH APPLIED TO SPORTS

John S Edwards (*editor*)
THE ESSENTIALS OF KNOWLEDGE MANAGEMENT

Navonil Mustafee (*editor*)
OPERATIONAL RESEARCH FOR EMERGENCY
PLANNING IN HEALTHCARE: VOLUME 1

---

The OR Essentials series
Series Standing Order ISBN 978–1–137–45360–0
(*outside North America only*)

You can receive future titles in this series as they are published by placing a standing order. Please contact your bookseller or, in case of difficulty, write to us at the address below with your name and address, the title of the series and the ISBN quoted above.

Customer Services Department, Macmillan Distribution Ltd, Houndmills, Basingstoke RG21 6XS

---

# Operational Research for Emergency Planning in Healthcare: Volume 2

Edited by

Navonil Mustafee
*Senior Lecturer in Operations Management,*
*University of Exeter Business School, UK*

First published 2016 by
PALGRAVE MACMILLAN

Palgrave Macmillan in the UK is an imprint of Macmillan Publishers Limited,
registered in England, company number 785998, of Houndmills, Basingstoke,
Hampshire RG21 6XS.

Palgrave Macmillan in the US is a division of St Martin's Press LLC,
175 Fifth Avenue, New York, NY 10010.

Palgrave Macmillan is the global academic imprint of the above companies
and has companies and representatives throughout the world.

Palgrave® and Macmillan® are registered trademarks in the United States,
the United Kingdom, Europe and other countries.

ISBN 978–1–137–57326–1

This book is printed on paper suitable for recycling and made from fully
managed and sustained forest sources. Logging, pulping and manufacturing
processes are expected to conform to the environmental regulations of the
country of origin.

A catalogue record for this book is available from the British Library.

A catalog record for this book is available from the Library of Congress.

Typeset by MPS Limited, Chennai, India.

# Contents

v

# List of Figures and Tables

## Figures

vii

## Tables

# 1
## Operational Research for Healthcare Emergency Planning at a Strategic Level

*N. Mustafee*

### 1.1 Context

Operational Research (OR) is the discipline that applies analytical methods to help make better and more informed decisions. Most of the quantitative techniques ('Hard OR') are mathematical, statistical or computational in nature; they are frequently used to arrive at optimal or near-optimal solutions to complex decision-making problems. 'Hard' OR is based on the assumption that systems are objective aspects of reality – they are generally independent of the observer; 'Soft' OR methods by contrast can best be characterized as assuming that a system is defined subjectively – it is a reflection of the observer's worldview (Wienke and Mustafee, 2015). Thus, 'Soft' OR expects the presence of a range of decision-makers or stakeholders who may all have differing and even conflicting objectives. The application of qualitative OR techniques in this sphere is to guide and structure the various stakeholders' discussions and build a shared understanding. Strategic level planning (which is the focus of Volume 2 of this book) is generally characterized by the presence and the active involvement of various actors in the decision-making process. Thus, 'Soft' OR can be used as a starting point for discussion regarding an appropriate resolution approach that all participants are prepared to implement.

OR is a vast field of study! A reference to the *'Wiley Encyclopedia of Operations Research and Management Science'* (Cochran et al., 2011) provides scholarly insights into the enormity of this discipline. The encyclopaedia is marketed as an 'unparallel undertaking' that is devoted towards the advancement of OR and is an eight-volume authoritative reference set made up of over 6,000 pages! The field of OR is also expanding! The *International Abstracts in Operational Research* (IAOR, n.d.) is an indicator of the growing literature in OR. IAOR indexes abstracts from OR/

MS journals as well as some specialized journals that are relevant to OR/ MS research (IAOR, n.d.). It is maintained by the *International Federation of Operational Research Societies (IFORS)* and is quoted to be the 'the only dedicated source for bibliographic and abstract information in operations research and management science' (IFORS, n.d.). It consists of 68,000 abstracts from over 145 journal titles (Miser, 2000); the number of journals has now increased to approximately 180. Mustafee and Katsaliaki (n.d.) report that in 1961 the first issue of IAOR listed work on models of common processes in 35 categories, on problems in 11 arenas of application and on 31 types of related theory development. By 1975, the numbers in these categories had reached 47, 34 and 53, respectively, and by 1998 they were 66, 43 and 77. In the specific case of healthcare OR there is evidence that this continues to be a growing area of research (Brailsford et al., 2009; Mustafee et al., 2010; Katsaliaki and Mustafee, 2011).

## 1.2   The triple lens

A way to describe the sheer enormity of OR content is through the identification of broad categories of *OR techniques*, their *domain of application (application area)* and *application context*. As mentioned in the introductory chapter of Volume 1 of this book, this is important because readers must not only build an understanding of the analytical methods that are discussed in this book, they should in addition possess domain knowledge which is specific to their area of work or study, and further, they should carefully consider the context of application since the choice of particular OR techniques can be largely dictated by specific problems that are to be solved! It therefore follows that this triple lens of technique-application-context will help readers to better appreciate the practical application of OR, and the 26 studies that have been presented in Volumes 1 and 2 of this book have been structured keeping this in mind (an outline of Volume 2 is presented in Table 1.1). Readers are referred to Chapter 1 of Volume 1 for examples of the broad categories of technique, application and context, which is based on a separate piece of research that focuses on the development of a classification scheme for OR/MS (Mustafee and Katsaliaki, n.d.).

## 1.3   Structure of volume two: a triple lens approach for the study of OR for emergency planning at a strategic level

The application of OR methods in healthcare has been widely reported in literature (Jun et al., 1999; Brailsford et al., 2009; Mustafee et al., 2010,

2013; Katsaliaki and Mustafee, 2011; Rais and Viana, 2011; Mustafee and Katsaliaki, 2015). Several studies have used these methods for emergency planning in healthcare. The two volumes of this book showcase studies that have applied OR methods for achieving heightened preparedness, better planning, and faster response to A&E and public health emergencies. The book covers four broad themes that are relevant to healthcare emergency planning. These are A&E, ancillary services, outbreak of epidemic and public health emergency response. A&E is core to emergency planning and the availability of adequate resources is crucial to saving lives. The second theme is that of ancillary services like ambulance service and healthcare supply chain. They support A&E and the wider healthcare operations. Planning for epidemics (the third theme) enables public health institutions to minimize the effect of outbreaks among the population. The final theme is on public health emergency response and it acknowledges the need for multi-agency planning using a qualitative approach to problem-solving. These themes intersect through the various parts and chapters of both the volumes of this book.

The focus of Volume 1 was on *OR for Emergency Planning at an Operational Level*. It consisted of 13 studies which were presented in three parts, namely, *OR for Locating Emergency Services* (Part I; three chapters), *OR for Operational Planning in Emergency Services* (Part II; six chapters) and *OR for Inventory Management in Emergency Services* (Part III; four chapters). The chapters included the application of mainly 'Hard' OR techniques, for example, mathematical modeling, MCDA, Bayesian decision model and discrete-event simulation (DES).

Volume 2 of this book is mainly on the application of *OR for Healthcare Emergency Planning at a Strategic Level*. It also includes a few literature review papers. Like Volume 1, this book consists of 13 studies which are organized under specific parts, namely, *OR for Assessment and Review of Emergency Services* (Part IV; Chapters 2–4), *OR for Policy Formulation in Emergency Services* (Part V, Chapters 5–6), *OR for Broader Engagement in Planning for Emergency Services* (Part VI, Chapters 7–10) and *Application of OR within the Wider Healthcare Context* (Part VII, Chapters 11–14). The chapters included in this volume are outlined in Table 1.1; for every chapter (except for Part VII) the table lists the OR technique, domain of application and context of use.

## 1.4   Overview of volume 2: A focus on strategic level planning

Following this introductory chapter, the book consists of 13 chapters that are organized into four parts. Part IV focuses on the *OR for Assessment*

*Table 1.1* An outline of volume 2 presented through the triple lens of technique-domain-context

| Volume 2 Chapter Number | The Triple Lens of Technique-Domain-Context | | |
| --- | --- | --- | --- |
| | OR Technique | OR Application Area (General / Specific) | OR Application Context |
| Chapter 2 | System Dynamics; Whole-systems Approach | Emergency Services / **Emergency and On-demand Health** | Whole-system review |
| Chapter 3 | Process Mapping; Discrete-event Simulation | Emergency Services / **A&E Department** | Assessing the impact of systems modeling in care redesign |
| Chapter 4 | Monte Carlo Simulation | Emergency Services / **First Responder** | Assessment of cardiac first responder schemes |
| Chapter 5 | Discrete-event Simulation | Emergency Services / **A&E Department** | Informing national policy development in A&E |
| Chapter 6 | System Dynamics | Emergency Services / **A&E Department** | Policy formulation in A&E |
| Chapter 7 | Qualitative System Dynamics | Emergency Services / **Acute Hospital** | Mapping of acute patient flows within the NHS |
| Chapter 8 | Critical Systems Thinking; Soft Systems Methodology | Public Health/ **Emergency Response** | Planning for a multi-agency counselling service that could be activated in the event of an emergency |
| Chapter 9 | Network-based Simulation | Public Health/ **Control of Epidemic** | Simulations for epidemiology as a pedagogical tool for public health education |
| Chapter 10 | Knowledge Management | Emergency Services / **Hospital and Ambulance Service** | Importance of taking a systems view of knowledge management |
| Chapter 11 | Literature review in the area of healthcare OR and modeling & simulation | | |
| Chapter 12 | Literature Review in the area of healthcare modeling & simulation | | |
| Chapter 13 | Literature review focusing on System Dynamics applications to European healthcare issues | | |
| Chapter 14 | Viewpoint on the contribution of OR in health from the context of UK NHS | | |

*and Review of Emergency Services* and is the subject of the next three chapters. In **Chapter 2** Brailsford et al. describe their use of qualitative and quantitative System Dynamics (SD) as part of a study that looked into whole-system review of emergency and on-demand healthcare in a city in England. They used interview data and qualitative SD to develop a conceptual map of possible patient pathways through the system; a quantitative SD model (stock-flow model) was then developed to simulate patient flows and to identify system bottlenecks. Mould et al. assess the impact of systems modeling in the redesign of an emergency department **(Chapter 3)** through two complimentary techniques, namely, process mapping and DES.  One finding from the study is that both process mapping of the patient pathway and simulation of the A&E can be valuable, though in some applications the simpler pathway mapping may alone be sufficient. Cairns, Marshall and Kee are the authors of **Chapter 4** in which they report the use of Monte-Carlo simulation to assess the effectiveness (including cost-effectiveness) of a public health scheme involving volunteer cardiac first responders. The scheme being assessed aims to improve survival of sudden cardiac arrest patients by reducing the time of emergency treatment (life-saving defibrillation); this is achieved through the active involvement of volunteers who are paged to respond to possible cardiac arrest incidents alongside the emergency medical services.

Part V of the book includes two studies on *OR for Policy Formulation in Emergency Services*. The study by Fletcher et al. (**Chapter 5**) describes a generic A&E simulation model that was developed by OR analysts within the Department of Health (DH). The primary purpose of the model was to inform the national policy team of significant barriers in achieving the national targets related to A&E. The model was used by stakeholders at the national level (DH, national A&E team) to discuss patient flows and the impact of potential policies. As the A&E model was developed to be a generic model its application was also possible at the local level, and indeed it was used as a consultancy tool to aid hospital trusts to improve their A&E departments. **Chapter 6** is a study by Lane, Monefeldt and Rosenhead, which was motivated by public concern over long waiting times for admissions. The authors developed a SD model to capture the interaction of demand pattern, A&E resource deployment, other hospital processes and bed numbers. The study revealed the interconnectedness of A&E service levels, bed provision and the experience of patients on waiting lists. One principal message that came out was that using A&E waiting times alone to judge the effect of bed reductions was a naïve approach.

Part VI is the Penultimate part of the book and concentrates on *OR for Broader Engagement in Planning for Emergency Services* and it consists of four chapters. Lane and Husemann present a study that uses qualitative SD for mapping the flows of acute patients within the NHS (**Chapter 7**). The UK Department of Health provided funding and broad direction for this study. The chapter mainly focuses on the activities associated with the three workshops wherein NHS staff were able to propose ideas for improving patient flows and on the basis of which a suite of maps of general acute hospitals were drawn up. The maps and ideas were then communicated back to the DoH and subsequently informed about the modernization of A&E. **Chapter 8** focuses on OR for disaster response. Planning related to Disaster Operations Management (DOM) generally takes place in multi-stakeholder environments, consisting of, for example, representatives from healthcare, fire brigade, police, disaster relief terms, politicians and indeed the vulnerable group who stand to be affected. In such environments the use of Soft OR methods like Soft Systems Methodology (Checkland, 1981), Qualitative SD, Strategic Option Development Analysis, etc. can be used for developing a shared understanding within this diverse group (Wienke and Mustafee, 2015). In Chapter 8 authors Gregory and Midgley report on one such 'Soft OR' study on multi-agency planning for disaster-response. The chapter describes how Critical Systems Thinking and methods from SSM were used in six, one-day workshops that were attended by representatives from 19 agencies (including four health authorities and the ambulance service) who came together to plan the basis for a counselling network that could be activated during an emergency. Further to the use of 'Soft OR' techniques (which are qualitative in nature), mathematical modeling, fuzzy sets, statistical techniques, decision theory and queuing theory have been used in relation to DOM, for example, for predicting environmental disasters, estimating damage, evacuation planning, among others (Wienke and Mustafee, 2015). Huang, Tsai and Wen are the authors of **Chapter 9**. The chapter focuses on the use of network-based simulation for teaching epidemiology. It is arguable that the use of public health simulations as a pedagogical tool enables students to better understand spreading situations; further it allows the analysis of disease patterns, prediction of epidemic dynamics and allows a safe environment for testing the possible effectiveness of public health interventions, all of which contribute towards better planning of emergencies associated with epidemic outbreak. There are also examples in Operations Management literature where business-simulation games like the *Blood Supply Chain Game* (Katsaliaki et al., 2014) have been used to train participants in making better decisions under pressure and in complex situations where an outcome arises from the interaction of multiple factors and interventions. A systems vision of knowledge management in emergency care is presented by authors Edwards, Hall and Shaw in **Chapter 10**; it draws upon research conducted in two healthcare organizations that appeared to be approaching knowledge management in a fragmented way and which prevented them from having a holistic view of the whole of the care process. The chapter explores the complexity of knowledge management in emergency healthcare and draws the distinction for knowledge management between managing local and operational knowledge, and global and clinical knowledge. As a summary of this part of the book, broader engagement in emergency planning could be achieved by involving multiple stakeholders (including the public) in the decision process, knowledge management and through the introducing of simulation and game-based learning.

Part VII of the book consists of four chapters and it focuses on the *Application of OR within the Wider Healthcare Context*; its purpose is to inform readers of the OR techniques that have been used in the wider healthcare context (which also includes emergency planning). The first three chapters are literature reviews in healthcare and provides evidence of the application of OR. In **Chapter 11** authors Brailsford et al. present a systematic approach towards the analysis of academic literature on modeling in healthcare. The aim of their study was to analyse the range of OR modeling approaches (this included qualitative systems modeling, mathematical modeling, statistical modeling, statistical analysis and simulation), together with the specific domains of application and the level of implementation. Katsaliaki and Mustafee **(Chapter 12)** employ a methodological approach for conducting a review of literature pertaining to healthcare simulation. Their review was restricted to the following four simulation techniques – Monte Carlo Simulation, DES, SD and Agent-based Simulation. They reviewed approximately 250 high-quality journal papers published between 1970 and 2007. The results present a classification of the extant literature according to the simulation techniques they employ; the impact of published literature in healthcare simulation; a report on demonstration and implementation of the studies' results; the sources of funding; and the software used. In **Chapter 13**, author Dangerfield takes a European perspective to review both qualitative and quantitative SD models that address healthcare issues. Bearing in mind the strategic orientation of SD modeling, the author highlights two main purposes for developing SD models in healthcare, namely, the model as a tool of persuasion and the model as a frame for evaluation of tactical studies. **Chapter 14** is the concluding chapter of this two-volume book. It presents a viewpoint by Royston on the past, present and future contribution of OR in UK healthcare. The viewpoint is also a piece of insightful commentary that draws on 30-odd years of the author's personal experience working in this area. The aim of this chapter is to stimulate reflective thinking and to promote proactive action among the readers of this book, who are indeed the OR practitioners, researchers, healthcare managers and policymakers of the future!

## 1.5   Chapter summary

This book (Volume 2) presents a collection of studies that have applied both qualitative OR (e.g., Problem Structuring Methods, Soft Systems Methodology, Critical Systems Thinking and Qualitative System Dynamics) and quantitative methods (e.g., Quantitative System Dynamics, Monte Carlo Simulation and Discrete-event Simulation) for strategic-level decision-making in the context of healthcare emergency planning. The studies focus on the use of OR for assessment of emergency services, its application in policy formulation and how such methods facilitate broader public engagement in emergency preparedness and response. Further the book presents rigorous reviews on the application of OR in the wider healthcare context. It is expected that the book will serve as an important reference source for policymakers, NHS trusts, managers, clinicians, researchers and OR practitioners working in this area.

### References

Brailsford, S. C., Harper, P. R., Patel, B. and Pitt, M. (2009). 'An Analysis of the Academic Literature on Simulation and Modelling in Healthcare'. *Journal of Simulation*, 3(3): 130–140.

Checkland, P. (1981). *Systems Thinking, Systems Practice*. Wiley: Chichester.

Cochran, J. J., Cox, Jr., L. A., Keskinocak, P., Kharoufeh, J. P. and Smith, J. C. (2011). *Wiley Encyclopedia of Operations Research and Management Science*. New York, US: John Wiley.

IAOR. (n.d.). International Federation of Operational Research Societies – International Abstracts in Operations Research (IAOR). Accessed May, 2015. http://www.palgrave-journals.com/iaor.

IFORS. (n.d.). International Federation of Operational Research Societies – IAOR. Accessed May, 2015. http://ifors.org/web/iaor/.

Jun, J. B., Jacobson, S. H. and Swisher, J. R. (1999). 'Application of Discrete-Event Simulation in Health Care Clinics: A Survey' *Journal of the Operational Research Society*, 50(2): 109–123.

Katsaliaki, K. and Mustafee, N. (2011). 'Applications of Simulation Research within the Healthcare Context'. *Journal of the Operational Research Society*, 62(8): 1431–1451.

Katsaliaki, K., Mustafee, N. and Kumar, S. (2014). 'A Game-Based Approach towards Facilitating Decision Making for Perishable Products: An Example of Blood Supply Chain'. *Expert Systems with Applications*, 41(9): 4043–4059.

Miser, H. J. (2000). 'The Easy Chair: What OR/MS Workers Should Know about the Early Formative Years of Their Profession'. *Interfaces* 30: 99–111.

Mustafee, N. and Katsaliaki, K. (n.d.). *A Keyword Classification Scheme for OR/MS*. Submitted.

Mustafee, N. and Katsaliaki, K. (2015). 'Simulation for Sustainable Healthcare' – Guest Editorial for the Special Issue on Modelling and Simulation for Sustainable Healthcare. *Journal of Simulation*, 9(2): 83–85. Palgrave Macmillan.

Mustafee, N., Katsaliaki, K. and Taylor, S. J. E. (2010). 'Profiling Literature in Healthcare Simulation'. *SIMULATION: Transactions of the Society of Modelling and Simulation International*, 86(8–9): 543–558.

Mustafee, N., Katsaliaki, K., Williams, M. D. and Gunasekaran, A. (2013). 'Healthcare Operations Management through Use of Simulation: An Introduction to the Special Issue'. *Journal of Enterprise Information Management*, 26(1 and 2): 5–7.

Rais, A. and Viana, A. (2011). 'Operations Research in Healthcare: A Survey'. *International Transactions in Operational Research*, 18(1): 1–31.

Wienke, A. and Mustafee, N. (2015). 'An Investigation of "Soft" Operations Research Methods to Inform Hybrid Simulation Studies on Environmental Disasters'. In *Proceedings of the 2015 Spring Simulation Multi-Conference (SpringSim'15) – ANSS Symposia*, 12–15 April 2015, Alexandria, VA: Society for Modelling and Simulation International (SCS).

# Part IV
# OR for Assessment and Review of Emergency Services

# 2

# Emergency and On-Demand Healthcare: Modeling a Large Complex System

S. C. Brailsford[1], V. A. Lattimer[2], P. Tarnaras[1] and J. C. Turnbull[2]

[1] University of Southampton, Southampton, UK
[2] School of Nursing and Midwifery, University of Southampton, Southampton, UK

*This paper describes how system dynamics was used as a central part of a whole-system review of emergency and on-demand healthcare in Nottingham, England. Based on interviews with 30 key individuals across health and social care, a 'conceptual map' of the system was developed, showing potential patient pathways through the system. This was used to construct a stock-flow model, populated with current activity data, in order to simulate patient flows and to identify system bottle-necks. Without intervention, assuming current trends continue, Nottingham hospitals are unlikely to reach elective admission targets or achieve the government target of 82% bed occupancy. Admissions from general practice had the greatest influence on occupancy rates. Preventing a small number of emergency admissions in elderly patients showed a substantial effect, reducing bed occupancy by 1% per annum over 5 years. Modelling indicated a range of undesirable outcomes associated with continued growth in demand for emergency care, but also considerable potential to intervene to alleviate these problems, in particular by increasing the care options available in the community.*

## 2.1 Introduction

In this paper, we describe an application of system dynamics to a very large, complex system: the entire healthcare system in the city of

Reprinted from *Journal of the Operational Research Society*, 55: 34–42, 2004, 'Emergency and On-Demand Healthcare: Modeling a Large Complex System', by S. C. Brailsford, V. A. Lattimer, P. Tarnaras and J. C. Turnbull. With kind permission from Operational Research Society Ltd. All rights reserved.

Nottingham, England, or to be more precise that part of it concerned with the delivery of emergency or 'unscheduled' care. The model was developed as part of a research project led by Dr Valerie Lattimer of the School of Nursing and Midwifery at the University of Southampton. This project, commissioned in 2001 by the (then) Nottingham Health Authority, was itself part of a larger, ongoing project in Nottingham, known as the Emergency Care–On Demand (ECOD) project.[1] In Nottingham, emergency hospital admissions have risen dramatically in recent years. The ECOD project was designed to look at the whole healthcare system, to determine why demand is so high, and to investigate what could be done to alleviate this pressure. The Southampton contribution involved carrying out a system review and providing research support to the ECOD project.

Emergency or unscheduled care can be provided either in hospital (the secondary sector) or in the community (the primary sector). Many emergency hospital admissions occur as a result of patient visits to a hospital Accident and Emergency (A&E) Department. Patients can also be admitted directly to the wards, usually as a result of a referral by a General Practitioner (GP). In both cases, some patients may arrive by ambulance whereas others travel to hospital independently. A third group of emergency patients are admitted directly from outpatient clinics. In the community, unscheduled care is provided in a number of ways. In normal surgery hours, patients may request urgent or same-day GP appointments. After the surgery is closed, patients wishing to see a doctor urgently usually need to contact an out-of-hours GP service. This may be a cooperative of local GPs or a commercial deputizing service. Very few individual GPs now provide their own out-of-hours cover. Other services are available, including NHS Direct, a national 24/7 telephone help-line where people can seek medical advice and information. Staffed by nurses, who can seek medical opinion or summon an ambulance if necessary, this service was intended to enable people to make better decisions about accessing healthcare. Nottingham has a well-established NHS Direct, which is integrated with the largest GP cooperative Nottingham Emergency Medical Services (NEMS). Patients calling out of surgery hours simply dial the NHS Direct number, and if a doctor's visit is required, will be transferred directly through to NEMS and given an emergency appointment.

Another Government initiative, launched a couple of years after NHS Direct, was the introduction of 'Walk-in Centres', often located in shopping centres or supermarkets,–where people can attend without an appointment. This is also a nurse-run system whose aim is to treat, or advise about, minor conditions, thus (in theory) freeing up the time of GPs and hospital A&E Departments to deal with more serious cases. Nottingham has had a Walk-in Centre since June 2000. Other community services providing health advice or access to the healthcare system include Social Services, pharmacist shops, the dental services, and community mental health teams. Finally, the '999' emergency services—Fire, Police and obviously the Ambulance Service—provide emergency care and access to the NHS system.

## 2.2   Background to the problem

Nottingham is a city of about 640 000 inhabitants in the East Midlands of England. The city is served by two acute NHS Hospital Trusts, Queens Medical Centre (QMC) and Nottingham City Hospital (NCH). Both are teaching hospitals. NCH has approximately 1000 beds. Of 77 230 admissions to NCH between April 2000 and March 2001, 25 755 (33%) were emergency admissions. QMC has 1441 beds, including approximately 1000 acute beds. QMC admitted 97 850 patients in 2000–2001, of whom 37 789 (39%) were emergency admissions. QMC has the only A&E department in the city. Outpatient attendances and in-patient admission rates are approximately three times the national average, although A&E attendances decreased slightly (1.5%) in 2000–2001 over the previous year. At both hospitals, there has been an increase in people needing emergency care for the past 3 years (see Table 2.1). The A&E department at QMC is one of the busiest in England, seeing over 120 000 patients between April 2000 and March 2001. All areas of the system are experiencing increasing pressures, manifesting itself in long waiting times for patients, stressed and overworked staff, hospital wards running close to capacity limits, and fewer elective (planned) admissions as the hospitals struggle to cope with the workload generated by the emergencies.

This problem is by no means confined to Nottingham. Recent reports by the UK Audit Commission[2,3] have highlighted the fact that despite

*Table 2.1*   Increases on the previous year's emergency admissions to Nottingham hospitals

|       | 1999–2000 | 2000–2001 |
| ----- | --------- | --------- |
| QMC   | 4.7%      | 5.6%      |
| NCH   | 2.3%      | 10.1%     |

some improvements in a few areas, by and large in England and Wales A&E waiting times, both to see a doctor and also to be admitted to hospital, have increased steadily since 1996. In 1996, about 72% of all patients were seen within 1 h of arrival in A&E, but this had fallen to about 53% by 2000. In 1996, about 89% of patients who needed in-patient care were admitted within 4 h, but this had fallen to 76% by 2000.[3] There is also significant unexplained variation between departments; there is a tendency for larger departments to have longer waits, but the association is weak—in fact, the Audit Commission found that the most significant single factor influencing waiting time was location in or out of London. Since 1996 patient numbers attending A&E in England and Wales have increased by 1% per annum, whereas the number of nurses has remained roughly the same.[3] Nurse workloads vary widely between departments (from less than 1000 to more than 2000 patients per nurse per annum). However, the total number of doctors has increased by 10% since 1998, especially in the more senior 'non-consultant career grades'.[3] This is not, therefore, a simple problem of supply and demand, neither is it a straightforward issue of maximizing the throughput of a production system. The Audit Commission report suggests that long waiting times are caused by 'a host of managerial and organizational differences as much by resources and staff levels'.[3]

The ECOD project grew out of an earlier initiative for winter crisis planning in Nottingham, when it became apparent that the 'crisis' was a chronic state of affairs rather than a temporary acute problem. A Steering Committee was set up early in 2001, containing representatives from all the healthcare providers in Nottingham, and a Project Team formed, chaired by a local GP and including a full-time project manager. The aim of the ECOD project was to develop a new Local Services Framework for emergency care, which would form the basis of future strategy in Nottingham. The University of Southampton team began work in August 2001 and completed the research project in April 2002. There were four key research questions to be addressed:

- How is the emergency/on demand system currently configured and what organisational systems, processes and responsibilities support it?
- What characteristics of demand, demand management and patient flows can be identified from retrospective analysis of activity data, observational data and the views of key informants?
- How should the emergency care/on demand system be developed to respond to health policy and local needs, and what are the economic implications?

- To what extent do community preferences account for current use of the emergency care/on demand system and how can they inform its development?

The research project itself has been described elsewhere[4] and comprised several strands, involving a literature review, activity data collection and analysis, stakeholder interviews and a patient preference survey.[5] In this paper, we shall describe the contribution of two simulation models, a system dynamics model of the whole system and a smaller discrete-event simulation model of the A&E department, in helping to provide answers to the first three of these four questions.

## 2.3   Choice of modelling approach

An early decision was whether to adopt a discrete or continuous simulation approach. Historically, there have been very few examples in the healthcare modelling literature of discrete-event simulation (DES) models for very large populations.[6] This is essentially because a DES model with over a hundred thousand entities (ie patients) would require a vast amount of computer memory and would be very slow to run. Despite advances in computing power and the use of efficient queue sorting techniques, DES models are still time-consuming to run, since every individual patient's 'life history' is modelled. Moreover, multiple iterations must be performed to account for random variation. These problems do not arise for system dynamics, which is not stochastic and does not model patients at the individual level.

System dynamics (SD) is an analytical modelling approach originally developed by Jay Forrester[7,8] in the 1960s in his work on 'industrial dynamics'. SD combines qualitative and quantitative aspects, and aims to enhance understanding of a system and the relationships between different system components. The concepts of feedback and causal effects are important in SD. Surprisingly, perhaps, there have been relatively few applications of SD in healthcare, compared with the vast number of DES applications.[9] Dangerfield and Roberts' SD models for HIV/AIDS are well known.[10] A more recent example is Townshend and Turner's model[11] for screening for *Chlamydia*, a major cause of infertility. Townshend and Turner chose SD partly because the populations in this model were large, and partly because SD could incorporate the feedback effects due to re-infection of treated people, and the reduction in the prevalence of *Chlamydia* after screening. Wolstenholme's model[12] was one of the first well-known applications of qualitative SD in healthcare, and showed that an (unintended) effect of the UK's 1993 Community Care Act would in fact be to increase social service spending. Another well-known SD example, focusing on A&E, is David Lane's model,[13] which was designed to explore the relationships between waiting times in A&E and bed closures. The argument was that bed reductions led to cancelled elective admissions and this led to more people presenting in A&E, partly as a direct result of the deterioration in their health and partly as a behavioural response by doctors wishing to get their patients admitted 'by the back door'. The key finding was that the major impact of bed shortages was not on emergency admissions, but was felt first on elective admissions, so that using A&E waiting times to measure the effect of bed shortages was misleading.

In the Nottingham study, we were dealing with a very large, complex system involving a population of over 600 000 potential patients. Furthermore, we considered that although the specific pathways followed by individual patients were of interest, they were of less importance than understanding the major flows of people through the 'front doors' to the NHS, and gaining insight into the general structure of the system and the relationships between its component parts. The problems experienced in A&E, for example, were not principally felt to be due to high variability in casemix or staffing levels, but more to the sheer volume of demand and consequent pressure on resources. Finally, we were less concerned with the waiting times of individual people than with the general flow of patients through the system, in order to identify bottlenecks. Thus, system dynamics was chosen as our modelling approach and we used both qualitative and quantitative aspects.

## 2.4   Phases of model development

### 2.4.1   Qualitative phase

The aim of this phase was to develop understanding of the ECOD system, not only by the research team but also by the stakeholders in the system. It was not merely a preliminary stage to the quantitative modelling, but was important in its own right. Many useful insights were gained as a result of the development of the conceptual map and through the interview process.

During August 2001, the research team made an orientation visit to Nottingham, in which a first-pass 'conceptual map' of the system was drawn up. The first stage of this was to list the 'front doors' or access points to the healthcare system, and then to expand this to show the connections between these access points and the other parts of the system. A highly simplified version of this map is shown in Figure 2.1.

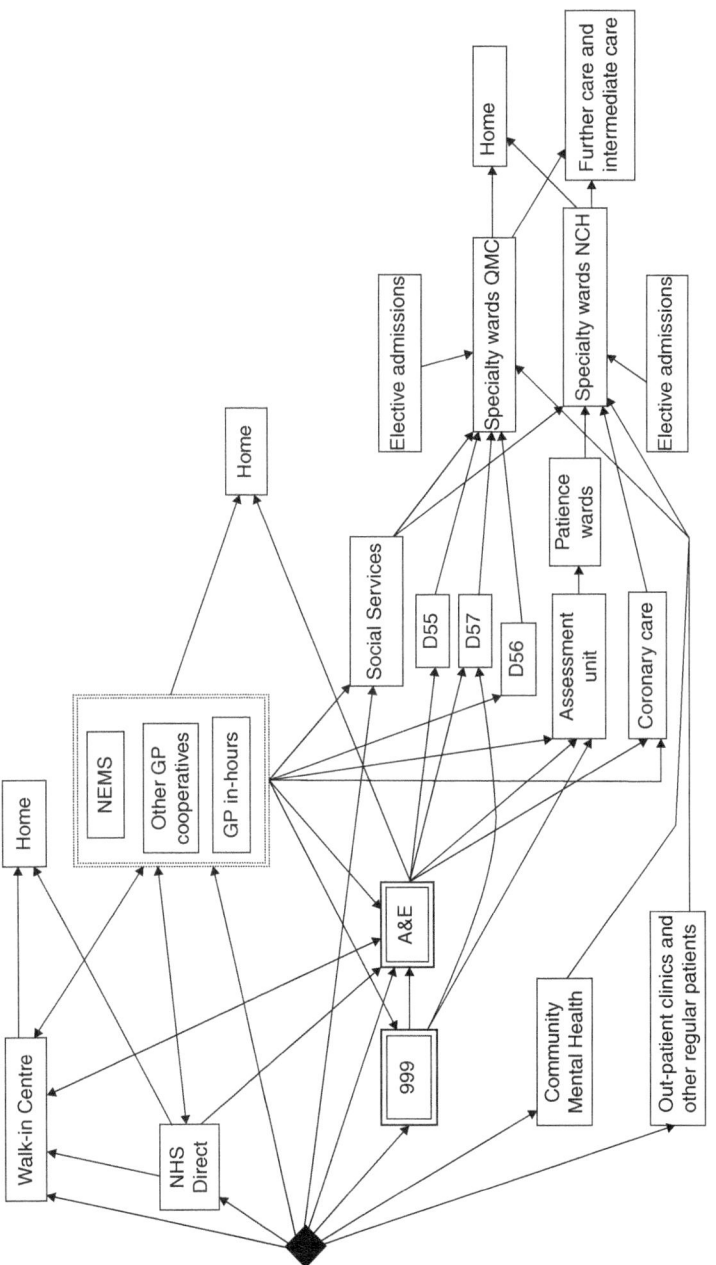

*Figure 2.1* Simplified 'conceptual map' of the emergency healthcare system in Nottingham. D55, D56 and D57 are acute admission wards in QMC

The diamond on the far left-hand side represents the patient's initial decision to contact the health service. The conceptual map was printed on A3 paper and used as the basis of 30 semi-structured interviews with key individuals from all the main healthcare providers, together with patient representatives. These interviews took place between September and November 2001. These 'stakeholders' were selected in consultation with the Project Team and the Steering Committee. The participants' initial agreement was sought by telephone and they were sent a copy of the interview schedule in advance, to allow time for preparation. All but one of the interviews were tape-recorded and later transcribed for analysis.

During the interviews, participants were asked about their work roles and the capacity they felt they had to influence the interface between their part of the system and other components. This led on to a discussion of the interfaces between components and the factors that might influence patient flows through the system. Participants were asked to draw on the map to show these influences and to annotate or alter the map in any way they felt appropriate. As a result a final agreed version of the map was derived, which was later used as the basis for a quantitative computer model of the system using the software STELLA.[14]

### 2.4.2   Quantitative phase

The aim of this phase was to facilitate experimentation with various potential changes in service configurations and demand rates. A stock-flow modelling approach was used, where stocks represented accumulations of patients (eg, waiting to see a GP, waiting for treatment in A&E, or occupying a bed in an acute admission ward) and the flows were the admission, transfer, treatment and discharge rates.

STELLA (also known as *ithink*) is a user-friendly package with a drag-and-drop user interface which allows the modeller to develop the model without the need for programming. The layout of the computer screen followed that of the conceptual map, so that the top half represented the primary care sector (in-hours and out-of-hours GP surgeries, NHS Direct and the Walk-in Centre) and the bottom half represented the secondary sector (the two main hospitals). In the middle was the Ambulance Service, Social Services and the A&E Department. We did not attempt to model every single hospital ward, but just the admissions wards. Onward transfers to the main specialty wards after a stay in an admissions ward were not modelled in detail, as we were concerned principally with patient flows within the emergency system. STELLA uses *submodels* to make the model more transparent by concealing

21

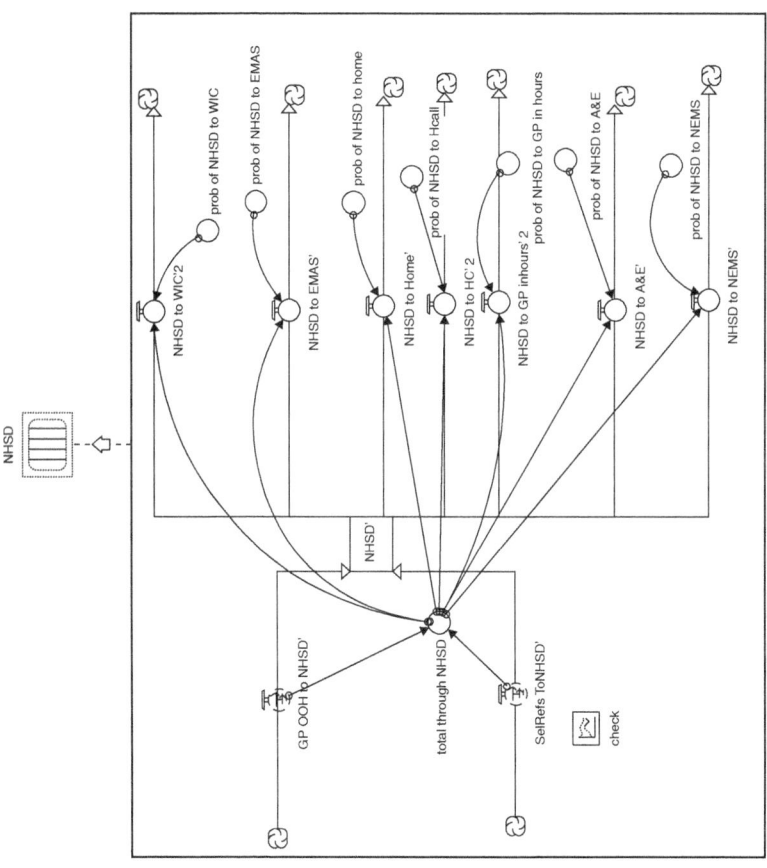

*Figure 2.2*  The NHS Direct submodel of the STELLA model

detail, and these were used for each of the sectors. We used a single submodel to represent all the main specialty wards in each hospital.

For example, Figure 2.2 shows the internal flows within the NHS Direct submodel. As a result of the integration of NHS Direct with the GP out-of-hours cooperative NEMS, patients may arrive from two sources, depending on the time of day. During surgery hours, every caller is an NHS Direct 'self-referral', but outside surgery hours some patients will be calling NHS Direct in order to contact NEMS. Inside the NHS Direct submodel, patients are routed on to one of seven possible destinations: the Walk-in Centre, the ambulance service, NEMS, the commercial out-of-hours GP deputizing service HealthCall, the in-hours GP surgery, A&E, or 'home', meaning given self-care advice over the telephone. In this and the other front door submodels, we were not concerned with patient waiting times, but rather with the proportions of patients routed on to other providers. The outflows from the NHS Direct submodel become inflows to the seven destination sectors.

Other submodels, for example, the Assessment Unit (the acute admissions unit at NCH) contain information about the bed capacity and the influence of various factors, such as patient age, bed occupancy rates and day of week on the length of stay. The model thus allowed a top-level, global view of the whole system, with the capability of drilling down to lower levels of detail in specific areas if necessary.

The STELLA model was populated with data for the year April 2000–March 2001, obtained from the various providers in Nottingham. These comprised the patient arrivals, broken down where possible by hour and day, sex and age band and where appropriate category of urgency; the source of the arrival, and the destination (eg emergency hospital admission, discharge home or elsewhere). Hospital length of stay data were derived from the Hospital Episode Statistics provided by the Department of Health.[15] This enabled flow balance cross-checking to be carried out, although the quality and level of detail of the data were variable. The outflow to B reported by A must equal the inflow from A reported by B. Unfortunately, no system-wide data were available for the in-hours GP sector, although we collected prospective data for a single week from four individual practices. We therefore had to rely solely on the hospital data regarding GP admissions, which essentially produced a discontinuity in the model for this particular flow.

As in all stock-flow systems, the contents of each stock or reservoir are updated at regular intervals by solving a set of difference equations representing the inflows and outflows from that stock. The choice of the time-step d*t* was difficult, given the wide range in activity durations (some only took minutes, others took days or even weeks), but we chose a value of d*t* equal to 2.4 h (0.1 days, 144 min). STELLA presents results in the form of graphs and tables, but most of our output was exported to Excel for analysis and presentation purposes. The output included the throughput of each 'front door' and the occupancy rates of each of the wards and hospital departments. STELLA allows the user to break down stocks and flows into subscripted arrays; for example, to classify patients by age, but it is not possible to combine an arrayed model with submodels. We decided that the benefits of using submodels outweighed the benefits of arrays, as we were able to account for age where necessary by using extra stocks, flows and auxiliary variables.

### 2.4.3  Model validation

The validation of SD models is a thorny topic. It has been argued[16] that validation of qualitative models should be carried out with the client as an ongoing dialogue during the model-building process, and is essentially a 'white box' process,[17] where the client knows, understands and trusts the internal structure of the model. The aim of qualitative models is not to produce point estimates or to 'optimize', but to gain insights into the system and learn about the way it behaves. On the other hand, quantitative SD models can be validated, in the same way as any other numerical simulation model,[16] by a 'black box' process[17] where emphasis is not on the model structure, but on the output it produces.

In our case, we used both approaches. We developed the model in close collaboration with the Steering Group during frequent visits to Nottingham. In addition to the inflow–outflow balance checking described above, we carried out 'black box' validation by running the model for the period April 2000 to March 2001, using the known arrivals data, and comparing the model output with real-life system performance data which had not been used in the construction of the model. For example, we used the total daily bed occupancy (formerly known as 'midnight bed state' data) supplied by the hospitals' Information Management and Technology Departments, and compared this with the corresponding model output by aggregating all the individual ward bed occupancies (see Figure 2.3), to give confidence that the model was producing sensible output. Similar plots were obtained for other output parameters such as individual ward occupancies.

24

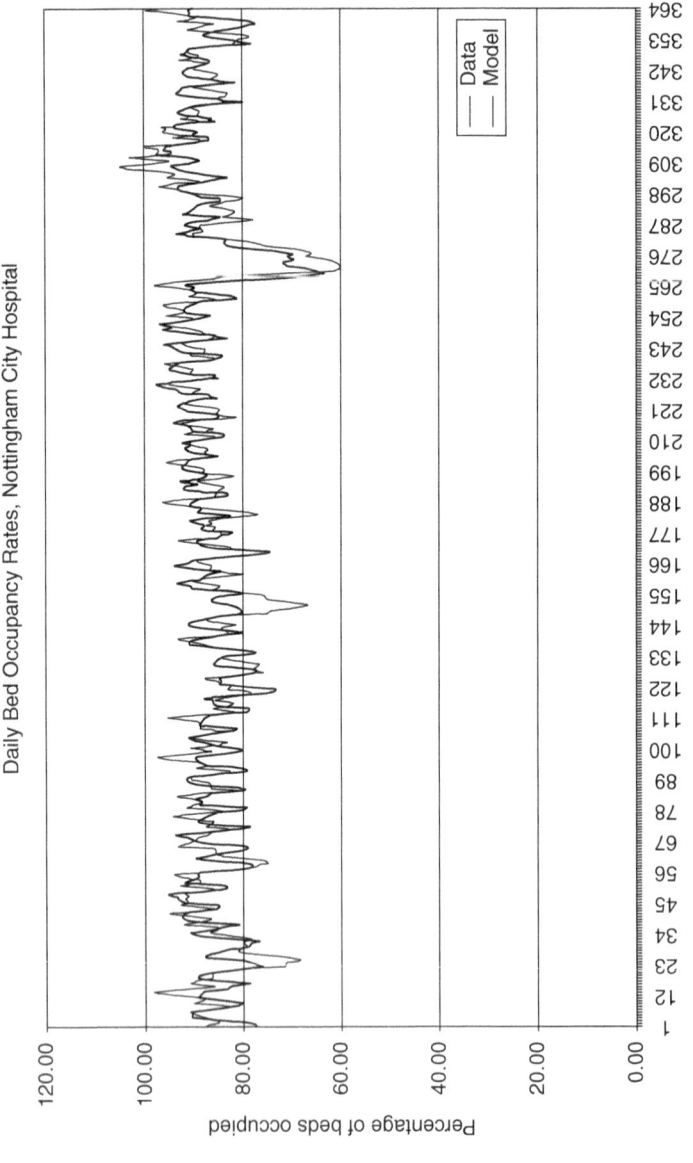

*Figure 2.3* Model validation, using total daily bed occupancy of NCH for 2000–2001

## 2.5   Scenario testing: model results

The Steering Committee suggested a range of scenarios for testing, based on the comments of the interview participants. For example, it was suggested that GPs are admitting some patients as emergencies in order to get investigations carried out, which could equally well be performed as day cases or even outpatients, because of the lack of suitable facilities. This is a similar behavioural response to that identified in Lane's study in London.[12] A community Diagnostic and Treatment Centre (DTC) where such tests could be carried out could therefore prevent many 'unnecessary' admissions.

A planning horizon of 5 years was used. The scenarios included the 'Doomsday scenario' (maintaining current growth in demand with no additional resources) and a variety of possible alternatives, including:

- 3% year-on-year growth in GP referrals for planned admissions,
- reduced emergency admissions for certain patient groups (eg the elderly or people with respiratory disease), for example, by the use of a DTC or other community initiatives,
- earlier discharge of the elderly to nursing homes,
- the effects of 'streaming' in the A&E department, that is, separate resources for certain patient groups.

The key outputs from the system map and STELLA model were initially, the insights gained into different parts of the system by people seeing it as a whole for the first time. Simple influence diagrams describing parts of the system were found to be a powerful tool in stimulating debate. For example, it could be argued that long waiting times in A&E are not necessarily always a bad thing, in that the expectation of a long wait might discourage 'inappropriate' attenders and lead them to seek help elsewhere, perhaps in the Walk-in Centre or by phoning NHS Direct. The patient preference study[5] showed that many people were indeed deterred by the prospect of a long wait and would only go to A&E if they felt they really needed to be there (eg, if they thought they needed an X-ray). Thus, inadequately thought-out initiatives designed to reduce waiting times in A&E might actually turn out to be counterproductive.

The first main result from the scenarios was that the system is currently operating dangerously close to capacity. This reinforced the message coming across from many of the stakeholder interviews. The model showed that if growth in emergency admissions continues at the current rate, both hospitals will see a significant decrease in the number

Table 2.2   Average percentage occupancy of both hospitals, assuming a sustained year-on-year decrease of 3% in emergency admissions of people aged over 60 years

|                | NCH  | QMC  |
|----------------|------|------|
| 'Status quo'   | 86.7 | 84.7 |
| 2000–2001      | 85   | 83   |
| 2001–2002      | 84   | 82   |
| 2002–2003      | 83   | 81   |
| 2003–2004      | 82   | 80   |
| 2004–2005      | 80   | 79   |

of elective admissions within 4 years. City Hospital, for example, could expect to see at least a 25% drop in elective admissions by 2005 (from 1100 per month in 2000–2001, to 700 in 2004–2005). The scenario where planned GP admissions were constrained to increase by 3% per annum was even worse, with *average* bed occupancies exceeding 100% by 2005 (assuming no additional resources).

The model also showed how small changes to one part of the system can have a considerable impact elsewhere in the system. For example, the effect on average total bed occupancy of sending 3% of patients aged over 60 to a DTC instead of admitting them is shown in Table 2.2. If a 3% reduction were maintained year-on-year for 5 years, a significant decrease in total occupancy could be achieved. The bed occupancy target for 2004 set by Government[18] is 82% and the current figures for QMC and NCH are 84.7 and 86.7%, respectively. Bagust et al[19] have used DES to show that it is risky to have average occupancy figures higher than 85%.

Interventions targeted at patients with specific health problems, such as respiratory conditions or ill-defined diagnoses, did have an effect, although it was not large. Reducing emergency admissions for patients with respiratory problems (by 20% per annum year on year for four years) reduced overall bed occupancy by approximately 2%, a small annual effect. However, the seasonal nature of the reductions in admissions gave increased benefits, as the January peak in occupancy was more significantly reduced relative to other months.

Interventions aimed at preventing 3 or 6% emergency admissions of patients over 60 years of age made a substantial difference in the model. Even without assuming any decrease in average length of stay, bed occupancy in both hospitals was reduced by 1% per annum over the 5-year duration. This is to be expected since people in this age group comprise around about half of all emergency admissions.

We evaluated the effect of early discharge for patients admitted as emergencies, who were subsequently discharged to nursing homes. Despite the common perception of 'bed-blockers', discharging these patients 2 days early made hardly any difference to overall occupancy rates, and there appeared to be surprisingly little potential for improvement in this area. We also investigated the effects of 7-day-a-week discharging from hospital. This showed a small decrease in occupancy, although care needs to be taken in interpreting the model results here, since the admission days for elective patients are currently planned to accommodate weekday discharging. However, some benefit might still be achieved. Overall, though, the model showed that the effects of discharging these people earlier were minimal compared with the effects of keeping them out of hospital in the first place.

## 2.6   The A&E model

We were asked to investigate the Government suggestion[18] that waiting times in A&E could be reduced by the provision of 'fast track' systems for minor injuries or illnesses. Patients streamed in this way would have their own waiting area and dedicated staff, and would not share resources with other A&E patients. Streaming patients appears counter-intuitive from a queueing theory perspective, until we take into account the fact that different categories of patients have different acceptable waiting times and hence different targets. Thus although some patients may have to wait for longer, their waiting time could still be within acceptable limits. For a description of how such a system might be implemented in practice, see Cooke *et al.*[20]

Unfortunately, system dynamics does not ideally lend itself to narrowly focussed systems involving resource-constrained queueing networks. For problems requiring this level of individual detail, discrete-event simulation is the method of choice.[6] A separate, very simple DES model for A&E was therefore rapidly developed using the software Simul8[21] and was populated with patient arrival and staff resource level data from the A&E department at QMC. Activity duration data were derived from the literature[2,22] as there was no time to gather primary data in this study.

On arrival in A&E, patients are initially prioritised into five urgency categories, where 1 denotes life-threatening conditions and 5 denotes minor injury or illness. This process is called triage. Category 1 patients are always seen immediately, but lower category patients are seen in priority order as resources permit and may have to wait. We investigated the streaming of minor cases (triage categories 4 and 5). We found that

*Table 2.3*  Results from the A&E streaming model

|  | Performance indicator | Without streaming | Streaming minor cases |
|---|---|---|---|
| Shared doctors | % Utilisation | 70 | 73 |
| Stream doctors | % Utilisation | — | 58 |
| Cat 2 treatment | % Queued less than 10 min | 96 | 83 |
| Cat 3 treatment | % Queued less than 60 min | 99 | 70 |
| Cat 4 treatment | % Queued less than 120 min | 87 | 100 |
| Cat 5 treatment | % Queued less than 240 min | 86 | 99 |

the permanent streaming of minor injuries was not an efficient use of clinical resources. Improvements were observed for the less urgent patients, but these were at the expense of patients in categories 2 and 3. The results for this scenario are shown in Table 2.3.

A flexible system appears to be required in which streaming is only triggered when waiting times reach a certain threshold. This is in accordance with the findings of Cooke *et al.*[20] A compromise solution for Nottingham may be to dedicate one doctor to the fast track patients, and have a second doctor on standby to join the first doctor if there is a sudden rush of minor cases. Other solutions may well involve the use of Emergency Nurse Practitioners to deal with less serious patients, releasing doctors to work with the more serious cases. Further simulation modelling work could help here, for example, in determining the threshold for initiating streaming.

## 2.7  Discussion

Both the qualitative and quantitative aspects of the system dynamics approach proved to be very useful in this project. The conceptual map provided a helpful structure around which to base the stakeholder interviews. Many participants commented on the value of seeing the whole system in its entirety, often for the first time, and on the insights they gained about how other parts of the system related to the part with which they were familiar. Although causal loop (influence) diagrams were not constructed for the entire system, they were used to gain insight into the behaviour of parts of the system.

The STELLA model was useful on two levels—firstly, naturally, for investigating specific scenarios in terms of patient flows and bottlenecks, but secondly (and perhaps equally importantly) as a device for provoking and facilitating discussion and comment. Interestingly, although the

Nottingham Steering Group were initially fascinated by the computer model and the visual and numerical output, they readily accepted the idea that the model gave an indication of the relative effects of different interventions rather than mathematically precise forecasts or point predictions. They were very keen to suggest alternative scenarios for testing, arising from the findings of earlier runs of the model.

This study was conducted in partnership with a health and social care community in Nottingham already committed to the concept of partnership working and the need for a 'whole systems approach' to development. The process and findings of this independent enquiry appear to have contributed to sustained local efforts to find better solutions for the benefit of the people of Nottingham, and have informed the articulation of a local service framework for emergency care. The SD model we have constructed has the potential to evaluate the impact of the real system developments that are now envisaged in Nottingham.

The approach adopted in Nottingham could easily be applied elsewhere. The process of stakeholder interviews and the development of a conceptual system map is a generic one which could be used anywhere. Emergency and on-demand healthcare systems in different geographical areas may differ slightly but will share many common features, and the STELLA model for Nottingham could easily be reconfigured for a different location and repopulated with the appropriate data. Much of the necessary data are now routinely collected by Trusts for management purposes. We believe this approach could make a substantial, practical contribution to the improvement of emergency healthcare delivery.

## Acknowledgements

We thank the health and social care staff who assisted us in the conduct of this study and Dr Stephen Shortt, Mr James Scott, Mr John MacDonald, Dr Doug Black and the local steering committee for their contribution. We also thank Mr Steve Baxter and Mr Shaun Leah for their assistance in providing data. Nottingham Health Authority funded the project but the views expressed in the paper are those of the authors alone.

## References

1. http://www.nottinghm-ha.trent.nhs.uk, downloaded Oct 21, 2002.
2. Audit Commission (1996). *By Accident or Design: Improving A&E Services in England and Wales*. HMSO: London.
3. Audit Commission (2001). *Accident and Emergency Acute Hospital Portfolio: Review of National Findings*. Audit Commission: London.

4. Lattimer VA *et al* (2004). Reviewing emergency care systems I: insights from system dynamics modelling. *Emerg Med J*, In press.
5. Gerard K *et al* (2004). Reviewing emergency care systems II: measuring patient preferences using a discrete choice experiment. *Emerg Med J*, In press.
6. Brailsford SC and Hilton NA (2001). A comparison of discrete event simulation and system dynamics for modelling healthcare systems. In: Riley J (ed) Proceedings from ORAHS 2000, Glasgow, Scotland, pp 18–39.
7. Forrester JW (1961). *Industrial Dynamics*. MIT Press: Cambridge, MA.
8. Forrester JW (1960). The impact of feedback control concepts on the management sciences. In: *Collected Papers of J.W. Forrester* (1975 collection), Wright-Allen Press: Cambridge, MA, pp 45–60.
9. Jun JB, Jacobson SH and Swisher JR (1999). Application of discrete-event simulation in health care clinics: a survey. *J Opl Res Soc* 50: 109–123.
10. Dangerfield BC and Roberts CA (1990). Modelling the epidemiological consequences of HIV infection and AIDS: a contribution from Operational Research. *J Opl Res Soc* 41: 273–289.
11. Townshend JRPan d Turner HS (2000). Analysing the effect of Chlamydia screening. *J Opl Res Soc* 51: 812–824.
12. Wolstenholme EF (1993). A case study in community care using systems thinking. *J Opl Res Soc* 44: 925–934.
13. Lane DC, Monefeldt C and Rosenhead JV (2000). Looking in the wrong place for healthcare improvements: A system dynamics study of an accident and emergency department. *J Opl Res Soc* 51: 518–531.
14. STELLA, High Performance Systems, 145 Lyme Road, Hanover, NH.
15. Department of Health (2002). *Hospital Episode Statistics*. Department of Health: London.
16. Lane DC (2000). You just don't understand me: modes of failure and success in the discourse between system dynamics and discrete event simulation, Working paper no. LSEOR 00.34, London School of Economics.
17. Pidd M (1998). *Computer Simulation in Management Science*, 4th edn. Wiley: Chichester.
18. Department of Health (2001). *Reforming Emergency Care*, Downloadable from www.doh.gov.uk/capacityplanning/reformfirststeps.htm.
19. Bagust A *et al* (1999). Dynamics of bed use in accommodating emergency admissions: stochastic simulation model. *BMJ* 319: 155–159.
20. Cooke MW, Wilson S and Pearson S (2002). The effect of a separate stream for minor injuries on accident and emergency department waiting times. *Emerg Med J* 19: 28–30.
21. Simul8, www.Simul8.com.
22. Shrimpling M (2002). Redesigning triage to reduce waiting times. *Emerg Nurse* 10: 34–37.

# 3
# Assessing the Impact of Systems Modeling in the Redesign of an Emergency Department

*G. Mould[1], J. Bowers[1], C. Dewar[2] and E. McGugan[2]*
[1]*School of Management, University of Stirling, Stirling, U.K.;*
[2]*Queen Margaret Hospital Punfirmline, U.K.*

*Systems modeling has been used to redesign care in the National Health Service in the United Kingdom. However, assessing the benefits of such modeling is problematic. This paper examines the impact of two complementary techniques, process mapping and simulation, in the redesign of Emergency Department (ED) systems. Using the example of one significant change prompted by systems modeling, the introduction of a new staff roster, the impact on patient-time in the ED is examined. Any assessment has to recognize the effect of changes in the environment, notably staff experience and volume of activity. Using a performance model that incorporates these variables, the main quantifiable impact of the new roster was identified as a reduction in the mean patient-time of 16 min, for the 87% of ED patients classified as minor. Attributing credit for any improvement requires care but systems modeling can provide valuable insights into the design of ED systems resulting in quantifiable improvements.*

## 3.1 Introduction

Many models of industrial and commercial operations management are being deployed in efforts to improve the delivery of healthcare services. In particular, the benefits of a variety of systems analysis and modeling tools have been demonstrated in many applications and there is now a major movement in the National Health Service (NHS) of the United Kingdom to exploit their potential on a wider scale (Proudlove *et al*, 2008). The

Reprinted from *Health Systems*, 2: 3–10, 2013, 'Assessing the Impact of Systems Modeling in the Redesign of an Emergency Department', by G. Mould, J. Bowers, C. Dewar and E. McGugan. With kind permission from Operational Research Society Ltd.

current paper explores the experience of using such tools in the redesign of an Emergency Department (ED) and in particular the application of the complementary techniques of process mapping and simulation.

Mapping the patient pathway is a well-established concept in healthcare and provides a practical basis for redesign. The pathway can be most useful in visualizing the patient's experience and the interdependence of the various processes, encouraging a systemic approach to improvement (Bragato & Jacobs, 2003). Pathway mapping can fulfill a variety of roles but its key benefit lies in its disciplined approach to assimilating knowledge from all those involved during the patient's care: a critical first step in the redesign process for any service (Mould *et al*, 2010). The patient pathway can take many forms: it may be a traditional systems analysis flow chart, a collection of post-it notes representing contributions from many staff, or an interactive computer-based model with capabilities such as hierarchical maps and electronic dissemination. The key challenge of mapping is to provide a high-level view, such that staff can develop a vision of the whole care system, while retaining the detail vital for safe and effective healthcare. Accessibility is a crucial characteristic and the pathway mapping has to encourage all staff to contribute, avoiding technical barriers that might discourage full staff participation in the redesign exercise.

In many examples of redesign, process mapping alone may be sufficient. However, some proposals require a more rigorous analysis and discrete event simulation provides a natural extension of process mapping. Simulation populates the pathway with flows of patients through the sequences of processes competing for limited resources, often within a stochastic environment. Simulation has been used in many studies of healthcare systems (Jun *et al*, 1999; Fone *et al*, 2003) to analyze current and proposed designs: it provides a basis for experiments with redesign options, assessing the service levels and developing insights into the system's constraints and identifying the resource contingencies required to deliver the desired service. In particular, simulation has been used in various studies of EDs (Fletcher *et al*, 2007; Kolker, 2008; Bowers *et al*, 2009; Gunal & Pidd, 2009). Although simulation has been employed widely, a systematic review (Fone *et al*, 2003) observed that there is little reported evidence describing the outcomes from healthcare simulation studies. The review was generally positive about the value of simulation in healthcare but the authors were uncomfortable about the lack of quantifiable evidence of the benefits.

The long-term success of systems' modeling in healthcare depends on feedback, and reviewing the impact of any intervention should be common good practice (Harper & Pitt, 2004). However, measuring this impact can be difficult and there are various possible explanations for the lack of published quantitative evidence about the benefits of systems modeling. The timescale implied by a longitudinal study can be problematic and it is often difficult to motivate the data collection required for pre- and post-implementation studies. Redesign interventions are usually part of an evolving program within a changing environment and attributing improvements to any one factor is difficult. While there are some exceptions (Vishwanath *et al*, 2010), rigorous comparisons of pre- and post-implementation are rare in the accounts of service innovations.

This paper examines the role of system's modeling and its impact on performance using a specific redesign intervention in an ED as an example. The study was part of a 3-year Knowledge Transfer Partnership between the University of Stirling and NHS Fife Health Board. The project explored the use of a variety of modeling methodologies in the support of the redesign of healthcare services. The objective was to assess the practical value of these approaches in a series of case studies, identifying good practice for wider dissemination.

## 3.2 Methods used for the redesign of Emergency Department systems

The NHS launched a widespread program of redesign across the United Kingdom (Department of Health, 2000), encouraging the use of various tools and techniques that have been found to be effective in industry. The intention was to transfer good practice into the NHS, while recognizing that some refinement in the tools and their implementation is often necessary to retain the critical focus on the needs of the patient (Bell *et al*, 2006). The redesign program was driven by a series of targets; one notable target is that patients attending an ED should not spend more than 4 h between arrival and their being discharged or admitted to a ward. In July 2005, NHS Scotland formed the Unscheduled Care Collaborative Programme (Scottish Executive, 2005) involving all 14 Health Boards in Scotland. This provided the forum for a nationwide redesign initiative to deliver improved services and most importantly faster treatment for patients. The program recommended that five 'Flow Groups' be formed to manage the redesign of unscheduled care, supported by a series of national events disseminating good practice. Flow Group 2 was responsible for the redesign of ED services but there was inevitably significant overlap with other Flow Groups, such as those examining medical admissions. The Flow Group was chaired by an ED consultant, with managers and clinicians from ED and associated services such as radiology, diagnostic laboratories and patient transport. Other members of the Flow Group provided statistical and analytical support, including systems modeling. The use of such multidisciplinary teams, with the genuine involvement of front line staff, has been identified as critical in transforming patient processes (Locock, 2003; Newell *et al,* 2003). The Flow Group met regularly to review progress against the 4-h target. Staff were very positive and were willing to offer suggestions for improving the organization of care, and contributed to implementing proposals. The initial work of Flow Group 2 in NHS Fife concentrated on three areas.

- Mapping the patient pathway through the ED and developing a complete, shared understanding of all of the activities and inter-related services involved in delivering ED care. This provided a basis for a structured, qualitative analysis of the system constraints.
- Matching resources with demand; an information system had been established that recorded the admission and discharge times of the patients in the ED, providing reliable data describing the patterns, and variability, in patient attendances at the ED. These demand data were compared with the availability of facilities and resources.
- Identifying and investigating the major causes of patients spending longer than the target 4 h in an ED. Typical problems may include waiting for assessment by a doctor, admission to a ward or transport home. Some issues may be within the control of the ED itself but others may arise from the dependencies on the operation of the whole hospital; interactions with other competing hospital systems may lead to delays in patient care.

### 3.2.1   Process mapping

The initial task was to examine patient flows through the ED mapping the processes involved in organizing and delivering treatment. The form of these pathway maps evolved during the study beginning with simple paper-based formats, then adapting more formal traditional flow-charting techniques with the aid of Microsoft Visio. This approach provided a more rigorous representation of the patient pathway but some staff found that the symbols acted as a barrier discouraging full participation in the redesign process. Furthermore, the map appeared complex: it was difficult to identify redundant tasks and the information flows and the physical flows of patients could not easily be distinguished. These problems were addressed by adopting a more sophisticated mapping tool. This made use of stylized icons, with clear signage distinguishing flows of patients and information, as illustrated in the x-ray sub-pathway of Figure 3.1. The maps were produced in HTML format to help their dissemination, via the intranet or in presentations, allowing for more feedback, and acceptance. Hyperlinks were adopted to support a hierarchy of maps: a high-level map depicted the overall pathway while the user could drill down for precise details of individual sub-pathways or processes in the overall map. The hyperlink capability also allowed additional information to be attached, describing timings, staff availabilities and resource requirements.

Pathway maps were constructed for each of four acute emergency pathways: Minor injuries; Emergency Department; Emergency Medical Admissions; Emergency Surgical Admissions. The new pathway maps had some unexpected benefits. The maps improved the group dynamics by encouraging junior staff to contribute to the review process: they were able to view the maps in their own offices and send comments by email, whereas in group discussions they might feel intimidated by more senior colleagues. Staff were able to appreciate the work done by others and could better understand their own role in the overall treatment plan. The pathway maps highlighted duplicate processes and the number of handovers between staff, encouraging critical questioning of current practice. In addition, the maps were a valuable training aid for clinical staff, in particular for Junior Doctors who spend six months in EDs as part of their general clinical training. The use of a consistent form of mapping also facilitated comparisons of the organization of ED care across different hospitals, helping identify good practice. In this example the comparison resulted in opening a more comprehensive medical assessment unit and a larger discharge lounge facilitating the flow of patients out of the ED.

The maps were developed over a period of two months and were used with considerable success, facilitating discussions about possible improvements among the full range of staff involved in ED care. This process led to many modifications in the patient pathway. Patients with 'minor' injuries were distinguished, allowing senior doctors to concentrate on more seriously ill 'major' patients. A dedicated ED porter was recruited to reduce delays for patients waiting to be transferred to other departments. The need for services such as physiotherapy and occupational therapy was considered at an earlier stage, organizing their provision in tandem with other processes and avoiding delays at the end

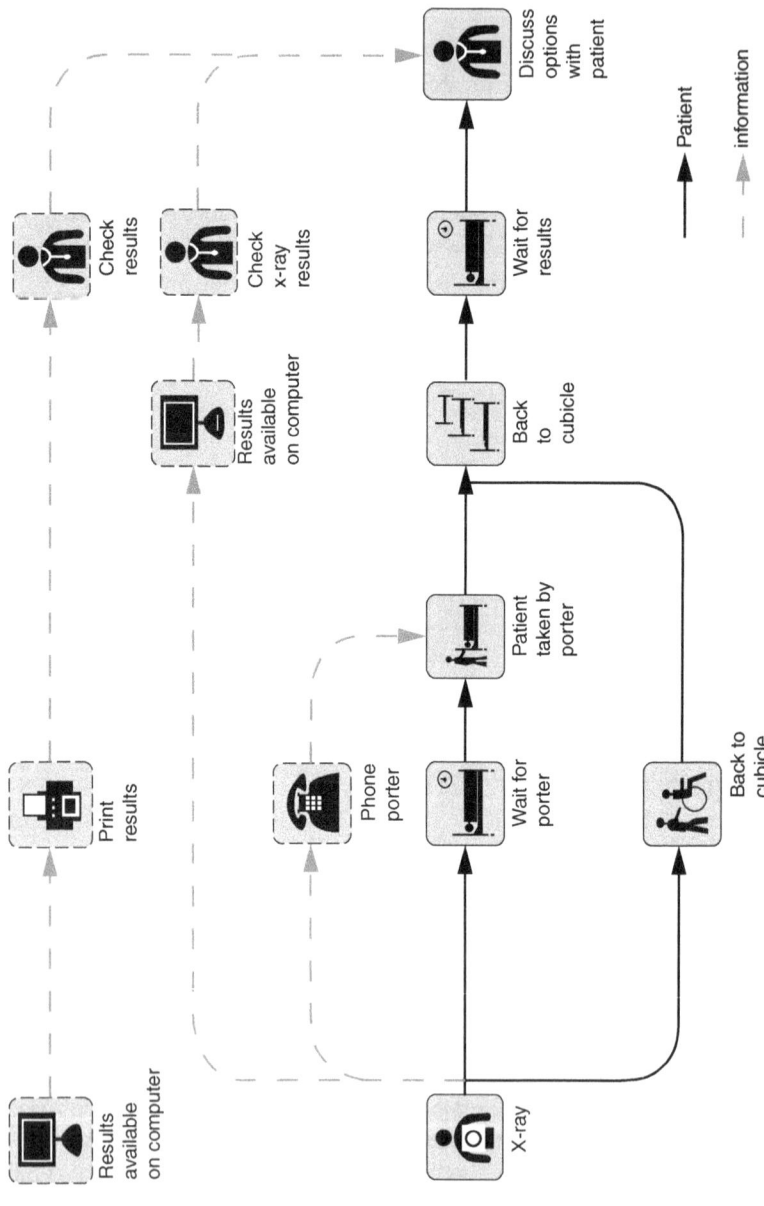

*Figure 3.1* An x-ray sub-pathway map using stylized icons distinguishing patient and information flows

of the patient pathway. Another significant source of delay was patient transport and these problems were reduced by the provision of a vehicle specifically for inter-hospital transfers.

### 3.2.2 Discrete event simulation

Many of the pathway modifications resulting from the process mapping were relatively cheap and their implementation was uncontroversial. However, the pathway mapping also identified a number of problem areas requiring a more substantial, quantitative analysis: process mapping alone did not have the capability to specify the details of a solution or provide a convincing justification for radical change. In particular, the pathway mapping focused debate on matching staff shift patterns with the typical demand for ED services. The problem had already been recognized, and a likely solution identified, but a more substantial analysis was desirable in order to persuade staff of the value of changing their working practices. A simulation model was developed using Simul8 to help provide these more rigorous quantitative analyses. A high-level illustration of the logic is shown in Figure 3.2.

Given the objective to match staff and demand more effectively, a key component of the simulation was the model of arrivals at the ED, and the services required by different categories of patients. Patients come from a variety of sources; their arrival is stochastic but the hourly mean arrival rate follows a clear profile as illustrated in Figure 3.3. This arrival pattern was captured with a non-homogeneous Poisson model, as employed in other analyses of service industries and unscheduled healthcare in particular (Swisher *et al*, 2001; Alexopoulos *et al*, 2008). In addition to the weekly patterns of demand, there was evidence of seasonal variation and a trend of increasing ED attendances. These variations were incorporated in a series of sensitivity analyses exploring different assumptions about future demand, and also the supply of resources. The ED distinguished patients as 'minor', requiring relatively simple treatment, or 'major', needing more sophisticated care and often admission to a hospital ward. These two categories were modeled as separate sources of arrivals, with a sub-category specifying the detailed pathway of the patient through the ED. The detailed pathways were modeled as sequences of activities describing the patient's route through the range of services illustrated in Figure 3.2. The ED has to interact with many hospital services shared with patients from other specialties, for example, inpatient wards, radiology, laboratories and patient transport. Furthermore, coordination with physiotherapy, occupational therapy

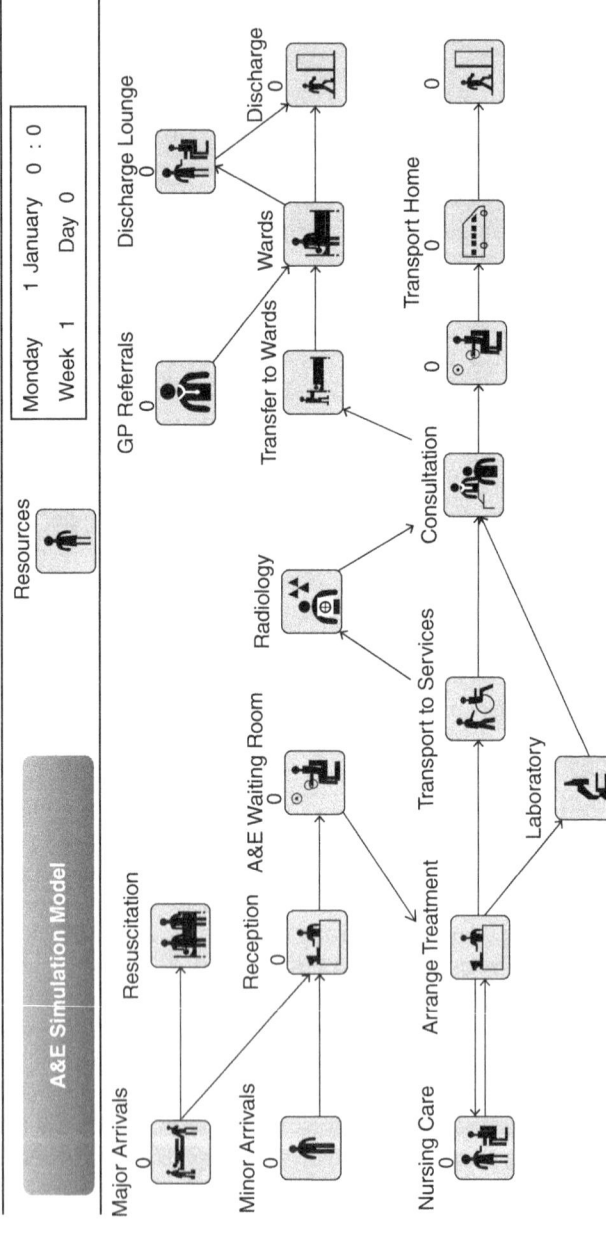

*Figure 3.2* Emergency Department (A&E) simulation model

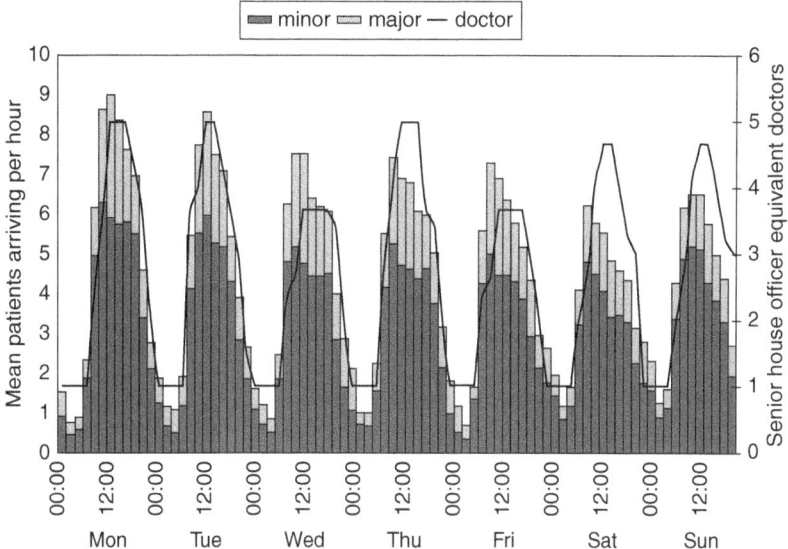

*Figure 3.3*  Variations in the mean ED arrivals compared with staff provision

and social services may be needed before patients can be discharged. One of the modeling challenges was to capture the critical details of these interactions without attempting to model the whole hospital (Gunal & Pidd, 2011): the interactions were modeled as restrictions on the availabilities of these shared services reflecting the patterns of use by non-ED patients.

Data from the routine information systems provided the basis for understanding the arrival patterns and the overall durations of patients' visits to the ED but these data were complemented by a patient tracking exercise providing detailed timings of the various activities. Normal distributions were adopted as models for the activity durations of most services. Many files of data were available from existing systems but it was not readily apparent which were really critical to the management's decisions; other vital data, such as the detailed activity durations, were missing and the focus of the simulation helped specify the additional data requirements clearly, as in the patient tracking exercise. The process of constructing the simulation enforced a disciplined data collection; this is a major benefit to simulation, providing practical assistance in establishing a basis for 'evidence-based management' (Walshe & Rundall, 2001).

## 3.3   Results

### 3.3.1   Addressing the 4-h breaches

The simulation outputs were designed to serve the key objective of reducing the number of patients spending more than 4 h in the ED. Figure 3.4 provides one example of an output, depicting the proportion of patients meeting the 4-h target as a function of the time of arrival at the ED, based on repeated trials of a simulation of ED activity for May-July a 24-h warm-up period was used with 20 trials for the duration of the period. This output contributed to the validation of the simulation, confirming that the model was a reasonable reflection of reality and a sound basis for assessing proposed changes. Figure 3.4 also provides estimates of the proportions being treated within 3 and 2 h to help staff appreciate the challenges of meeting tougher targets in the future. Other simulation outputs were designed to help understand possible causes of the breaches, summarizing key statistics such as intermediate waits for different services and the utilization of key staff.

### 3.3.2   Modifying staff allocation

Figure 3.3 incorporates data describing the typical shift pattern over a typical week. The time taken to treat a patient was dependent on the doctor's grade, for example a staff grade doctor could be expected to treat approximately twice as many patients as a Senior House Officer (SHO). The staff provisions were weighted to reflect this variation in

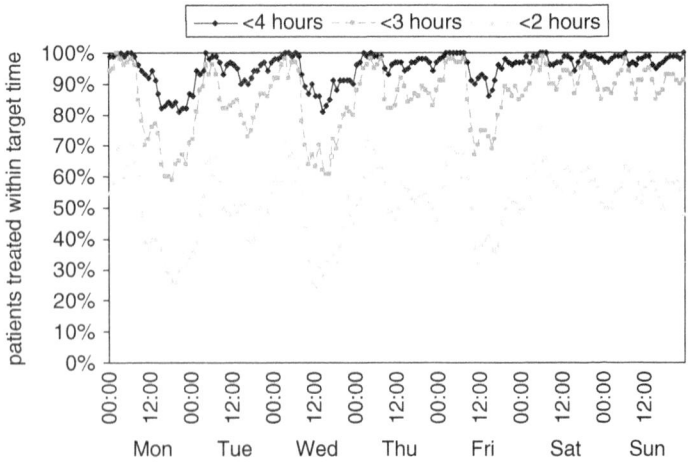

*Figure 3.4*   Proportions of patients treated within the target times

doctors' capacities, producing a simple measure of 'SHO equivalent'. Figure 3.3 suggested a possible mismatch of demand and staffing with relatively few staff compared with patient arrivals on Monday, Wednesday and Friday. The effects of this staffing profile are apparent in Figure 3.4: the simulation suggested that fewer patients are treated within the target times on these days. This result corresponded with experience and, having established that the model was reasonably accurate, a number of simulation experiments were undertaken to explore various options and notably new staffing profiles. These experiments suggested that some small but useful reductions in patient-time in the ED could be achieved relatively easily. The simulation experiments and the comparisons of supply and demand resulted in changes to the staff roster. ED staff judged the innovation to be successful, contributing to an overall reduction in patient-time in the ED. But rigorous assessment of the impact of such interventions and attributing the improvements to specific interventions is problematic. Innovations were often undertaken in parallel while the large variability in patient need made it difficult to detect unambiguous evidence of reductions in patient-time. However, the introduction of the new staff roster provided an opportunity to attempt a more rigorous assessment: the roster was a specific, well-defined and independent innovation; a comparison of performance pre- and post-implementation should provide quantitative evidence of its impact.

### 3.3.3   Measuring Emergency Department performance

One recommended route to long-term success in healthcare systems' modeling is to adopt a complete project life cycle incorporating a project review and an assessment of the outcome of any intervention (Harper & Pitt, 2004). In attempting to identify evidence of an impact of systems modeling in the ED, the scope of the quantitative assessment was limited to just one innovation, the introduction of the new staff roster, and a single measure, the patient-time in the ED. This was a clearly defined change at a specific date with a relatively simple quantitative measure; hence, it might be expected that the impact could be easily detected. The use of patient-time as a target has received much attention in the U.K.'s NHS and there is considerable debate about the possibility of the target distorting clinical decisions (Bevan & Hood, 2006; Bevan, 2009; Gubb, 2009). However, evidence from both statistical analyses of mortality data (Freeman *et al*, 2010) and interviews with staff (Mortimore & Cooper, 2007) suggest that while there is potential for an adverse effect on the quality of care, this is not a widespread problem. Given the prominence of the target, considerable efforts were taken to ensure the integrity of the data: gaming was possible but the patient-time data can generally be regarded as robust. Other countries do not adopt a single target for patient-time and other measures of performance may be used though these measures are usually inter-related; one alternative measure is the proportion of ambulance diversion due to a lack of capacity in the ED but this is strongly related to patient-time (Kolker, 2008). Simplistic implementation of a single target for patient-time in an ED can produce adverse effects but the target provides a useful focus that improves care for many patients.

### 3.3.4   Assessing the impact of the change in staffing

The study examined the change in time spent by patients in the ED during the six months spanning the implementation of the new staff roster at the beginning of August. This roster entailed a general increase in staffing mainly junior doctors to enable a better match of resources to demand on weekdays but no change at weekends as demand was lower and staffing was judged to be adequate. Table 3.1 notes that the mean time in the ED for minor patients on weekdays fell from 100 min to 94 min, with a reduction from 200 to 195 min for major patients. There was an associated fall in the number spending more than 4 h in the ED, suggesting the new staff roster may have improved performance, though further changes were needed if the 4-h target was to be met.

However, this simple comparison of mean times in the ED is mislead-ing: it ignores the fact that there was a reduction of 8% in the number of patients attending the ED. A further factor that might have influenced

*Table 3.1* Comparing patient-times in ED weekdays before and after the implementation of the new staff roster

|  | Minor | | Major | |
|---|---|---|---|---|
|  | May–Jul | Aug–Oct | May–Jul | Aug–Oct |
| Mean time (mins.) | 100 | 94 | 200 | 195 |
| No. patients |  |  |  |  |
| Total | 6376 | 5814 | 1255 | 1208 |
| >4 hours | 285 | 223 | 303 | 277 |
| 3–4 hours | 498 | 444 | 353 | 348 |
| 2–3 hours | 1040 | 887 | 327 | 292 |
| %>4 hours | 4.5% | 3.8% | 24.1% | 22.9% |
| %3–4 hours | 7.8% | 7.6% | 28.1% | 28.8% |
| %2–3 hours | 16.3% | 15.3% | 26.1% | 24.2% |

*Table 3.2*  Comparing patient-times in ED at weekends

|  | Minor | | Major | |
| --- | --- | --- | --- | --- |
|  | May–Jul | Aug–Oct | May–Jul | Aug–Oct |
| Mean time (mins.) | 98 | 109 | 172 | 197 |
| No. patients | 2707 | 2462 | 407 | 437 |

the ED performance was the rotation of junior doctors that occurs in August: the cycle of the doctors' training program implies that new junior doctors arrive in August and their relative lack of experience may well affect the time taken to treat patients in the ED. Evidence for the possible effect of this influx of new junior doctors is provided in a comparison of performance at weekends, when there was no change in the staff roster. Table 3.2 notes that despite a reduction of 7% in minor patient activity at weekends, the mean time spent by minor patients in the ED increased by 11 min; this might be explained by the relative inexperience of the new doctors.

The possible effects of activity in the ED and the junior doctors' experience were investigated in a one-way between-groups analysis of covariance, incorporating variables describing:

$y_i$ = time spent in the ED by patient $i$

$x_{1i}$ = 0 if pre-staff roster change; 1 if post-staff roster change

$x_{2i}$ = number of arrivals at the ED during the hour preceding the arrival of patient $i$

$x_{3i}$ = junior doctors' experience in months at the date of arrival of patient $i$

where $x_3$(August) = 1 ... $x_3$(October) = 3 ... $x_3$ (July) = 6

Preliminary checks were conducted to ensure there was no violation of the assumptions of normality, homogeneity of variance homogeneity of regression slopes, and reliable measurement of the covariate. The results of the analysis of covariance are summarized in Table 3.3.

The analysis identified a significant improvement in performance for minor patients attending ED on weekdays, when the time in ED was controlled for the number of patients attending and the experience of the junior doctors; $F(1,12,186) = 33.7$, $P<0.001$, $\eta^2 = 0.003$. Both of the covariates, $x_{2i}$, $x_{3i}$ had a significant effect on patient-time in the ED. However, there is much residual variation reflecting the variability inherent in healthcare where individual patients' needs are often

Table 3.3   Incorporating the effect of experience and activity

| Covariance analysis | F | P | $\eta^2$ | Mean[a] | |
|---|---|---|---|---|---|
| | | | | Pre | Post |
| No control | | | | 99.8±1.9 | 94.1±1.8 |
| Experience & activity | 33.7 | <0.001 | 0.003 | 104.8±2.9 | 88.6±3.1 |

[a] Mean minutes spent by minor patients in the ED on weekdays, with 95% confidence interval.

unpredictable. Although the statistical model provides a useful basis for comparing the mean performance, it is not suitable for assessing individual patients' experiences.

The mean treatment time, adjusted for the changes in ED activity and staff experience over the period, fell from 105 min in May–July to 89 min in August–October. Hence, it can be concluded that the improved staffing roster reduced the mean treatment time by 16 min for this group of patients, compared with the expected mean time if there had been no change to the staffing. The same analysis did not produce statistically significant results for minor patients at weekends: this might have been expected since there were no changes in staffing levels at weekends and any differences in performance might be attributed to activity and junior doctor experience. The analysis also failed to identify a significant change for the major patients for either weekdays or weekends; major patients tend to have more complex care requirements and their time in the ED is dependent on the availability of a range of resources. These patients tend to be treated by senior doctors and hence the change in junior doctors shift patterns had little effect on this category of patients. There is a possibility that the Hawthorn effect made a contribution to the improvements (Leonard & Masatu, 2006); however, the time scale of the project was not sufficient to establish whether or not the improvement was sustained in the long term.

## 3.4   Clinical and managerial experience with systems modeling

While the simulation can claim some credit in encouraging the change to the staff roster, its main role was acting as a catalyst for change rather than revealing any radical insights. This was an experience typical of other interventions: staff are already aware of the need for change but the process of logically assembling the information, as required for the simulation, and demonstrating the likely effects of proposals helped win the support of all stakeholders. In this study, revising the shift patterns had always been a consideration but the structured evidence from the simulation experiments stimulated action. Healthcare systems modeling involves many uncontrollable variables, and it is unrealistic to expect simulation to provide an accurate forecast of future performance. However, simulation can contribute to helping staff understand their systems and encourage more rigorous evidence-based decision making.

The change in the staff roster was just one innovation introduced as part of a bigger redesign program in the ED. While many of the innovations could have been made without sophisticated systems modeling, the contribution of simulation was sufficiently encouraging that the approach was used in further successful applications in NHS Fife, for example, in capacity planning in the orthopedic and ENT outpatient departments. The experience illustrated in this case study of systems modeling in an ED was typical of other departments. Process mapping of the patient pathway, using a standardized clear structure that encourages staff involvement, makes a substantial contribution to redesign of healthcare systems. Converting the patient pathway into a more powerful simulation model can be a valuable development allowing options to be assessed rigorously. However, simulation requires more analytical skills and time: this is often not justified and process mapping alone may be adequate if the options are limited and the decisions are uncontroversial.

## 3.5   Conclusions

The application of systems modeling in supporting a program of improvement in ED care was regarded as a significant success by staff leading to further applications. Accessible process mapping of the patient pathway and simulation of the ED system can both be valuable, though in some applications the simpler pathway mapping is sufficient. However, quantitative assessment of the impact is challenging, even when limiting the analysis to one specific innovation, a new staff roster, and an apparently unambiguous performance measure, patient-time in the ED. Simple comparisons of performance pre- and post-implementation can be misleading and changes in both the external and internal environment have to be considered. Extending the comparison to include the effects of both the changes in the volume of activity at the ED and also the experience of the junior doctors, it became apparent that the introduction of the new staff roster had resulted in a significant reduction in patient-time in the ED. The mean time for minor patients fell by 16 min but other patients, with a higher priority for resources, were not so dependent on the staff availability and did not benefit from the innovation. However, service innovations are often part of a larger program of change and apportioning credit for any improvement in performance requires care.

## References

Alexopoulos C, Goldsman D, Fontanesi J, Kopald D and Wilson JR (2008) Modeling patient arrivals in community clinics. *Omega International Journal of Management Science* **36(1)**, 33–43.

Bell D, McNaney N and Jones M (2006) Improving health care through redesign. *British Medical Journal* **332(7553)**, 1286–1287.

Bevan G (2009) Have targets done more harm than good in the English NHS? No. *British Medical Journal* **338(7538)**, 3129.

Bevan G and Hood C (2006) Have targets improved performance in the English NHS? *British Medical Journal* **332**, 419–422.

Bowers J, Ghattas M and Mould G (2009) Success and failure in the simulation of an accident and emergency department. *Journal of Simulation* **3(3)**, 171–178.

Bragato L and Jacobs K (2003) Care pathways: the road to better health services? *Journal of Health Organization Management* **17(3)**, 164–180.

Department of Health (2000) The NHS plan: a plan for investment, a plan for reform. HMSO, London. [WWW document] http://www.dh.gov.uk/en/Publicationsandstatistics/Publications/PublicationsPolicyAndGuidance/DH_4002960 (accessed 25 May 2012).

Fletcher A, Halsall D, Huxham S and Worthington D (2007) The DH accident and emergency department model: a national generic model used locally. *Journal of the Operational Research Society* **58(12)**, 1554–1562.

Fone D, Hollinghurst S, Temple M, Round A, Lester N, Weightman A, Roberts K, Coyle E, Bevan G and Palmer S (2003) Systematic review of the use and value of computer simulation modelling in population health and health care delivery. *Journal of Public Health Medicine* **25(3)**, 325–335.

Freeman JV, Croft S, Cross S, Yap C and Mason S (2010) The impact of the 4 h target on patient care and outcomes in the emergency department: an analysis of hospital incidence data. *Emergency Medical Journal* **27(12)**, 921–927.

Gubb J (2009) Have targets done more harm than good in the English NHS? Yes. *British Medical Journal* **338(3130)**, 3130.

Gunal MM and Pidd M (2009) Understanding target-driven action in emergency department performance using simulation. *Emergency Medical Journal* **26(10)**, 724–727.

Gunal MM and Pidd M (2011) DGHPSIM: generic simulation of hospital performance. *ACM Transactions on Modeling and Computer Simulation* **21(4)**, article 23, doi: 10.1145/2000494.200496, http://doi.acm.org/10.1145/2000494.2000496 (accessed 19 September 2012).

Harper PR and Pitt MA (2004) On the challenges of healthcare modelling and a proposed project life cycle for successful implementation. *Journal of the Operational Research Society* **55(6)**, 657–661.

Jun JI, Jacobson SH and Swisher JR (1999) Application of discrete-event simulation in health care clinics. *Journal of the Operational Research Society* **50(2)**, 109–123.

Kolker A (2008) Process modeling of emergency department patient flow: effect of patient length of stay on ED diversion. *Journal of Medical Systems* **32(5)**, 389–401.

Leonard KL and Masatu MC (2006) Outpatient process quality evaluation and the Hawthorne effect. *Social Science and Medicine* **63(9)**, 2330–2340.

Locock L (2003) Healthcare redesign: meaning, origins and application. *Quality and Safety in Health Care* **12(1)**, 53–57.

Mortimore A and Cooper S (2007) The 4-hour target: emergency nurses views. *Emergency Medical Journal* **24(6)**, 402–404.

Mould G, Bowers J and Ghattas M (2010) The evolution of the pathway and its role in improving patient care. *Quality and Safety in Health Care* **19(5)**, 1–6.

Newell S, Edelman L, Scarbrough H, Swann J and Bresnan M (2003) Best practice development and transfer in the NHS: the importance of process as well as product knowledge. *Health Services Management Research* **16(1)**, 1–12.

Proudlove N, Moxham C and Boaden R (2008) Lessons for lean in healthcare from using six sigma in the NHS. *Public Money & Management* **28(1)**, 27–34.

Scottish Executive (2005) An introduction to the unscheduled care collaborative programme. Scottish Executive, St Andrew's House, Edinburgh, Scotland. [WWW document]   http://www.scotland.gov.uk/Resource/Doc/141079/0034895.pdf (accessed 25 May 2012).

Swisher JR, Jacobson SH, Jun JB and Balci O (2001) Modeling and analyzing a physician clinic environment using discrete-event (visual) simulation. *Computers and Operations Research* **28(2)**, 105–125.

Vishwanath A, Singh SR and Winkelstein P (2010) The impact of electronic medical record systems on outpatient workflows: a longitudinal evaluation of its workflow effects. *International Journal of Medical Informatics* **79(11)**, 778–791.

Walshe K and Rundall TG (2001) Evidence-based management: from theory to practice in health care. *Milbank Quarterly* **79(3)**, 429–457.

# 4

# Using Simulation to Assess Cardiac First-Responder Schemes Exhibiting Stochastic and Spatial Complexities

*K. J. Cairns[1], A. H. Marshall[1] and F. Kee[2]*
[1]*Centre for Statistical Science and Operational Research, Queen's University Belfast, Belfast, UK; and* [2]*UKCRC Centre of Excellence for Public Health (NI), Queen's University Belfast, Belfast, UK*

*A Monte-Carlo simulation-based model has been constructed to assess a public health scheme involving mobile-volunteer cardiac First-Responders. The scheme being assessed aims to improve survival of Sudden-Cardiac-Arrest (SCA) patients, through reducing the time until administration of life-saving defibrillation treatment, with volunteers being paged to respond to possible SCA incidents alongside the Emergency Medical Services. The need for a model, for example, to assess the impact of the scheme in different geographical regions, was apparent upon collection of observational trial data (given it exhibited stochastic and spatial complexities). The simulation-based model developed has been validated and then used to assess the scheme's benefits in an alternative rural region (not a part of the original trial). These illustrative results conclude that the scheme may not be the most efficient use of National Health Service resources in this geographical region, thus demonstrating the importance and usefulness of simulation modelling in aiding decision making.*

## 4.1 Introduction

Decision making in healthcare delivery has been aided through the use of Operational Research techniques (Brandeau *et al*, 2004; Davies and Bensley, 2005; Romeijn and Zenios, 2008). Methods used include

Reprinted from *Journal of the Operational Research Society*, 62: 982–991, 2011, 'Using Simulation to Assess Cardiac First-Responder Schemes Exhibiting Stochastic and Spatial Complexities', by K. J. Cairns, A. H. Marshall and F. Kee. With kind permission from Operational Research Society Ltd.

linear and nonlinear optimisation, network and integer programming, data envelopment analysis, goal programming, dynamic and stochastic programming, data-mining, mathematical modelling, decision trees, forecasting, queuing models, Markov processes, quality management, soft OR, heuristics, decision support tools and simulation.

In particular the formulation of simulation-based models (Fone *et al*, 2003; Brailsford, 2007; Taylor *et al*, 2009) can support decision-makers in examining issues such as public health interventions, providing further insight beyond that obtained from observational trials. For example, simulation-based models have the potential to enable decision-makers to consider numerous further scenarios under safe and relatively inexpensive conditions. Furthermore, building simulation-based models within an economic evaluation, such as a cost-effectiveness analysis (based on both costs and effectiveness), provides a method for comparing healthcare interventions in an objective fashion. Indeed, modelling is now required by the National Institute of Clinical Excellence (NICE) to support economic evaluations in making recommendations for the use of new technologies (National Institute for Clinical Excellence, 2004).

A number of simulation-based modelling techniques are available (Jun *et al*, 1999; de Jong, 2002; Cooper *et al*, 2007; Kuljis *et al*, 2007) such as decision trees, system dynamics, Markov models, multi-agent simulation, Monte-Carlo simulation and discrete event simulation. The choice of modelling technique(s) deployed depends upon the system that is being modelled (eg are there interactions between individuals; are chronic diseases being considered) but should adequately capture the mechanisms surrounding any possible intervention.

The purpose of this research is to develop a simulation-based model to assess the effectiveness and cost-effectiveness of a mobile-volunteer First-Responder (FR) Public Access Defibrillation (PAD) scheme. The public health scheme being considered involves the recruitment of mobile-volunteer cardiac First-Responders (FRs) across a geographical region. These volunteers are paged to respond to possible Sudden-Cardiac-Arrest (SCA) incidents alongside the Emergency Medical Services (EMS). The scheme aims to improve survival of SCA patients, through reducing the time until administration of life-saving defibrillation treatment (Kern, 1998).

The assessment of the effectiveness and cost-effectiveness of such a public health scheme is important before further investment may be made. Whilst much research has gone into assessing the benefits of these PAD schemes at fixed sites (eg Walker *et al*, 2003; The Public Access Defibrillation Trial Investigators, 2004), conclusions from various

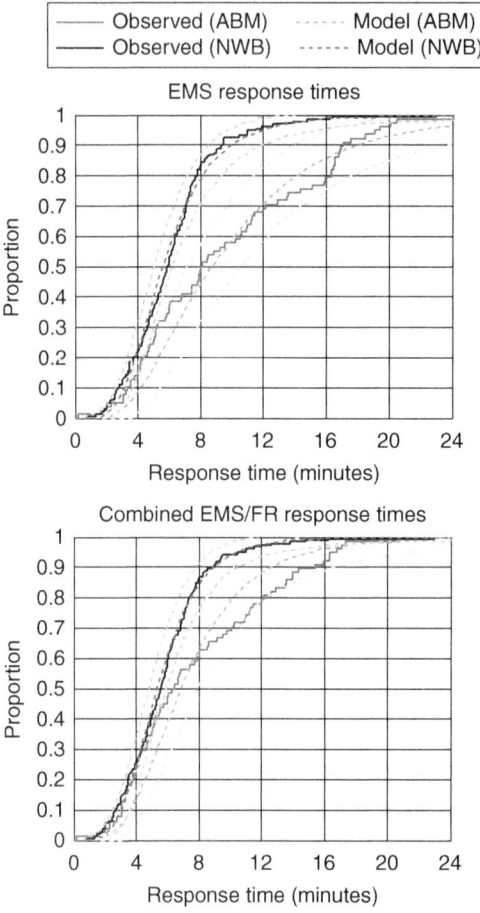

*Figure 4.1* Cumulative response-time distributions are illustrated for the two geographical regions considered in the Northern Ireland-Public Access Defibrillation (NI-PAD) trial: North and West Belfast (NWB); and Antrim, Ballymena and Magherafelt district councils (ABM). The figure illustrates the response-time distributions on considering only the Emergency Medical Services (EMS) response, or the best combined EMS/First Responder (FR) response. In each plot, the solid lines illustrate the observed response-time distributions while the dotted lines illustrate the pointwise median and 95% central confidence interval output from the simulation model

mobile-volunteer observational trials produce conflicting and varying results (Joglar and Page, 2002; Capucci *et al*, 2002).

Our previous results from the Northern Ireland-Public Access Defibrillation (NI-PAD) trial (Moore *et al*, 2008) also highlight this varying impact of mobile-volunteer cardiac FR schemes in different geographical regions. In this trial, data were collected from two different geographical regions: (i) the urban residential region of North and West Belfast (NWB); and (ii) Antrim, Ballymena and Magherafelt district councils (ABM), composed of numerous remote rural areas inter-dispersed with many large/small towns and villages. Differences were visualised in the underlying EMS response (see the cumulative response-time distributions in Figure 4.1), with responses typically faster in the more urban NWB region. The extent of the improvements in response times (because of FRs) also differed between the two geographical regions, with the relative impact of the FRs appearing larger in the less urban ABM region.

This current research has therefore attempted to model the varying impact of mobile cardiac FR schemes in different geographical regions, as opposed to assuming the impact observed in one geographical region will occur in another, as seen in other cost-effectiveness analyses (Nichol *et al*, 2003; Mears *et al*, 2006).

To achieve this, a Monte-Carlo simulation-based model has been developed which is able to quantify effects at a population level by combining the detail complexity found in simulating the life histories of individuals. For example, this type of model is able to consider the stochastic and spatial nature of the occurrence of cardiac arrests across time and space. It can also incorporate the many intricacies found in running a mobile-volunteer rota-based scheme (Cairns *et al*, 2008); and can take account of the varying response times of the EMS and FRs to incidents at different locations and times; and can model the varying long-term survival of patients.

The following sections describe the simulation-based model that has been developed, including details of its validation. The model's potential to assess the impact of the scheme in other geographical regions/under different volunteer configurations is illustrated below, where simulated results are presented for a selected rural region of the United Kingdom (UK), not part of the original NI-PAD trial.

## 4.2 Methodology

The simulation-based model wishes to assess the benefits of interventions (through comparison of (i) response times; (ii) lives saved and

(iii) Quality-Adjusted-Life-Years (QALYs) gained), together with their associated costs.

The first of the two health interventions considered is the typical situation where the initial emergency response treatment of SCA patients is provided by the EMS, who administer defibrillation and Advanced Life Support (ALS). The alternative health intervention scheme considered involves the simultaneous response of both the EMS and mobile FRs to SCAs. In this scheme FRs administer defibrillation until the arrival of the EMS (in cases where they arrive before the EMS), with ALS administered by the EMS. The FR scheme deployed is assumed similar to that implemented in the NI-PAD trial. For example, FRs were trained in the use of Automated-External-Defibrillators (AEDs) based on the Resuscitation Council (UK) 2000 guidelines, with retraining occurring every 6 months. FRs were on a rota when they were 'on-call' to carry AEDs and pagers. The simultaneous dispatch of FRs, alongside the EMS, was facilitated through Automated-Internet-Paging. FRs were paged to emergencies coded 'Cardiac-Arrest' by the Advanced-Medical-Priority-Dispatch-System (AMPDS) (v11.1 Priority Dispatch Corp) software, within a given geographical region. The geographical paging zone of each individual FR was a circular region, identified by its central location and radial distance.

### 4.2.1   Structure of simulation model

The analysis considers the life history for each SCA patient within the geographical region of interest over a 5-year period, with the overall scheme impact assessed through combining individual life histories. For each SCA that occurs, the EMS and any FR response times are quantified and are used in determining a patient's survival-to-hospital discharge. Figure 4.2 provides a schematic of the timeline of SCA patients, as considered within the model. The model considers both the short-term (survival-to-hospital discharge) and the long-term survival of patients.

The simulation-based model was built in Matlab (Math-Works, version R2007b). Statistical analyses were performed using SAS (version 9.1).

### 4.2.2   Simulation model component: sudden cardiac arrest cases

SCAs are simulated to occur throughout a selected geographical region according to its demographic make-up. The number within any one particular Census Output Area (COA) is modelled by a Poisson process (Skogvoll and Lindqvist, 1999; Marshall *et al*, 2006):

$$\text{Number of SCAs in COA } i \text{ in 1 year} \sim \text{Poisson}\left(\lambda_i = \sum_{j,k} P_{jk} N_{ijk}\right)$$

53

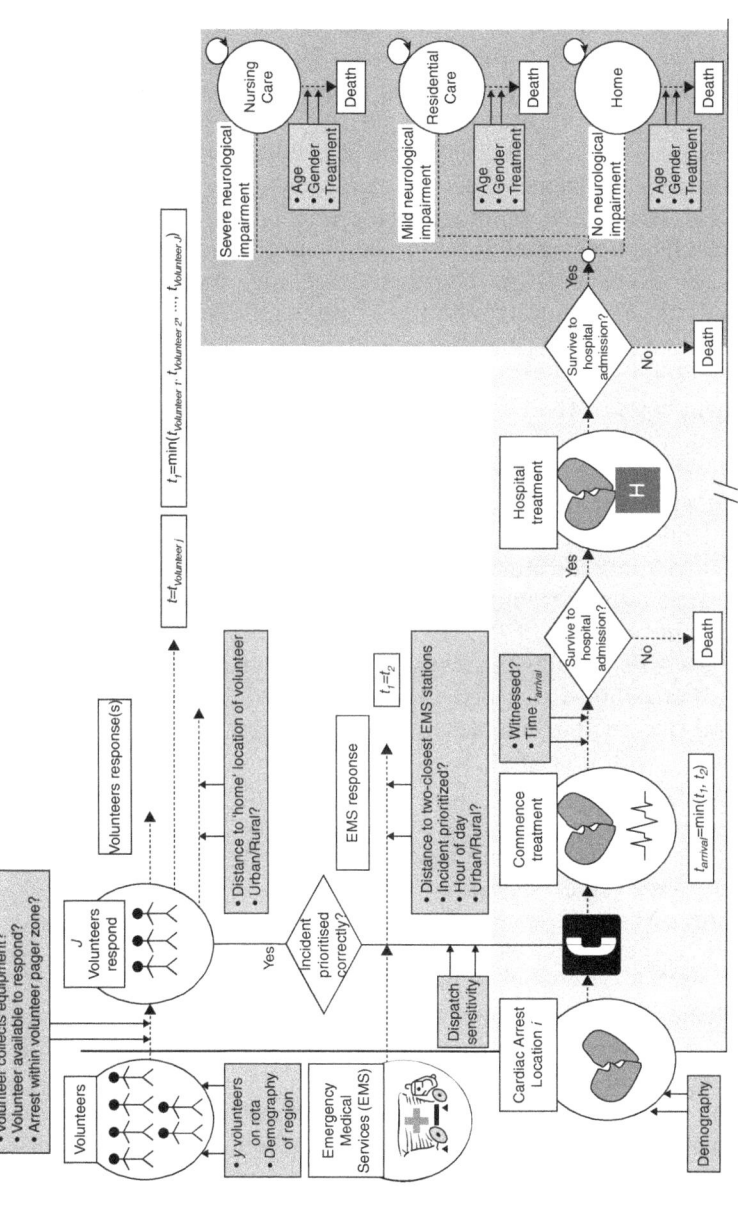

*Figure 4.2* Model schematic of the timeline of Sudden Cardiac Arrest (SCA) patients. The model considers both the short-term (survival-to-hospital discharge) and the long-term survival of patients. Variables that influence any part of the timeline are given in grey boxes

where $P_{jk}$ is the probability of SCA over 1 year, for persons in a given 5-year age-group $j$ and gender $k$, and $N_{ijk}$ is the number of people in COA $i$ from the 5-year age-group $j$ and gender $k$. $P_{jk}$ is principally based on the number of incidents recorded by the World Health Organisation's MONICA project in Belfast (Tunstall-Pedoe et al, 1994), according to gender and age-group over the period 1983–1993. Data prospectively obtained from the NI-PAD trial (Moore et al, 2006, 2008) as well as multiple source surveillance of death certificate data in Northern Ireland were also used in determining $P_{jk}$. $N_{ijk}$ is obtained using population demographic information from the UK census (Census, 2001).

For each simulated SCA, the patient's age, their gender, the hour of day, and the geographical location are used in other parts of the model.

### 4.2.3    Simulation model component: costs

The main costs of the FR scheme considered include employment of a Community-Defibrillation-Officer to recruit, train, and co-ordinate volunteer FRs on a rota. Costs also include equipment, advertising and support administration costs over a 5-year period (West and Hamilton, 2007). Note however FRs are not assumed to receive any additional wages for training and attendance at incidents, other than fuel expenses.

The model also accounts for hospitalisation (Peberdy et al, 2003; Department of Health, 2006; Private Health Care UK, 2007) and long-term care costs of individuals (Curtis and Netten, 2006; Owens et al, 1997). It is assumed that patients with no/mild neurological impairment receive an Implantable-Cardioverter-Defibrillator (ICD) and an angiogram, with a proportion receiving coronary artery bypass graft/angioplasty. A proportion of patients with moderate neurological impairment are assumed to receive an angiogram and angioplasty. Costs for these cases, together with long-term care costs (under the baseline scenario) are given in Table 4.1.

Future costs were discounted at a rate suggested by Gold et al, 1996.

### 4.2.4    Simulation model component: short-term survival

Possible improvements in response times between the two health interventions can result in differences in the proportions of patients that die before hospital discharge (Valenzuela et al, 1997).

Within the model, the survival of patients whose SCA is witnessed and whose initial rhythm is ventricular fibrillation (VF) is modelled depending on the response-time interval. A logistic-regression equation (Valenzuela et al, 1997) is used in this case, assuming that CPR and defibrillation are performed 1 and 2 minutes, respectively, after arrival

*Table 4.1* Input data for simulation model: costs

| Costs (£) | Estimate | Reference |
|---|---|---|
| Cost of implementing cardiac FR PAD scheme (example) | 474 256 | West and Hamilton (2007) |
| *Hospital stay for patient:* | | |
| who dies before discharge | 2162 | Peberdy *et al* (2003); Department of Health (2006); Private Health Care UK (2007) |
| discharged alive with no/mild neurological impairment | 34 540 | Peberdy *et al* (2003); Department of Health (2006); Private Health Care UK (2007) |
| discharged alive with moderate neurological impairment | 13 040 | Peberdy *et al* (2003); Department of Health (2006); Private Health Care UK (2007) |
| discharged alive with severe neurological impairmment | 10 154 | Peberdy *et al* (2003); Department of Health (2006); Private Health Care UK (2007) |
| *Weekly cost of care for:* | | |
| moderately neurologically impaired | 398 | Curtis and Netten (2006) |
| severely neurologically impaired | 424 | Curtis and Netten (2006) |
| Yearly ongoing cost of ICD | 6168 | Owens *et al* (1997) |
| Discount rate for future costs and effects (%) | 3 | Gold *et al* (1996) |

of assistance, as suggested. For those patients not in witnessed-VF, their probability of survival is assumed to be relatively small (Moore *et al*, 2008) (Table 4.2).

The witnessed-VF status of patients is determined in two stages (based on NI-PAD trial data results (Moore *et al*, 2008)). First, only a proportion of cases are assumed as witnessed (Table 4.2). For those patients that are witnessed, the probability that their initial rhythm is VF is represented by the following logistic-regression equation model, dependent on the time to arrival of assistance.

Equation (1): Logistic-regression equation used to represent the probability that a witnessed SCA patient's initial rhythm is VF:

$$\text{Prob(VF| witnessed)} = \frac{1}{1 + \exp\left[-0.601 + 0.149 \times t_{arrival}\right]} \tag{1}$$

To incorporate costs of additional non-survivors going to hospital, the expected number of additional hospital non-survivors is assumed to follow an observed ratio of hospital admissions to discharges (Kim *et al*, 2001).

### 4.2.5   Simulation model component: long-term survival

A number of assumptions are made regarding patients surviving post-hospital discharge (using sources other than the NI-PAD experience, Table 4.3). It is assumed that patients with severe neurological impairment require long-term nursing care; those with moderate neurological impairment require residential care. Valuations of the quality-of-life of SCA survivors are derived from cohort studies (Gage *et al*, 1996; Nichol *et al*, 1999). The proportions of patients with moderate/severe neurological impairment are derived from a retrospective cohort study (Pell *et al*, 2006).

State-transition Markov models are used to model long-term survival (Briggs and Sculpher, 1998). Lifetables are used as part of the Markov

*Table 4.2*   Input data for simulation model: short-term survival

| Short-term survival probabilities | Estimate | Reference |
|---|---|---|
| P(SCA is witnessed) | 0.372 | Moore *et al* (2008) |
| P(survival \| non-(witnessed VF) SCA) | 0.005 | Moore *et al* (2008) |
| P(hospital admission surviving to discharge) | 0.432 | Kim *et al* (2001) |

Table 4.3    Input data for simulation model: long-term survival

| Long-term survival parameters | Estimate | Reference |
|---|---|---|
| *Quality-of-life utility:* | | |
| Severe neurological impairment | 0.1 | Gage *et al* (1996) |
| Moderate neurological impairment | 0.2 | Gage *et al* (1996) |
| No/mild neurological impairment | 0.8 | Nichol *et al* (1999) |
| *Probabilities/risk parameters:* | | |
| P(no/mild neurological impairment) | 0.813 | Pell *et al* (2006) |
| P (moderate neurological impairment \| either moderate or severe neurological impairment) | 0.837 | Pell *et al* (2006) |
| Annual probability of death due to SCA without ICD | 0.086 | The AVID Investigators (1997) |
| Relative risk of death due to SCA with ICD | 0.43 | The AVID Investigators (1997) |
| Relative risk of death due to severe neurological impairment | 1.1 | Nichol *et al* (2003) |

model for age-specific mortality from unrelated causes (Office for National Statistics, 2008). The increased risk of death because of SCA after insertion/no insertion of an ICD was derived from a randomised trial (The AVID Investigators, 1997). This disease-specific mortality rate is combined with each patient's age-specific mortality rate. Those with severe neurological impairment are also assumed to be at increased risk of death (Nichol *et al*, 2003).

### 4.2.6 Simulation model component: response-time improvements

Improvements in response times because of the FR scheme can be quantified through modelling both EMS and FR response times to each SCA incident.

### 4.2.7 Response-time improvements: modelling EMS response times

A parametric accelerated failure-time model has been used to model EMS response times. This model fully parameterizes the EMS response-time distribution (which is necessary for the simulation purposes of this analysis) and accounts for the effect of multiple covariates on the response. On the basis of examining 75 219 emergency incidents (across Northern Ireland) this research highlights that the EMS response typically depends on the geographical location of an incident, with $r_1$ and $r_2$, the radial distances from the 1st and 2nd closest EMS station, influencing response. The hour of day also influences response, and has been incorporated into the model through 4 categories: 0–7, 8–9, 10–13, and 14–23 hours. The response is also influenced by region type (urban/rural), and to a lesser extent, the AMPDS prioritisation coding. The most apt underlying distribution was found to be that of the log-logistic.

### 4.2.8   Response-time improvements: modelling FR rota

The model aims to mimic the FR rota scheme deployed to ascertain FR responses. Whilst research has been carried out into developing the most effective rota for volunteers (Cairns *et al*, 2005), the simulation model has also been built to assume volunteers are recruited across the selected geographical region, where their locations are in line with the geographical distribution of the underlying potential recruitable population (ie persons aged 18+) (Census, 2001). Thus in this case, the number of FRs in each COA on the rota in any given week is given by a multinomial distribution with parameters $y$ (the total persons on the rota scheme in any given week) and $p$, representing the proportion of the selected geographical region's potential recruitable population in each COA.

The radial distance of the geographical paging zone of each individual FR can be varied in the model. The optimal distance can vary depending on the geographical region being considered. For example, during the NI-PAD trial, pagers zones in the more remote ABM region were set to 15 miles, whilst in the urban NWB region the zone was 3 km.

A factor has been incorporated into the model to account for volunteers on the rota not always collecting their AED/pager (as found during the NI-PAD trial). It was also observed that while numerous FRs may have been paged to any one particular SCA incident, individuals FRs typically only responded to around 30% of incidents to which they were paged during the NI-PAD trial (Table 4.4).

The model also incorporates the sensitivity of the dispatch mechanism. FRs were not paged to all SCA incidents during the NI-PAD trial (Cairns *et al*, 2008), given the dispatch mechanism used firstly required SCAs to be reported to the EMS as emergencies, and secondly required the AMPDS software to correctly prioritise SCAs as 'Cardiac-Arrest'. The sensitivity of the dispatch mechanism was found to be significantly lower in the rural ABM region at 40.2% (95% Confidence Interval (CI) 31.4–49.4%) in comparison to that observed in the urban NWB region namely 60.0% (95% CI 54.8–64.7%) (Fisher's exact test: $p < 0.001$). This

*Table 4.4* Input data for simulation model: parameters of FR scheme

| Parameters of cardiac FR scheme (assumed for illustrative example) | | Reference |
|---|---|---|
| Number of volunteers on rota | 31 | NI-PAD Investigators (2007) |
| Radial distance of paging zone for FRs (miles) | 15 | NI-PAD Investigators (2007) |
| Probability volunteer on rota collects their AED | 0.8 | NI-PAD Investigators (2007) |
| Probability an individual FR responds to a paged incident | 0.3 | NI-PAD Investigators (2007) |
| Sensitivity of the dispatch mechanism | 0.4 | NI-PAD Investigators (2007); Cairns *et al* (2008) |

difference may be due in part to differences in the length of time the AMPDS software has been operational in the two regions (Heward *et al*, 2004). However, there may also be regional-based reasons for these differences.

### 4.2.9 Response-time improvements: modelling FR response times

A separate parametric accelerated failure-time model has been used to model individual FR response times. Analysis of the NI-PAD trial data found that FR response times to incidents depend on the location of the SCA relative to location of the mobile FR (a trend also found in modelling EMS response times). Several different methods of quantifying geographical location information were tested, the most apt was found to use the radial distance between the location of the FR's home and the SCA incident, denoted $r_{FR}$. FR response times were found to differ significantly in the two observational regions (Likelihood Ratio Test, $p = 0.003$), with responses typically 1.34 times longer in the urban NWB region, at comparable $r_{FR}$ distances (Figure 4.3). This urban congestion factor has thus also been included in the FR response-time model.

## 4.3  Validation of the simulation model

A core component of the model, not present in other cost-effectiveness analyses assessing mobile-volunteer cardiac FR schemes, involves representing response times of the EMS and FRs accurately. Numerous validation checks have been carried out examining the response times produced by the model, to ascertain the model's validity.

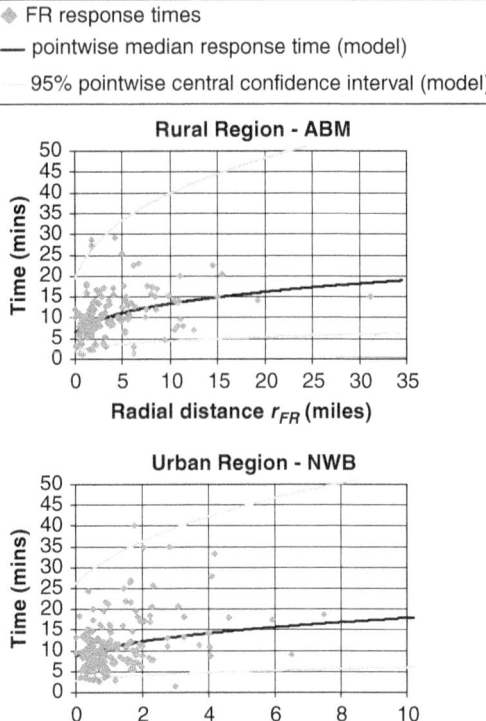

*Figure 4.3*  The NI-PAD trial FR response-time data in the urban/rural region is illustrated as a function of the radial distance $r_{FR}$ (see main text) by diamonds. The pointwise median and 95% central confidence interval for the FR response times from the parametric accelerated failure-time model are also illustrated

The observational NI-PAD trial data were used at the validation stage to assess whether the overall conclusions drawn by the model are in general agreement with those observed. Thus simulations were carried out considering the two geographical regions part of the NI-PAD trial, namely NWB and ABM. Apart from selecting different geographical regions, the only other parameter differences were in (i) the volunteers on the rota each week (7 volunteers in NWB; 13 in ABM); (ii) the geographical paging zone distance (3 km in NWB; 15 miles in ABM) and (iii) the dispatch sensitivity (60% in NWB; 40% in ABM).

Table 4.5 illustrates that the model output agrees with a number of the key statistics observed from the observational trials, capturing

*Table 4.5* Comparison of key statistics observed from the observational trials in North and West Belfast (NWB) and Antrim, Ballymena and Magherafelt (ABM), compared with model output (median values together with 95% central confidence intervals are indicated)

| Statistic | Geographical region | | | |
|---|---|---|---|---|
| | NWB | | ABM | |
| | Observed | Model | Observed | Model |
| Number of SCAs FRs are paged to | 106 | 92 | 49 | 55 |
| | | [74, 111] | | [41, 70.5] |
| Proportion of paged incidents responded to by FRs (%) | 68.3 | 63.8 | 80.0 | 82.4 |
| | | [53.8, 73.4] | | [70.4, 91.5] |
| Proportion of paged incidents reached by FRs before EMS (%) | 12.9 | 11.1 | 40.0 | 36.9 |
| | | [4.9, 18.7] | | [24.1, 50.0] |

the variation between geographical regions. For example, the model is in agreement with that observed for the number of SCAs FRs were paged to (a statistic that depends on the generation of SCA incidents, and the sensitivity of the dispatch mechanism). Similarly, the model is in agreement with that observed for the proportion of paged incidents responded to by FRs (a statistic that depends on the rota scheme deployed and the availability of FRs to respond).

Figure 4.1 illustrates the agreement between the response times output by the model and those observed in the NI-PAD trial. The model captures the underlying differences in the EMS response times between the two geographical regions. It also captures the changes in the response-time distributions as a result of the FRs, with a smaller 'shift' being observed in NWB compared with ABM (on comparison of EMS response times to combined EMS/FR response times).

## 4.4   Illustrative application of model

To present some of the information output from the model and to illustrate its potential, simulated results are presented for a selected region of the UK, not part of the original NI-PAD trial. The comparison of interventions was made for a primarily rural region encompassing Cookstown,

Dungannon Fermanagh, and Omagh district councils (population 185 795 (Census, 2001), area 4410 km², Figure 4.4).

For the purposes of presentation of results, the impact of running a 31-person rota scheme for 5 years has been considered (in line with costing developed by West and Hamilton, 2007). The geographical paging zones are set to 15 miles, with the sensitivity of the dispatch mechanism set to 40% (see Table 4.4 for baseline scenario parameter values). Furthermore FR response times in this geographical region are assumed to be comparable to the predominately rural ABM region, thus the urban congestion factor is not used explicitly in generating FR response times.

The model predicts that within this region, 930 (95% CI 871–990) SCA incidents occur over the 5-year period. This is in line with expected given population demographics (Woollard, 2001; Moore et al, 2006).

With the baseline 31-person rota described, at least one FR attempts to respond to 87.6% (95% CI 84.0–90.8%) of SCAs to which they were paged. Figure 4.5 illustrates the typical number of FRs that would respond to paged SCA incidents based on this rota configuration. The model predicts that at least one FR would arrive at least 1 min before the EMS in the case of 44.6% (95% CI 39.6–49.7%) of the paged SCA incidents. This corresponds to 17.8% (95% CI 15.4–20.3%) of all SCAs.

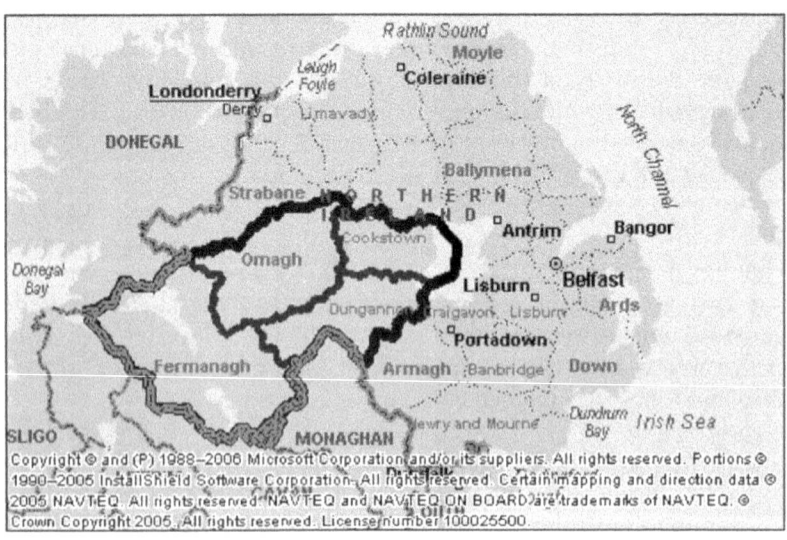

*Figure 4.4* Map illustrating the geographical region where the impact of a FR scheme has been assessed through simulation. It encompasses Cookstown, Dungannon, Fermanagh, and Omagh district councils

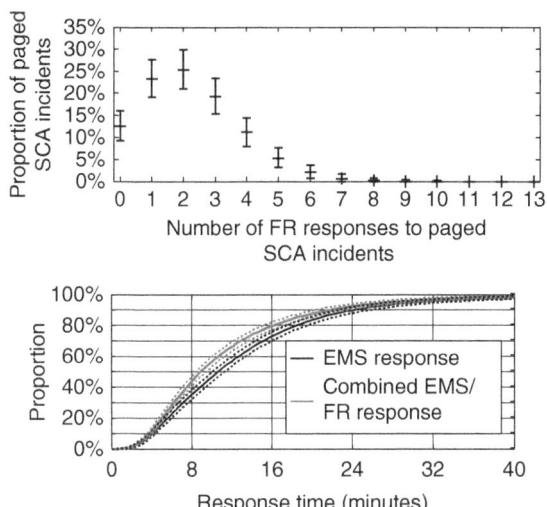

*Figure 4.5* Figure illustrating the number of FRs that would typically respond to paged SCA incidents in the selected geographical region, based on the 31-person rota. (95% central confidence intervals are indicated by error bars.) The simulated cumulative response-time distributions (with 95% central confidence intervals) under the two interventions: (EMS only versus combined EMS/FR) are also presented

Simulated response times are thus improved in this geographical region through the addition of the FR scheme, as shown in Figure 4.5. The median EMS response over the 5-year period is 10.7 min (95% CI 10.1–11.3 min) compared with 8.9 min (95% CI 8.4–9.4 min) under the combined EMS/FR response. With only the EMS response, 35.0% (95% CI 32.0–38.1%) of SCA incidents are reached within 8 min, compared with 43.8% (95% CI 40.6–47.0%) under the combined EMS/FR response.

For 96.3% of simulations (under the baseline scenario), the FR scheme results in at least one additional survivor (to-hospital discharge). Figure 4.6 illustrates the probability distribution for the number of additional lives saved. The model predicts that 2.4% (95% CI 1.5–3.4%) of SCA lives would be saved under EMS compared with 2.8% (95% CI 1.8–3.9%) under the combined EMS/FR response.

The model predicts that the average life-years gained in the case of the additional survivors is 8.2 (95% CI 1.3–23.1). The additional QALYs gained over the course of the 5-year period are 13.5 QALYs (95% CI 0.0–42.8; interquartile range [IQR] = 6.3–22.5).

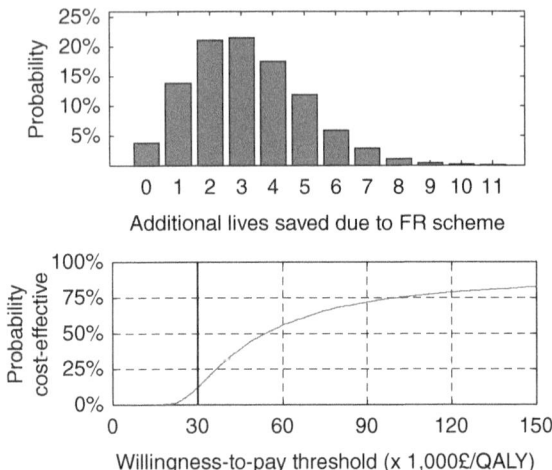

*Figure 4.6*   Figure illustrating the probability distribution for the number of additional lives saved due to the FR scheme in the selected geographical region (ie the number of additional patients now surviving to hospital discharge). The cumulative distribution of the Incremental Cost-Effectiveness Ratio for the illustrative example mobile FR scheme is also presented

The incremental cost-effectiveness ratio (ICER) (that is, the incremental costs incurred divided by the QALYs gained) is £54 234/QALY (IQR = 36 699 to 101 385) upon comparison of the two interventions (Figure 4.6).

## 4.5   Conclusions

A Monte-Carlo simulation-based model has been constructed to assess a public health scheme involving mobile-volunteer cardiac First-Responders. The model produced goes beyond observational trial results, which have shown varying impact. It aims to model the stochastic and spatial complexities inherent in a scheme involving mobile-volunteers, so that the improvements in response times in different geographical region/rota schemes can be quantified, and, in turn, so that the conclusions drawn from the cost-effectiveness analysis reflect the geographical region being considered.

The potential of the model has been illustrated through considering the scheme's impact in a rural region of the UK. In this case, the ICER ratio was less than the nominal National Health Service (NHS) NICE threshold of £30 000 (Evans *et al*, 2004) in 12.2% of simulations

(Figure 4.6), suggesting that the scheme may not be the most efficient use of NHS resources. However, as seen from the observational trial data (Figure 4.1) this scheme could start to address the existing imbalance in emergency response provision between rural and urban regions. Additionally it may be useful to monitor the changing costs of the components of the model. (If the cost of a particular aspect were to decrease, the scheme could then become a more cost-effective option.) The simulation model presented can be readily used to perform one-way sensitivity analyses (to assess if conclusions made would differ as a result of changes in single parameter estimates). Furthermore second order (multiple-parameter uncertainty) probabilistic sensitivity analyses can be readily integrated into this research's model. These techniques, combined with the model presented, thus aim to improve the information being provided to decision-makers in assessing such a public health scheme.

In conclusion, this paper has developed a sophisticated model to replicate the impact of mobile-volunteer cardiac FR schemes. In doing so it demonstrates the importance of simulation modelling as a tool for decision makers.

## Acknowledgements

This work was supported by a commissioned research grant from the Research and Development Office of the DHSSPSNI (Department of Health, Social Services and Public Safety Northern Ireland). KJC is also supported through an Engineering & Physical Sciences Research Council (EPSRC) RCUK Academic Fellowship. The authors specially thank the members of the NI-PAD team and its collaborators.

## References

Brailsford SC (2007). Tutorial: Advances and challenges in healthcare simulation modeling. In: Henderson SG, Biller B, Hsieh M-H, Shortle J, Tew JD and Barton RR. (eds). *Proceedings of the 2007 Winter Simulation Conference*. ACM Press: New York, pp 1436–1448.

Brandeau ML, Sainfort F and Pierskalla WP (2004). *Operations Research and Health Care: A Handbook of Methods and Applications*. Kluwer Academic Publishers: Dordrecht.

Briggs A and Sculpher M (1998). An introduction to Markov modelling for health economic evaluation. *Pharmacoeconomics* 13: 397–409. http://www.herc.ox.ac.uk/downloads/supp_pub/markov, accessed 19 January 2010.

Cairns KJ, Marshall AH and Kee F (2005). A Public Access Defibrillation Trial in Urban and Rural Communities in Northern Ireland: Developing the Roster Model. In: Tsymbal A and Cunningham P (eds). *Proceedings of the 18th IEEE*

*International Symposium on Computer-Based Medical Systems (CBMS)*, Dublin, pp 497–502, IEEE Computer Society Press: Los Alamitos.

Cairns KJ, Hamilton AJ, Marshall AH, Moore MJ, Adgey AAJ and Kee F (2008). The obstacles to maximising the impact of public access defibrillation: An assessment of the dispatch mechanism for out-of-hospital cardiac arrest. *Heart* **94**: 349–353.

Capucci A, Aschieri D, Piepoli MF, Bardy GH, Iconomu E and Arvedi M (2002). Tripling survival from sudden cardiac arrest via early defibrillation without traditional education in cardiopulmonary resuscitation. *Circulation* **106**: 1065–1070.

Census (2001). Northern Ireland Census 2001 output, http://www.nisranew.nisra. gov.uk/census/Census2001Output/index.html, accessed 19 January 2010.

Cooper K, Brailsford SC and Davies R (2007). Choice of modelling technique for evaluating health care interventions. *J Opl Res Soc* **58**: 168–176.

Curtis L and Netten A (2006). *Unit costs of health and social care*. Personal Social Services Research Unit (PSSRU), University of Kent, Kent.

Davies R and Bensley D (2005). Editorial for special issue: Meeting health challenges with OR. *J Opl Res Soc* **56**: 123–125.

de Jong H (2002). Modeling and simulation of genetic regulatory systems: A literature review. *J Comput Biol* **9**: 67–103.

Department of Health (2006). NHS Reference Costs 2005–06, http://www.dh.gov. uk/en/Publicationsandstatistics/Publications/PublicationsPolicyAndGuidance/ DH_062884, accessed 19 January 2010.

Evans C, Tavakoli M and Crawford B (2004). Use of quality adjusted life years and life years gained as benchmarks in economic evaluations: A critical appraisal. *Health Care Manag Sci* **7**: 43–49.

Fone D, Hollinghurst S, Temple M, Round A, Lester N, Weightman A, Roberts K, Coyle E, Bevan G and Palmer S (2003). Systematic review of the use and value of computer simulation modelling in population health and health care delivery. *J Public Health Med* **25**: 325–335.

Gage BF, Cardinalli AB and Owens DK (1996). The effect of stroke and stroke prophylaxis with aspirin or warfarin on quality of life. *Arch Intern Med* **156**: 1829–1836.

Gold MR, Siegel JE, Russell LB and Weinstein MC (1996). *Cost-effectiveness in Health and Medicine*. Oxford University Press: New York.

Heward A, Damiani M and Hartley-Sharpe C (2004). Does the use of the Advanced Medical Priority Dispatch System affect cardiac arrest detection? *Emerg Med J* **21**: 115–118.

Joglar JA and Page RL (2002). Automated external defibrillator use by police responders: Where do we go from here? *Circulation* **106**: 1030–1033.

Jun JB, Jacobson SH and Swisher JR (1999). Application of discrete-event simulation in health care clinics: A survey. *J Opl Res Soc* **50**: 109–123.

Kern KB (1998). Public access defibrillation: A review. *Heart* **80**: 402–404.

Kim C, Fahrenbruch CE, Cobb LA and Eisenberg MS (2001). Out-of-hospital cardiac arrest in men and women. *Circulation* **104**: 2699–2703.

Kuljis J, Paul RJ, Stergioulas LK (2007). Can health care benefit from modeling and simulation methods in the same way as business and manufacturing has? In: Henderson SG, Biller B, Hsieh M-H, Shortle J, Tew JD and Barton RR (eds).

*Proceedings of the 2007 Winter Simulation Conference*, ACM Press: New York, pp 1449–1453.

Marshall AH, Cairns KJ, Kee F, Moore MJ, Hamilton AJ and Adgey AAJ (2006). A Monte Carlo simulation model to assess volunteer response times in a public access defibrillation scheme in Northern Ireland. In: Lee DJ, Nutter B, Antani S, Mitra S and Archibald J (eds). *Proceedings of the 19th IEEE International Symposium on Computer-Based Medical Systems (CBMS)*, Salt Lake City, pp 783–788, IEEE Computer Society Press: Los Alamitos.

Mears G, Mann NC, Wright D, Schnyder ME and Dean JM (2006). Validation of a predictive model for automated external defibrillator placement in rural America. *Prehospital Emergency Care* 10: 186–193.

Moore MJ, Glover BM, McCann CJ, Cromie NA, Ferguson P, Catney DC, Kee F and Adgey AAJ (2006). Demographic and temporal trends in out of hospital sudden cardiac death in Belfast. *Heart* 92: 311–315.

Moore MJ, Hamilton AJ, Cairns KJ, Marshall A, Glover BM, McCann CJ, Jordan J, Kee F and Adgey AAJ (2008). The Northern Ireland Public Access Defibrillation (NIPAD) study: Effectiveness in urban and rural populations. *Heart* 94: 1614–1619.

National Institute for Clinical Excellence (2004). Guide to the Methods of Technology Appraisal. NICE: London.

Nichol G, Stiell IG, Hebert P, Wells GA, Vandemheen K and Laupacis A (1999). What is the quality of life for survivors of cardiac arrest? A prospective study. *Acad Emerg Med* 6: 95–102.

Nichol G, Valenzuela T, Roe D, Clark L, Huszti E and Wells GA (2003). Cost effectiveness of defibrillation by targeted responders in public settings. *Circulation* 108: 697–703.

NI-PAD Investigators (2007). The Northern Ireland-Public Access Defibrillation (NI-PAD) study report. Volume 1.

Office for National Statistics (2008). Interim life tables for Northern Ireland (2004–06), http://www.statistics.gov.uk/downloads/theme_population/Interim Life/ILTNI0608Reg.xls, accessed 19 January 2010.

Owens DK, Sanders GD, Harris RA, McDonald KM, Heidenreich PA, Dembitzer AD and Hlatky MA (1997). Cost-effectiveness of implantable cardioverter defibrillators relative to amiodarone for prevention of sudden cardiac death. *Ann Intern Med* 126: 1–12.

Peberdy MA, Kaye W, Ornato JP, Larkin GL, Nadkarni V, Mancini ME, Berg RA, Nichol G and Lane-Trultt T (2003). Cardiopulmonary resuscitation of adults in the hospital: A report of 14 720 cardiac arrests from the National Registry of Cardiopulmonary Resuscitation. *Resuscitation* 58: 297–308.

Pell JP, Corstorphine M, McConnachie A, Walker NL, Caldwell JC, Marsden AK, Grubb NR and Cobbe SM (2006). Post-discharge survival following pre-hospital cardiopulmonary arrest due to cardiac aetiology: Temporal trends and impact of changes in clinical management. *Eur Heart J* 27: 406–412.

Private Health Care UK (2007). Coronary angioplasty costs in the UK, http://www.privatehealth.co.uk/hospitaltreatment/whatdoesitcost/coronary-angioplasty/, accessed 19 January 2010.

Romeijn HE and Zenios SA (2008). Introduction to the special issue on operations research in health care. *Opns Res* 56: 1333–1334.

Skogvoll E and Lindqvist BH (1999). Modeling the occurrence of cardiac arrest as a Poisson process. *Ann Emerg Med* **33**: 409–417.

The AVID Investigators (1997). A comparison of antiarrhythmic drug therapy with implantable defibrillators in patients resuscitated from near-fatal ventricular arrhythmias. *N Engl J Med* **33**: 1576–83.

The Public Access Defibrillation Trial Investigators (2004). Public-Access Defibrillation and survival after out-of-hospital cardiac arrest. *N Engl J Med* **351**: 637–646.

Taylor SJE, Eldabi T, Riley RJ and Pidd M (2009). Simulation modelling is 50! Do we need a reality check? *J Opl Res Soc* **60**: S69–S82.

Tunstall-Pedoe H, Kuulasmaa K, Amouyel P, Arveiler D, Rajakangas AM and Pajak A (1994). Myocardial infarction and coronary deaths in the World Health Organisation MONICA Project. Registration procedures, event rates, and case-fatality rates in 38 populations from 21 countries in four continents. *Circulation* **90**: 583–612.

Valenzuela TD, Roe DJ, Cretin S, Spaite DW and Larsen MP (1997). Estimating effectiveness of cardiac arrest interventions: A logistic regression survival model. *Circulation* **96**: 3308–3313.

Walker A, Sirel JM, Marsden AK, Cobbe SM and Pell JP (2003). Cost effectiveness and cost utility model of public place defibrillators in improving survival after prehospital cardiopulmonary arrest. *BMJ* **327**: 1316–1320.

West J and Hamilton A (2007). First Response for Northern Ireland: Discussion Paper, Northern Ireland Ambulance Service.

Woollard M (2001). Public access defibrillation: a shocking idea? *J Pub Health Med* **23**: 98–102.

# Part V
# OR for Policy Formulation in Emergency Services

# 5
# The DH Accident and Emergency Department Model: A National Generic Model Used Locally

*A. Fletcher[1], D. Halsall[1], S. Huxham[1] and D. Worthington[2]*
[1]*Department of Health, Leeds, UK; and* [2]*Lancaster University, Lancaster, UK*

*The Department of Health (DH) Accident and Emergency (A&E) simulation model was developed by Operational Research analysts within DH to inform the national policy team of significant barriers to the national target, for England, that 98% of all A&E attendances are to be completed (discharged, transferred or admitted) within 4 hours of arrival by December 2004. This paper discusses why the model was developed, the structure of the model, and the impact when used to inform national policy development. The model was then used as a consultancy tool to aid struggling hospital trusts to improve their A&E departments. The paper discusses these experiences with particular reference to the challenges of using a 'generic' national model for 'specific' local use.*

## 5.1 Introduction

The Economics, Statistics and Operational Research (ESOR) division in the Department of Health (DH) provide analytical modelling and advice to policy leads on the design and implementation of DH policy, in public health and the National Health Service (NHS) in England. The primary author led analytical support in DH from December 2002 on the NHS Plan Target that by December 2004, 98% of patients arriving at Accident and Emergency (A&E) departments in England should be completed, that is, admitted, discharged or transferred, within 4 h. Approximately 13 million people attend around 200 'major' A&E

Reprinted from *Journal of the Operational Research Society*, 58: 1554–1562, 2007, 'The DH Accident and Emergency Department Model: A National Generic Model Used Locally', by A. Fletcher, D. Halsall, S. Huxham and D. Worthington. With kind permission from Operational Research Society Ltd. All rights reserved.

departments in England every year, with no barrier to attendance at any time. Around 80% of attendees are discharged home, 20% being admitted to an inpatient hospital bed. This target was a major national performance indicator and at the time, the NHS was receiving significant increases in funding. It was important that targets such as this were seen to be delivered as evidence that NHS performance was being modernized and improved to meet patients' expectations.

In December 2002, the national figure was 78% completed within 4 h. ESOR were asked to identify the key issues faced by A&E departments, and barriers to delivery of the target. An analytical programme of work was developed, which included the work described in this paper.

This paper has three main sections. The first part covers the development and application of a 'generic' simulation model in Simul8 (2006, http://www.simul8.com/, 29 September 2006) of a 'typical' A&E department to help policy leads understand the flows of patients in A&E departments. Aims, methodology, model design, model calibration and validation, and examples of national use of the model are covered.

We then describe an opportunity that subsequently arose to apply this generic model in hospital trusts and the associated results. This is of interest because it addressed a real problem, and also provided the opportunity to investigate the practical pros and cons of applying a generic model to specific problem situations.

Finally, we summarize these experiences and reflect on them in the context of some current simulation modelling debates.

## 5.2   Aims of the generic national model

Within the programme of analytical work to support the national policy team in helping the NHS to improve A&E departments, a key requirement was to effectively communicate the issues facing a typical A&E department. The generic national model was designed to contribute in this area. Specific aims for the model are summarized as follows:

- show, visually and numerically, how an A&E department works (key outputs being 4-h performance by patient group and overall);
- build a consensus within DH about the key issues facing A&E;
- identify 'quick wins' to improve A&E;
- communicate the effects of variability in demand and service provision;
- show what success and failure look like;
- run high-level 'what if' scenarios to quantify the potential impact of key policy options;

- direct available DH resources into the correct areas;
- establish a baseline of performance and issues in a 'typical' department to measure changes against.

The customer for the model was the national DH emergency care team. This was made up of emergency care policy leads, nursing and clinical advisers and programme managers, with overall national responsibility for delivering the A&E target. The primary author was the analytical lead within this team. In terms of building the model, the nursing and clinical advisers were key in terms of defining processes to model to ensure realism.

## 5.3 Methodology for the generic national model

Discrete event simulation is known to have potentially substantial benefits in communicating issues visually and numerically to stakeholders. Given the aims of the work, it was felt that discrete event simulation could help build common understanding in the national policy team of 'baseline' performance and issues in A&E at a time when improvement strategies were often driven by anecdote rather than evidence. Two of the authors also had substantial experience in industry applying discrete event simulation to improve industrial processes. Specific benefits anticipated from use of discrete event simulation were:

- recognized success in replicating and improving pathways of multiple processes,
- ability to model individuals,
- visual impact when working with different stakeholder groups,
- ability to run 'what ifs' quickly.

## 5.4 Model design

### 5.4.1 Lessons from elsewhere

Jun *et al* (1999) provide an extensive review of 117 papers on the application of discrete-event simulation in health care. A&E department models are common, and are the focus of at least 12 of them. The reported work included models examining patient routing and flows (eg using a fast track lane in minor care), scheduling of resources (eg matching staffing to demand) and staff sizing and planning (eg the mix and numbers of staff), all of which were important issues to incorporate into our generic model. There is also a wide range of other recently published experience of A&E models. In this literature, there is more evidence of specific A&E

models (ie to one department) than generic. Many examples are in non-English Emergency Rooms (Badri and Hollingsworth, 1993; Gonzalez and Perez, 1994; Blake and Carter, 1996; Rossetti *et al*, 1999; Baesler *et al*, 2003; Blasak *et al*, 2003; Centeno *et al*, 2003; Mahapatra *et al*, 2003; Miller and Ferrin, 2003; Samanha and Armel, 2003; Wiinamaki and Dronzek, 2003; Miller *et al*, 2004; Sinreich and Marmor, 2004; Takakuwa and Shiozaki, 2004); which have different designs to English A&E. Key outputs are typically time in A&E, queue length and staff/room utilization. Models often include A&E medical, nursing and clerical staffing, examination cubicles, diagnostics, decision to admit and bed management. Specific patient types are often modelled, often by time of day and day of week. Models occasionally directly model capacity constrained bed systems, diagnostic departments and surgery, but more often as capacity unconstrained time distributions. Techniques used are mainly discrete event simulation, but there is also evidence of scheduling, queuing models and system dynamics. Design is usually through discussion with local experts. Data collection is generally through computerized records, also occasionally using work study and local consultation. Validation is discussed less, but is usually through comparison with computerized records, and/or 'open box' type validation with local experts. Improvement scenarios include workforce scheduling, changed roles, bed management, fast track patients, diagnostic changes and overall capacity changes. Implementation is not widely discussed, but there is some evidence to suggest that both generic and specific models have similar designs and they have been used with success rates approximately equal among them.

As discussed, a lot of this is experience in foreign departments where patient flows can differ significantly from England. Those developed in England include Lane *et al* (2000), who developed a system dynamics model of an A&E department, output being patient time in A&E, issues being demand profiles, patient testing, doctor utilization and bed management. Komashie and Mousavi (2005) describe a specific detailed A&E model, also including a Medical Admissions Unit, the key output being patient time. Modelled issues were around changes in bed capacity and demand patterns. As will be seen later, models described in the literature were similar to the issues modelled here.

We have seen that valuable lessons can be learnt from the literature on the key model building issues of model scope, design, performance indicators, analytical techniques, data collection, validation, improvement scenarios and implementation. The literature suggests that generic models were not noticeably less successful than models specific to one A&E department.

In addition to learning general lessons from the research literature, our interest in model re-use, see for example Robinson *et al* (2004), required that we looked seriously for, and obtain access to any models that might be considered for re-use. DH contacts made us aware of a model developed at Oldham hospital. This model was not published, but had a good reputation, was recent, had already been applied locally to model total time in A&E and was available immediately.

We learnt a good deal from this model, but we ultimately built a new model for a variety of reasons:

- While the model included the key 'bottleneck' processes, we had agreed with the national clinical leads, it also contained many locally specific processes that were not nationally appropriate. For example, it included the formal initial triage of patients by nurses, whereas guidance from the NHS Modernisation Agency had led to many trusts dispensing with this process.
- The model used the traditional patient groupings of the 'Manchester' triage system, which categorized patients by urgency of need. However, most A&E departments had moved away from this to a simple minor/major patient split—we wished to reflect this 'new world'.
- The Oldham model had a more detailed process flow than required in a national model.

Our decision not to use the Oldham model was driven by confidence in our ability to build a national model without the issues identified above with somebody else's (specific) model. However, numerous lessons (and some process time data) were taken from the model and it was a significant aid in the design stages. Significant amounts of traditional work study had been conducted to generate the process times in the Oldham model. As described later, this helped give some validity to the assumptions used in the national model. We were also encouraged by their experience that it was possible to accurately model an A&E department using discrete event simulation.

We therefore developed the A&E model (in Simul8) within DH, with the help of targeted external consultancy support. Early iterations of the model were developed in the first part of 2003, with the first set of detailed survey data available in July 2003 for validation.

## 5.5   Model structure

In partnership with the national clinical and nursing advisers, we established generic flows through A&E departments of three types of patients (minor, major and admitted). These patient types had been defined and 'marketed' to the NHS by the NHS Modernisation Agency whose role was to spread good practice across the NHS. The most complex flow of subprocesses is for the admitted patients and is summarized in Figure 5.1.

To interpret, for admitted patients the patient arrives in A&E and queues if necessary for an 'initial assessment' by a junior or senior doctor. Diagnostic tests in the form of X-rays or blood tests may be required, in which case, interpretation of the results are needed, also by a doctor. Some sort of treatment process may be required, followed by a 'decision to admit' by the hospital admitting team. Following this, the patient may wait for an inpatient bed to become available, described as 'trolley waits'.

Process flows for major and minor patients are similar, but neither group experiences waits for beds, and the minor group is also assumed not to experience a wait for a decision to admit.

There were two important features of the model design that should be highlighted:

- The model had three patient flows: minor, major and admitted patients. These are modelled separately for visual and communication purposes. However, although minor patients are usually streamed effectively at the 'front door', many major patients are indistinguishable from admitted patients in the early stages of their journey. Hence, the model implies a false, retrospective clarity. This issue was weighed against ease of communication, the latter consideration winning the argument.
- In line with much of the literature reviewed, processes outside the control of the A&E department such as diagnostic tests, decision to admit and admission were not modelled as capacity constrained processes, but as capacity unconstrained time distributions. The impact of these processes on the patient journey was represented, but lack of detailed data in these areas and the need for model simplicity meant that detailed capacity constrained submodels of these processes were not attempted.

## 5.6   Model outputs

Some example outputs from the model are shown in Figure 5.2. These are just a small selection of numerous communication devices.

The first table shows modelled 4 h performance overall, and by patient group, and the variability in these measures by week (typical model

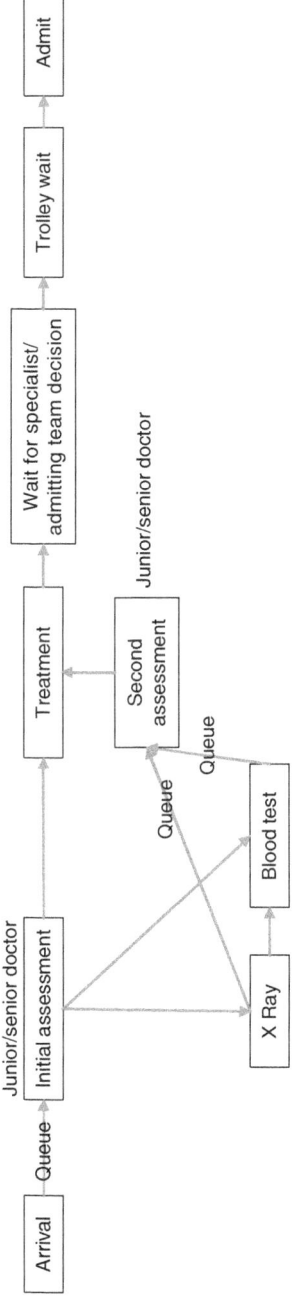

*Figure 5.1* Flows of admitted patients through A&E departments

| Overall A&E 4-hr Performance | | | |
|---|---|---|---|
| | Min % | Avg % | Max % |
| Overall | 90 | **91** | 91 |
| | | | |
| Admitted | 71 | **75** | 79 |
| Major | 89 | 91 | 94 |
| Minor | 95 | 97 | 97 |

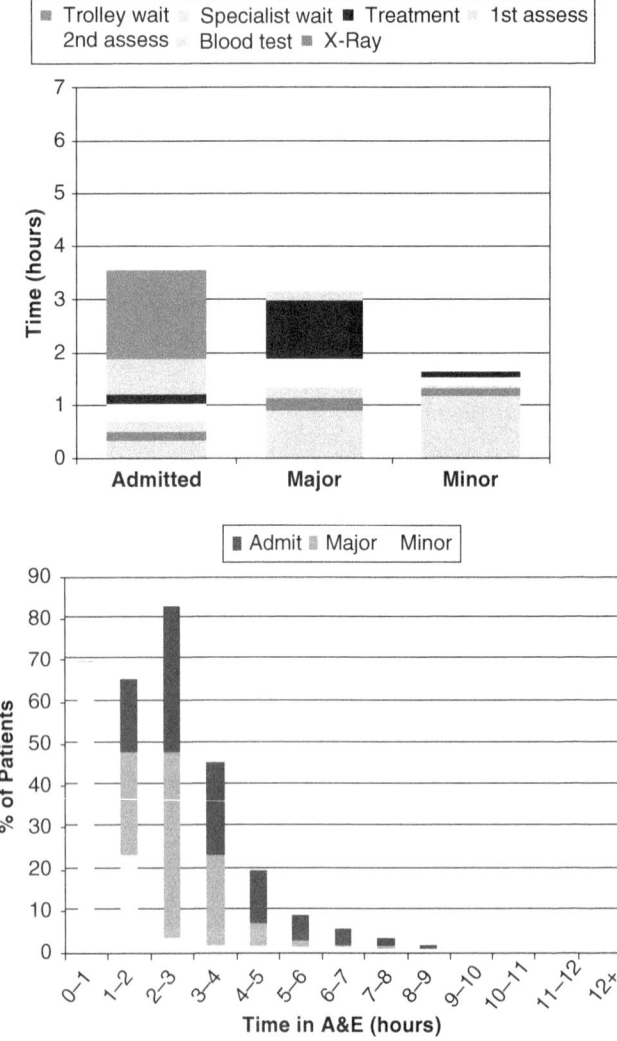

*Figure 5.2*  Example outputs from one run of the National A&E model

run length was 20 weeks). In this run, 75% of admitted patients spent less than 4-h in the A&E department overall, but by week this varied between 71 and 79%.

The right hand bar chart shows the numbers of patients completed in 0–1, 1–2 h, etc., by patient group. In this case, the majority of minor patients are completed very quickly, whereas significant percentages of major and admitted patients require over 4 h.

The final graph shows the average time in each process on the patient journey for each patient group, hence improving understanding of the key reasons for breaches of the 4 h target.

## 5.7  Model calibration

The model was to represent a 'typical' A&E department rather than a particular one, so the challenge of calibrating the model was unusual.

A typical demand profile was obtained from a detailed 7-day survey of a random sample of trusts which were asked to record, for every patient attending A&E in a 7-day period:

- patient group (ie minor, major, admitted);
- date/time of arrival;
- date/time of completion;
- age;
- if the patient was a breach, what process contributed the longest part of the patient's journey.

The survey was designed and run by ESOR and external consultants. The first survey was run in May/June 2003 (and rerun subsequently). Twelve responses from trusts were received, which were indicative of national performance at that time.

Other sources of data were National DH statistics (QMAE), national medical workforce census, Audit Commission, A&E Surveillance Centre, advice from national clinical and nursing advisers and the Oldham model—and were used to set total patient demands, staffing levels, waits for beds, patients requiring diagnostics and decisions to admit. See Table 5.1 for details.

The initial setting of process times (apart from waits for beds) were based on the data from Oldham and expert opinion. However, because the crucial requirement for the generic model was that it should generate 'typical' problems, these times were adjusted until the incidence level of breaches and key reasons matched those observed in the survey.

*Table 5.1* Data used to populate the national A&E model

| Data | Description | Sources |
|---|---|---|
| Size of A&E department | Total number of attendances per annum | National DH statistics |
| Split by patient group | Percentage of attendees in the minor, major and admitted patient groups | A&E 7-day survey |
| Demand profile by hour of day | Percentage of attendees in each patient group every hour | A&E 7-day survey |
| Staff profile per hour of the day | Number of doctors and decision making nurses every hour | Doctors from national medical workforce census. Nurses from Audit Commission data |
| Process times | Minimum, average and maximum times in every process | Waits for bed from national DH statistics. Other process times were inferred from the reasons for breach in A&E 7-day survey |
| Use of diagnostics | Percentage of patients in each patient group that require X-rays and Blood Tests | A&E Surveillance Centre— Birmingham University |
| Decision to admit | Percentage of major patients that required a decision (not) to admit | Advice from national clinical and nursing advisers and local A&E models |

This issue is discussed further in the next section, as in many circumstances this 'fixing' of input parameters to reproduce observed output parameters should not be allowed.

Variability in demand by patient group was generated using inter-arrival times drawn from a negative exponential distribution (changed every hour to allow for demand profiles). Variability in process times was taken from national statistics where available, plus the Oldham model and advice from clinical and nursing advisers. Simple triangular distributions were used to aid communication. A basic analysis indicated that the model produced similar patterns in weekly 4 h performance to those observed in A&E performance at trust level.

### 5.7.1 Validation

Pidd (1999) discusses two key validation techniques—'black box' and 'open box' validation. Black box validation is where the model output is numerically tested against known characteristics of the system. Predictive accuracy is important. Open box validation is a critical assessment of the variables and relationships in the model. Performed in partnership with experts on the system being modelled, it generates mutual agreement that the model accounts for the key 'real world' issues. Both validation techniques were used here.

### 5.7.1.1   Black box validation

Failure of black box validation would normally require that the analyst should refer back to the real world to revisit the model. However, in this case the model was a communication tool representing a 'typical' A&E department. There was no particular real-world department to check against. In fact, as noted earlier, because the model was designed to represent the key characteristics of a 'typical' A&E department, it was assumed that discrepancies between the model and a 'typical' A&E department could be corrected by adjusting process times. The black box test was therefore whether it replicated knowledge generated in the national 7-day survey. The steps taken were as follows:

- take an average sized A&E department (DH statistics);
- split into patient groups of average sizes (7-day survey);
- apply the arrival distributions by time of day for each patient group (7-day survey);
- take an average staffing level of doctors and nurses and generate staffing rotas broadly matching the arrival patterns;
- adjust process times until the distributions of reasons for breach matched the survey;
- in parallel, check that the modelled 4-h performance by patient group replicated the survey;
- finally, ensure the system variability replicated the weekly variability in 4 h performance of a typical trust by adjusting process time variability.

Data from the Oldham model was also very useful in this process as it give an indication of average and variability in process times in a real A&E department. This data was used to crosscheck the generated process times.

This validation process took some time, and was a trial and error-based iterative approach. Where conflicts arose, 4 h performance by patient group took precedence—this was felt to be more accurate than information on reasons for breach. Eventually, the 4h performance by patient group was reflected exactly, and modelled primary reasons for breach were within around 5–10% of survey results. In February 2004, the model was revalidated against a much larger (around 80 trusts) 7-day survey.

We note in passing that this black box validation process has been somewhat unusual because of the intended generic purpose of the model, and hence the absence of any particular real system to compare against. The process has also been 'usual' in the sense that it has been limited by the available data. For example, 7-day surveys for other parts of the year might have given the chance to test the model's validity for different operating conditions.

### 5.7.1.2    *Open box validation*

After the black box validation, open box validation was conducted. The national clinical and nursing adviser and other A&E consultants were shown the model and asked whether the bottleneck process times and broad patient flows looked 'right'. For example, junior doctors were noted to tend to take longer to treat patients and to have higher utilization; and the visual build-up of patients in the waiting room and waiting for beds in the middle of the day was noted (with great feeling!) to match the A&E consultants' experiences. Finally, the model builders also visited a number of A&E departments to 'walk through' the process with local experts, giving confidence to the model builders that the model reflected reality.

## 5.8    Application of the generic model at national level

The result of the validation process was a baseline model with the following characteristics:

- an average sized A&E department;
- with average demand splits by patient group;
- and average arrival patterns by time of day;
- average staffing levels, profiled to the demand pattern;
- inferred process times consistent with average 4 h performance for each patient group and average distributions of reasons for breach.

The baseline model represented an imaginary trust, but was a good representation of the issues facing a 'typical' trust. By modifying the baseline model, it was fairly simple to replicate variability issues—of good or poorly performing trusts, large or small trusts, trusts with particular staffing issues, trusts with issues at a particular stage of its process, trusts with atypical patient mixes and trusts with atypical arrival patterns. Four examples of the ways in which it was used are described next.

### 5.8.1 'What if' scenarios for national A&E team

The model was used for seminars with the national A&E team to discuss patient flows and the impact of potential policies. 'What if' scenarios enabled the national team to focus on aspects of the patient journey with the biggest potential to improve A&E performance. Not only a 'typical' department was considered, but also 'good' and 'poor' performers. These interactive sessions helped to generate a common understanding of issues in A&E in the national team. Internal discussion papers were subsequently written that addressed these key issues. Key scenarios investigated were:

- nursing staff required to run a dedicated minor stream;
- extra staff/reduced consultancy times;
- moving demand from A&E;
- extra demand at night time and weekend;
- improved diagnostics;
- better bed availability;
- improving the decision to admit process;
- changing working practices/responsibilities.

### 5.8.2 What does a 98% department look like?

In the early stages of the A&E project, there was much national debate about whether 98% performance in A&E was achievable and sustainable given the variability in demand and complexity of patient flows. The model was used to identify process times and service levels at each bottleneck process required to reach a sustained performance of 98%. The clinical advisers advised whether these process times were achievable. Some processes such as assessment required a certain time to be clinically safe, and others such as X-ray/blood test had fixed process times. This exercise was valuable in generating common understanding that a 98% target was achievable, and what a successful A&E department might look like.

### 5.8.3 Resources to deal with 'minor' demand

The model was run to illustrate the required nursing staff that would be required to deal with a dedicated stream of minor patients. This was compared with the equivalent number (and cost) of doctors that would be required, with assumptions on process times. The significant number of nurses required (over a thousand) was used to inform workforce policy in A&E.

### 5.8.4   Deflection of demand

The potential to improve A&E departments by deflecting minor patients away from A&E was investigated. This showed that it would not be a successful policy. Most of the delays in A&E are caused by whole hospital issues such as waits for beds and diagnostics. Releasing A&E clinical staff from dealing with minor patients would not help with these issues, and the average performance on the remaining, more complex case mix would be lower than that of the mix with minor patients included.

### 5.8.5   NHS improvement initiatives

The NHS Modernisation Agency ran A&E improvement programmes for all acute trusts. The model was demonstrated at numerous events to facilitate discussion with NHS participants on the issues facing A&E departments, and encourage them to pursue their own analysis and modelling endeavours. The sessions received highly positive feedback from participants, with numerous requests to use the model. (Local use is discussed later.) Results from the model, allied to the 7-day survey results, also fed into guidance issued by the NHS Modernisation Agency to the NHS around improvements to the waits for bed, waits for specialists and waits for assessment processes.

## 5.9   Application of the generic model at a local level

By Spring 2004, the model had fulfilled its national purpose. However, following a demonstration of the model to the head of the national A&E 'Intensive Support Team' (IST) (whose role was to help trusts struggling with the A&E Target), it was felt that the tool could have local benefit to some of these trusts. In theory, if the trust could provide an accurate local 7-day survey and staffing profiles, the model could be used to model that trust in detail to show where high impact interventions might be.

There also presented an important learning opportunity for ESOR to investigate whether a nationally developed OR model could be used to improve local NHS services. A full time OR analyst (Sally Huxham) was recruited to take the model to trusts nominated by the IST lead and to attempt to use it to aid improvement.

### 5.9.1   Experience with local trusts—the consultancy process

Between Summer 2004 and early 2005, we took the model to 10 trusts, partly nominated by the IST, but also a proportion of those that volunteered following the demonstrations of the model at national MA

*Table 5.2*  The consultancy process—numbers of trusts reaching each stage

|  | | Number of trusts |
|---|---|---|
| 1 | Initial demo of the generic model to key stakeholders in the trust (A&E consultants, A&E managers, nurses, performance directors, analysts). | 10 |
| 2 | Work with local analysts to get accurate data on demand, staffing, process times, performance by patient group, reasons for breach. | 8 |
| 3 | Replicate the performance of the trust from the key parameters with the model and agree with trust. | 5 |
| 4 | Run 'what if' scenarios on potential improvement strategies. | 5 |
| 5 | Implement improvement strategies. | 3 |
| 6 | Test if the predicted improvements were made. | 0 |

events. Trusts were prioritized according to A&E 4h performance. Others were nominated, but had difficulties bringing together key stakeholders. Our target consultancy process would have completed all stages in Table 5.2. The actual numbers of trusts that made it to each stage are shown in the right-hand column.

At first glance, this table implies that the exercise was a failure—no trusts reached the end of the process. However, this reaction would underestimate the benefits achieved by reaching intermediate stages.

For example, for some of the trusts reaching stage 1, this was the first time that key stakeholders had convened to consider issues facing their A&E department. Using the generic national model (with national data) to facilitate these discussions was surprisingly effective in generating a common understanding of local issues. Sometimes it was possible to rapidly adjust the model data to illustrate local issues. For example, one trust felt their staff were not allocated optimally to match the demand. They were immediately shown the effects of mismatches between demand and resource using national data. This provided the incentive to resolve their local issues. In other cases, particular local issues such as waits for beds, diagnostics and admitting team opinions were discussed using the national model.

At stage two, many trusts obtained new insight into local issues from the exercise of finding or improving the quality of the required data.

For those trusts that reached stages 3 and 4, running the 'what if' scenarios on the agreed validated model enabled prioritization of improvement strategies. However, time constraints driven by the looming A&E target meant that many strategies were adopted in parallel, making measurement of individual improvements impossible. For example, one trust's suspicion that they did not have enough examination cubicles was well founded, and investment in this was supported, but this change was introduced in parallel with other measures. Hence, unambiguous progress to stages 5 and 6 was rare.

### 5.9.2   Obstacles to local application of the generic model

As implied in Table 5.2, local use of the model could have been more effective. At the outset, our main worries about applying the generic model locally were around those instances where local patient flows were so different from model assumptions that modelling became meaningless. We did encounter cases where local practice was significantly different from the national model assumptions. Examples were different patient routings (eg extra triage), staff responsibilities and behaviours, admission techniques, local patient groupings and assumptions around resources required for trolley waits.

However, these did not provide major obstacles to progress, as with some modelling expertise they could always be overcome by one of the following three methods:

- Flexible use of input data into the existing model structure (eg putting two real-life processes into one modelled process). The structure of the generic model was unchanged, but a local interpretation of the input data was required.
- Small changes to the structure of model. For example, because examination cubicles were a key constraint in one trust, these were quickly added to the model.
- Some issues were resolved by exporting modelled data to Excel and adding extra analysis offline. An example of this was a fast track admission process in one trust that could not be formally included in the model structure.

In fact, the more crucial obstacles to progress were not related to the generic nature of the model, and were as follows:

- *Data quality*: This was poor in most of the visited trusts. In some cases, this prevented effective model use. Unfortunately this issue is a common experience in the NHS.
- *Organizational dysfunction*: The trusts were chosen because they were struggling to meet the A&E target. However, a key reason for the struggle in many cases was organizational dysfunction. Problems in

A&E are often a symptom of whole hospital issues. For example, if inpatient beds, the admission process, or diagnostics are under capacity or managed ineffectively, the effects are seen in A&E. However, for the A&E model to be used effectively, all these stakeholders must be active and well-informed participants. As noted above, stage one of the consultancy process often helped resolve such issues, but this was not always the case.

- *Motivation*: Some trusts only paid 'lip service' to the process, which may have been seen as being forced on them by DH. For example, this often manifested itself at the point where the trust needed to make significant effort to find and/or improve data.
- *Changes in A&E departments*: Most trusts were employing numerous mechanisms over different time periods to improve A&E performance. It was therefore often difficult to validate the model locally and/or to identify the impact of individual changes.

## 5.10 Discussion and conclusions

### 5.10.1 Development and application of a generic model

The work described in this paper was primarily concerned with developing and applying a generic simulation model for a 'typical' A&E department. The work has been successful in this respect, achieving most of the objectives set for it. It provided:

- a visual and analytical representation of a typical A&E department;
- illustration of the impact of variability of demand and process in A&E;
- a facilitation tool to focus national resources onto the key issues;
- the ability to run 'what if' scenarios, both visually and analytically;
- the ability to illustrate what success would look like.

The particular challenges in OR terms with use at national level were:

- *Finding the appropriate 'level' of modelling*: Designing the model so it was not overspecific to particular A&E departments, but detailed enough to explain national issues to an appropriate level. Required input data needed to be as simple as possible. Striking this balance required numerous revisions of the model in development stages. For example, waits for bed at specialty level were not modelled to avoid unnecessary complexity.
- *Data*: Interpreting the available national data and using it appropriately, making allowances for known inaccuracies.

- *Communication and consultancy skills*: Facilitating sessions to explain and run the model and build common understanding. Interpretation of results and use of the model in innovative, unanticipated ways.

We felt that the project was successful in the first two of these challenges in producing a model at an appropriate level of detail that used available data appropriately. On the third point, the seminars were successful in terms of feedback from participants, the common understanding that they generated, and the targeting of national efforts. However, in retrospect, some of the local effort with the model may have been better spent on these sessions.

### 5.10.2    Local application of the generic model

A secondary concern of the work was to use the generic model to help individual trusts that were struggling to meet the A&E target. The main obstacles to effective use of the generic model were external to the model—particularly organizational and data quality issues. Where these were resolved, the model was flexible enough to resolve specific local issues, through different interpretations of the input data, small changes to the model structure or small amounts of offline analysis. For none of the 10 trusts did we reach the end of our target consultancy pathway, but significant benefits were achieved from the intermediate stages.

On more general modelling issues, the work provided some interesting case study evidence to contribute to debates surrounding model re-use, generic models and model validation.

### 5.10.3    Model reuse

An important current debate in simulation modelling concerns model reuse. Robinson *et al* (2004) discuss dimensions of this, including a spectrum of reuse, from 'code scavenging' up to full model reuse and weighing these considerations against development cost. A cycle of 'grabbing and gluing' old ideas/models/pieces of code, running them, using them if workable, otherwise rejecting and retrying is proposed. The key benefits of model reuse are identified as time, cost and consistency of output; obstacles being the time/cost required on projects to support reusability, plus systems architecture issues. Pitfalls are around the required level of abstraction, and the potential for 'force fitting' inappropriate models.

In the work described in this paper, reuse of the Oldham model was seriously considered. Reuse of the model was eventually rejected for practical reasons related to the costs of adopting a model which was not designed with reusability in mind, and the relatively low costs of building a new model. However, reusing ideas, data and concepts from the Oldham model made a valuable contribution to our work, and this additional aspect of model reuse should perhaps be included in the debate around simulation model reuse.

### 5.10.4 Generic modelling

A different perspective on model reuse also appears under the heading of 'generic modelling' and can be seen as attempts to use system architectures which facilitate reuse. In a study which concerns the simulation of emergency departments in Israel, Sinreich and Marmor (2004) suggest three levels of genericity—the most generic being high levels of abstraction that can model any system and scenario, the least generic being those that can model only one specific system. In the middle are models at medium abstraction that can model any provider of a similar process. Sinreich and Marmor claim that it is possible to model the emergency departments using a medium level of abstraction, on the grounds that in their extensive study of five hospitals, the processes received by patients depended much more strongly on the characteristics of the patients than on the particular hospital where they were seen. Without specifically doing either, they go on to imply two important uses of such generic models:

- to model a typical hospital to gain general insights about service improvements;
- to model a specific hospital to address specific local issues.

In this paper, we provide concrete examples of both types of usage. In doing so we support the suggestion that modelling a 'typical' department using a generic model with 'typical' inputs has value. In passing we also note that, as with much operational research, working for a client who wishes to gain general insights is a different situation from that often faced by academics who have the added challenge of trying to interest managers in the general insights provided by their models.

On the issue of local usage of a generic model we distinguish two different circumstances. If the purpose of the study is to model/predict the impact of local decisions, much work remains to be done as local input data is needed for calibration and local performance data for validation. In addition, local circumstances may require some modification of model structure. Nevertheless, the generic model was found to be a good starting place in the hands of those who had built and understood the model. Our experience of trying to reuse previous models suggests that generic models may be less advantageous as a starting point in the hands of others.

If on the other hand the purpose of a local model is to generate interest and facilitate debate of alternative methods of improving performance, the experience of this project is that a generic model may be all that is required.

### 5.10.5  Validation

As described earlier, the process of validating the generic model described here was rather different than is traditionally suggested in text books. The validation process used was a mixture of black box and open box validation. In particular, input parameters were adjusted to reproduce the desired output, but with open box validation overseeing the process to ensure that this resulted in a reasonable, transparent and believable model.

### 5.10.6  Further work

This experience of the potential value of generic models has motivated the primary author's current research which focuses on the development of a generic model to examine whole hospital issues in dealing with emergency demand, and the applicability of such a generic model locally.

### Acknowledgements

Members of the DH emergency care policy team—particularly Mark Davies, Helen Miscampbell, Claire Howland, Jane Cummings. Martin Reddy and Lis Nixon from the IST. Matthew Cooke on validation. Roger Quincy, Numerous ESOR colleagues for advice and support. Roger Kirby at Oldham hospital. Staff at participating NHS trusts.

### References

Badri M and Hollingsworth J (1993). A simulation model for scheduling in the emergency room. *Int J Oper Prod Mngt* **13**(3): 13–24.
Baesler F, Jahnsen H and DaCosta M (2003). The use of simulation and design of experiments for estimating maximum capacity in an emergency room. *Proceedings of the 2003 Winter Simulation Conference*, New Orleans, USA.
Blake J and Carter M (1996). An analysis of emergency room wait time issues via computer simulation. *Int J Opns Res* **34**(4): 263–273.
Blasak R, Armel W, Starks D and Hayduk M (2003). The use of simulation to evaluate hospital operations between the emergency department and a

medical telemetry unit. *Proceedings of the 2003 Winter Simulation Conference*, New Orleans, USA.

Centeno M, Giachetti R and Linn R (2003). A simulation-ILP based tool for scheduling ER Staff. *Proceedings of the 2003 Winter Simulation Conference*, New Orleans, USA.

Gonzalez B and Perez P (1994). Evaluation of alternative functional designs in an emergency department by means of simulation. *Simulation* **63**(1): 20–28.

Jun J, Jacobson S and Swisher J (1999). Applications of discrete-event simulation in health care clinics: A survey. *J Opl Res Soc* **50**: 109–123.

Komashie A and Mousavi A (2005). Modelling emergency departments using discrete event simulation techniques. *Proceedings of the 2005 Winter Simulation Conference*, Orlando, USA.

Lane D, Monefeldt C and Rosenhead J (2000). Looking in the wrong place for healthcare improvements: A system dynamics study of an accident and emergency department. *J Opl Res Soc* **51**: 518–531.

Mahapatra S *et al* (2003). Pairing Emergency Severity Index 5-level triage data with computer aided system design to improve emergency department access and throughput. *Proceedings of the 2003 Winter Simulation Conference*, New Orleans, USA.

Miller M and Ferrin D (2003). Simulating six sigma improvement ideas for a hospital emergency department. *Proceedings of the 2003 Winter Simulation Conference*, New Orleans, USA.

Miller M, Ferrin D and Messer M (2004). Fixing the emergency department: A transformational journey with EDSIM. *Proceedings of the 2004 Winter Simulation Conference*, Washington, DC, USA.

Pidd M (1999). *Tools for Thinking: Modelling in Management Science*. Wiley: New York.

Robinson S *et al* (2004). Simulation model reuse: Definitions, benefits and obstacles. *Simulation Model Pract Theory*, 479–494.

Rossetti M, Trzcinski G and Syverud S (1999). Emergency department simulation and determination of optimal attending physician staffing schedules. *Proceedings of the 2003 Winter Simulation Conference*, New Orleans, USA.

Samanha S and Armel W (2003). The use of simulation to reduce the length of stay in an emergency department. *Proceedings of the 2003 Winter Simulation Conference*, New Orleans, USA.

Sinreich D and Marmor Y (2004). A simple and intuitive simulation tool for analyzing emergency department operations. *Proceedings of the 2004 Winter Simulation Conference*, Washington, DC, USA.

Takakuwa S and Shiozaki H (2004). Functional analysis for operating emergency department of a general hospital. *Proceedings of the 2004 Winter Simulation Conference*, Washington, DC, USA.

Wiinamaki A and Dronzek R (2003). Using simulation in the architectural concept phase of an emergency department design. *Proceedings of the 2003 Winter Simulation Conference*, New Orleans, USA.

# 6
# Looking in the Wrong Place for Healthcare Improvements: A System Dynamics Study of an Accident and Emergency Department

D. C. Lane, C. Monefeldt and J. V. Rosenhead
*The London School of Economics and Political Science, University of London*

*Accident and Emergency (A&E) units provide a route for patients requiring urgent admission to acute hospitals. Public concern over long waiting times for admissions motivated this study, whose aim is to explore the factors which contribute to such delays. The paper discusses the formulation and calibration of a system dynamics model of the interaction of demand pattern, A&E resource deployment, other hospital processes and bed numbers; and the outputs of policy analysis runs of the model which vary a number of the key parameters. Two significant findings have policy implications. One is that while some delays to patients are unavoidable, reductions can be achieved by selective augmentation of resources within, and relating to, the A&E unit. The second is that reductions in bed numbers do not increase waiting times for emergency admissions, their effect instead being to increase sharply the number of cancellations of admissions for elective surgery. This suggests that basing A&E policy solely on any single criterion will merely succeed in transferring the effects of a resource deficit to a different patient group.*

Reprinted from *Journal of the Operational Research Society*, 51(5): 518–531, 2000, 'Looking in the Wrong Place for Healthcare Improvements: A System Dynamics Study of an Accident and Emergency Department', by D. C. Lane, C. Monefeldt and J. V. Rosenhead.

## 6.1 Introduction

### 6.1.1 Accident and emergency and the crisis in British health care

The National Health Service (NHS) has been in semipermanent crisis during two decades of government restraints on public sector expenditure. Despite the election of a new government in May 1997, problems continue (*Independent*, 16.8.97, *Daily Telegraph*, 5.5.99). Among the indicators of crisis have been repeated reorganisations, closure of facilities, over-worked junior doctors, lengthy waiting lists, cancellation of scheduled admissions to hospital, and depletion of budgets before the year end leading to curtailment of activity. In recent years public and political concern has focused in particular on the performance of Accident and Emergency departments at acute hospitals.

Accident and Emergency (A&E) provides access to hospital services for urgent cases. The A&E (or casualty) department is used both by individuals brought by ambulance and by those presenting themselves for treatment. The latter, in particular, include people whose medical conditions vary widely in severity. A&E therefore performs a sorting function, deals itself with a range of less seriously ill patients and assesses more serious cases for admission as inpatient. Only 15–20% of patients arriving at A&E require admission to beds on hospital wards.[1]

Public concern has focused on excessively long waiting periods at A&E, particularly for those requiring admission. Official guidelines specify that patients requiring treatment as inpatients should be allocated to a bed within two hours.[2] Although these standards apply only to the time elapsed after a decision to admit, they are nevertheless routinely broken in many hospitals. The spectacle of sick people whose condition merited admission as inpatients waiting overnight on trolleys, or even being treated in ambulances parked outside the unit (*Guardian*, 12.1.96), has provoked widespread criticism. At times A&E units have become so congested that they have been 'closed to blue lights'— even emergency ambulances are barred and diverted to other hospitals (*Evening Standard*, 17.12.96).

A variety of explanations has been offered for the A&E crisis, a recent report providing a comprehensive account of possible factors.[3] One commonly held view attributes it to the closure of more than one in ten acute hospital bed in the early to mid 1990s (*Guardian*, 12.1.96 and 14.1.97). Resulting bed shortages not only delay A&E admissions, but also cause cancellations of scheduled non-emergency admissions which may in turn generate additional future emergency cases. Certainly there has been a surge of attendances at A&E, up some 17% in London over a similar period.[4]) It has been argued that this represents a behavioural response by patients and their GPs to the difficulty of gaining admission through the referral procedure.[1]

Another possibly factor implicated in the A&E crisis is beds 'blocked' by fit patients whose discharge is prevented by lack of community care resources. Government waiting list reduction initiatives have also been blamed, since giving precedence to those who have been waiting longest may dislodge more serious cases, which may then require emergency admission. Another plausible mechanism is that competition on price, promoted since 1990 by the internal market in health services, has increased bed occupancy rates to a level where there is inadequate slack left to cope with demand variations. All of these explanations implicate one or more aspect of the then government's policies on the NHS in the deterioration of A&E performance. The governmental response was, typically, to urge hospitals to manage their beds more effectively—but also to permit hospitals to employ doctors in A&E departments beyond agreed quotas (*Daily Telegraph*, 12.1.96).

### 6.1.2  Origins of this present study

'Casualty Watch' is a project established in 1992 as a response to public concern that cuts in the NHS were producing an inadequate casualty service and harming patients. It is run by Southwark Community Health Council (South London) with funding from a number of sources. (Community Health Councils are statutory bodies representing community views on health service provision.) Casualty Watch monitors the performance of A&E departments throughout London, and some further afield. Its volunteers make simultaneous co-ordinated monthly visits to A&E units, collecting data on the numbers and waiting times to date of patients currently in A&E. These surveys enable the trend in performance to be tracked, and publicised.

The work reported here arises out of a collaboration between Casualty Watch and the Department of Operational Research at the London School of Economics in a joint effort to explore the causes of observed delays in casualty. The modelling expertise was provided by LSE, while orientation to the problem area, judgements on design choices, and introductions to stakeholders were supplied by Casualty Watch.

System dynamics was selected as the appropriate modelling medium, and the initial model was developed through two MSc student projects in 1995 and 1996. From October 1996 a nine month project was established, funded partly by Casualty Watch and partly by LSE, to turn the resulting prototype into a fully operational model. A close working relationship was established with the A&E department of an inner London teaching hospital—which for confidentiality reasons we will refer to as 'St. Dane's'. The model has been calibrated with access to information held by St. Dane's staff and the hospital database.

### 6.1.3 Contents of this paper

This paper reports on the A&E system dynamics model and on its use to explore the dynamics of the system of which A&E is a part. The second section outlines the principal features of an A&E department, justifies the choice of system dynamics, proposes a focus for the model and then describes its structure. The following section presents an analysis of the outputs of a 'Base Case' simulation and addresses model validity. This Base Case is then compared with a number of scenarios involving changes in bed capacity and demand pattern. A final section derives lessons from these experiments, draws some general policy conclusions, and identifies where further work needs to be performed.

## 6.2   Model conceptualisation and formulation

In this section we first describe the activities in and around an A&E department. We then justify the use of system dynamics, present the focus of our modelling study and give an overview of the model formulation.

### 6.2.1   Initial conceptualisation of the A&E system

The specific focus of this research was on the response of A&E waiting times to reductions in bed capacity. For this purpose we can conceptualise the A&E system in terms of two areas: the community; and the hospital, with the relevant functions of the hospital sub-divided into three: (1) the A&E department; (2) the management of elective patients; and (3) the wards. These can be characterised as follows:

*The Community*

Patients flow into the hospital from the surrounding community and are subsequently discharged back into it. There are two main patient groups: emergency patients (arriving by ambulance or making their own way to hospital); and elective patients. The rate at which emergency patients arrive in the A&E department depends on many characteristics of the community: density and average age of the population, accessibility to other hospitals etc. The rate of scheduled elective admissions depends on the capability of the hospital (scale of facilities, range of services offered etc.) and the characteristics of the catchment area. Both of these rates were treated as exogenously determined, and represented using historical time-series data (see Figure 6.4).

The rate at which patients are discharged back into the community influences hospital occupancy and is related to length of stay. The various factors affecting the length of time patients stay in hospital[5-7] are aggregated into a single value for this parameter.

### The Hospital—A&E department

Many elements make up the time which elapses between a patient arriving in A&E and, if necessary, leaving the department to go to a bed on one of the wards (Figure 6.1). Patients follow different pathways through A&E before they are eventually admitted (if indeed they are). Patients arriving in A&E are triaged and registered and then wait for an initial consultation with an 'A&E doctor' (either a Senior House Officer or Registrar in A&E). The number of A&E doctors on duty varies during a day. Patients may be treated and discharged, or may be the subject of further clinical appraisal and testing prior to treatment and discharge. More severe cases are referred to a 'Specialty Doctor', a member of a specialty support team called to A&E from elsewhere in the hospital. Such patients may undergo further test procedures and then be treated and discharged. Alternatively, they may be admitted to a ward for treatment. The main procedures necessary to determine whether hospital admission is required for emergency patients are shown in Figure 6.1.

### The Hospital—management of elective patients

Elective patients are individuals requiring non-urgent medical treatments who stay on a waiting list until scheduled for treatment. Treatments for which such patients are waiting are primarily 'surgical', for example hip replacement, but also 'medical', for example chemotherapy. Such treatments are scheduled well in advance, and patients are admitted to wards the day before their treatment and 'prepped' by nurses.

On their scheduled day of admission patients are asked to contact the hospital, when they may be told that their admission is confirmed; or that it is cancelled; or they may be asked to wait at home in the hope that ward rounds later in the day will free-up a bed. A small proportion of patients are unable to keep their appointment, or cancel it themselves, and they lose their scheduled slot.

Elective patients who are allocated a bed are admitted onto a ward. This is true for those whose admission is confirmed early and for those

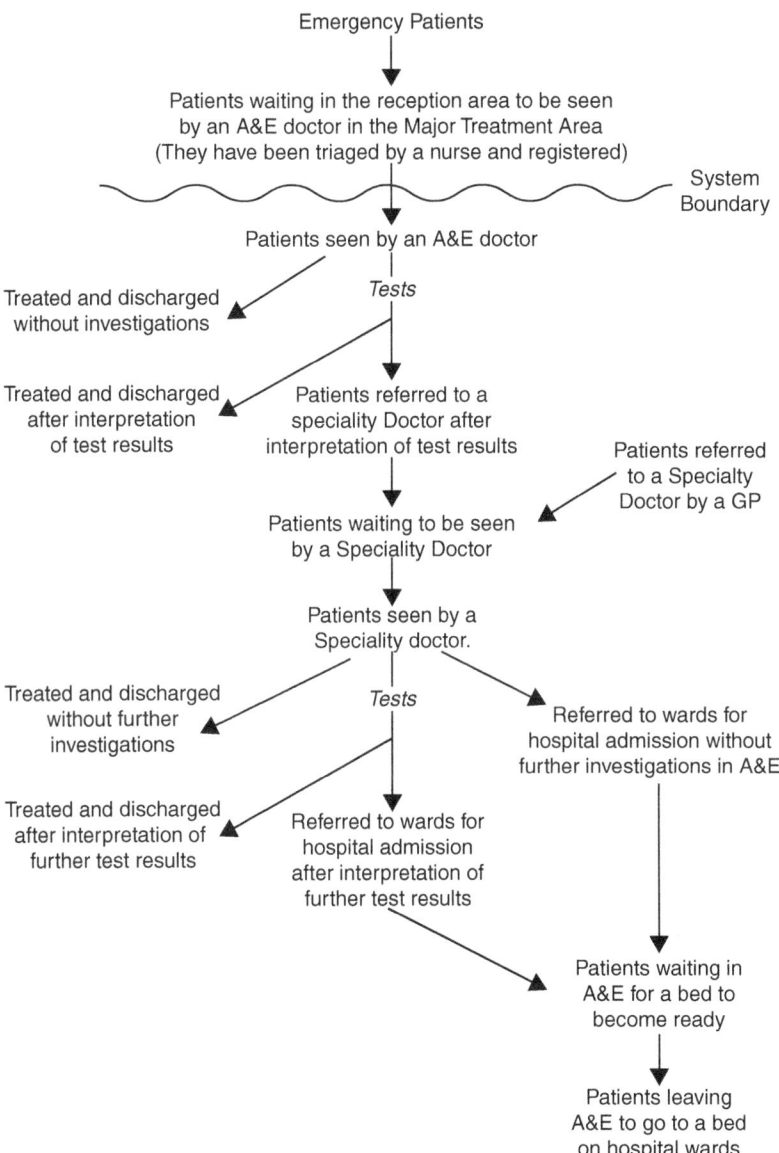

*Figure 6.1* Schematic representation of A&E elements, processes and pathways included in the system dynamics model

found a bed only later in the day. Consequently, these elective patients arrive on the wards throughout the day, though rarely reaching them later than early evening.

Some elective patients who fail to have a bed allocated to them can be accommodated overnight in St Dane's 'hotel unit'. On the following day these patients must rapidly be found a bed and then prepped for treatment that day. Only a small proportion of patients can be handled in this way.

*The Hospital—wards*

The rate at which a hospital can admit new patients—emergencies or electives—is influenced by the management and staffing of beds. Because lack of available beds on wards may contribute to delays in A&E, a model must incorporate information about bed occupancy, the ratio of the accumulated number of patients on the wards to the total number of hospital beds. As occupancy rises, increasing priority is known to be given to admitting the urgent patients from A&E, whilst pre-scheduled admissions increasingly need to be cancelled.

Patients are discharged from wards during normal opening hours. In principal, this frees a bed. However, patients must first be prepared and their associated files duly processed, and beds have to be identified, cleaned and got ready. This all takes nursing time and nurses have other duties; during daylight hours continuing patients need more attention and in consequence there is an increased 'turnover interval' before emptied beds become available.

### 6.2.2   The use of system dynamics

Healthcare systems have been the subject of previous simulation studies. Here we briefly review this work and show the relevance of the system dynamics approach.

The culture of the NHS leads to a focus on individual patients and this generally predominates in studies of A&E.[8–10] It is therefore not surprising that modellers have, broadly speaking, tended to use discrete event simulation (DES) to generate detailed results concerning the handling of patients with stochastically-generated attributes.[11,12] However, a consequence has been studies whose predominant focus has been on isolated areas within a hospital[13–15] or on the treatment histories of specific types of patients.[16,17]

System dynamics modelling[18] can play a different role in probing healthcare systems. A general discussion of this role may be found elsewhere[19] so is stated only briefly here. As with all modelling approaches, the application of system dynamics produces losses as well as gains. Examples of the former are the loss of the effects of stochastic variation and of resolution down to individual patient, or condition level. However, the gain, put simply, is that considering aggregated variables encourages both a systemic view of the interactions of patient flows and information, and a more strategic perspective of the management of the system. It is widely accepted by healthcare professionals that healthcare provision cannot he understood by looking at factors in isolation.[20] By encouraging the study of how different processes interact to produce effects, system dynamics offers a rigorous approach for bringing that interconnectedness insight into focus. Our decision to use the approach in this specific case had two components.

Firstly, the main purpose of this study was to investigate the sensitivity of waiting times to hospital bed numbers, a factor external to A&E. However initial conceptualisation revealed the need to consider other such external factors (demand patterns, elective patients). By adopting a stance of 'conceptual distance',[21] the system dynamics approach allows us to consider this broad range of interactions.

Secondly, modern software[22] and group processes[23] produce models which are both more technically representative and more persuasive to their users. In this study we worked closely with those who had knowledge of the system. By accessing their 'mental databases' as well as formal sources,[18] we were able to build a transparent model which they accepted as realistic in its formulations. The model became a 'visual learning environment',[24,25] helping users to understand why structure produced behaviour (the Base Case), and how behaviour varied under different conditions (the Policy Analysis). Making a complex and compelling mathematical model accessible to healthcare professionals can contribute powerfully to the policy making process, generating rigorous analyses for use in a broader political context.

### 6.2.3 Model focus: the dynamic hypothesis

In this section the main feedback processes within an A&E department are presented. An hypothesis concerning the resulting dynamic behaviour is also discussed. These two elements provide the main focus for this study.

A system dynamics model is a causal theory of how behaviour is generated by a social system.[18,26,27] Such models need a clear 'dynamic hypothesis'; a description of a feedback structure, combined with a 'reference model, or description of the system behaviour that the structure is thought to generate.[28] A simulation model can test this dynamic hypothesis. The dynamic hypothesis described below served as a guide for model construction and for subsequent policy experiments.

Although no two A&E departments have the same problems, the nature of the main factors is clear.[1] There are two main patient groups interacting to influence the availability of beds on the wards. The principal interactions are shown in Figure 6.2 as a causal loop diagram.[29] The main feedback loops are all balancing loops (a change in the value of one variable is counter-acted by the operation of that loop).

Loops B1 act to drain the number of emergency patients in A&E, loop Bla by discharging the majority directly from A&E and loop B1b by admitting them to hospital wards. The various waiting times for patients result from the separate delays involved in the various activities within A&E. Most of the detail of the model therefore resides in the extensive disaggregation of loop Bla into the separate activities described previously (Figure 6.1).

Loop B2 acts to control the occupancy level on wards; by restricting—and even shutting down—emergency admissions, loop B2 ensures that patients are not admitted unless there is free bed capacity.

Loop B3 has the same goal of controlling bed occupancy but acts by influencing the rate of elective admissions. Again, bed capacity is a limiting variable.

Loop B3 also controls loops B4 whose two components together share the goal of reducing the backlog of scheduled elective patients. This is achieved either by admission to wards (loop B4a) or by cancellation (loop B4b). If there is room to accommodate all of the elective scheduled admissions then the elective admission rate will equal the desired elective admission rate (B4a), otherwise, a greater burden falls on B4b. The operation of B2 has priority over the operation of B3.

The previous government's claim constituted a desired behaviour of the above system.[30–32] The case might run as follows: decreasing acute bed capacity increases occupancy levels and so makes up for the beds lost; hospitals can accommodate the same number of patients and so the emergency admission rate—and hence A&E patients waiting times—remain unchanged. In reference mode terms: a downward step in bed capacity yields upward adjustment in occupancy and no change in waiting times.

We therefore have a system structure (Figure 6.2) and a desired behaviour. Together, these form the dynamic hypothesis to be tested.

### 6.2.4   Formulation of model structure and equations

This section outlines the key elements of the model formulation. The most detailed sub-model concerns the A&E department itself. This

101

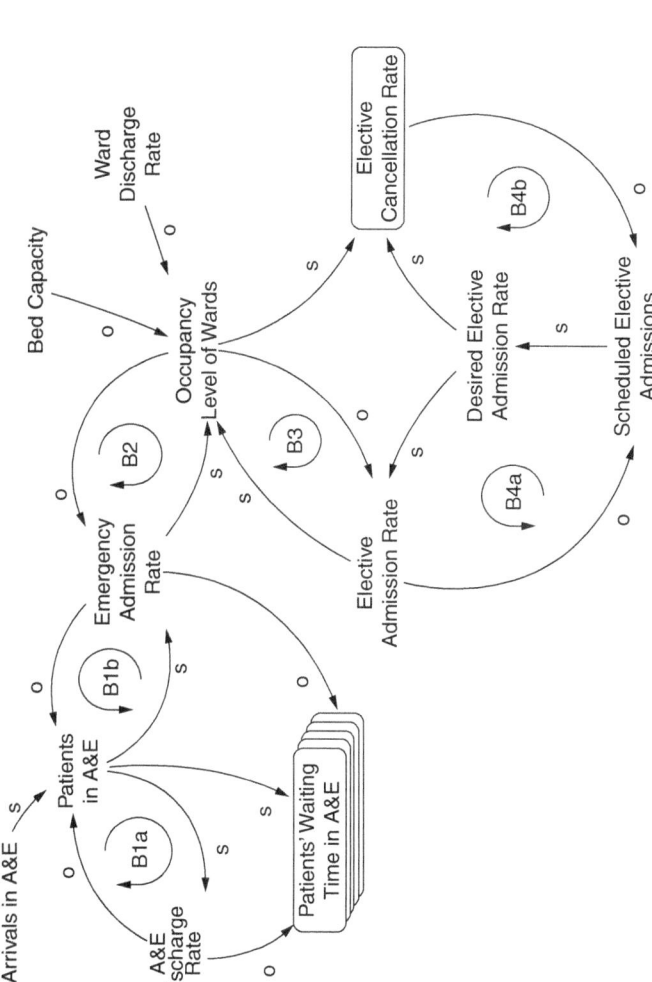

*Figure 6.2* Causal loop diagram of the main effects determining waiting times in an A&E department. The polarities of the causal links read as: s = variables move in the same direction, *ceteris paribus*; o = variables move in opposite directions, *ceteris paribus*. Boxes indicate performance measures for the model

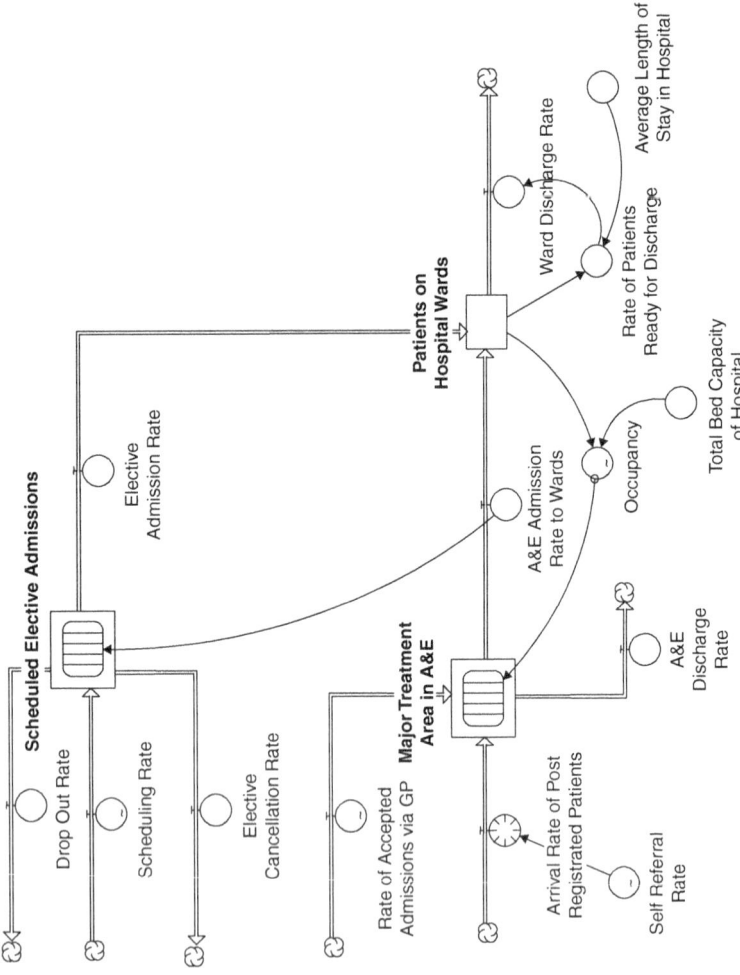

*Figure 6.3* Stock/flow diagram of the A&E system dynamics model. Only the high level map is shown: the two boxes with vertical grills open to reveal the full, 194 equation model

formulation represents the processes described above, shown schematically in Figure 6.2. The model also incorporates the handling of elective patients as described earlier, the map in Figure 6.3 being only a simplified representation. As patients are scheduled, they are modelled as flowing into a stock (Scheduled Elective Admissions). Individuals waiting at home, travelling to the hospital and those who have stayed overnight in the hotel unit are all included in this stock. Some patients fail to keep their appointment (Drop Out Rate). Others have their treatment cancelled because the hospital does not have of Hospital beds available to admit them (Elective Cancellation Rate). The remainder are admitted onto a ward for treatment (Elective Admission Rate). Admissions and cancellations both on the day before treatment and on the actual day of treatment are brought together in these two flows.

The model was constructed using the iThink software,[22] on a Macintosh. The model's core had nine stocks and 160 other variables, whilst a further nine stocks and 16 other variables calculated the performance measures. Although the software allows all of this structure to be displayed graphically, it was overlaid with a simplified map which allows the systemic interactions of the model to be effectively presented (Figure 6.3).

## 6.3   The Base Case simulation: calibration, analysis and model validation

This section treats simulation output. The Base Case run of the model is described and illuminates further aspects of the functioning of the actual system. The section closes with a discussion of model validity.

### 6.3.1   Base Case output generation, performance measures and preliminary analysis

The calibration of arrival rates, for both patient types, was derived from historical data, with supplementary information from the hospital Bed Manager. This data, uprated for annual increase, produced a 24 hour cycle of arrivals (averaged over days of the week, see Figure 6.4) of 220 emergency patients, of whom about 40 require admission; and 110 scheduled elective patients assumed to arrive evenly from 9.00 to 17.00. Bed capacity was 800.

To exclude initialisation transients, the model was run for six simulated days, yielding a repeating 24 hour cycle, or 'steady state'. Summary statistics from these runs are shown in Tables 6.1 and 6.2. Unless otherwise stated, these performance measures have been calculated from the steady state region and are averages across that daily cycle.

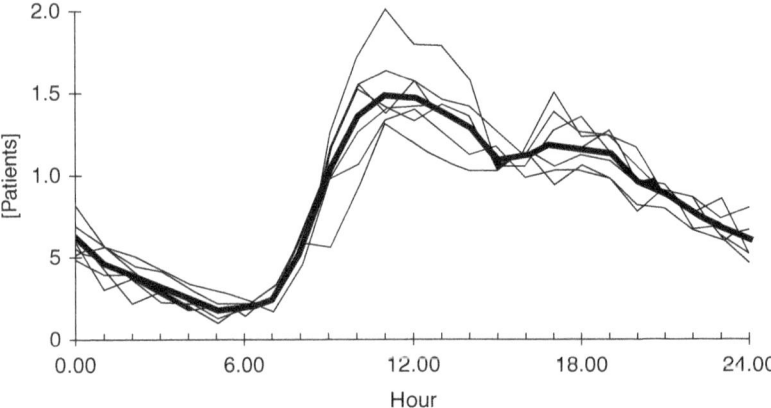

*Figure 6.4*  Average number of emergency patients arriving in A&E department in hourly intervals. Thin lines: arrival numbers for each of the days of the week. Bold line: hourly data averaged across days of the week

*Table 6.1*  Performance measures for the Base Case Model run

| | Average time to A&E Dr. Consult. [Hours] | Average time to DTA [Hours] | Total waiting time (min. <u>avg</u>. max) [Hours] | Average % elective cancellations [%] | Average daily hospital occupancy [%] | Average daily A&E Dr. Util. [%] |
|---|---|---|---|---|---|---|
| *Base Case* 800 Beds and normal demand | 1.3 | 3.6 | 4.2, <u>5.9</u>, 8.4 | 16.2 | 94.6 | 92.1 |

The measures calculated included daily averages across all patients for the delays from registration to: (1) consultation with an A&E doctor; (2) decision to admit and, (3) admission to wards. The daily minimum and maximum of the last of these—the total waiting time—was also calculated. Other measures track daily average figures for percentage of elective cancellations, proportion of A&E doctors' time spent with patients and hospital bed occupancy.

The output of the 'Base Case' simulation was used to analyse the functioning of the A&E admission system in finer detail. Figure 6.5 displays the average time taken to complete each stage of the process, plotted against the hour of the day when that stage is completed.

The top line in Figure 6.5 shows the waiting times averaged across all those emergency patients subsequently admitted to a ward. Under

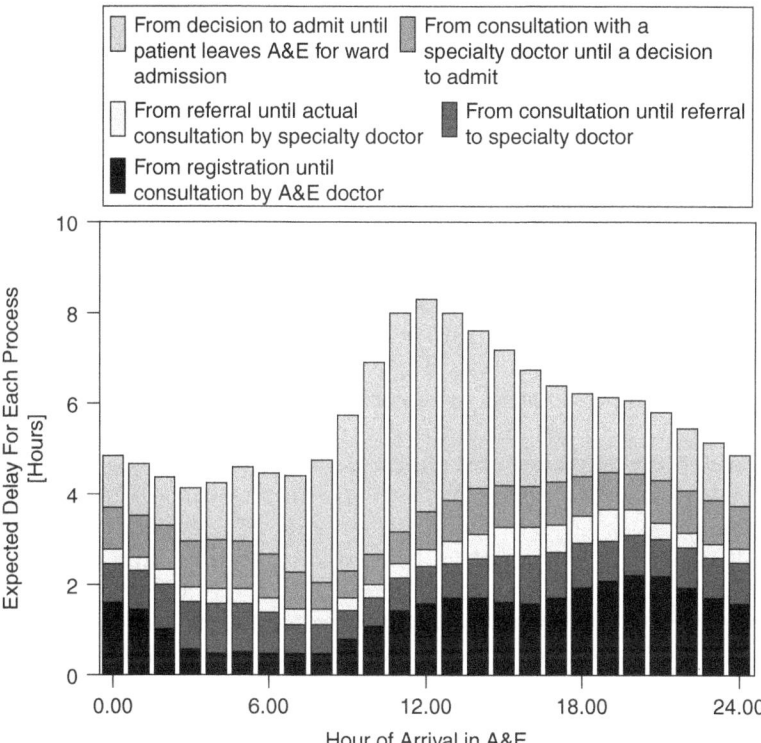

*Figure 6.5* Emergency patient waiting time to reach different stages in A&E (Base Case simulation output)

normal conditions patients spend at least four and as much as eight and a half hours in the A&E department, depending on their time of arrival, before being given a bed. Considerable variation may be seen in two components of this total: the time from registration until being seen by an A&E doctor and the time waiting in A&E from the decision to admit until leaving A&E for hospital admission. The underlying reasons for these two delays are analysed below.

### 6.3.2 Waiting time from registration until completion of A&E doctor consultation

The graph for time waiting to be seen, and then being seen, by an A&E doctor (Figure 6.5) shows a single deep trough in the morning, and afternoon and evening peaks. This is only partly explained by the emergency patient arrival pattern. Another factor is the variation in the roster arrangements for A&E doctors. At the time of this study, the number of A&E doctors on duty at St. Dane's ranged from a peak of seven in the afternoon to a trough of two in the early hours of the morning.

Four A&E doctors cope with the backlog of a busy evening and are fully utilised (Figure 6.6, Graph 1), until by 3 am average patient waiting time is down to its minimal level of 25 minutes. This situation is maintained, with reduced staffing until 8 am. Although the number of doctors steps up steadily from 7:00 until reaching its maximum complement by early afternoon, this is not sufficient to keep pace with the rise in emergency patient arrivals (Figure 6.4). The situation is exacerbated by a crowding effect as the A&E cubicles become full. It then becomes more difficult to administer the patients who are waiting and so the time expended by a doctor finding and giving an initial consultation to a patient rises (note that this is a minor reinforcing loop). A&E doctors therefore work flat out for the rest of the day. The backlog of patients only reduces in late afternoon but a second, evening, rush of arrivals causes backlog to increase again. During the evening, therefore, delay in consultations rises again, producing the second peak.

The waiting time from registration to A&E doctor consultation and the associated utilisation of A&E doctors is therefore seen to result from the combination of the pattern of arrival of emergency patients and the specific A&E doctor roster.

### 6.3.3 Waiting time from decision to admit until admission to ward

The largest component of patient waiting time arises from delays in the ward admission process. This delay, which displays steep peaks and troughs, is co-produced by the arrival and discharge patterns and the bed turnover interval, as well as by elements of the procedure for managing elective patients.

Patients are discharged from the hospital from 9:00 until 17:00; in the model these discharges occur at an aggregated rate corresponding to an average stay of six days. Hospital staff estimated that in the late evening and early morning the bed turnover interval is relatively low (average one hour), while from midday until late in the afternoon it is generally high (up to five hours). In principle this difference is generated endogenously but it was represented in the model as an exogenous time series.

At 9:00 patients begin to be discharged from wards (Figure 6.6, Graph 3). However, the turnover interval starts to increase just as more patients

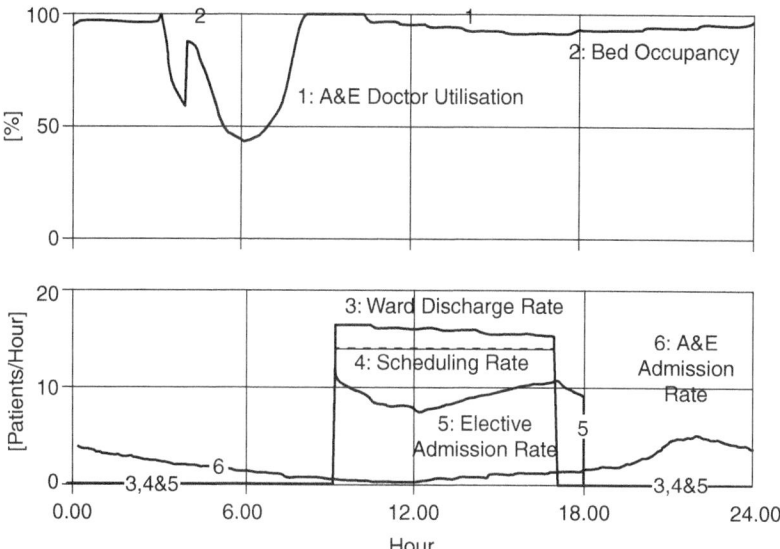

*Figure 6.6* Outputs from the Base Case run of the model

start to arrive in A&E (Figure 6.4). Bed occupancy falls (Figure 6.6, Graph 2) and delays to A&E patients mount. Crowding also plays a part. An A&E patient must be accompanied to a ward by a porter and a nurse from A&E. As A&E becomes more pressured during the late afternoon and early evening, it becomes increasingly difficult to spare nurses to do this. This second crowding effect limits the former's ability to take up the opportunity of an available bed (for which, in principle, they have priority) which are snapped up for any elective patients seeking admission.

Elective patients intended for treatment the following day are scheduled to arrive throughout normal daytime hours (Graph 4) and those that can be admitted are a component of the elective admission rate (Graph 5). However, from 9:00 to 12:00 priority is afforded to those elective patients held overnight in a hotel unit whose treatments are scheduled on this day. Such patients make up the remainder of the elective admission rate. After 12:00 such patients cannot be prepped in time and their treatment is cancelled. Consequently, all of the elective admission flow in the afternoon consists of patients intended for treatment the following day. This continues until 18:00. when some will be held over in the hotel unit for admission on the day of their treatment, and the remainder are cancelled.

During the evening and the early hours of the morning these dynamics have a knock-on effect on the time spent by A&E patients awaiting a bed. Although no patients are discharged from wards during this time, the delay resulting from the lengthened turnover interval means that beds released by earlier discharges are continuing to become available. In the absence at these hours of elective patients seeking admission, they are filled by waiting A&E patients. There is a surge in such admissions around 22:00 (Graph 6). This is associated with the late evening reduction in turnover time and also with the accumulated wave of A&E arrivals, phase-shifted beyond the period of elective patient admissions.

### 6.3.4   Model validation

For system dynamicists—as with other simulators[33]— validity, 'accumulates gradually as the model passes more tests' (Reference 34, p. 209). Therefore the treatment of validity should ideally run in parallel with the description of the model and its runs. For clarity we have instead consolidated the discussions of validation here. The treatment is brief— validation and the modelling process are the subjects of separate, more detailed, documents.[35,36]

The validation tests specific to system dynamics are well established,[26,34] being divided into those focusing on model structure and those relating primarily to simulated behaviour. We outline the application of these tests to the A&E model and then describe the team involved in performing them.

*Structure-based validation test*

These tests concern formulation and ensure that the model is suitable for its purpose and is consistent with the real system. To test suitability for purpose we focus inwards on the model, checking for dimensional consistency and ensuring that formulations hold for extreme input values. In this way we confirmed that the model was well posed.

Testing structural consistency involves judging the model's representativeness.[33] The close links with St. Dane's allowed us to discuss the structure with people familiar with the A&E system. This ensured that the model structure captured their perceptions of the actual processes operating in the real system. Validity was further enhanced by confirming the correspondence of model parameters to information available.

## Behaviour-based validation tests

These tests use model simulations to probe further the validity of its construction. The paucity of recorded data made it impossible to perform a full behaviour reproduction test[37] and so a process of triangulation was used, involving both subjective, qualitative analysis of time series and objective, quantitative summary data. Graphs of model variables were presented to our collaborators along with the performance indicators. This output was judged to be realistic and convincing (mode, scale and phase being within 10% of observed behaviour) by those with day-to-day experience of the real system.

The above judgements were made from the Base Case. However, model validity was further enhanced by applying tests to the policy analysis runs described below. These scenarios can be seen as extreme condition testing[34] and the diagnosis of surprise behaviour.[38] The policy analysis runs lead to the generation of insights and sensitivity analysis was also undertaken to test the robustness of those insights.[26,34] The group process used to create the model meant that these simulations could be studied and judged reasonable by our collaborators.

## The modelling team

The validation of a model of this type requires the exercise of judgement both by experienced modellers and by individuals with knowledge of the actual system. The core team for this study consisted of the authors (acting as modellers and facilitators) and staff from St. Dane's. Our collaborators included: the Registrar and other physicians from A&E, the Bed Manager, the Site Nurse Practitioner, other nurses and staff from other specialisms and from the test laboratories. In addition, aspects of the model formulation were checked with staff from the Southwark Community Health Council and we also benefited from the experience of staff in Casualty Watch, the London Ambulance Service and the Emergency Bed Service.

The details of how this team worked to create the model are recorded elsewhere.[36] Here we merely comment that this spread of individuals gave us access to both hospital databases and a range of judgmental estimates. However, it was the LSE team and the Registrar of St. Dane's who were responsible for checking each model assumption, element of formulation and parameter value used.

## 6.4   Policy analysis: exploring scenarios using model simulations

The initial motivation for the research described here was to test the hypothesis that restrictions of bed capacity would not lead to increased waiting times in A&E. However, in the course of developing the model it became evident that waiting time is only one of a number of measures of system performance. Also, discussion with our collaborators indicated that other simulation experiments might be of interest. The developed model was therefore used to conduct a range of simulation experiments for comparison with the Base Case. The principle scenarios involved changes in bed capacity and in A&E demand, with values of the key performance measures shown in Table 6.2. Other policy runs explored the effects of combined capacity and demand changes, and of a crisis event consisting of a sharp temporary demand increase. See Reference 39 for further details.

### 6.4.1   Bed capacity scenarios

System behaviour was simulated for bed capacities between 700 and 900, the range chosen by our collaborators to be of interest. These scenarios tested the implicit government hypothesis that the closure of hospital beds would not affect the standard of service provided to the community.

The resulting performance measures (Table 6.2) and analysis of the various outputs of the runs, reveal the extreme similarity of the three simulations; there are only trivial differences in output graphs. This counter-intuitive result[38,40] might appear to support the above hypothesis. However, average daily occupancy increases only slightly as bed numbers are reduced, such changes being insufficient to substitute for the lost beds. The explanation for this apparent paradox lies in the figures for elective cancellations, which are revealed as extremely sensitive to bed capacity. As hospital beds are removed more elective patients have their treatments cancelled. With 100 fewer beds, in order to deliver approximately the same waiting time to emergency patients, cancelled non-emergency treatments almost double in absolute terms.

This response can be explained using the causal loop diagram of Figure 6.2. Balancing Loops B1, B2 and B3 together control the flow of patents onto wards. Specifically, B3 controls the balance between

Table 6.2  Consolidated performance measures for the various policy analysis runs of the model

| | Average time to A&E Dr. Consult. [Hours] | Average time to DTA [Hours] | Total waiting time (min. avg. max) [Hours] | Average % elective cancellations [%] | Average daily hospital occupancy [%] | Average daily A&E Dr. Util [%] |
|---|---|---|---|---|---|---|
| **Bed capacity scenarios** | | | | | | |
| 700 beds | 1.3 | 3.6 | 4.2, 5.9, 8.4 | 30.4 | 95.4 | 92.1 |
| 800 beds (Base) | 1.3 | 3.6 | 4.2, 5.9, 8.4 | 16.2 | 94.6 | 92.1 |
| 900 beds | 1.3 | 3.6 | 4.2, 5.9, 8.4 | 7.8 | 90.0 | 92.1 |
| **Demand pattern scenarios** | | | | | | |
| *Demand increase* | | | | | | |
| 0% | 1.3 | 3.6 | 4.2, 5.9, 8.4 | 16.2 | 94.6 | 92.1 |
| 1% | 1.4 | 3.7 | 4.3, 6.0, 8.4 | 16.5 | 94.6 | 93.6 |
| 2% | 1.6 | 3.8 | 4.7, 6.2, 8.5 | 16.8 | 94.6 | 95.5 |
| 3% | 1.7 | 4.0 | 4.9, 6.3, 8.5 | 17.1 | 94.7 | 97.5 |
| 4% | 1.9 | 4.2 | 5.3, 6.6, 8.6 | 17.4 | 94.7 | 99.4 |
| ≥5% | $\to \infty$ | $\to \infty$ | $\to \infty$ | n/a | n/a | n/a |
| *Crisis day* | | | | | | |
| Crisis day | 1.9 | 4.0 | 4.2, 6.1, 8.8 | 16.4 | 94.6 | 94.7 |
| Crisis day + 1 | 3.8 | 6.0 | 7.5, 8.8, 10.6 | 17.3 | 94.7 | 99.5 |
| Crisis day + 2 | 2.7 | 5.0 | 6.8, 7.6, 8.9 | 17.7 | 94.7 | 99.5 |
| Crisis day + 3 | 1.7 | 4.0 | 5.0, 6.4, 8.4 | 17.7 | 94.7 | 98.1 |
| Crisis day + 4 | 1.3 | 3.6 | 4.2, 5.9, 8.4 | 17.1 | 94.7 | 92.2 |
| **Combined scenario** | | | | | | |
| 700 beds and 7% increase in demand (+ A&E Dr. response) | 2.3 | 4.6 | 6.0, 7.1, 8.8 | 32.5 | 95.5 | 99.5 |

B4a and B4b. By shifting greater weight to B4b and cancelling elective admissions, the hospital manages—even with reduced bed numbers—to keep ward occupancy at a level which leaves virtually unaffected the waiting time for emergency patients. The elective cancellation 'safety valve' removes the expected distortive effects on B2, and hence B1.

The response of the hospital occupancy performance measure indicates that the various processing capacities involved in admission activities result in a limited ability to take advantage of additional beds.

### 6.4.2  Demand pattern scenarios

Two scenarios involving changes solely to the demand pattern are outlined below.

*Permanent changes in demand*

The response of the model to permanent changes in the number of emergency patients presenting was examined. The aim is to explore how the system—with today's staff and bed resources—would behave in situations of increased load. Such increases could be caused either by the permanent closure of a casualty unit in a nearby hospital, or by a generalised increase in demand in line with long term trends.[41] For reasons explained below, the model was simulated for permanent changes in emergency demand of up to 5%. The results are shown in Table 6.2.

Elective cancellations once again increase, though to a smaller extent. This is because A&E patients form a minority of all admissions, so that an increase in A&E demand results in a smaller proportionate increase in total admissions. However, small changes in demand have appreciable effects on patients' total waiting time, primarily because of the increase in delay before consultation with an A&E doctor. With a 4% increase, patients spend an average of three-quarters of an hour more in A&E. Higher levels of arrivals also produce increases in the daily averaged utilization of A&E doctor, with free doctor capacity decreasing steadily. However with increases up to 4% there is still some free doctor capacity at certain hours of the day. Patients do experience delays for consultations, but there is just sufficient staff to cope with the workload over a 24-hour cycle. Note, however, that with a 4% increase in demand doctor utilisation reaches virtually 100%.

Beyond 4%, this gradually deteriorating balance collapses. There is no slack A&E doctor capacity to cope with the extra arrivals, a backlog of patients awaiting initial consultation accumulates without bound and, even with staff working at maximum capacity, the waiting time rises continuously. The system therefore fails to reach a steady state and the performance measures can no longer be calculated. Interestingly, the cause of this collapse is not bed capacity, but rather insufficient provision of A&E doctors.

*A crisis event*

On the 27th of February 1997 St. Dane's experienced a demand 13% above normal. We simulated a similar temporary demand increase to test whether the model would reproduce past behaviour, and to offer a cause and effect description of the pressures on staff and long waits for patients that were observed on that day. The model was run with a transient 13% increase in the emergency patient arrival rate lasting 24 hours. Table 6.2 and Figure 6.7 summarize these effects.

The system takes until Crisis Day +5 to return to normal. For the reason described above, the effects on elective cancellations are small, the main effect being a bottleneck at the first consultation stage. Until the system restabilises, all patients arriving in A&E experience prolonged delays, due to the abnormal backlog of patients awaiting consultation. A&E doctors are working under increased pressure even on Crisis Day +2. All doctors work constantly from midday on the Crisis Day until the morning of Crisis Day +3. These simulation results were entirely consistent with the experiences of our collaborators.

### 6.4.3 Combined scenario

In the final scenario a situation was simulated with 700 hospital beds and a 7% increase in demand. Since A&E doctors are overwhelmed by demand increases above 4%, de-bottlenecking this stage was necessary. We therefore increased the consultation rate by 3%, crudely simulating faster working in response to the increased demand. This scenario therefore explores system behavior under reasonable predictions of increased demand if a policy of further reduction in bed numbers to achieve NHS economics was implemented (Figure 6.8 and Table 6.2).

Total waiting time for patients increases, the greatest contribution occurring in the morning, the experience of patients arriving on wards around 7:00 exemplifying the effect (Figure 6.8). These emergency patients have waited six and a half hours before admission, compared with four and a half hours in the Base Case. This increase has a single main component, the delay before obtaining a first consultation, which

114

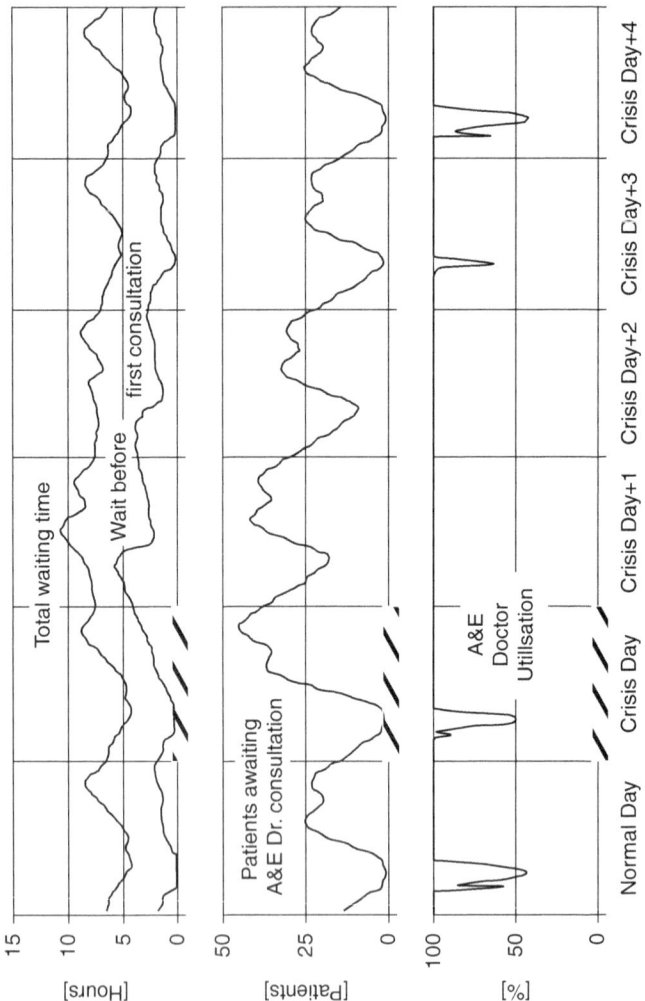

*Figure 6.7* Simulation of a crisis event

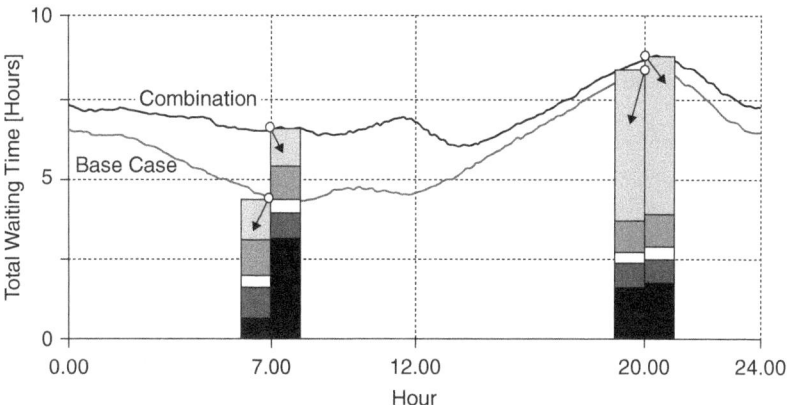

*Figure 6.8* Comparison of total waiting time under normal conditions (Base Case) and in the scenario of combined demand increase and bed reduction, with illustrative decomposition into stages of waiting

has increased fivefold, reaching three hours. This results from the loading on A&E doctor capacity caused by the demand increase.

The afternoon and evening increases in the total waiting time are smaller. Patients admitted to wards at 20:00 have waited less than half an hour extra in total, which is largely in the increased delay prior to first consultation (Figure 6.8). Nevertheless, patients arriving on wards at 20:00 have waited almost nine hours since arriving in A&E. In this scenario the 'safety valve' of elective patient cancellations—up to 32.5%—copes with the reduced bed capacity. At times when loop B4b is available (Figure 6.2) it is used to control waiting times, and the penalty of a mismatch between demand and resources is substantially transferred to a different performance measure.

## 6.5 Comments and conclusions

This work yields specific, practical lessons for A&E, as well as more general conclusions for the management of the system of which A&E is a part. Additionally, elaborations and further uses of the model are possible.

### 6.5.1 Lessons from the simulations

Conclusions drawn from the Base Case and policy analysis runs described in the previous sections are detailed below. Although they apply formally only to situations comparable to those studied at St. Dane's, because they are robust to reasonable parameter changes, their wider relevance is quite evident.

### The Base Case

The analysis indicates that much of the waiting time experienced before admission is inevitable: the constituent processes (Figure 6.1) are many and simply take time. However, at St. Dane's the restricted A&E doctor capacity in the morning and the limited availability of beds in the afternoon produce avoidable additional delay. The average daily occupancy level of 92%, above the 80–85% recommended by the British Association of Accident and Emergency Medicine,[42] and the high A&E doctor utilisation indicate an intensive use of resources. Nevertheless, capacity is insufficient to deal with demand: waiting times are high and scheduled elective admissions are regularly cancelled. This is a system with little room for maneuver and with few 'efficiencies' waiting to be squeezed out.

### Bed capacity scenarios

Bed occupancy was shown to be relatively insensitive to total bed capacity. These scenarios indicate that without changes in both A&E and ward staffing, there are limits to how fast new patients and used beds can be made ready. These simulations demonstrate that enhanced bed occupancy levels cannot alone compensate for further bed reductions. Instead, the burden is borne elsewhere: the 'safety valve' of elective cancellations compensates for any bed loss. An implication is that the appropriate choice of indicators is crucial in judging the performance of the system. Taking an holistic view of the healthcare system within which A&E is embedded, it becomes evident that delays to patients in A&E and elective cancellations must be jointly assessed; they are linked and compensating measures.

### Demand pattern scenarios

Scenarios with permanent demand changes show that despite increased elective cancellations, both bed occupancy and utilisation of A&E doctors approach 100%. Eventually the system collapses, though it is the earliest process—consultation with an A&E doctor—which is overwhelmed. The 'Crisis Event' simulation suggests that the system can cope with a demand pulse, but only at the cost of dramatic four day increases in elective cancellations, staff utilisation and A&E patient waiting times.

*Combined scenario*

This scenario emphasises the error of the dynamic hypothesis. There is even less slack in this system, and it can reasonably be inferred that it is highly exposed to a crisis event or to a reduction in staff capacity due to illness.

### 6.5.2   General policy conclusions

The principal message of this study is that using A&E waiting times alone to judge the effect of bed reductions is systemically naive. Developments in multiple performance indicators[43] recapitulate an old idea: complex systems must be monitored using a corresponding variety of signals.[44] By concentrating solely on A&E delays—important as these are—the original dynamic hypothesis provides misleading, indeed dysfunctional, guidance to policy. The hypothesis encourages policy makers to look in the wrong place for healthcare improvements because it implicitly discounts the effects of cancelling elective patients. However, this 'safety valve' is not without its costs. Even with current bed numbers, headlines such as "Girl's heart surgery cancelled five times" (*Guardian*, 12.9.96) are all too numerous. Patients waiting on lists for elective admission are the victims in the battle for beds on wards, because of the priority necessarily allotted to emergency patients.

This study reveals the interconnectedness of A&E service levels, bed provision and the experience of patients on waiting lists. Bringing that interconnectedness to life via simulation can, in principle, also provoke a discussion on appropriate measures of performance. A&E departments do not exist in isolation. Policy must be based on an understanding of how they relate to pre-hospital circumstances, to the rest of the hospital and to care in the surrounding community,[1] and a set of performance measures reflecting this broad view should appropriately inform policy making.

### 6.5.3   Possible elaboration of the model

The model reported here concentrates on short timescale effects, aggregates patient attributes and has a simplified representation of a hospital. These limitations were appropriate for the questions which the study team wished to address. Nevertheless, a number of elaborations could illuminate a range of related issues.

*De-bottlenecking*

The simulated system collapse provoked by inadequate provision of A&E doctors masks other effects. The model can be run with this capacity scaled up in order to reveal the effects of increased demand on other system elements, therefore informing judgements on priorities for the provision of additional resources.

### Longer timescale effects

Models operating with a longer timescale could explore a range of effects. Scenarios in which staff operate at permanently high utilisations could incorporate the effect of downward spiralling productivity exacerbating individual workload and so further degrading productivity.[45] It might also be possible to investigate the longer tern effects of cancelling elective admissions, since those so dislodged cycle back into an aging chain, emerging with a higher priority, either because of the duration of their wait or because they become emergency cases. High occupancy and/or demand levels can increase pressure to free up beds, leading to inappropriately early discharge. Modelling this effect would allow the consideration of the extra demand (some of it on A&E) created by consequent re-admissions.[46] Lastly, the phenomenon of so-called 'bed blocking' caused by the low provision of community care services interacts with factors already represented in the model.[7] Incorporating this interaction would extend the model to an area of growing concern.

### Hospital clusters

To test the ability of A&E services to respond to demand surges, it would be desirable to consider the resilience of a network of hospitals across which a demand surge would be shared. (Possible sources of such a surge include a major accident, or the closure of A&E to admissions at one or more hospitals within the network). Such a 'Cluster Model' is currently under discussion.

### Feedback control of A&E doctor roster

In its current form the model stimulates a complex system with inputs in order to understand the nature of the response mechanism. The system dynamics approach prompts us to see how endogenous feedback effects might be improved: to this end we have been developing improved policies for controlling the rostering of A&E doctors.

In conclusion, we feel that the system dynamics model reported in this paper offers a tool which enables decisions on health care priorities to be soundly based on systemic analysis and so has the potential to improve the quality of the healthcare that is delivered.

## Acknowledgements

We would like to thank staff at Casualty Watch, London Ambulance Service, the Emergency Bed Service, Southwark Community Health Council, the Department of Health and particularly all of the staff at the collaborative hospital for the time that they contributed to this study. Without the access and personal involvement that they afforded us, this work would not have been possible.

## References

1. Audit Commission (1996). *By Accident or Design: Improving A&E Services in England and Wales.* HMSO: London.
2. Department of Health (1996). *The Patient's Charter.* HMSO: London.
3. NHS Confederation Royal College of Physicians (1997). *Tackling NHS Emergency Admissions: Policy into practice.* NHS Confederation: Birmingham.
4. Department of Health (1998). *Outpatient and Ward Attenders, England: Financial year 1996–1997.* HMSO: London.
5. Hadfield J, Yates D and Berry A (1994). The emergency department and the community: model for improved cooperation. *J Roy Soc Med* **87**: 663–665.
6. Lane DC (1994). System dynamics practice: a comment on a case study in community care using systems thinking. *J Opl Res Soc* **45**: 361–363.
7. Audit Commission (1997). *The Coming of Age: Improving care services for older people.* Audit Commission Publications: Abingdon.
8. Dale J, Green J, Reeds F and (1995). Primary care in the accident and emergency department: 1. Prospective identification of patients. *Brit Med J,* **311**: 423–426.
9. Leydon GM, Lawrenson R, Meakin R and Roberts JA (1996). *The Cost of Alternative Models Of Accident and Emergency Care: A systematic review.* Report to North Thames Regional Health Authority: London.
10. Middleton EL and Whitney FW (1993). Primary care in the emergency room: a collaborative model. *Nurs Connect* **6**: 29–40.
11. Davies R and Davies H (1994). Modelling patient flows and resource provision in health systems. *Omega* **22**: 123–131.
12. Paul R (1995). Outpatient clinics. *OR Insight* **8**(2): 24–27.
13. O'Kane PC (1981). Simulation model of a diagnostic radiology department. *Eur J Opl Res* **6**: 38–45.
14. Riley J (1995). Visual interactive simulation of accident and emergency departments. In: Kastelein A, Vissers J, van Merode GG and Delesie L (eds). *Proceedings of ORAHS 21 Managing Health Care Under Resource Constraints.* Eindhoven University Press: Maastricht, pp 135–141.
15. Altinel IK and Ulas E (1996). Simulation modelling for emergency bed requirement planting. *A Opl Res* **67**: 183–210.
16. Romanin-Jacur G and Faechin P (1987). Optimal planning of a pediatric semi-intensive care unit via simulation. *Eur J Opl Res* **29**: 192.
17. Mejia A, Shirazi R, Beech R and Balmer D (1998). Planning midwifery services to deliver continuity of Care. *J Opl Res Soc.* **49**: 33–41.
18. Forrester JW (1961). *Industrial Dynamics.* MIT Press: Cambridge, MA.

19. Taylor KS and Lane DC (1998). Simulation applied to health services: opportunities for applying the system dynamics approach. *J Health Services Res and Policy* **3**: 226–232.
20. Lane DC (1999). *System Dynamics Modelling of Patient Flows Through Acute Hospitals*. Report for the NHS Executive: London.
21. Richardson GP (1991). *Feedback Thought in Social Science and Systems Theory*. Univ. Pennsylvania: Philadelphia.
22. Richamond BM, Vescuso P and Peterson S (1990). *iThink Software Manuals*. High Performance Systems, 145 Lyme Road, Hanover, NH 03755, USA.: Hanover NH.
23. Lane DC (1992). Modelling As Learning: a consultancy methodology for enhancing learning in management teams. *Eur J Opl Res* **59**: 64–84.
24. Lane DC (1995). On a resurgence of management simulations and games. *J Opl Res Soc* **46**: 604–625.
25. Lane DC (1997). From discussion to dialogue: A case study using an interactive system dynamics modelling a approach (De la discussion an dialogue: one étude de cas d'utilisation interactive de la dynamique des systémes). *Revue des Sys de Décis* **6**: 251–281.
26. Richardson GP and Pugh AL (1981). *Introduction to System Dynamics Modelling with DYNAMO (republished edition)*. Productivity: Cambridge, MA.
27. Lane DC and Smart C (1996). Reinterpreting generic structure: evolution, application and limitations of a concept. *Sys Dyn Rev.* **12**: 87–120.
28. Randers J (1980). Guidelines for model conceptualisation. In: Randers J (ed). *Elements of the System Dynamics Method*. MIT Press: Cambridge, MA, pp 117–139.
29. Goodman MR (1974). *Study Notes in System Dynamics*. MIT Press: Cambridge, MA.
30. Tomlinson B (1992). *Report of the Inquiry into London's Health Service, Medical Education and Research*. HMSO: London.
31. Kings Fund Commission (1992). *London Health Care 2010: Changing the Future of Services in the Capital* King's Fund: London.
32. Department of Health (1993). *Making London Better* HMSO: London.
33. Lane DC (1995). The Folding Star: a comparative reframing and extension of validity concepts in system dynamics. In: Shimadar T and Saeed K (eds). *Proceedings of the 1995 International System Dynamics Conference: Volume I—Plenary Program*. Gakushuin University and the International System Dynamics Society: Tokyo, pp. 111–130.
34. Forrester JW and Senge PM (1980). Tests for building confidence in system dynamics models. In: Lagasto AA, Forrester JW and Lyneis JM (eds). *System Dynamics: TIMS Studies in the Management Science*. North-Holland: Oxford, pp 209–228.
35. Monefeldt C and Lane DC (1997). A&E Model: Validation notes. *LSE research Notes*.
36. Lane DA and Monefeldt C (1999). Client involvement in simulation model building: hints and insights from a case study in a London hospital. LSE OR Department Working Paper Series LSE OR 99/32.
37. Sterman JD (1984). Appropriate summary statistics for evaluating the historical fit of system dynamics models. *Dynamica* **10**: 51–66.

38. Mass NJ (1991). Diagnosing surprise model behavior: a tool for evolving behavioral and policy insights (1981). *Sys Dyn Rev* **7**: 68–86.
39. Lane DC, Monefeldt C and Rosenhead JV (1998). Looking in the wrong place for healthcare improvements: A system dynamics study of an accident and emergency department. *LSE OR Department Working Paper Series* **LSEOR 98.23.**
40. Forrester JW (1970). Counterintuitive behaviour of social systems. In: *Collected Papers of Jay W Forrester (1975 collection).* Wright-Allen Press: Cambridge, MA pp 211–244.
41. Fry L (1960). Casualties and casuals. *Lancet* **1**: 163–166.
42. Royal College of Surgeons of England (1993). *British Association for Accident and Emergency Medicine Directory 1993.* Royal College of Surgeons of England: London.
43. Kaplan RS and Norton DP (1992). The balanced scorecard— measures that drive performance. *Harvard Bus Rev* **Jan/Feb:** 71–79.
44. Ashby WR (1956). *An Introduction to Cybernetics.* Chapman & Hall: London.
45. Homer JB (1985). Worker Burnout: A dynamic model with implications for prevention and control. *Sys Dyn Rev* **1**: 42–62.
46. Audit Commission (1992) *Lying in Wait: The Use of Medical Beds in Acute Hospitals.* HMSO: London.

# Part VI
# OR for Broader Engagement in Planning for Emergency Services

# 7

# System Dynamics Mapping of Acute Patient Flows

*D. C. Lane and E. Husemann*
*London School of Economics, London, UK*

Department of Health staff wished to use systems modelling to discuss acute patient flows with groups of NHS staff. The aim was to assess the usefulness of system dynamics (SD) in a healthcare context and to elicit proposals concerning ways of improving patient experience. Since time restrictions excluded simulation modelling, a hybrid approach using stock/flow symbols from SD was created. Initial interviews and hospital site visits generated a series of stock/flow maps. A 'Conceptual Framework' was then created to introduce the mapping symbols and to generate a series of questions about different patient paths and what might speed or slow patient flows. These materials formed the centre of three workshops for NHS staff. The participants were able to propose ideas for improving patient flows and the elicited data was subsequently employed to create a finalized suite of maps of a general acute hospital. The maps and ideas were communicated back to the Department of Health and subsequently assisted the work of the Modernization Agency.

## 7.1 Introduction

In the United Kingdom the majority of healthcare is provided by the state, funded from general taxation. The provider—the National Health Service, or 'NHS'—is organized via a complex web of geographically based coordinating bodies and semi-autonomous hospital trusts. The NHS has around 90 000 physicians and 300 000 nurses. It handles one

Reprinted from *Journal of the Operational Research Society*, 59: 213–224, 2008, 'System Dynamics Mapping of Acute Patient Flows', by D. C. Lane and E. Husemann. With kind permission from Operational Research Society Ltd.

million scheduled visits to GPs, 33 000 unscheduled visits to A&E and 25 000 operations daily. Each of these days costs £140 million (Euros 210 million) (Royston, 2005, www.mashnet.org.uk). Although public support for a system of universal healthcare, 'free at the point of delivery' and equitable in its handling of individuals, has remained high, over the last two decades there has been an increase in public concern about unacceptable performance on various fronts. The three Labour administrations first elected to office in 1997 have had the improvement of patient experience within the NHS as a continuing campaigning point and many improvement programmes and policy innovations have resulted.

This paper concerns the development and use of a hybrid form of qualitative mapping derived from system dynamics (SD) (Forrester, 1961) and used to study flows of acute patients within the NHS. The DoH provided funding and broad direction, with the aim of improving the experience of patients within the NHS. This paper briefly describes all stages of the project but concentrates on the activities associated with the workshops.

## 7.2   Initiating the project

The DoH's Health Services Division ('HSD') initiated the project, prompted by an SD simulation study of A&E waiting times. That study dealt with patients in A&E but also with those on wards and on waiting lists for scheduled operations. By taking an aggregate view it had been possible to create a broad-brush model of the system and then parameterize it with reference to a collaborating hospital (Lane *et al*, 2000, 2003). A short account (Lane *et al*, 1998) had been distributed throughout the NHS and was seen by staff in the HSD who made contact with a view to extending the work by setting the handling of acute patients in an even wider context. Their initial idea was to become more familiar with approaches for building broader models; ones which dealt with various interconnected NHS processes involving acute patients. At this stage, the different experiences with modelling that NHS staff and the DoH had had informed their ideas on the shape that any project should take.

A recent review concluded that one of the 'unique selling points of significant strength within the British OR research agenda [is] . . . applications in health care' (Bouyssou *et al*, 2004) and this is evidenced by a previous *JORS* collection on this topic (Davies and Bensley, 2005). So DoH staff have experience of a range of OR approaches. This range includes 'problem structuring methods' (PSMs), which help different stakeholders to explore and then agree on a problem definition (Rosenhead, 1989) and some 'soft' systems approaches (Checkland, 1996). Tools from the SD field were also known (Royston *et al*, 1999) but the concentration was on the qualitative 'systems thinking' popularized by Senge (1990). Methods were developed for applying the systems thinking tools of causal loop diagrams and archetypes specifically to healthcare issues, these becoming known in the NHS as 'whole systems working' (Pratt *et al*, 1999). At the more quantitative end of OR approaches, DoH staff in the internal 'Economics and OR' (EOR) groups have a record of analysis of patient flows (Bensley *et al*, 1995) and they, along with other groups working with the NHS, have a long and continuing history of such analysis (Davies and Davies, 1994; Millard and McClean, 1996; Bennett and Worthington, 1998; Gallivan *et al*, 2002; Brailsford *et al*, 2004). Generally this work has used discrete event simulation and concentrated on specific parts of hospitals or particular treatment types (Harper and Shahani, 2002; Ashton *et al*, 2005; Griffiths *et al*, 2005).

An interest in bringing more breadth into their models, combined with an understanding that healthcare systems contain multiple interconnections, attracted DoH staff to the idea of experimenting further with the usefulness of SD. They wanted a process which ensured that any models did not present themselves as 'black boxes', understood only by their expert builders (Lane, 1992; Pidd, 1992). However, they also wanted something distinct from the PSM-like mapping approach of systems thinking. They saw a need for a systems modelling approach involving formal representations of system structure which also preserved the spirit of their PSM work by drawing many people into the analysis, not just a small group with specialist training in the approach. The range of interests described here resulted in the DoH agreeing to fund the research project. The exact focus of the project is outlined next.

## 7.3   Project purpose and scope

Though initiated by the DoH's HSD this study was aimed at contributing to the work of the Emergency Services Action Team ('ESAT') a high-level policy group reporting to the Secretary of State for Health. The project details were agreed with a Steering Committee of staff members from HSD and from elsewhere in the DoH, including the EOR Division. The main features that were agreed fitted the HSD's needs, while remaining within their very practical funding and timing/access constraints. These features were threefold; the organizing concern of the project, the main elements of the work and the intended outputs. These are now described briefly.

The concern was broad, being: 'the wider patterns of patient management in acute hospitals, and patient blockages in the whole system'. As well as considering existing patient experiences and the quality of service provided, we would look at what might happen to patients if different levels of resources were applied or if different treatment pathways were used. The idea was to identify possible ways of improving things.

We agreed the following three main elements of the work. First, creating an interim qualitative system map of a 'general acute hospital', that is hospitals admitting urgent as well as scheduled cases. Second, running workshops for invited NHS staff (who were assumed to have no previous SD experience). The workshop aims were to allow the correction of the map, and to facilitate discussions about ways of improving patient management. Subsequent analysis and summarization of the workshop responses was the third element.

The two intended outputs flowed directly form these elements. First, the workshops would provide an opportunity to assess the benefit of applying SD ideas within the NHS, particularly involving staff not expert in the approach. Second, ESAT and HSD would receive a report on the re-worked system map, along with a set of systemically informed suggested interventions for improving the processes of patient management.

This was an exciting opportunity, affording excellent access to NHS professionals.

## 7.4    Designing an approach: practical constraints and methodological issues

The ambitious aims combined with the practical constraints of the project had raised some methodological issues. The Steering Committee wanted 20–30 NHS staff involved in the daily work of patient treatment to take part in the project and to suggest improvements. The knowledge provided by this group would be the 'database' of the project (Forrester, 1992), the workshops acting as a channel for their ideas, with HSD and ESAT receiving those ideas. The modelling was constrained to being qualitative only. The resulting map had to be as general as possible and approved by all participants. Finally, time with the participants would be strictly limited; the workshops were restricted to a half day.

As referred to earlier, the tools of SD modelling have the potential to contribute distinctively to healthcare issues this being recently evidenced by work in a special issue of the *American Journal of Public Health* (Homer and Hirsch, 2006; Leischow and Milstein, 2006; Sterman, 2006). The question here was which selection of tools would best suit the needs of this project. Given the constraints specified by DoH, the participative development of an SD simulation model was not appropriate. Ways exist for developing such models with groups (Vennix, 1996; Andersen and Richardson, 1997), including groups of healthcare workers (Vennix and Gubbels, 1992). However, these require more time commitment from participants than this project afforded and would arguably not achieve the large-scale staff involvement that was required. On the other hand, we had concerns about the extent to which systems thinking alone could make a contribution in this case. PSMs can help groups agree a common definition of the problem and help them explore ways of dealing with it (Rosenhead, 1989). This can involve mapping to represent ideas. In contrast, SD focuses on the causal mechanisms of a system and how they might produce different modes of behaviour over time. A rigorous understanding of that structure/behaviour link requires equation formulation, parameterization and model simulation. The version of SD popularized by Senge (1990) introduced feedback thinking to a broad audience in the form of word/arrow 'causal loop diagrams'. However, many readers did not follow Senge's advice about the benefits of simulation models. The resulting systems thinking movement has an ambivalent relationship with the SD field. The field's originator, Jay Forrester (1994), commented: 'Systems thinking is coming to mean little more than thinking about systems, talking about systems, and acknowledging that systems are important. In other words, systems thinking implies a rather general and superficial awareness of systems'.

Simply ignoring feedback certainly can significantly reduce the effectiveness of policies (Sterman, 1989; Kleinmuntz, 1993) and so systems thinking can be very helpful because it sensitizes people to the possible existence and consequences of feedback. Nevertheless, there are limits to the contribution that such maps can make. System dynamicists are very aware of the need for a rigorous approach to understanding behaviour (Sterman, 1994b; Moxnes, 1998). Maps alone cannot achieve this (Richmond, 1994; Booth-Sweeney and Sterman, 2000) and there are particular problems with the maps used in the whole systems working approach—causal loop diagrams (Richardson, 1986; Lane, 2000, 2008; Warren, 2004) and archetypes (Sterman, 1994a; Lane, 1998).

The project therefore needed a mapping approach located somewhere between systems thinking mapping and SD simulation, an approach which offered more rigour via its maps but which could be implemented within the tight constraints of the project. The approach that we subsequently designed for the project had two parts (see Figures 7.1 and 7.2). The preliminary activities were planned to consist of interviews with DoH and NHS staff and site visits to three hospitals. These would be followed by three workshops around Britain and analysis of the contributions elicited during them.

Methodologically, the most important mapping decision was to use stock/flow diagrams—SFDs (Forrester, 1961, 1968). This allowed for the representation of system stocks and flows along with information feedback effects. However, as described later, this required the subsequent creation of both a conceptual framework to introduce these maps to participants and an associated set of questions to help them use them.

A key question was how to balance the content and process aspects of the project (Eden, 1987). Clearly we had to provide some modelling

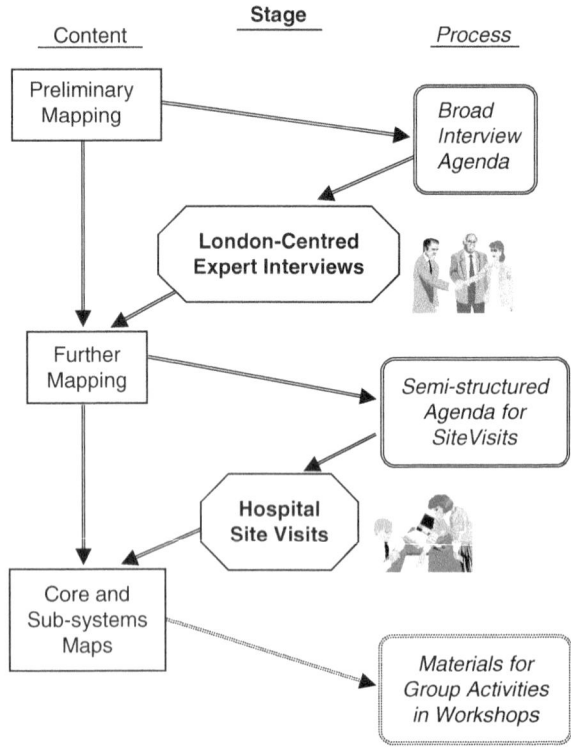

*Figure 7.1*   Preliminary activities in the acute patient flow mapping project

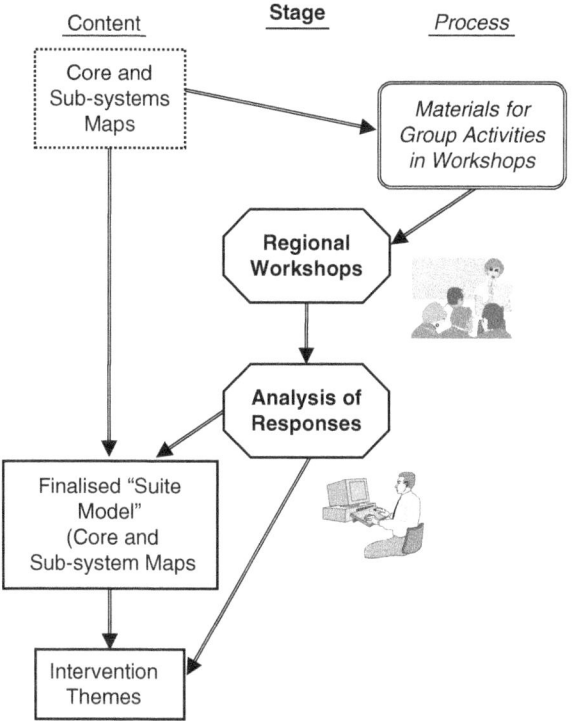

*Figure 7.2*  Workshop activities

content involving sound systems analysis. Also needed, however, was a number of appropriate group processes which would help participants to work with that analysis and make them feel involved and committed (Eden *et al*, 1983). The following account describes both the content and process aspects. It deals with the preliminary activities in a single section but then devotes more space to the workshop activities.

## 7.5   Preliminary activites

These activities are illustrated in Figure 7.1. We started with some preliminary mapping of patient flows based on previous experience from the A&E project and examination of DoH reports. The broad aspirations of the project meant that flows of patients between many different parts of the NHS had to be included. This tentative content generated questions for the subsequent interviews.

To further improve the quality of the maps interviews were undertaken with individuals in London: three with DoH experts and two with senior NHS staff in hospitals. Using the preliminary maps and the interviewee responses we did further mapping. At this stage we had a single map, showing stocks of patients and flows of patient movements, as well as influencing factors. We used this to create an approach for the site visits. The single map contained a great deal of detail. It included the processing of patients by GPs, by A&E departments and by out-patient clinics. We included in the maps patients scheduled for elective surgery. Finally, we represented the flow of patients into community care.

We conveyed this complexity during the site visits using one overall map and a series of different versions which also included more detail of one of the different sectors just mentioned. We photocopied the maps onto A1 paper and used them as the basis of the interviews. Essentially, this overall map created a context for the discussion. Staff were then shown the various other maps and asked to comment on their deficiencies and adequacies. This approach meant that rather than swamping interviewees with all of the information collected in one go, they were instead able to respond to different parts in detail at different times, in turn focussing the discussion on each aspect of acute patient management. However, across the whole series of interviews the contents of all of the maps was exposed to critical comment.

We used this approach during visits to three hospitals: Peterborough, Oxford Radcliffe and King's London. The comments collected led to the idea that the project needed a slightly different approach to the mapping and workshops. We therefore created a Core Map which gave an overview of patient flows (both acute flows and other presentation pathways) and then a series of separate, more detailed maps which concentrated on the detailed features of some of the sub-systems.

## 7.6   Conceptual framework for NHS resources and pathways

The workshop-related activities are illustrated in Figure 7.2. A critical element was the design of a process that would help the attendees to understand the existing maps, to comment on them, and then to work with the mapping symbols to create ideas about how to change the system. It was at this point that the practical constraints and methodological issues described above became most relevant to the approach used. Something was required which could be used with very little prior knowledge but which still offered a level of rigour by drawing on key SD ideas and helping people to represent their understanding of how the system components fitted together and influenced patient services. What we came up with was a hybrid approach with SFDs, involving a 'conceptual framework' and an associated, healthcare-related set of five generic questions.

To ensure that the SFDs could be used by NHS staff with no previous SD background, SFD mapping was introduced using a 'conceptual framework' for mapping treatment stages, patient flows and influencing factors (Figure 7.3). Those stock/flow ideas were then used to ask healthcare workers a series of five questions which were both very general in systems terms but also tailored to the requirements of the NHS. The framework and questions were designed to interest NHS staff and to draw them into a discussion concerning the larger maps.

The framework is couched in commonsense language yet within it lurk some powerful ideas from SD. The rectangles are state variables; in SD language, stocks or levels. The double-lined arrows indicate flows. These influence stocks via accumulation or draining processes. The round valves and taps indicate the amount of patients moving between treatment stages. The single lines show instantaneous causal influences.

We introduced the framework using a simplified healthcare example; patients waiting for some type of treatment. After diagnosis the patients go onto a waiting list (box lower left). Perhaps it is possible to perform the treatment on an outpatient basis. In that case the patient moves fairly quickly up the day care flow on the left of the figure and out of this little system. Otherwise the patient must wait for admission to a ward (doubled-lined arrow into central box), which naturally requires that a bed be free. The treatment happens when the necessary resources are applied and the patient recovers on the ward (box lower right) before being discharged.

This example visualizes some of the influences on the service that patients receive. It also serves to help people learn the language of SFDs. This then helps them to understand the more complex SFD maps and to think in stock/flow terms. It also relates the five generic questions to stock/flow thinking. Those questions come down to the mnemonic 'ABCDE' (Figure 7.3).

'A' stands for 'Alternative Pathways'. In the example a patient might be treated elsewhere than in hospital and so takes a different (upward) path. Generally, the framework encourages users' creativity by asking the question: *Are there possible alternative pathways along which patients could be processed?*

'B' stands for 'Blocking Resources'. In the example, patients cannot be admitted without free beds. This contains the idea that most

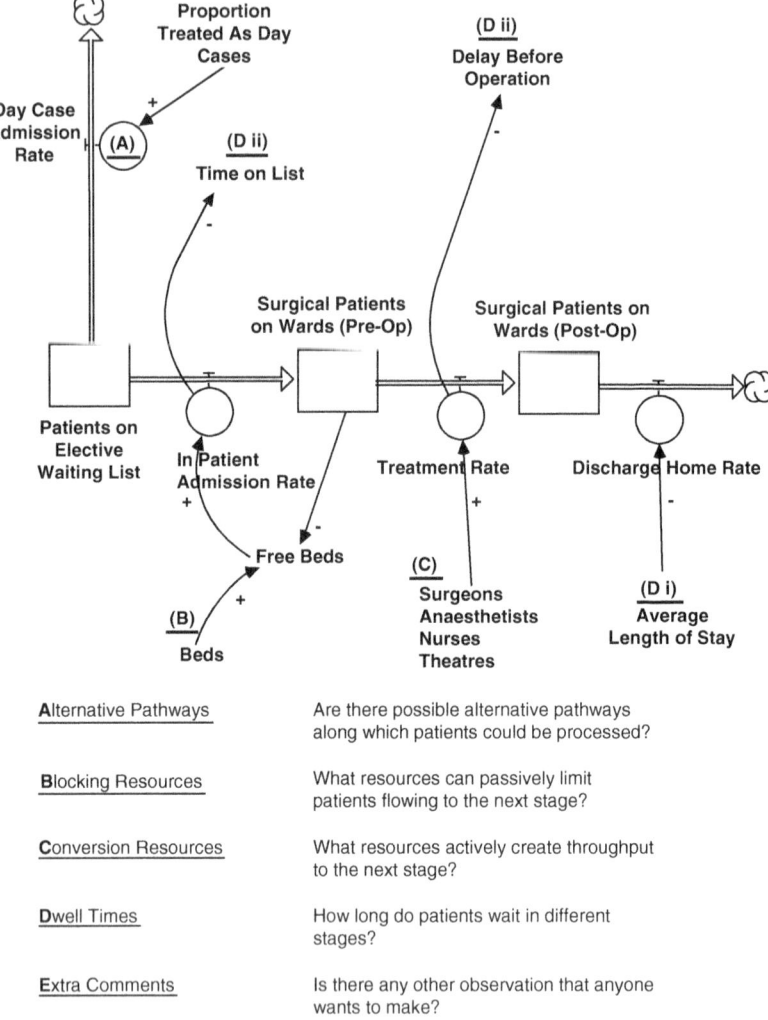

*Figure 7.3* Conceptual framework for NHS resources and pathways

stocks have finite capacity, so when they are filled their inflows are blocked, or shut down. The general question is: *What resources can passively limit patients flowing on to the next stage?*

'C' is 'Conversion Resources'. If B's are passive then C's are active. In many cases patients convert from one healthcare stage to the next because resources such as surgeons and operating theatres are brought to bear. The framework poses the question: *What resources actively create throughput to the next stage?*

'D' is 'Dwell Times in Stages'. These durations come in two forms. Sometimes D's are simple inputs (Di): in the example the average length of stay is the recuperation time; adding more nurses will not reduce this. Alternatively, D's can be outputs (Dii): as in the two cases here (waiting for admission and waiting for an operation) D's can depend on flow rates which themselves depend on B and C type resources. Here the framework makes people ask: *How long do patients wait in different stages?*

'E' stands for 'Extra Comments'. This is a catch-all which allows users to express any other thought or idea which did not seem appropriate or was in any way excluded by the previous categories. So: *Is there any other observation that anyone wants to make?*

The mnemonic was chosen to assist the discussions by helping participants remember and understand the set of questions being posed. In systems thinking terms this framework embodied some simple but powerful mapping symbols and some fundamental ideas from SD. The A's explore range of possible conserved flows (=treatment paths) and therefore help users to think about the different stocks (=treatment stages) that might exist. The B's are a non-technical way of looking for negative feedback loops and flow shutdown non-linearities. The C's adopt a resource-based view (Wernerfelt, 1984) of why flows actually take place, what their enabling influences are. Finally, the D's are important performance measures. However, they also distinguish between two important concepts in SD: those dwell times resulting from 'uncapacitated delays' (Di, resource-independent inputs) and dwell times arising from 'capacitated delays' (Dii, resource-dependent outputs). The ABCDE mnemonic therefore aimed to deliver both process and content benefits.

This framework also visualizes some of the influences on patients' experience and on the quality of service that they receive. The A's elicit comment on whether patients are directed to the part of the NHS most appropriate for their needs. The B's evoke effects which stop patients receiving the service they would wish for, while the C's deal with the resources which advance their treatments. Finally, the D's bring to the surface a key aspect of patient experience and service quality: the waiting times encountered in moving through the NHS.

We sent this framework to the NHS staff who had agreed to attend the workshops. We also sent a copy of the Core Map (see Figure 7.4) and

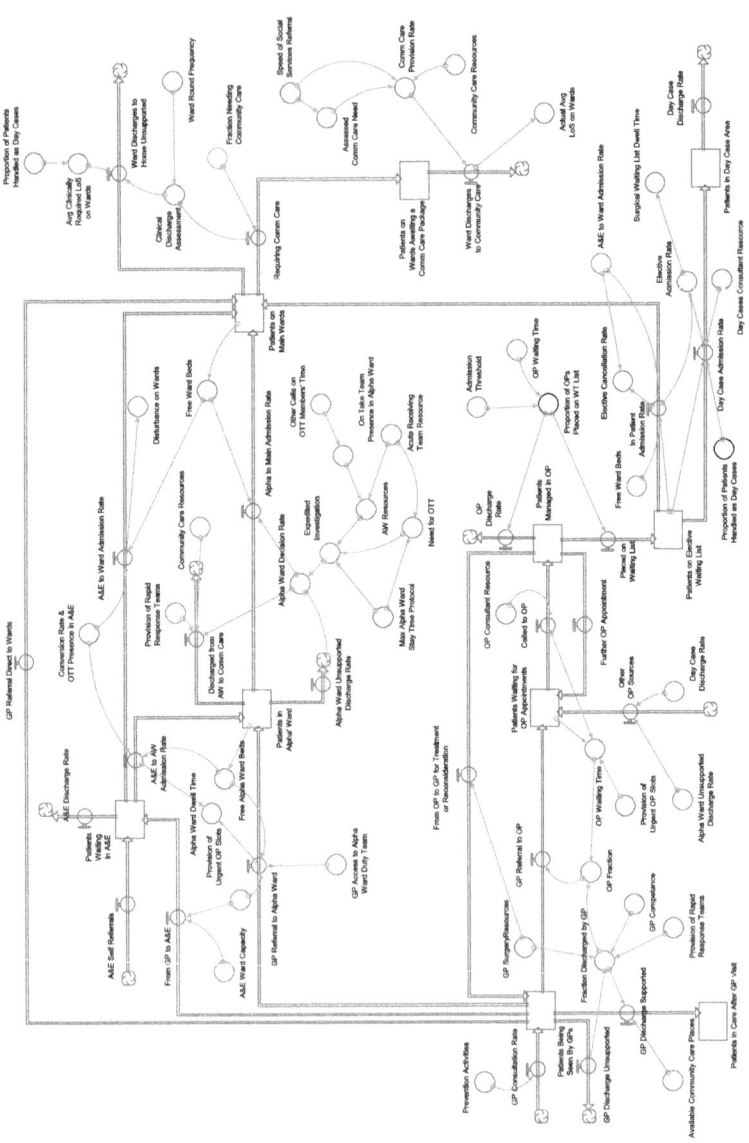

*Figure 7.4* Core Map of pathways for acute patients

asked them to spend a few minutes looking at these materials in preparation for the day. To support the use of this framework we created other materials. These are described next, in the context of the workshop.

## 7.7   Running the workshops

Three workshops were run over a 2-week period in London (at the headquarters of the British Medical Association), Sheffield and Manchester. In total, 43 people attended the workshops, drawn from middle to senior levels in the NHS, all involved in the daily work of patient treatment. These included hospital bed managers, A&E physicians, healthcare strategists, a Director of Nursing, a Social Services manager and a manager from the Ambulance Service. This group therefore represented a broad cross-section of NHS activities.

The format of the day is shown in Table 7.1. During the informal start each participant received a personalized pack of materials. By way of introduction, both the core map and the conceptual framework were reviewed, and the format and intended benefits of the day described. Participants were then split into four groups of three or four people (each participant's pack designated a group, arranged to get a good mix of job functions). To obtain a degree of triangulation, two groups looked at the work of local doctors and two at how emergency treatment works. In prepared break-out rooms, each had four items to work with (A0 charts taped to the wall). These were: the core map, the conceptual framework, a detailed sub-map of their area with ABCDE points indicated, a task structure listing a set of ABCDE questions concerning the experience of patients flowing through the area of the system. Examples of these last are shown in Figure 7.5 and Table 7.2. Group members

*Table 7.1*   Format of the three workshops

| | |
|---|---|
| 9:30 | 'Meet & greet' period |
| 10:00 | Presentation: Introduction and scene-setting |
| 10:30 | First pair of parallel group tasks: |
| | 2 × GP Activities          2 × A + E Activities |
| 12:00 | First plenary feedback session |
| 12:30 | Lunch |
| 13:00 | Second pair of parallel group tasks: |
| | 2 × Main wards Activities   2 × 'Alpha Wards' Activities |
| 14:15 | Second plenary feedback session |
| 14:45 | Presentation: What will/could happen next |
| 15:00 | Close |

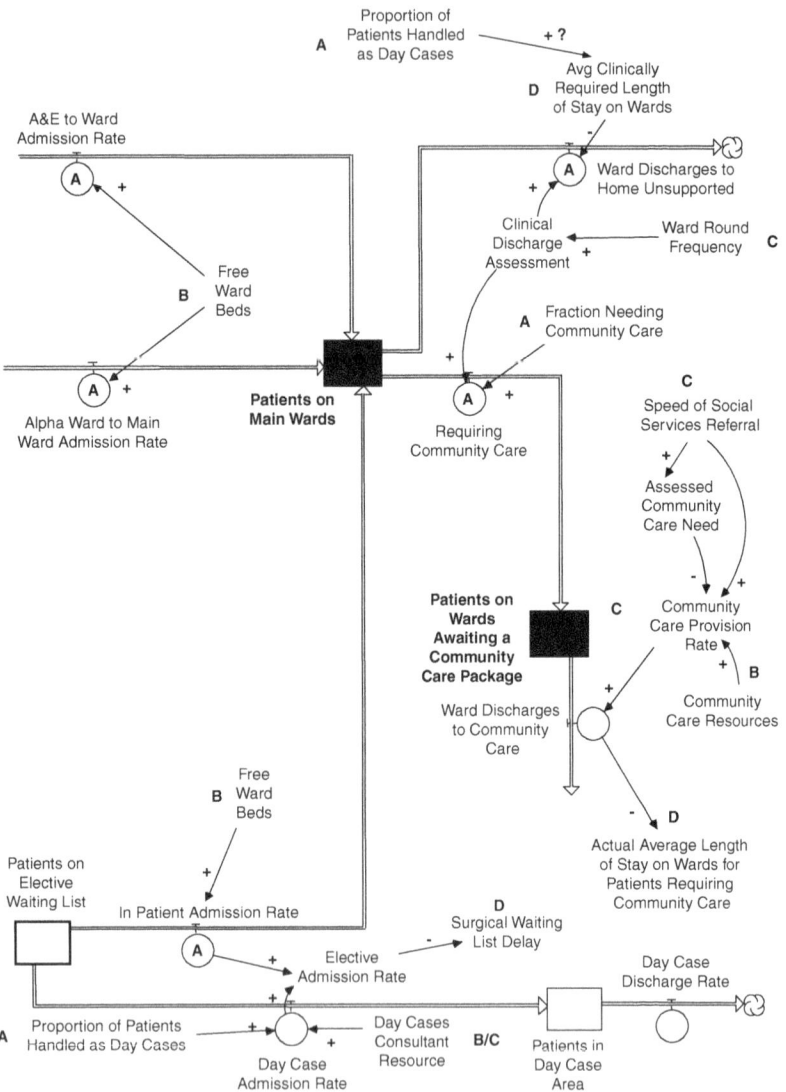

*Figure 7.5* Sub-map of the acute patient flows into and out of a hospital's main ward

*Table 7.2* Detailed task structure for acute patient flows into and out of a hospital's main wards

---

Main Wards Task Structure
*Please use the following framework to structure your group discussion.*
*Write your comments on the flip-chart, labelling them 'A1', 'A2' etc.*

*Alternative pathways*
(A1) Flowing into and out of the two main rectangles, are there any *additional* important pathways (A)?
(A2) What influences the 'Proportion of Patients Handled as Day Cases'? What are the advantages and disadvantages of increasing this proportion? (eg does the Length of Stay for the remaining in-patients rise?)
(A3) Is the value of the variable 'Fraction Needing Community Care' that you experience too high or too low? In which direction would you like to change this value and how would you do it?

*Blocking resources on flows*
(B1) For each of the pathways on the map, are there any *additional* Blocking Resources other than 'Free Ward Beds' and 'Community Care Resources' (B) that limit the flow rate to the next stage?
(B2) What interventions could possibly be made to the Blocking Resources to reduce these flow limiting effects?
(B3) Indicate your judgement of the potential importance of these interventions to removing the block using the scale:
   1. Slight          3. Important
   2. Worthwhile   4. Very Important

*Conversion resources on flows*
(C1) For each of the pathways flowing out of and into (this activity), are there any *additional* resources that are needed to make the flow to the next stage possible?
(C2) Which Conversion Resources (C) would you wish to increase in order to speed up ('de-bottleneck') each of the flows?
   1. Minor          3. Large
   2. Appreciable   4. Very Large

*Dwell times stages*
(D1) Which of the two Dwell Times shown (D) cause you the most concern? Mark them on the following scale:
   1. Appropriate duration          3. Longer than necessary
   2. A little longer than desirable   4. Far Longer that necessary
(D2) What actions could be taken to reduce the Dwell Times (D)?

*Extra comments that you want to make*
Any other observations, issues or questions which you would like to record.

---

were asked to use the sub-map and deal with the questions on the task structure. A designated 'recorder' wrote responses on flipchart pages.

The majority of participants found the framework and the maps self-explanatory. A little encouragement and clarification helped the remaining participants to join in. The groups fairly rapidly adopted the language and symbols of stocks and flows as a way of handling existing and alternatives treatment pathways. Causal links were equally unproblematic. Generally, participants found the provided maps reasonable and useful. When they agreed changes they drew new stocks, flows and links onto the maps. In this way inaccuracies were corrected and important new elements introduced.

The ABCDE question convention worked. In process terms, participants related well to the questions, understanding their main point but feeling able to discuss possibilities in a creative manner while 'operating' within each set question. The simple ABCDE naming made group members remind others of questions still to be asked, or prompt the group to cycle back to overlooked questions. It was also clear that individual questions were being answered in the broader, more systemically aware, context provided by the maps and with consideration of the system complexity that those maps illustrated.

In plenary one group from each task briefly presented their observations and comments from all other participants followed.

After lunch four different groups were formed (Table 7.1), concentrating on main hospital wards and what had been labelled 'alpha wards' (specialist wards where a concentration of resources allows more rigorous discharge protocols; patients thought to require only short stays are dealt with here). Again, these groups had detailed sub-maps and task structures with ABCDE questions. Another plenary feedback session followed. The day closed with a description of how the project would go forward.

## 7.8   Post-workshop activities

The workshops generated annotated maps, flipchart responses to the ABCDE questions, tapes of the plenary sessions and contemporaneous notes from the group work. The final stage therefore involved the analysis of these materials (Figure 7.2).

The first part of this was the finalization of the maps. System dynamicists aim for maps to have high 'face validity' (Forrester and Senge, 1980; Frankfort-Nachmias and Nachmias, 1992). In a workshop setting emphasis falls on the subjective understanding that groups have of how a system works now, and how it might be made to work (Eden *et al*, 1979; Checkland, 1995). Workshop participants had questioned and changed the maps thereby increasing the level of confidence that they were accurate and included the most important system elements. Creating final versions was straightforward and did not require major reworking. Emerging from this analysis was the 'Suite Model', a set of SFDs derived from the Core Model and the five detailed sub-maps. Having been subjected to the comments, changes and corrections of the workshops, this expressed the participants' shared understanding of the stocks, flows and influences of the different parts of the NHS through which acute patients (and others) pass, as well as displaying the understanding of the system which gave rise to the proposed changes.

The second part of the post-workshop analysis involved finding the general ideas and themes that participants had come up with about those possible ways of intervening to improve patient experience. The various materials were analysed to form clusters of related ideas. In the task structures (see Table 7.2) participants had been asked to rate the importance of their ideas in a way similar to that used in Likert Scales (Frankfort-Nachmias and Nachmias, 1992). This, combined with a simple frequency count of related ideas, made it possible to extract a rich set of 'intervention themes' from the material generated by the workshops.

## 7.9   Project outputs

The innovative features of the project concern the following elements. First, the conceptual framework for mapping acute patient flows, second, the health-specific—yet generic—ABCDE question sets and associated detailed SFDs. However, what should be emphasized is the practical use of these materials by NHS staff in the workshops, during which the different elements were used in conjunction. These features relate to the two intended outputs of the projects: an assessment of the benefits of applying SD with NHS staff not expert in the modelling approach, and the production of an internal report recording the system maps and the suggested interventions.

The Steering Group made a positive assessment of SD as a result of this work. The set of hybrid materials had been created and successfully used. Additing together the workshop participants and the early interviews, the materials had been put to the test by around 50 NHS staff (an improvement on the project target of 20–30). As described, participants found the maps useful and the questions meaningful.

The discussions helped communication among participants concerning knowledge of how the system was put together and helped them to think through the opportunities for, and consequences of, any changes using a broader, more systemic understanding. The project produced the Suite Model representing the majority of acute hospitals. These qualitative maps employed the iconograpy of stocks and flows to show the main patient flows of such hospitals along with more detailed maps of other processes. Although the content of this work was specific, in more general terms it demonstrated that the thinking of SD could be used to illuminate the functioning of ·healthcare systems. It demonstrated that mapping could be used not only in the PSM style of agreeing a problem definition but as a means of creating, exploring and agreeing actual modifications to the structure of the system in question.

It seems apropriate to quote the comments from two of the senior DoH staff on the project's Steering Committee. One wrote of the workshops, 'Colleagues who were involved in these discussions found the discussions very useful in clarifying their understanding of emergency services'. Assessing the benefits of SD, a second wrote that the project, 'improved the cognition by senior managers, working in the [A&E] services environment, of how the various components of the Acute Health care system were interrelated.'

The various maps were contained within the final report on the project, the production of which was the second intended project output. As a record of the events, all workshop attendees received a copy and its contents were subsequently communicated to ESAT (see below). The report recorded much of the detail of the project, including process maps and participant responses. The workshop responses, cross-referenced with the maps themselves, gave rise to a set of proposals for improvements in the management of acute patients. Some were ideas known already to a few who were present but the workshops gave them an opportunity to explain and explore them with other NHS staff. This helped all to consider the ideas in a broader context, or communicated them to a wider group of NHS staff—along with the reasons why they were thought useful.

The internal report presented these proposed changes in two clusters, or 'intervention themes'. One concerned ways of intervening to get a faster flow of patients along the existing pathways within the acute healthcare system. The ideas in this theme concerned; the more active management of patient progress, increased resource flexibility to cope with demand surges, a wide range of changes in NHS working and career practices to make the service more flexible, the provision of more resources/funding to extend present processes (and/or to create new delivery paths), and movement towards an all day, 7 days a week availability of facilities. The other cluster of proposed interventions concerned ways of changing parts of the systems so that patients are handled in the most appropriate part of that system. These ideas involved: minimization of variations of conditions dealt with at any point in the system (achieved by more filtering of patients and by the concentration of advanced healthcare resources in specific places), and increased availability of information to patients and healthcare workers.

The internal report described all of these in greater detail, however, a sketch of one may be helpful. An interesting aspect of the patient filtering idea was the insight that more patients could be kept away from hospitals by the appropriate redeployments of healthcare assets. Assets could be 'forward deployed; into GP surgeries (to allow a greater range of tests and treatments to be administered) or into NHS Direct (an emergency telephone service from which healthcare advice could be given). These initiatives would have the effect of avoiding admissions. There could also be 'backward deployment' of assets. For example, into home support for post-operative recuperation or into the creation of 'step down wards' which act as a bridge between main wards and a return to life back in the community. These ideas were aimed at enabling patients to be discharged from hospitals as quickly as possible. Such filtering took the view that automatically admitting all sick people to hospitals was old-fashioned and wasteful. As an alternative, many patients could be dealt with closer to home, with less disruption of their social support network and less chance of their becoming 'institutionalized', a common problem with elderly patients as long hospital stays can result in their losing their independence. With lower level healthcare being provided via different services there would then be less variation in the conditions of hospitalized patients; these facilities would be focused on the treatment of severely ill patients.

Space restriction prevents further discussion here. Even so, it merits emphasizing that systems mapping helped participants to look outside their functional specialisms when discussing such ideas. It was noticeable in the discussions that working with the maps allowed participants to judge proposals in a richer context, informed by the system maps that they were all referring to. Consequently, problems with some ideas were uncovered while new possibilities were invented. This is expressed in a comment by one of the workshop participants; 'There is no point focussing on one solution: all areas must be adressed'.

## 7.10   Beyond the project

This work showed that a version of SD mapping could be used successfully by NHS staff. It added to a number of positive experiences that the DoH's EOR Division had with SD. In the words of a member of the Steering Group, the 'project represented a successful use of SD particularly in a learning context' (The DoH has gone on to conduct other SD studies and this interest is continuing. For example, at the September 2005 launch meeting of MASHnet, a network for modelling and simulation in healthcare the DoH's Head of OR, Geoff Royston, expressed his belief that SD offered a uniquely powerful combination of analytical power and user transparency (Royston, 2005)).

The specific proposals for improving patient experience were fed back into the DoH and, hence, the NHS. This work was presented to ESAT at BMA House, reporting on both the specific results and the general mapping approach. The report itself, in the words of one of the Steering Committee members, 'has informed the modernisation of [A&E] services initially through an [A&E] task force and subsequently through the Modernisation agency.' Another Committee member completes the story of the project described in this paper: 'In policy terms, [the] work made an important contribution to work on improving A&E departments. [The] report showed how relatively simple modifications in physical arrangements and treatment pathways might improve the delivery of service . . . [the] report also helped to inform the work of the Accident and Emergency Modernisation Programme, a £15 million capital investment programme overseen by an expert taskforce that was also charged with developing proposals for modernisation of service delivery in A&E. The A&E task force . . . discussed [the] findings in some depth. I know that they found this work useful in developing models of future service delivery. . . . The task force recommendations are now being implemented by the National Patients' Access Team, a Government agency working with acute hospital.'

### Acknowledgements

We are greatful to the Department of Health for initiating this project and to all of the NHS staff who contributed their time to it. This project was funded by the Research and Development Division of the Department of Health.

### References

Andersen DF and Richardson GP (1997). Scripts for group model building. *Syst Dyn Rev* **13**: 107–129.

Ashton R, Hague L, Brandreth M, Worthington D and Cropper S (2005). A simulation-based study of a NHS walk-in centre. *J Opl Res Soc* **56**: 153–161.

Bennett JC and Worthington DJ (1998). An example of a good but partially successful OR engagement: Improving outpatient clinic operations. *Interfaces* **28**(5): 56–69.

Bensley DC, Watson PC and Morrison GW (1995). Pathways of coronary care— A computer-simulation model of the potential for health gain. *IMA J Math Appl Med Biol* **12**: 315–328.

Booth-Sweeney L and Sterman JD (2000). Bathtub dynamics: Initial results of a systems thinking inventory. *Syst Dyn Rev* **16**: 249–286.

Bouyssou D, Forder R, Merchant S, Nance R, Pierskalla W, Roper M, Ryan D and van der Duyn Schouten F (2004). *Review of Research Status of Operational Research in the UK.* EPSRC/ESRC/ORS. Swindon, UK.

Brailsford SC, Lattimer VA, Tarnaras P and Turnbull JC (2004). Emergency and on-demand health care: Modelling a large complex system. *J Opl Res Soc* **55**: 34–42.

Checkland PB (1995). Model validation in soft systems practice. *Syst Res* **12**: 47–54.

Checkland PB (1996). *Guidelines for the Use of 'Soft Systems' Methodology.* Information Management Group of the NHS Executive: Winchester.

Davies R and Bensley D (2005). Meeting health challenges with OR (special issue). *J Opl Res Soc* **56**: 123–125.

Davies R and Davies H (1994). Modelling patient flows and resource provision in health systems. *Omega* **22**: 123–131.

Eden C (1987). Problem solving or problem finishing? In: Jackson MC and Keys P (eds). *New Directions in Management Science.* Gower: Aldershot: UK, pp 97–107.

Eden C, Jones S, Sims D and Gunton H (1979). Images into models: The subjective world of the policy maker. *Futures* **February**: 56–62.

Eden C, Jones S and Sims D (1983). *Messing About in Problems.* Pergamon Press: Oxford.

Forrester JW (1961). *Industrial Dynamics.* MIT Press: Cambridge, MA.

Forrester JW (1968). *Principles of Systems.* MIT Press: Cambridge, MA.

Forrester JW (1992). Policies, decisions and information sources for modelling. *Eur J Opl Res* **59**: 42–63.

Forrester JW (1994). System dynamics, systems thinking, and soft OR. *Syst Dyn Rev* **10**: 245–256.

Forrester JW and Senge PM (1980). Tests for building confidence in system dynamics models. In: Lagasto AA, Forrester JW and Lyneis JM (eds). *System Dynamics: Tims Studies in the Management Sciences.* North-Holland: Oxford, pp 209–228.

Frankfort-Nachmias C and Nachmias D (1992). *Research Methods in the Social Sciences*, 4th edn. Edward Arnold: London.

Gallivan S, Utley M, Treasure T and Valencia O (2002). Booked inpatient admissions and hospital capacity: Mathematical modelling study. *Br Med J* **324**: 280–282.

Griffiths JD, Price-Lloyd N, Smithies M and Williams JE (2005). Modelling the requirement for supplementary nurses in an intensive care unit. *J Opl Res Soc* **56**: 126–133.

Harper P and Shahani AK (2002). Modelling for the planning and management of bed capacities in hospitals. *J Opl Res Soc* **53**: 11–18.

Homer JB and Hirsch GB (2006). System dynamics modeling for public health: Background and opportunities. *Am J Pub Health* **96**: 452–458.

Kleinmuntz DN (1993). Information processing and misperceptions of the implications of feedback in dynamic decision making. *Syst Dyn Rev* **9**: 223–237.

Lane DC (1992). Modelling as learning: A consultancy methodology for enhancing learning in management teams. *Eur J Opl Res* **59**:64–84.

Lane DC (1998). Can we have confidence in generic structures? *J Opl Res Soc* **49**: 936–947.

Lane DC (2000). Diagramming conventions in system dynamics. *J Opl Res Soc* **51**: 241–245.

Lane DC (2008). The emergence and use of diagramming in system dynamics: A critical account. *Syst Res Behavior Sci* **25**, forthcoming.

Lane DC, Monefeldt C and Husemann E (2003). Client involvement in simulation model building. Hints and insights form a case study in a London hospital. *Health Care Mngt Sci* **6**: 105–116.

Lane DC, Monefeldt C and Rosenhead JV (1998). Emergency—but no accident— a system dynamics study of an accident and emergency department. *OR Insight* **11**(4): 2–10.

Lane DC, Monefeldt C and Rosenhead JV (2000). Looking in the wrong place for healthcare improvements: A system dynamics study of an accident and emergency department. *J Opl Res Soc* **51**: 518–531.

Leischow SJ and Milstein B (2006). Editorial: Systems thinking and modeling for public health practice. *Am J Pub Health* **96**: 403–405.

Millard PH and McClean SI (eds) (1996). *Go with the Flow: A Systems Approach to Healthcare Planning.* London: Royal Society of Medicine Press: London.

Moxnes E (1998). Not only the tragedy of the commons:Misperceptions of bioeconomics. *Mngt Sci* **44**: 1234–1248.

Pidd M (1992). *Computer Simulation in Management Science*, 3rd ed. Wiley: Chichester.

Pratt J, Gordon P and Plamping D (1999). *Working Whole Systems: Putting Theory into Practice in Organisations.* King's Fund: London.

Richardson GP (1986). Problems with casual-loop diagrams (originally published in 1976). *Syst Dyn Rev* **2**: 158–170.

Richmond B (1994). Systems thinking/system dynamics: Let's just get on with it. *Syst Dyn Rev* **10**: 135–157.

Rosenhead J (ed) (1989). *Rational Analysis for a Problematic World: Problem Structuring Methods for Complexity, Uncertainty and Conflict.* Wiley: Chichester.

Royston G (2005). Modelling and simulation in health: Potential, achievement and challenge. *Presentation at the MASHnet launch event*, WBS, 20th September.

Royston G, Dost A, Townshend J and Turner H (1999). Using system dynamics to help develop and implement policies and programmes in health care in England. *Syst Dyn Rev* **15**: 293–313.

Senge PM (1990). *The Fifth Discipline: The Art and Practice of the Learning Organization.* Doubleday/Currency: New York.

Sterman JD (1989). Modelling managerial behaviour: Misperceptions of feedback in a dynamic decision making experiment. *Mngt Sci* **35**: 321–339.

Sterman JD (1994). Beyond training wheels. In: Senge PM, Roberts C, Ross R, Smith B and Kleiner A (eds). *The Fifth Discipline Fieldbook*. Nicholas Brealey Publishing: London, pp 177–184.

Sterman JD (1994). Learning in and about complex systems. *Syst Dyn Rev* **10**: 291–330.

Sterman JD (2006). Learning from evidence in a complex world. *Am J Pub Health* **96**: 505–514.

Vennix JAM (1996). *Group Model-building: Facilitating Team Learning Using System Dynamics*. Wiley: Chichester.

Vennix JAM and Gubbels JW (1992). Knowledge elicitation in conceptual model building: A case study in modeling a regional Dutch health care system. *Eur J Opl Res* **59**: 85–101.

Warren K (2004). Why has feedback systems thinking struggled to influence strategy and policy formulation? Suggestive evidence explanations and solutions. *Syst Res Behav Sci* **21**: 331–347.

Wernerfelt B (1984). A resource-based view of the firm. *Strat Mngt J* **5**: 171–180.

# 8

# Planning for Disaster: Developing a Multi-Agency Counselling Service

*W. J. Gregory and G. Midgley*
*University of Hull*

Multi-agency planning is becoming increasingly important to organisations, especially those concerned with delivering services for the benefit of the community. This paper describes how a modified version of the methods from soft systems methodology (SSM), chosen through methodological reflections informed by critical systems thinking, was used to support the planning of a multi-agency counselling service that could be activated in the event of a disaster. Representatives of nineteen agencies were involved in this exercise, working together in six, one-day workshops. Feedback from participants, using four evaluation criteria (derived from the principles of SSM and the stated priorities of workshop participants), suggests that the methods of SSM, modified as described, show a great deal of promise as a support to multi-agency planning.

## 8.1 Introduction

This paper describes a set of six, one-day workshops where representatives from nineteen agencies, in a County in the North of England, came together to plan the basis for a counselling network that could be activated in the event of a disaster. We will begin by describing the phenomenon of multi-agency working, which provides an important challenge to operational researchers and systems practitioners seeking to support the provision of services to local communities. We will then

Reprinted from *Journal of the Operational Research Society*, 51(3): 278–290, 2000, 'Planning for Disaster: Developing a Multi-Agency Counselling Service', by W. J. Gregory and G. Midgley. With kind permission from Operational Research Society Ltd.

go on to outline our initial contacts with the multi-agency group, and detail our decision to use the methods offered by soft systems methodology (SSM).[1,2] This decision was informed by critical systems thinking (CST) which, amongst other things, asks researchers to choose or design methods according to their own and stakeholders' perceptions of the situation being dealt with.[3-5] The choice of SSM methods was therefore not automatic, but seemed to us to offer the best way forward in the circumstances.

Having provided the necessary background, we will proceed to detail our intervention, focusing in particular on the difficulties we experienced in co-ordinating debate (resulting in some modifications of the SSM methods). We will also discuss the learning outcomes generated from the process. We will then reflect on the intervention in the light of feedback from participants, arguing that our work can be considered successful according to four criteria (generated from the priorities of participants and the stated purposes of SSM). This will allow us to reach some conclusions about the utility of the methods of SSM for supporting multi-agency planning.

## 8.2 Multi-agency working

In recent years there has been an increasing emphasis on multi-agency working—the practice of organisations working together in partnership. It has been a growing trend in the profit-orientated business sector,[6-8] and has also been increasingly evident in the area of public service provision (health, housing, child protection, etc.) where public, private and voluntary organisations are often expected to collaborate for the benefit of the community. This collaboration has been the subject of extensive study.[9-13] However, while the rhetoric of multi-agency working has permeated most service providing organisations, it is becoming apparent that its practice can be quite problematic. Watson,[14] for example, reviewing twenty recent studies of housing provision, points out that a significant theme is the noticeable lack of effective co-operation between organisations, despite expressions of good intentions. The literature[14-18] suggests that problems obstructing co-operation include differences in organisational culture and working practices; legislation requiring different things of different agencies; obscure or inadequate planning structures; a lack of clarity regarding accountability; poor understandings of conflict management; short-term financial planning; power imbalances between agencies; perceptions of hidden political agendas; and a lack of mutual trust.

Despite these problems, it is likely that the trend towards further multi-agency working will continue. This is because no public service organisation can meet all community needs, and gaps in provision are apparent, so co-operation between organisations is required to ensure that duplication of services is avoided, and coverage becomes progressively more comprehensive. Indeed, in a recent study[15] of the views of a variety of stakeholders in the housing system for older people (service users, carers, campaigners and professionals), there was widespread agreement that the continued existence of a diversity of agencies (public, private and voluntary) is a strength, and that multi-agency working is a key principle for the future of service development.

Multi-agency working therefore presents a challenge for operational researchers and systems practitioners seeking to support the provision of services to local communities. While quantitative operational research (OR) methods have been used for multi-agency decision support on occasion,[19] as far as we are aware the multi-agency challenge has never before been addressed by proponents of soft systems methodology (SSM). Checkland[20] has used SSM to work on a project with the National Health Service (NHS) (the public-sector health system in the UK), focusing on the NHS internal market. While he explored the views of people in other agencies as part of this study, his purpose was to gain insights into the NHS rather than to directly support multi-agency working. Similarly, Cohen and Midgley[21] describe the use of the methods of SSM (operated through a critical systems perspective) to support multi-disciplinary team-building: although the team in question included people drawn from a variety of different agencies, they were actually employed by a single organisation. The intervention described in this paper, in which nineteen agencies co-operated in the design of a counselling service to be activated in the event of a disaster, therefore offers a new test for the application of the methods of SSM.

## 8.3   Initial contacts with the multi-agency group

Our first introduction to the possibility of undertaking this project came when we were approached by the Chair of the multi-agency working party that had been set up to develop plans for a counselling service that could be activated in the event of a disaster. We were told that the working party had been meeting for about 18 months, but had achieved very little in terms of comprehensive planning. This was because the situation was perceived as so complex that participants found themselves unable to come up with an effective plan that satisfied all their requirements. In particular, they knew that their disaster response had to be multi-agency, because no single organisation had the resources to go it alone, but they anticipated real problems in harmonising their different views and working practices. The idea of the intervention was to support the working party in generating a sufficiently cohesive plan to warrant putting an application for funding in to Social Services. We said that we would like to explore the situation before deciding if and how we might help.

We were sent written details of the work undertaken so far, together with information about the constitution of the working party. The agencies represented were as follows: four Health Authorities (providers of health services); the Ambulance Service; the Fire Brigade; the Police; the Police Welfare Service; Victim Support (a voluntary organisation linked with the Police, offering counselling to people affected by crime); CRUSE (a voluntary organisation offering bereavement counselling); the Samaritans (a voluntary organisation offering crisis counselling); a local Association of Counsellors; the Emergency Psychological Service; the Council of Churches; two University departments; Emergency Planning (County Council); and Social Services (County Council).

We were then invited to a meeting of the working party at which we were expected to make a proposal for providing support. In between receiving the written material and attending the meeting, we made contact with a selection of working party representatives. The purpose of this was to see if their reasons for wanting an intervention (if indeed they did want one) mirrored those given by their Chair. We were particularly keen to talk with people from the voluntary sector, as the Chair was a Social Services representative and the idea was that the group should eventually apply for funding from Social Services. This put the statutory agencies (especially Social Services) in a pivotal position, and we wanted to know if this caused any problems in terms of the participation of other groups.

These initial discussions revealed that there *was* a difference of view between the voluntary and statutory agencies. The latter wanted to develop a 'professional' service, with selected employees in various caring professions paid a retainer to be on call in the event of a disaster. In contrast, the voluntary organisations envisaged a 'volunteer' service, with the names of a large number of potential, unpaid counsellors kept on file to be contacted when necessary. However, the voluntary agency representatives agreed with the Chair that, whichever vision was followed, the planning task was so complex that they really did need support. Also, they felt that it was important to get *something* done;

the 'professional' service would be better than nothing. Importantly, everybody we talked with said that open communication was possible in the group: nobody said that they feared representing their views, or felt that the results of the planning had been determined in advance by any single agency.

## 8.4   Designing the methods

Based on these preliminary discussions, the researchers developed a proposal to put to the working party. Both of us are involved in the theoretical, methodological and practical development of critical systems thinking (CST), which we have used to inform a number of other interven-tions.[15,21-24] This was also influential in the development of our proposal to the working party, so we will give some brief details of CST before moving on to discuss our decision to draw upon the methods from SSM.

### 8.4.1   Critical systems thinking

CST is an approach to intervention which Midgley,[25] building on the work of several other authors,[4,26,27] suggests is based around three themes for debate:

- *critical awareness*—examining and re-examining taken-for-granted assumptions, along with the conditions which give rise to them;
- *improvement*—*defined* temporarily and locally, but in a widely informed manner, taking issues of power (which may affect the definition) into account; and
- *methodological pluralism*—using a variety of intervention methods in a theoretically coherent manner, becoming aware of their strengths and weaknesses, to address a corresponding variety of issues.

These are inevitably an over-simplification of the range of issues considered important by critical systems thinkers, but are useful for indicating the general interests pursued by proponents of the perspective.

Being explicit about the third of the above themes for debate, methodological pluralism, is important because of the tendency of some practitioners in the OR and systems communities to specialise in the use of a very limited set of methods which are then applied in every project. Critical systems thinkers have argued for some time that this restricts the flexibility and responsiveness of practitioners involved in interventions.[3-5,28,29]

Methodolgoical pluralism usually finds its practical expression in the combination of methods to suit the researchers' and other stakeholders' perceptions of the situation in which an intervention is taking place. This practice of combining methods has been called *creative design*.[30] In the creative design process, methods are drawn from a variety of sources, synthesised, and operated through a methodology guided by an understanding of CST (there are several CST-inspired methodologies in the literature[31-36]). Much more rarely, one method is drawn upon in its 'pure' form. This was the case in the intervention reported upon in the current paper, the methods being drawn solely from SSM.[1,2]

### 8.4.2 Choosing the methods

It seemed abundantly clear from our initial investigations into the relationships between people on the working party that methods were needed to structure the problems and facilitate debate. However, we made the judgement that any use of methods involving the researchers in an 'expert' role with regard to the production of a design would have been highly problematic, and there were two reasons for this. Firstly, disaster planning is a specialised activity of which we had no prior knowledge. The expertise resided in the agencies. Secondly, we felt that, given the large number of stakeholder organisations involved, any proposals that were developed without their participation would have failed to engender their commitment. Indeed, this is a common problem in OR and systems practice: the need to foster commitment through participation is one of the strongest arguments for the use of problem structuring methods (sometimes called 'soft OR' or 'soft systems thinking').[37] There was no evidence of problems that might have prevented a debate-orientated approach from working, or which would have made debate a sham (such as coercion or insincerity on the part of those controlling resources), so we proceeded with this line of thinking.

The question then was, which problem structuring method(s) should we use? Because of the difference of opinion between the voluntary and statutory agency representatives, we were tempted to use a method like strategic assumption surfacing and testing (SAST).[38] This asks people with different ideas about strategy to justify their position to others before a synthesis of viewpoints is sought. However, to be operated effectively, SAST really needs the strategic options to be clearly defined in advance,[39] and the complexity of the situation made this condition difficult to satisfy. In addition, the likely outcome would have been a general direction which the working party could pursue, but little concrete detail. An alternative approach might have been interactive planning (IP).[40] This asks participants to generate a list of 'desired properties' of the ideal system (in this case, the ideal disaster response counselling system), which participants can then use to generate more concrete plans. However, most of the examples of IP in practice seem to indicate that planning takes some considerable time,[40] and even in situations where planning is truncated, the result is often a plan that needs to be worked towards over many years.[21] With this project, it was clear that plans needed to be generated quickly so that an application for funding could be submitted within a period of months, and the application had to detail activities that could be implemented in the subsequent one or two years (the longer the period of implementation needed, the more likely it would be that a disaster would occur before the response system was in place).

After exploring various options and combinations of options (in the spirit of critical systems thinking) through dialogue between ourselves, we decided to base our proposal on the methods of soft systems methodology (SSM).[1,2] SSM has the advantage of allowing participants in debate space to develop their ideas as they go along, thereby supporting them in getting to grips with complexity. The outputs, in terms of the identification of specific activities that need to be undertaken, can also be quite detailed. We felt that this would be useful given the short term goal of submitting a funding application. Finally, it was obvious that we were only ever going to be able to help the group 'kick start' their planning activities, and that a lot more work would need to be done once we had left and the funding application had been submitted: in common with some other problem structuring methods, SSM claims to provide participants with a planning 'language' that people can use to guide their discussions over the longer term— SSM is not only useful for one-off interventions.[1,2] We felt that this 'language' could help prevent the working party from getting into a similar 'stuck' situation in future.

At the meeting with the working party, the participants readily accepted our proposal. However, we made it clear that we wanted to set up a series of full-day workshops so that people could clear their minds of everyday work concerns and thereby be more creative. We also wanted to use the first couple of workshops to train participants in the use of SSM so that they would not be wholly reliant on us for support. This caused a serious problem for the group. They had wanted to work in relatively short evening meetings, and had not anticipated our desire for training. After a lengthy discussion, they decided that it *would* be possible to have full-day workshops, as long as there were no more than three blocks of two days each, spread over one month. This inevitably meant abandoning the idea of training participants beforehand, as we anticipated that the group would need the whole six days for planning. This is a compromise we were prepared to make on the grounds that participants would gain some familiarity with the language of SSM while engaged in the process of problem structuring.

We also explored one other issue at the meeting, and that was whether there were any further agencies, not yet represented on the working party, who could usefully be involved. Missing a key stakeholder with a different perspective on the situation could have posed problems in the longer term, as that person or group could have access to critical information affecting the potential success of the whole operation. The group reflected on their membership, but couldn't think of anyone else who should be involved.

## 8.5   Soft systems methodology

SSM was developed by Checkland and co-workers.[1,2] It encourages participants in the intervention to generate issues through on-going explorations of their perceptions, allowing people to model desirable future human activity. Given the necessary commitment from individuals involved in and affected by possible changes, these models of future human activity can be used as a basis for guiding actual human activity in the world. However, to ensure that the models will indeed be useful, it is necessary for participants to relate them back to their perceptions of their current situation.

Earlier versions of SSM were criticised for being consensus orientated: stressing the need for all participants to move towards a common understanding, regardless of whether this is in everyone's interests.[41–43] However, Checkland and Scholes[2] clarify that, while participants might make 'accommodations' with one another (agree to put aside their differences on a temporary basis to achieve common goals), SSM does not have to be used to generate a single action plan: it may simply be used to explore different perspectives so that people can gain insights into each other's thinking. Nevertheless, in most planning situations (including the one reported in this paper), it is common for people to express the desire to produce a way forward that they can all commit to.

Checkland and Scholes[2] describe two 'modes' of using SSM: mode 1 is the use of their specific methods, while mode 2 is the expression of their methodological idea (comparing models of future human activity with perceptions of the current situation) through the use of any methods the researcher cares to draw upon. The suggestion is that, as researchers get more practiced, they can move away from mode 1 towards mode 2 applications. In this paper we are concerned with mode 1 only: use of the methods as described by Checkland and Scholes.[2]

To maximise the accessibility of the argument, we will follow Checkland[1] in describing the methods of SSM as if they are operationalised in seven stages of activity. However, Checkland always stresses the *iterative* nature of SSM—that is, one moves backwards and forwards between the various stages as and when necessary.

SSM is usually (but not always) conducted in a workshop format involving a general group discussion. Workshop participants are asked to (iteratively) follow the stages set out in Figure 8.1 (taken from Checkland[1]). This figure is briefly explained in the text below (the numbers in brackets refer to the numbers in Figure 8.1), but the reader should consult the original literature on SSM[1,2] for further details.

Firstly, the problem situation is considered in an unstructured form (1). Then the participants are required to express their understandings

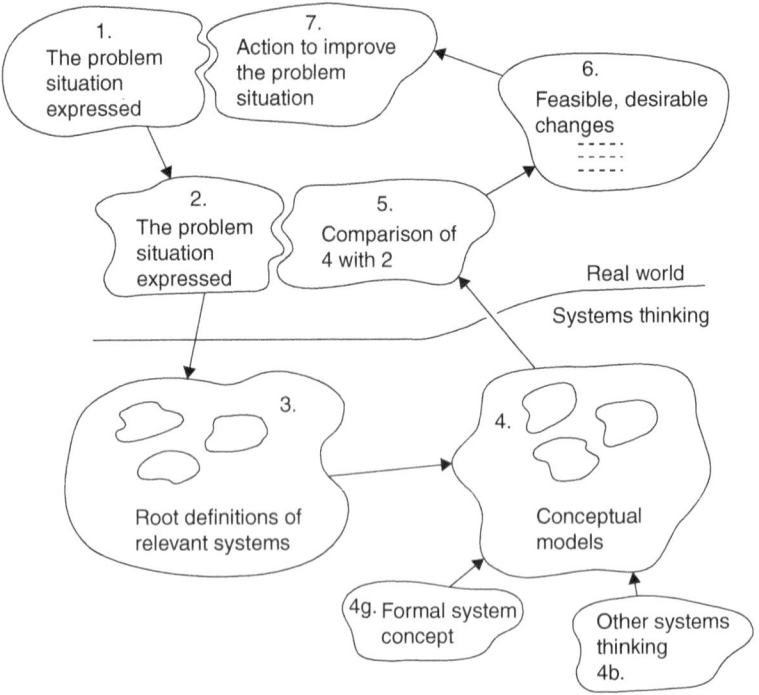

*Figure 8.1*   Soft systems methodology (from Checkland)

in a 'rich picture' (2), a visual representation of the situation people currently perceive. It is usually a mess of drawings and arrows showing the interconnections between the various facets of the situation.

Secondly, it is necessary to identify possible 'relevant systems' that might be designed to improve the situation (3). These have to be precisely defined to ensure common understanding amongst participants, and to do this a 'root definition' can be compiled for each relevant system. This is a statement of what the relevant system is all about. The adequacy of the root definition can be tested by use of a mnemonic, CATWOE, each letter of which refers to a different facet of the relevant system that should be explored in creating the root definition. CATWOE stands for: Customers (those who might be harmed, as well as beneficiaries), Actors (those who will be involved in making the system work), Transformation process (an identification of a 'raw material' that the system will transform into an 'end product'; for example, volunteers may be transformed into trained counsellors by a training system), Weltanschauung (the world view underlying the wish to make a transformation), Owners (those who have the power to stop the system from working), and Environmental constraints (things that have to be taken as given by the system). By exploring these aspects of a relevant system, participants in debate begin to develop common understandings and concretise the root definition.

A 'conceptual model' is then produced for each relevant system (4). A conceptual model is a 'map' of the key human activities that would need to be undertaken if the system were to become operational. Activities are first listed, then arrows are used to link them to show which ones need to be done first, and how the activities support one another. Once a conceptual model is complete, a comparison can be made with the rich picture to make a judgement about whether those activities would indeed make a difference to the problem situation (5). Then an action plan for making desirable and feasible changes can be developed (6), leading to action for improvement (7).

## 8.6  The process of application

Below, we detail our process of application. In writing up this intervention we have followed the 'stages' as detailed above, but (as Checkland and Scholes[2] indicate should be the case) the group moved iteratively between the stages, comparing, contrasting and changing things, so that in the end everything, from the identification of relevant systems through to the design of specific activities, came to be harmonised.

We found it necessary to modify the methods of SSM in a number of ways. The first of these was a decision to begin the workshops with an exercise designed specifically to explore the nature of a 'disaster' prior to embarking on the production of rich pictures.

### 8.6.1   Exploring disasters

We felt that a preliminary exercise was necessary because we had seen references to definitions of disasters in the written material we had been sent, and we had also spoken to several people who had claimed that it was important to be able to define what a disaster actually is before an appropriate counselling response could be identified. The written definitions usually said something like 'more than four people killed in any one incident'. Our immediate thought was, does this mean that 200 people injured in a football stadium is *not* a disaster? Or that a serious radioactive leak from a nuclear power station, where nobody is killed outright but deaths are expected in the long term, is not a disaster? It seemed to us that disasters are so varied that they are impossible to characterise with a single phrase of use to everyone. If we were right, then this would be important. It would have been easy to have started the SSM process with a restricted definition of what the group was dealing with, only to find that a counselling service had been designed that was unresponsive to disasters that fell outside the official definition. If we were wrong on this, and the group *could* define a disaster in a watertight manner, then we were happy to go with it.

Participants were asked to work in pairs to identify a real disaster and list its defining properties on a poster. Following this, people circulated around the room reading all the posters before coming together in a large group to discuss the results. The participants recognised that there was no single definition of what constituted a disaster, although common themes emerged. Some participants still wanted to try to pin a definition down, but the majority agreed with our own first thoughts that a restrictive definition might prevent the design of a sufficiently flexible system. It was therefore decided to keep an open mind on what constitutes a disaster, at least until more understanding had been generated.

### 8.6.2   Producing rich pictures

We then moved on to the first SSM method, production of rich pictures. At this point we divided the participants into two small groups, working in separate rooms. We felt that this was necessary because of the size of the larger group (nineteen people), which resulted in a rather 'strained' atmosphere in the disaster exploration exercise (described above), with a number of people not actively contributing to discussions. We allocated participants to groups ourselves, rather than allowing them to self-select who they worked with, as we wanted to ensure that both groups contained representatives from the statutory agencies, the emergency services and the voluntary sector.

We held a feedback session once the rich pictures had been completed, where a representative from each group presented their work to everybody else (unfortunately, the drawings have not been preserved, so cannot be reproduced here). The problem situation described in each of the pictures was quite similar, although both groups had identified complexities that the other had not thought of. These were left on the walls throughout the workshops as reminders of the 'mess' which the groups were trying to handle. They were also altered periodically throughout the workshops as peoples' ideas were clarified.

At an emotional level, the group were at a low point when they had finished their rich pictures, and we were not surprised at this. They felt that they had identified a lot of interrelated problems, simply confirming their worry that the whole thing might be far too complex to deal with. Nevertheless, we were able to make clear our own belief that the next stage of the process, identifying relevant systems, would directly address their concerns.

### 8.6.3 Identifying relevant systems

The following day, participants went back into their separate groups and were asked to think about what discrete (but interrelated) systems would be necessary to create a counselling network and ensure that it functions effectively in the event of a disaster. At the beginning of the process of identifying relevant systems, the groups appeared to be stuck with feelings of anger. They were frustrated that they had so far only identified problems (in the rich pictures), and that there seemed to be an unbridgeable gap between this and designing solutions. Several participants questioned the facilitators, suggesting that the methods we were using could not help. It took some considerable self-control not to give in and start the process of identifying relevant systems ourselves, but to have done this would have risked dependence on us for ideas, or alternatively would have set us up as scapegoats for the participants' frustration if our ideas had appeared inadequate.

Instead, we asked them to reflect on the rich pictures again and try to identify some general themes (not necessarily focusing on local areas of the rich pictures) that might be addressed. Themes slowly began to emerge, and were listed on a flip-chart, but the groups were still unsure about how they could move from these to the identification of relevant systems. To get the process moving, we asked if anyone could identify just one thing (initially) that could be done to improve the situation. Once somebody had taken a risk and identified a possible relevant system, other ideas immediately followed. The mood turned from depression to excitement in a very short period of time.

Each small group produced a poster which described the relevant systems they felt were important, and they then presented this to the large group. The output from the two groups was noticeably different, and the relevant systems were therefore debated in the large group and a list was finalised. At this point participants asked for clarification about how long it would take to explore the relevant systems further (testing them using the CATWOE mnemonic and developing conceptual models). It became apparent that not all the relevant systems could be explored in the time available. Participants therefore chose what they felt were the immediately important ones, and committed to explore the others in their own time after the workshops had finished. Each group took three relevant systems for further exploration.

### 8.6.4   Exploring the relevant systems

The next task was to examine the relevant systems in more detail to ensure the development of a common understanding of what each was about. The groups used the CATWOE mnemonic for this purpose, but root definitions were not produced. This is because both the researchers and participants felt that enough clarity would be engendered by the CATWOE exercise, and not much added value would be gained by having protracted discussions about the precise wording in root definitions. This phase involved much debate, and the mention of 'CATWOE' led to numerous quips about cats causing grief! These remained with us throughout the rest of the workshops. Needless to say, the interjection of this sort of humour helped the process, and we believe that it significantly improved participants' grasp of what was required at this stage.

It was when we joined the two groups together again for feedback that the first major problem surfaced. While it had *appeared* that there was mutual understanding when everyone first decided that each small group would work on three relevant systems, the CATWOE exercise showed this to be an illusion. There were two types of problem. Firstly, when representatives from the small groups presented their CATWOEs, there were significant disagreements over fundamental issues (such as what the transformation process was and who the actors should be) between the presenters and those who had not been involved in developing the CATWOEs; and secondly, while each of the relevant systems had appeared to be discrete when they were originally identified, they had been elaborated in such a manner that there were now major areas of overlap. Unsurprisingly given this situation, people from each of the small groups began to advocate for their own relevant systems against those of their 'competitors'.

Tempers became frayed at this point. Some participants made the comment that, having felt like they had made enormous progress identifying the relevant systems, they were now back at square one with too much complexity. Interestingly, a suggestion was made that the groups had ended up replicating the two separate visions that they had started with (a 'professional' versus a 'volunteer' service), despite our efforts to ensure that the groups were well mixed in terms of agency representation. It actually emerged at this point that the two visions were not the property of two separate camps (the statutory agencies and the voluntary sector) as we had originally been led to believe, but cut across agency boundaries. By sheer chance we had replicated the division in the constitution of the two groups. People went home at the end of this discussion in an angry and dispirited mood and we were left to consider how to deal with the situation at the next meeting.

### 8.6.5   Whole system modelling

We felt that, uncomfortable though it may be, the only viable solution was for the group to face the problem head-on. It was under the considerable pressure of needing to find a way to facilitate this that we once again modified the methods of SSM. We decided to work with the whole group, taking each of the relevant systems they had defined (plus the ones that they were yet to think about in detail) and get them to do two things. Firstly, to identify problems of disagreement and overlap, and deal with these in open debate. The goal was to reach accommodation and redefine the relevant systems in such a way that they became discrete once again. Secondly, to examine how the relevant systems, if created, would operate together holistically. This meant creating a model for the whole disaster response counselling system, showing links between key elements. We will discuss each of these aspects of the task in turn, starting with the business of redefining the relevant systems.

Emotionally speaking, the first couple of hours working on the redefinitions were exceptionally difficult. There was still a lot of anger in the room, and people were struggling just to understand the mess they had created, let alone deal with it. However, the breakthrough came when, at more or less the same moment, those championing the 'professional' vision realised that there was far too much work for a professional team to manage, while those pushing the 'voluntary' vision realised that it would be impossible to ensure a quality service if there was no centralised selection and training system. There was a sudden synergy. The resolution was to propose a core, professional team to manage the selection and training of a wider pool of volunteers.

Once this breakthrough had been achieved, the task was much easier. The relevant systems were redefined in line with the new thinking. As the process of redefinition began to gather steam, we introduced the idea of showing the links between the relevant systems to create a unified vision of the whole system. Doing this proved to be a turning point. By the time they had developed a model for the whole proposed disaster response counselling system, the atmosphere was electric. This was no doubt partly in contrast with the earlier feeling of negativity, but by the end of the day people were saying that they finally had a concrete vision of where they were heading, and a real pride in its innovative nature. There was a palpable sense of achievement. The model of the whole system is presented in Figure 8.2.

One thing should be noted concerning this technique of modelling the whole system. In our workshop, as people began to draw links between the relevant systems, gaps became evident. Several new relevant systems had to be defined to fill these gaps and make the system complete. This is an important observation because it indicates that, up until that point, the relevant systems had just been seen as parts without regard to the functioning of the whole. We therefore suggest that the addition of this new stage into the SSM process, which we call *whole system modelling,* represents an improvement to the systemic nature of SSM.

### 8.6.6   Conceptual modelling

Having developed the whole system model, participants then reflected once more on the time constraints of the workshops. They decided that it would still only be feasible to explore six of the relevant systems in further detail. They split up into two groups, taking three relevant systems each. Once again, they made a commitment to explore the others after the workshops. For each of the six relevant systems, the participants set about developing conceptual models: models of related human activities that would need to be put into place if the relevant systems were to become a reality.

Now, in order to express the human activity systems in a parsimonious manner, so that a whole conceptual model can be comprehended at once, Checkland and Scholes[2] suggested that each model should

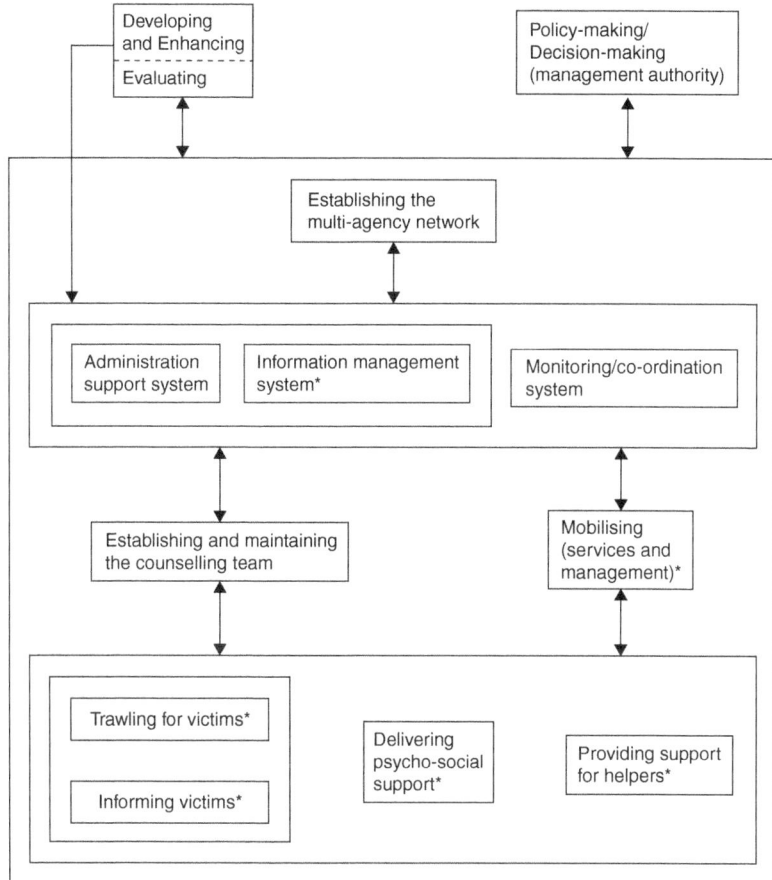

\* = Relevant systems elaborated into conceptual models

*Figure 8.2*   Whole system model of the disaster response system

be restricted to 7 plus-or-minus 2 elements. This number was chosen because, according to Miller,[44] human short-term memory can only contend with 7 plus-or-minus 2 'chunks' of information. However, the workshop participants said that they found this guideline impossibly restrictive. We put Check-land and Scholes's[2] point that each element of the conceptual model could be opened up, and a new conceptual model built to explain it, so that a hierarchy of models is created. However, they rebelled against this, seeing it as excessively complex and time consuming. We got them to try it out, but they continually insisted on getting down to the lowest level of detail straight away, so after a while we gave up trying to persuade them.

The six conceptual models that they eventually built had an interesting characteristic. In most cases the activities were organised into clusters, with relationships between the clusters made clear. One example in which the clustering is particularly noticeable is given in Figure 8.3. We will not go into detail about the content of this conceptual model. What is important is its form. There are four sectors in the diagram representing different arenas of action in time and space, and within each sector is a cluster of activities. Essentially, what the participants managed to do with this and the other models is provide *sets* of human activity systems, diagrammed in systemic relationship with one another.

### 8.6.7   Creating an action plan

The final stage in this project was the creation of an action plan. Checkland and Scholes[2] suggest that this is a particularly important aspect of an intervention because it involves 'reality checking': relating the conceptual models back to perceptions of people's current situation. As participants reached the end of the conceptual modelling phase, some anxiety surfaced with regard to the practicality of the outcome. While they said that they had definitely found it useful modelling the human activity systems, as it made what needed to be done to create the disaster response counselling service more concrete, they were nevertheless afraid of the gap that still existed between these models and the practicalities of making the activities happen. They wanted to use their last workshop to identify how this was to be done, which was exactly what we had planned.

The method we initially used was the one that Checkland and Scholes[2] claim is most widely practised in the application of SSM. The sets of human activities within each conceptual model were examined in terms of whether they already existed, who did (or should do) them, what the resource implications were, whether they linked with activities in other relevant systems, whether those links already exited, and who was, or should be, responsible for them. Other relevant comments were also recorded, and several new activities that would need to be developed were identified.

A great deal of detail was generated through this exercise, and this actually intensified the anxiety of participants. By the end of the morning, several people were saying that there was just too much to be done. An intense fear was expressed by one or two people that what they had planned was not really practical at all. At this point we asked

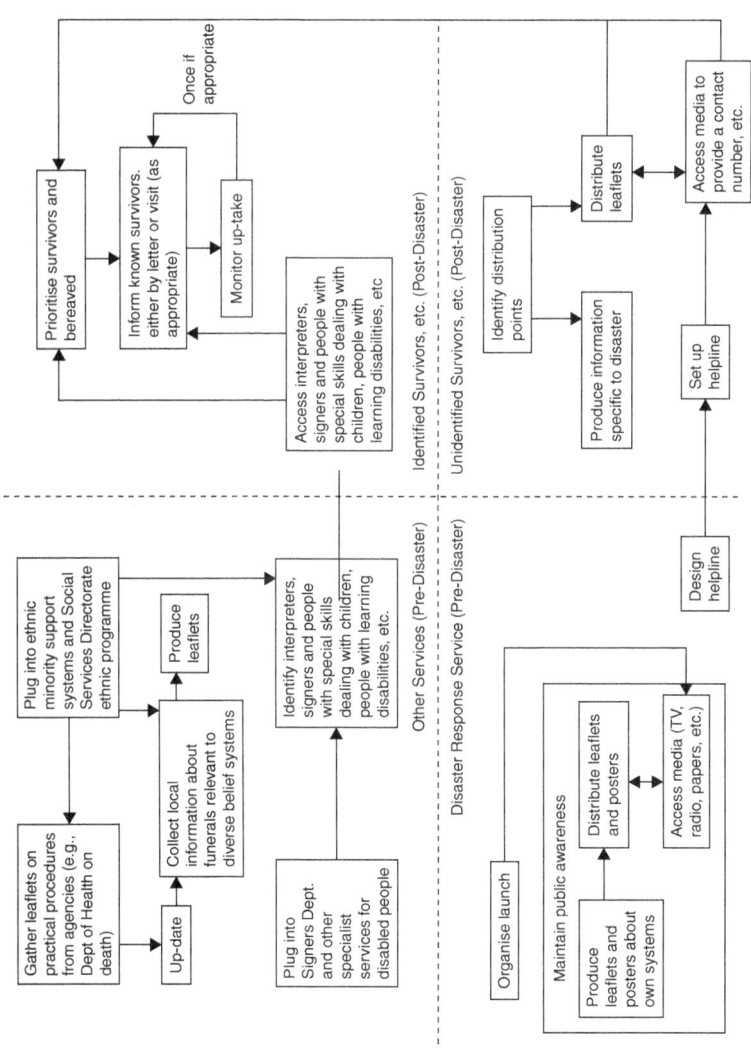

*Figure 8.3*  Conceptual model of 'informing victims'

participants to step back from the situation and revisit the original purpose of the exercise: to plan a large, multi-agency service from scratch
so that funding could then be sought for its implementation. Further
discussion clarified the fact that producing the application for funding was an immediate priority, and that the resources asked for would
have to be sufficient to allow personnel to undertake the key activities
identified through the workshops. Once this insight had been achieved,
it became obvious that a more systematic prioritisation exercise was
needed. The decision to undertake this exercise allowed participants
to feel more confident and motivated once again.

The action plan was reviewed in order to add a time dimension to it.
Actions were designated as short-, medium- or long-term. The whole list
was then taken away, with the idea that the actions needed in the short-
term would be placed on the agenda of the next unfacilitated meeting
of the working party. This allowed participants to finish the workshop
in an up-beat mood (focused rather than ecstatic), determined to take
the work forward.

## 8.7    Learning outcomes

Having detailed our process of application of SSM, we can now highlight the learning outcomes of this project for the participants. One
form of learning can be found in the *content* of the conceptual models
(and the whole system model), and another form of learning was about
the *process* of working together.

### 8.7.1    Content learning

The full set of conceptual models have been published elsewhere,[45]
so here we have just reproduced a typical example (Figure 8.4) which
shows the core activities of 'delivering psycho-social support'.

Below we present, in text form, the group's conclusions about the
kinds of activities required for an effective post-disaster counselling service
to be set up and run. However, only an overview has been provided:
it would be perfectly possible to provide a detailed rationale for most
of the individual activities in the conceptual models, but this would
exceed the space available to us. Nevertheless, we hope that these outcomes of the participants' learning, even in this summary form, will
be useful to people in other geographical areas who need to undertake
similar planning activities.

Referring back to Figure 8.2, the participants worked out the whole
system model as follows. They began with 'establishing the multi-agency

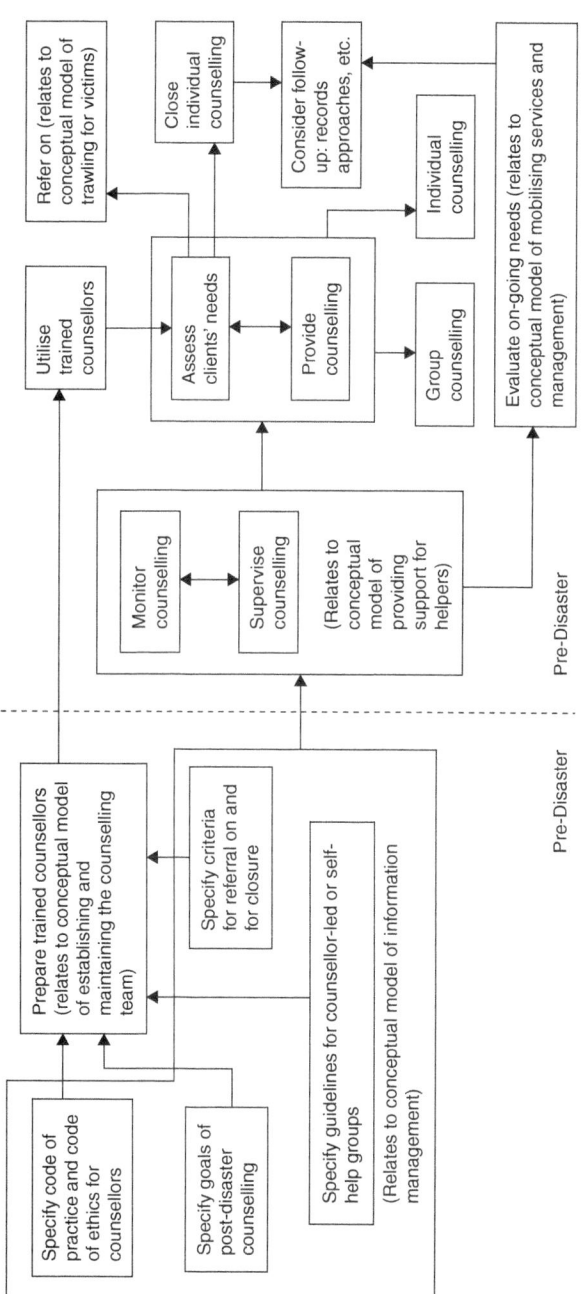

*Figure 8.4* Conceptual model of 'delivering psycho-social support'

network' (which had obviously already been started). This can be found centred at the top of the large box in Figure 8.2. They then diagrammed the management of the disaster response counselling system (the 'administration support system', the 'information management system' and a 'monitoring/ co-ordination system') in relation to 'establishing the multi-agency network'. Flowing from (and feeding back to) management are the activities of 'establishing and maintaining the counselling team' and 'mobilising services and management'; and flowing from these (and also feeding back to them) are the activities involved in making the system work on the ground in the event of a disaster ('trawling for victims', 'informing victims' of the services available, 'delivering psycho-social support' and 'providing support for helpers'). The term 'helpers' refers to the counsellors, who would themselves need counselling to deal with the experience of working with victims. The whole system is also subject to evaluation and policy decisions from the contributing agencies (see the top of Figure 8.2).

Each of the six relevant systems that were elaborated into conceptual models are also described below.

Figure 8.3 shows the conceptual model of 'informing victims'. The participants divided the model into four sections. On the left are those activities which would have to be undertaken in preparation for a disaster: they include activities to be undertaken by the multi-agency project itself (bottom left) and those which would have to be undertaken by selected individual agencies (top left). On the right are activities of information provision to be undertaken in the event of a disaster: some are geared towards providing information to known survivors and relatives (top right) and some (bottom right) are designed to reach survivors who nobody yet knows about (this is because, in a disaster, people sometimes leave the scene in a state of shock without making contact with the emergency services).

Figure 8.4 shows the conceptual model for actually delivering the psycho-social support. In preparation for any disaster (see the left hand side of Figure 8.4), there is the business of designing codes of practice, guidelines, etc., which feeds into the training of counsellors. When a disaster happens (the right hand side of Figure 8.4), counsellors are brought on stream: they assess needs and provide counselling of various kinds. Their work is supervised, monitored and evaluated with a view to making decisions on addressing the longer-term needs of clients through appropriate follow-up procedures. In this model, counsellors not only have the capacity to provide individual and group counselling themselves, but can also refer people on to other agencies.

The group also explored what it would mean to provide support for helpers—that is, training and counselling for the counsellors themselves. First they listed all the activities associated with recruiting trainers (the paid staff whose job it would be to train the volunteers). Then a range of training and counselling activities were identified, underpinned by the need to make explicit the expectation that helpers will need support. This had to be made explicit in order to counter the 'macho' culture that still prevails amongst some emergency services personnel: this culture prevents helpers from seeking help themselves because they fear that they will be ridiculed by their colleagues. While it was planned that most of the trainers would be drawn from the Health and Social Services, who have far less of a 'macho' culture than (for example) the Fire Service and Police, it was nevertheless considered important to ensure that a strongly supportive culture is created from the start.

A variety of activities associated with providing supervisory and debriefing support to counsellors were identified. It was argued that a worker should be recruited on a temporary basis (most likely a secondment from a neighbouring area) to provide some independent input to the support system. This is because so many people in the 'caring' agencies know each other, and many people move jobs from one agency to another within the locality: there may therefore be a fear amongst some personnel of being allocated a supervisor who could turn up as a colleague a year or two later. Someone recruited from outside the area was therefore viewed as a necessity.

A variety of activities (in preparation for a disaster, and in the event of one) associated with 'trawling for victims' were identified too. While the participants thought that 'trawling for victims' was a rather macabre phrase, they felt that it accurately expressed what is needed. To prevent long-term psychological damage to individuals, it is vital that as many victims as possible are contacted and offered a service as soon as possible after the disaster has happened. Ideally, victims should be identified at the scene, but this is not always possible—either because of the nature of the disaster (if a wide area is affected); because there are 'indirect' victims (relatives of the dead and injured); or because people have walked away without telling anyone. Therefore, a whole set of activities have to be undertaken relating to the need to locate victims and pass information to them.

Then there are activities associated with 'mobilising services and management'. In preparation for a disaster, some planning activities are needed to ensure that an appropriate response can be triggered. Once a disaster has happened, there is a necessity to make sure that the system is activated effectively by (amongst other things) convening the co-ordinating team (which has responsibility for managing the counselling response); making assessments of the situation; linking with other agencies (in the locality and elsewhere); and deploying resources.

Finally, there is a need for effective information management. In preparation for a disaster, an information system needs to be devised, especially to keep records of counsellor availability. While some participants assumed that this should be a computer system, the facilitators opened this assumption to analysis by playing devils advocate and arguing for a paper records system. The participants realised that the availability of personnel with knowledge of the computer system could not be guaranteed in the event of a disaster, and in some disasters electricity generation may be affected too, making computers inoperable. They therefore decided that a paper record system, available at more than one location, would be less vulnerable to malfunction on the day.

When a disaster actually happens, a wide range of information needs to be collected from a variety of sources, collated and utilised. The many sources of this information were identified by the group, and mechanisms for collating and using it discussed.

Having provided an overview of the *content* learning undertaken by participants (for more detail, see the full set of conceptual models[45]), we can now move on to discuss their learning about *process*.

### 8.7.2  Process learning

The participants' learning about process can be assessed partly through our own reflections, and partly by discussing the results of a debriefing exercise we undertook immediately after the workshops had finished. This took the form of an open debate in which people talked about their impressions of the workshops. We also made telephone contact with the Chair of the group one month, one year and two years following completion.

At our debriefing session, people said that they had a much better understanding of the positions of other people, as well as what was needed to construct their counselling service, and had built far closer working relationships than they had previously. There were numerous instances of learning about each others' practices which proved vital in enhancing mutual understanding. For example, some of the agencies were unaware of the details of plans that had already been worked out (by the County Council Emergency Planning Department, Social Services and the four Health Authorities) for the provision of hospital and other facilities in the event of a disaster. The details were important because counselling would have to be provided alongside these other services.

There was also a great deal of learning about the different priorities of agencies. For instance, some people put great emphasis on the provision of psychological support to those on the front-line, such as the emergency services (police, fire and ambulance). However, while two of the emergency services welcomed this, the representative of the third said that his agency had its own support system fulfilling a clearly specified function for the organisation: dealing with post-traumatic stress in order to minimise absenteeism from work. He felt that his senior management team would be against the idea of staff seeking external counselling from a system that may not take account of the organisation's wish to minimise absenteeism. Initially, this agency representative strongly resisted the idea of providing any psychological support to emergency services personnel, but an accommodation was reached when details were worked out about how internal agency counselling services could interface with the wider system in a manner that would be acceptable to them.

At the debriefing session, everybody expressed pleasure at the fact that they had achieved some key accommodations (such as the one described above), and had thereby generated a unified vision of the service to be developed. Some of these accommodations were highly significant, dissolving major differences between agency representatives. Perhaps the most striking was the one described earlier in which those championing a 'professional' vision and those wanting a 'volunteer' service both realised that there were important problems with their positions. A moment of synergy resulted in an accommodation in which it was agreed that professionals would be used to train volunteers. This represents learning at two levels: learning about a new possibility for service provision, and learning that the group has the internal capacity to deal effectively with major differences of opinion in order to secure a result that can satisfy everybody. We suggest that having 'breakthrough' learning experiences such as this gives confidence to a group that it can handle future internal problems, and thereby encourages individuals to feel it is worthwhile committing energy to the group's collective work.

Apart from the task-orientated learning that takes place within workshops, Checkland and Scholes[2] also talk about the value of people learning a problem-structuring language that they can use to facilitate further debates once the researcher has left. We did not have high hopes of the group continuing to use SSM once the workshops were over because our original idea of training the participants in the method had been rejected. We had the distinct impression that the group wanted this to be a one-off intervention. However, in his telephone conversations with us, the Chair reported something interesting. One month after the workshops he stated that the group had found it very difficult indeed to complete the exercise (elaborating on the relevant systems not fully dealt with in the workshops) without us present as facilitators. He said that they had only been partially successful in this regard, and had become bogged down in debate. However, a year later, although the group was not *routinely* using SSM, the Chair reported that they occasionally drew upon aspects of it to clarify particularly sticky problems. Therefore, for example, they might return to the output of the workshops for guidance when they felt that they had lost their way, or they might do an impromptu CAT WOE to harmonise their understandings. Some limited learning about the use of SSM had therefore taken place.

## 8.8   Feedback on the intervention

This intervention was completed several years ago, and we believe that sufficient time has passed to judge its success or failure. Judgements about the success of the intervention can be made in terms of the claims for the value of SSM made by Checkland and Scholes,[2] and also in terms of the priorities of the working party.

Checkland and Scholes[2] stress that the *process* of an SSM intervention is as important as the content of any plans that are drawn up. It should foster a spirit of team learning, and facilitate accommodations between participants. As described above, the workshop participants unanimously expressed the view that important learning outcomes, including some key accommodations, had been achieved. One year on, the Chair of the working party said that the vision and team spirit had been maintained, partly through continued joking references to CATWOEs, etc., which reminded them all of the team-building 'ordeal' they had gone through.

Checkland and Scholes[2] also talk about the value of providing a problem-structuring language that people can use to facilitate future learning. The intervention was less successful in this regard, but (as indicated earlier) some limited assimilation of the language of SSM did take place.

The success of the intervention can also be judged in terms of the priorities of the working party. One major priority was that the workshops should support them in gaining enough clarity to make a strong bid for funding from Social Services. One year later, the Chair confirmed that a bid had been put together, and full funding for all their proposed activities had been granted. Implementation was therefore proceeding as planned.

Finally, there would be little point in spending time on systemic planning if the resulting system failed when it came to be used. After two years the Chair said that there had not been a disaster in the locality, but there had been one in a neighbouring County. One aspect of the group's planning related to the need to activate their system in the event that help was required elsewhere. This is indeed what happened in the case of the incident in the neighbouring County, and the Chair said that all ran smoothly. Indeed, the incident was reported on national TV, and special mention was made by journalists of the speedy and efficient psychological support made available to victims.

## 8.9 Conclusions

In this paper we have described an intervention, undertaken from a critical systems perspective, in which representatives drawn from nineteen different agencies came together to plan the development of a disaster-response counselling service. To provide support, the methods of SSM were used (and were modified to deal with various contingencies encountered during the intervention). In reflecting on the intervention in the light of feedback from participants, we found that it was largely successful, both in terms of what one would expect given the stated purposes of SSM, and in terms of what the participant group hoped to achieved. The case study therefore provides evidence for the utility of this adapted version of SSM in multi-agency contexts. In particular, it is striking to note that useful plans were produced in a very short time (six days of workshops spread over a one month period) when, according to participants, eighteen months of previous meetings had failed to produce adequate results.

## References

1. Checkland P (1981). *Systems Thinking, Systems Practice*. Wiley: Chichester.
2. Checkland P and Scholes J (1990). *Soft Systems Methodology in Action*. Wiley: Chichester.
3. Midgley G (1990). Creative methodology design. *Systemist* **12**: 108–113.
4. Flood RL and Jackson MC (eds) (1991). *Critical Systems Thinking: Directed Readings*. Wiley: Chichester.
5. Flood RL and Romm NRA (eds) (1996). *Critical Systems Thinking: Current Research and Practice*. Plenum: New York.
6. Contractor F and Lorange P (eds) (1988). *Cooperative Strategies in International Business*. Lexington Books: Lexington, MA.
7. Nohria N and Eccles R (eds) (1992). *Networks and Organisations*. Harvard Business School Press: Cambridge, MA.
8. Alter C and Hage J (1993). *Organizations Working Together*. Sage: London.

9.  Stein SL, Garcia F, Marler B, Embreebever J and Garrett CJ. (1992). A study of multi-agency collaborative strategies: did juvenile delinquents change? *J Commun Psychol* **20**: 88–105.
10. Buckley R and Bigelow DA (1992). The multiservice network: reaching the unserved multi-problem individual. *Commun Mental Health J* **28**: 43–50.
11. Scheffel AL, Swanson EA, Potter M and Triolo PK (1992). A nursing camp: a multi-agency cooperative effort. *J of Nursing Admin* **22**: 53–57.
12. Kendrick A (1995). The integration of child care services in Scotland. *Children and Youth Services Rev* **17**: 619–635.
13. Sutton M (1996). *Implementing Crime Prevention Schemes in a Multi-Agency Setting: Aspects of Process in the Safer Cities Programme.* HMSO: London.
14. Watson L (1997). *High Hopes: Making Housing and Community Care Work.* Joseph Rowntree Foundation: York.
15. Midgley G, Munlo I and Brown M (1997). *Sharing Power: Integrating User Involvement and Multi-Agency Working to Improve Housing for Older People.* Policy Press: Bristol.
16. Fargason CA, Barnes D, Schneider D and Galloway BW (1994). Enhancing multiagency collaboration in the management of child sexual abuse. *Child Abuse & Neglect* **18**: 859–869.
17. Kintrea K (1996). Whose partnership? Community interests in the regeneration of a Scottish housing scheme. *Housing Studies* **11**: 287–306.
18. Yerbury M (1997). Issues in multidisciplinary teamwork for children with disabilities. *Childcare Health & Develop* **23**: 77–86.
19. Papamichail KN, French S (1999). Generating feasible strategies in nuclear emergencies—a constraint satisfaction problem. *J Opl Res Soc* **50**: 617–626.
20. Checkland P (1997). Rhetoric and reality in contracting: research in and on the NHS. In: Flynn R and Williams G (eds). *Contracting for Health.* Oxford University Press: Oxford.
21. Cohen C and Midgley G (1994). *The North Humberside Diversion from Custody Project for Mentally Disordered Offenders: Research Report.* Centre for Systems Studies: Hull.
22. Midgley G and Floyd M (1990). Vocational training in the use of new technologies for people with disabilities. *Behav and Inform Technol* **9**: 409–424.
23. Gregory WJ, Romm NRA and Walsh MP (1994). *The Trent Quality Initiative: A Multi-Agency Evaluation of Quality Standards in the National Health Service.* Centre for Systems Studies: Hull.
24. Midgley G, Munlo I and Brown M (1998). The theory and practice of boundary critique: developing housing services for older people. *J Opl Res Soc* **49**: 467–478.
25. Midgley G (1996). What is this thing called critical systems thinking? In: Flood RL and Romm NRA (eds). *Critical Systems Thinking: Current Research and Practice.* Plenum: New York.
26. Jackson MC (1991). The origins and nature of critical systems thinking. *Sys Pract* **4**: 131–149.
27. Schecter D (1991). Critical systems thinking in the 1980s: a connective summary. In: Flood RL and Jackson MC (eds). *Critical Systems Thinking: Directed Readings.* Wiley: Chichester.
28. Jackson MC (1987). Present positions and future prospects in management science. *Omega* **15**: 455–466.

29. Flood RL (1989). Six scenarios for the future of systems 'problem solving'. *Sys Pract 2*: 75–99.
30. Midgley G (1997). Developing the methodology of TSI: from the oblique use of methods to creative design. *Sys Pract* **10**: 305–319.
31. Flood RL and Jackson MC (1991). *Creative Problem Solving: Total Systems Intervention*. Wiley: Chichester.
32. Gregory WJ (1992). *Critical Systems Thinking and Pluralism: A New Constellation*. PhD thesis, City University, London.
33. Flood RL (1995). *Solving Problem Solving*. Wiley: Chichester.
34. Flood RL and Romm NRA (1996). *Diversity Management: Triple Loop Learning*. Wiley: Chichester.
35. Ulrich W (1983). *Critical Heuristics of Social Planning: A New Approach to Practical Philosophy*. Haupt: Berne.
36. Midgley G (1997). Mixing methods: developing systemic intervention. In: Mingers J and Gill A (eds). *Multimethodology: The Theory and Practice of Combining Management Science Methodologies*. Wiley: Chichester.
37. Rosenhead J (ed) (1989). *Rational Analysis for a Problematic World*. Wiley: Chichester.
38. Mason RO and Mitroff II (1981). *Challenging Strategic Planning Assumptions*. Wiley: New York.
39. Jackson MC and Keys P (1984). Towards a system of systems methodologies. *J Opl Res Soc* **35**: 473–486.
40. Ackoff RL (1981). *Creating the Corporate Future*. Wiley: New York.
41. Mingers JC (1980). Towards an appropriate social theory for applied systems thinking: critical theory and soft systems methodology. *J Appl Sys Anal* **7**: 41–50.
42. Jackson MC (1982). The nature of soft systems thinking: the work of Churchman, Ackoff and Checkland. *J Appl Sys Anal* **9**: 17–29.
43. Mingers JC (1984). Subjectivism and soft systems methodology—a critique. *JAppl Sys Anal* **11**: 85–103.
44. Miller GA (1956). The magical number seven, plus-or-minus two, or some limits on our capacity for processing information. *Psychol Rev* **63**: 81–97.
45. Gregory WJ and Midgley G (1999). Planning for disaster: developing a multi-agency counselling service. Research Memorandum no. 23. Centre for Systems Studies, Business School University of Hull, Hull.

# 9

# Simulations for Epidemiology and Public Health Education

*C.-Y. Huang[1], Y.-S. Tsai[2] and T.-H. Wen[3]*
[1]*Chang Gung University, Taoyuan, Taiwan;* [2]*National Chiao Tung University, Hsinchu, Taiwan; and* [3]*National Taiwan University, Taipei, Taiwan*

*Recent and potential outbreaks of infectious diseases are triggering interest in predicting epidemic dynamics on a national scale and testing the efficacies of different combinations of public health policies. Network-based simulations are proving their worth as tools for addressing epidemiology and public health issues considered too complex for field investigations and questionnaire analyses. Universities and research centres are therefore using network-based simulations as teaching tools for epidemiology and public health education students, but instructors are discovering that constructing appropriate network models and epidemic simulations are difficult tasks in terms of individual movement and contact patterns. In this paper we will describe (a) a four-category framework (based on demographic and geographic properties) to discuss ways of applying network-based simulation approaches to undergraduate students and novice researchers; (b) our experiences simulating the transmission dynamics of two infectious disease scenarios in Taiwan (HIV and influenza); (c) evaluation results indicating significant improvement in student knowledge of epidemic transmission dynamics and the efficacies of various public health policy suites; and (d) a geospatial modelling approach that integrates a national commuting network as well as multi-scale contact structures.*

## 9.1 Introduction

Network-based simulation approaches have gained acceptance as trustworthy means of investigating a wide variety of epidemics (Boccara and Cheong, 1993; Axelrod, 1997; Gilbert and Troitzsch, 1999; Alfonseca *et al*,

2000; Barrett *et al*, 2003; Huang *et al*, 2004, 2005b; Schneeberger *et al*, 2004; Ferguson *et al*, 2005; Hsieh *et al*, 2005, 2006; Sumodhee *et al*, 2005; Stroud *et al*, 2007). For the purposes of training students and novice researchers, epidemiology instructors from many disciplines are collaborating with simulation researchers to recreate the transmission dynamics of infectious diseases and to improve our understanding of the efficacies of public health policies (Huang *et al*, 2005a; Hsieh *et al*, 2006). However, computational epidemiology researchers and instructors are still addressing individual problems involving movement and contact patterns among millions of people of different ages and with different professions, educational levels, marital/partner statuses, and levels of epidemiological resistance (Boccara and Cheong, 1993; Barrett *et al*, 2003; Huang *et al*, 2004, 2005b).

In addition, emerging and re-emerging infectious disease outbreaks can develop randomly and unexpectedly depending on the breadth of early stage outbreaks, numbers of randomly imported cases, infected individuals' responses, and contacts with other susceptible individuals (Barrett *et al*, 2003; Huang *et al*, 2004, 2005a, b). Public health policies executed by health authorities also directly and indirectly affect epidemic dynamics and spreading situations (Hsieh *et al*, 2005). Furthermore, improper implementation and the inappropriate timing of public health policy activation occasionally produces such secondary impacts as disease concealment and social discrimination against infected patients and the health care employees who work with them (Huang *et al*, 2004). In spite of these factors, most students and novice researchers in public health and related disciplines still use questionnaires or field investigation techniques when studying epidemic outbreaks—a process that prevents many from gaining a macro view of epidemic dynamics or from assessing the potential efficacies of public health policies for prevention and control.

Network-based simulations are proving successful for solving individual movement and contact problems, exploring epidemic dynamics, and assessing the efficacies of public health policies (Barrett *et al*, 2003; Huang *et al*, 2004, 2005b; Schneeberger *et al*, 2004; Ferguson *et al*, 2005; Hsieh *et al*, 2005, 2006; Sumodhee *et al*, 2005; Stroud *et al*, 2007). In previous studies we have applied our social network simulation experiences to the transmission dynamics of_HIV, SARS, and influenza in Taiwan (Huang *et al*, 2004, 2005b; Hsieh *et al*, 2005, 2006; Sumodhee *et al*, 2005). In this paper we will explain our proposal for a four-category framework based on demographic and geographic properties, discuss ways of applying network-based simulation approaches to undergraduate students and novice researchers, and describe our experiences simulating the transmission dynamics of two infectious disease scenarios in Taiwan (HIV and influenza). In doing so, we hope to clearly illustrate existing challenges to building network-based epidemic simulations. We hope that our pre-analysis framework and two application examples will assist epidemiology students and novice researchers in their efforts to predict the transmission dynamics of emerging and re-emerging infectious diseases, as well as to improve current public health policies and immunization strategies.

## 9.2   Simulations for epidemiology and public health education

Using computer simulations as a pedagogical tool is now common in many scientific technology training and the teaching of science concepts (Liao and Sun, 2001; Colpitts, 2002; Hsieh *et al*, 2006). Computer simulations are also being used in epidemiology disciplines to support educational and training efforts based on constructivist learning principles. In addition to mitigating learner obsession with the minutiae of complicated procedures described in epidemiological textbooks (Wenglinsky, 1998), simulations provide multiple opportunities for 'learning by doing' (Oehme, 2000). Constructivists believe that learners draw upon prior knowledge when forming new schema via discovery learning (Bruner and Lufburrow, 1963). When confronted with a new stimulus, learners apply their own knowledge bases to accommodate new information and to alter their existing schema (Piaget, 1978). When constructive learning processes are embedded in epidemic simulations, students can learn by doing, have more and better opportunities for discovering interesting primary and secondary epidemic issues, and gain hands-on experience for dealing with real-world public health issues.

Instructional simulations exemplify problem-based learning. Originally developed for medical education in the early 1970s, problem-based learning is now considered a core teaching model in over 60 medical schools (Savery and Duffy, 1995). The use of simulations for learning and teaching has two characteristics that make it compatible with the theoretical foundations of problem-based learning:

1. *Engagement.* Students often request epidemic simulations to assist with learning and to gain a sense of engagement with real-world epidemiology problems. This allows for the introduction of related concepts to the learning process. There is no 'perfect' simulation, but

simulations can still support meaningful learning experiences as long as scenario limitations are taken into account (Aldrich, 2004).

2. *Interaction flexibility.* Epidemic simulations can be used with interaction and feedback methods to illustrate how infectious diseases are spread under different conditions and circumstances (Aldrich, 2004). Epidemiology problems are usually complicated and rarely have single 'correct' answers, which encourages learners to repeatedly manipulate parameters. With sufficient practice, learners or novice researchers can learn how to transfer their new knowledge to real-world infectious diseases.

Learning through epidemic simulations has at least three potential benefits:

1. *Operational.* Epidemiology problems often require examinations of the influences of various public health policies in specific environments. Using the SARS outbreak of 2003 as an example, epidemiologists may want to measure the potential impacts of public health policies, but it is impossible to do so when running real-world experiments. Epidemiology instructors and students can examine the influences of different public health policies in different regions, and execute 'what-if' experiments to study the emerging behaviours of infections when irrelevant health policies are temporarily removed. In short, simulations can be optimized for learning (Bertsche *et al*, 1996).
2. *Observational.* Users can take epidemic simulation processes and adjust their scales for observation purposes, slow them down, or speed them up (Sumodhee *et al*, 2005). Epidemic simulations not only allow novice researchers to practice professional skills without having to invest large amounts of resources, but are also recognized as an efficient approach to reviewing or proving epidemiological concepts. This protects them from having to jump into high-risk situations for learning purposes. In classrooms, post-simulation reports allow teachers to determine which concepts their students have mastered (Levy *et al*, 1995; Hargrave and Kenton, 2000; Klein *et al*, 2004).
3. *Construction.* Epidemic simulations can be used to create or explore environments. Using public health policy assessments as an example, learners can practice predicting developments that might result from different combinations of public health policies. In classrooms, epidemiology instructors can exert relatively precise control over knowledge construction and accumulation (Hargrave and Kenton, 2000).

Processes and goals associated with learning via epidemic simulations differ from those associated with traditional classroom and textbook-centred learning. Epidemic simulation scenarios are often open-ended and poorly defined (Hsieh *et al*, 2005), and problems frequently arise after simulations are started. We therefore suggest that novices be required to use instruction-based manuals to run epidemic simulations and to create professional quality reports or presentations of their learning results. Teacher preparation time will vary depending on the required epidemiology background, scenario construction requirements, and instruction needed to help learners formulate problem statements, collect data, run simulations, and create reports. Evaluative techniques for learning results also differ from those used in traditional classroom settings, and require some training on the part of instructors.

In light of the amount of required background knowledge (Hargrave and Kenton, 2000), we suggest using pre-instructional time to teach public health policy assessment and epidemic outbreak prediction skills, and post-instructional time to teach skills in epidemic simulation construction and analysis. Both are appropriate for learning-by-doing experiences. We designed a five-step epidemiology teaching process: (a) introducing epidemiology knowledge and background scenarios; (b) preparing a pre-test for guiding students to key properties of an epidemiology issue; (c) creating step-by-step instruction-based epidemic simulations with appropriate sample data, user manuals for operating epidemic simulations, and experiment design examples; (d) unrestrained operating time, which allows students to construct and develop their own experiments; and (e) post-tests or final presentations to evaluate student understanding of the issue.

Since disease scenarios often have no single or absolute approach, it is difficult to evaluate how well novice learners understand the operational aspects of simulations. One potential solution is to design constructive pre-tests and post-tests. Using epidemic simulations associated with public health policies as an example, novice learners may be asked to compare the efficacies of different combinations of public health policies before and after an epidemic simulation is run. In addition, we have observed that novice learners exhibit wide differences in terms of controlling simulation parameters (Hsieh *et al*, 2006), and therefore suggest that parameters be used as an evaluation criterion.

## 9.3   Network-based epidemic simulations

Compared to agent-based simulations, network-based simulations rely more on relationships among individuals. Recent mathematical studies and experimental simulations indicate that the topological features of social networks exert considerable influence on the transmission dynamics and critical thresholds of infectious diseases, thereby supporting subtle analyses that agent-based simulations are incapable of performing (Moore and Newman, 2000; Barrett *et al*, 2003; Huang *et al*, 2004, 2005a,b; Sumodhee *et al*, 2005; Kao *et al*, 2006). Accordingly, epidemiologists are focusing on the transmission dynamics of specific network models to investigate in the spread of emerging infectious diseases.

Network-based simulations entail computer entities that imitate contact patterns between individuals and apply state-of-the-art computing technology to study the movement of heterogeneous individuals. Lattice graphs have been applied for purposes of determining distance relationships between individuals. For example, von Neumann and Moore neighbourhood concepts are commonly used in two-dimensional lattice graphs in which one node's four or eight adjacent nodes are defined as neighbours, respectively (Gilbert and Troitzsch, 1999). The use of two-dimensional lattice graphs allows for the easy representation and measurement of geographic spatial and distance concepts. In contrast, random graphs support features associated with casual contacts among mobile individuals in addition to the low degree of separation commonly observed in social networks.

Two major modelling issues associated with network-based epidemic simulations must be considered: choosing an appropriate network model, and integrating knowledge and properties of epidemiology issues into that model. Different epidemiology issues require different network topology structures for building epidemic simulations based on specific contact patterns. For example, both sexual contact and illegal drug use cause HIV infections and diffusion, but their network topology structures are very different. Sexual contact networks should be scale-free to reflect the power-law statistical distribution of sex partners, but bipartite networks are more likely to accurately reflect needle sharing among injecting drug users (IDUs). Several network model types can be adopted, including daily contact networks that make use of individual activity records (Barrett *et al*, 2003; Stroud *et al*, 2007) or bipartite networks composed of individuals and most frequently visited places (eg homes, train stations, school buses, workplaces, restaurants) (Kao *et al*, 2006).

Data granularity and detail also affect network topology structures: if a disease control agency can trace all IDU activities, it is possible to use identified matches to build a relatively precise daily contact network.

In contrast, simulations performed by researchers limited to knowing specific locations where IDUs congregate require more assumptions regarding contact patterns. Static demographic data (eg age, gender, profession, educational level, marital status) can be represented as the social network attributes of nodes. In addition to well-constructed and appropriate assumptions, individual movement and contact patterns require support in the form of demographic, geographic, and transportation data—for instance, average daily movement statistics for railway passengers between counties and cities, statistical distributions of family members per household in each county, numbers of employees in workplaces, and numbers of students in classrooms. For novice researchers interested in network-based epidemic simulations, these requirements pose significant challenges to the collection and analysis of demographic, geographic, and related statistical data on individual movement and contact patterns.

In response to a wide variety of geographic and demographic restrictions, we divided all network-based epidemic simulations into four categories. The first category reflects the use of real contact tracing for constructing small-scale individual-to-individual contact networks. Using the 2003 SARS outbreak as an example, health authorities in Taiwan and Singapore attempted to construct contact histories for all infected individuals in order to quarantine anyone who had come into contact with a carrier.

The second category consists of individuals and locations, with individuals passively connected by activity locations. For example, saunas and bars frequented by homosexuals can be viewed as activity locations bridging susceptible individuals with HIV carriers; for illegal drug users, infection locations include syringes and chemicals used for drug dilution. To construct social networks for illegal drug users, epidemiologists must determine how many times a user shares a syringe with other users during 1 week/month, or how many users share the same diluting agent in a single session.

The third category reflects individual neighbourhood concepts using statistical geographic properties. In the absence of real contact data, epidemiologists may need to build a specific and customized social network using well-constructed and appropriate interaction and contact assumptions. In previous studies we proposed a Cellular Automata with Social Mirror Identity Model (CASMIM) consisting of two layers: the upper layer is a simplified multi-agent system for simulating heterogeneous cohorts, and the lower layer contains two-dimensional cellular automata for retaining the geographic mobility of individuals and for representing real-world activity spaces (Figure 9.1) (Huang *et al*, 2004, 2005b). The social mirror identities that connect the two layers establish CASMIM as a small-world social network and preserve the properties of individuals who interact with their neighbours within two-dimensional geographic spaces. Those properties reflect such activities as long-distance movement and daily visits to fixed locations.

The fourth category frequently requires significant support in the form of demographic or geographic data. For example, Ferguson's Southeast Asian influenza simulation (Ferguson *et al*, 2005) uses statistical data for group density, household size, age distribution, school and workplace size, and individual travel information. The spread of HIV among homosexuals serves as a negative example—that is, movement, location, and means of sexual contact are less obvious, making it more difficult to build a network-based HIV epidemic simulation (Sumodhee *et al*, 2005).

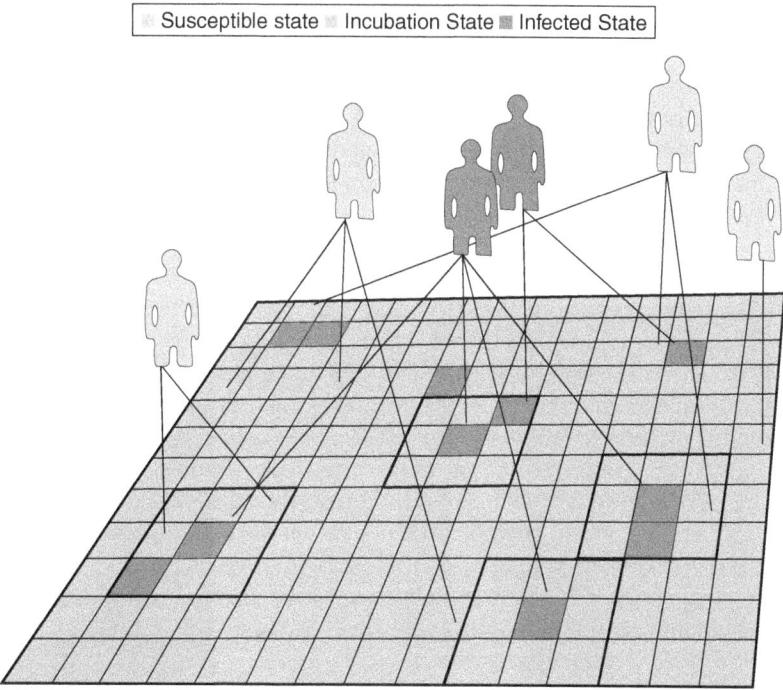

*Figure 9.1*   Cellular Automata and Social Mirror Identity Model (CASMIM)

The four properties considered most important for building network-based epidemic simulations are:

1. *Time scale.* In the case of HIV diffusion via heterosexual intercourse, frequency distributions of sexual behaviours over 1 month or 1 year show power-law distribution features (Schneeberger *et al*, 2004), but the same is not true when the time scale is reduced to 1 day or 1 week. It is also important to remember that different diseases have different incubation periods (5 days for SARS *versus* 6 months to 20 years for HIV) and immunization periods.
2. *Geographic scale.* Care must be taken when selecting this scale. Whereas CASMIM can be applied to simulate SARS outbreaks in modern cities such as Taipei or Singapore, simulating multi-region epidemic dynamics requires additional demographic data. One possible solution is building a separate CASMIM for each city and measuring transportation flow between paired cities. For example, a new form of influenza tends to be expressed as a large-scale epidemic, therefore models for countries that have multiple regions require the consideration of cross-border transportation networks. Building a social network for any modern city with an established mass transportation system must assume a strong and varied mix of human movement, which can affect considerations of inter-regional transportation.
3. *Data dependency.* Data granularity determines the best method for building a network model. Using homosexual HIV diffusion as an example, a situation in which data are limited to frequency distributions of sexual contact restricts modellers to using abstract von Neumann and Moore neighbourhood concepts (Huang *et al*, 2005b). However, if movement within a high-risk contact group can be traced, modellers can create simulations capable of predicting further development.
4. *Extendability.* Due to the diversity of data collected for epidemiology issues, simulations of specific infectious diseases often require modifications to existing network models. For example, the homogeneous mixing hypothesis used in random networks assumes that all members of a group are well-mixed (ie equal probabilities exist for contact between any two members), but data on sexual contact or needle sharing do not support this hypothesis. Therefore, extendibility is a major concern when applying an existing network model to new epidemic simulations.

In the next two sections we will share our modelling experiences to construct network-based epidemic simulations. We applied an event-driven programming concept to implement the user and input/output interfaces of epidemic simulations. In addition to providing specific statistical reports and charts presenting experimental results, the two epidemic simulations let learners use browser windows to observe real-time infection situations in an agent society. For a detailed description of our epidemic simulations, please contact the corresponding author.

## 9.4 HIV simulation

According to annual statistics presented by Taiwanese health authorities (World Health Organization (WHO), 2003), the number of HIV-1-infected patients increased nationally from 861 in 2003 to 1519 in 2004 to 3386 in 2005 (Table 9.1). The proportion of IDUs in this population increased from 8.6% in 2003 to 35.8% in 2004 to 71% in 2005 (Sumodhee *et al*, 2005). In light of these sharp increases, government agencies initiated several projects aimed at identifying at-risk populations and controlling the rate of new infections. Due to our success

*Table 9.1* Numbers of HIV-1 infections in Taiwan from January 1984 to December 2008

| Year | Number of HIV-1 cases per year |
|------|-------------------------------|
| 1984 | 9 |
| 1985 | 15 |
| 1986 | 11 |
| 1987 | 12 |
| 1988 | 29 |
| 1989 | 43 |
| 1990 | 36 |
| 1996 | 277 |
| 1997 | 348 |
| 1998 | 401 |
| 1999 | 478 |
| 2000 | 530 |
| 2001 | 654 |
| 2002 | 771 |
| 2003 | 861 |
| 2004 | 1519 |
| 2005 | 3386 |
| 2006 | 2924 |
| 2007 | 1935 |
| 2008 | 1752 |

simulating the 2003 SARS outbreak (Huang *et al*, 2004, 2005b), we were asked by the Taiwan Centers for Disease Control (CDC) to collaborate with Professor Yi-Ming A. Chen of the AIDS Prevention and Research Center of National Yang-Ming University to build a network-based epidemic simulation capable of predicting HIV-1 infections among Taiwanese IDUs.

### 9.4.1   Data collection

We used data on HIV-positive Taiwanese gathered between 1984 and 2008. In addition, between November 2004 and December 2006 we collected HIV-1-seropositive blood samples and conducted questionnaire interviews with 518 inmates living in four detention centres and two prisons across Taiwan; 3% were teenagers, 73% adults, and 24% adults 60 years of age or older (mean age 32.6±77.7). The large majority (505, or 97.4%) described themselves as IDUs. The women in our sample were three times more likely than their male counterparts to have had sex partners who were also IDUs (65.8% *versus* 19.4%). On average, each IDU shared a drug dilution chemical with two or three other IDUs between two and three times per month; 86.9% stated that they had shared at least a heroin diluent, and 98% said they had shared either diluent or syringes. Results from a logistic regression produced 17.2, 34.0, and 46.7 odds ratios for sharing heroin diluent, sharing syringes, or sharing both diluent and syringes, respectively. In summary, the major causes of HIV-1 infection among the IDUs in our sample were identified as syringe sharing, heroin dilution sharing, low education level, and number of IDUs using the same syringe.

### 9.4.2   Simulation model

Since our data were limited to the average number of syringe- and diluent-sharing events per month and average number of persons sharing them per occasion, we treated users as abstract neighbours when developing a bipartite network model based on our social mirror identity concept (Figure 9.2). The model consisted of two layers connected by social mirror identities: an upper layer representing real-world high-risk locations and a lower layer for simulating IDUs. The individual labeled 'P' in Figure 9.2 visited more high-risk places than the other IDUs; 'L' marks a frequently visited gathering place.

The time unit used in this simulation was equivalent to 1 month in the real world; results and epidemic curves are reported for each year. We used the average number of syringe and diluent-sharing events per month to represent the number of social mirror identities owned by

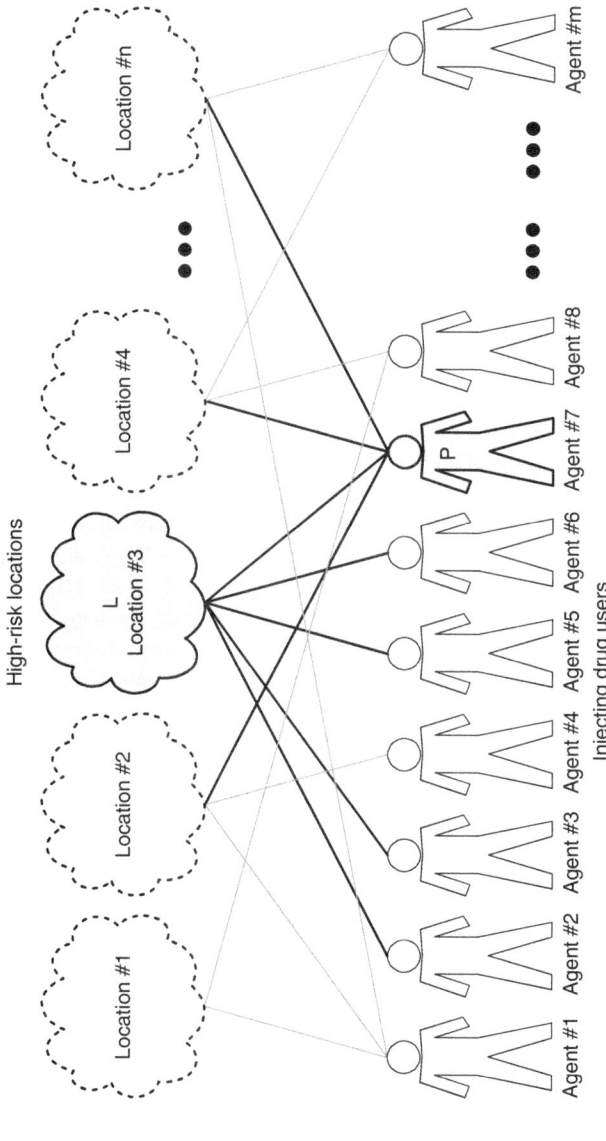

*Figure 9.2* Bipartite relations among injecting drug users (IDUs) and their meeting locations

a lower layer IDU. For the upper layer we used the average number of persons sharing either syringes or a chemical diluent during each occasion to represent the number of IDUs gathered at a high-risk location (Figure 9.2). Real-world IDU gathering places are located throughout the country and in multiple locations in individual cities, meaning that the spread of HIV among different high-risk locations has no effect on local spreading. In contrast, note that our SARS simulation CASMIM incorporated the effect of local spreading, meaning that SARS could still spread to any other location via transmission between local neighbours in the absence of social mirror identities or shortcuts. Since these high-risk locations are not adjacent, the same CASMIM is inappropriate for simulating HIV transmission among IDUs.

While we were able to obtain data on the statistical distribution of shared syringe and diluent events, we had no data on the statistical distribution of IDUs visiting each location. According to the most common topological features of social networks, we assumed that this reflects a power-law connectivity distribution. However, we had insufficient empirical data for model validation—especially since the reported number of infected individuals may not have contained concealed cases. This situation shows how difficult it is to build an HIV epidemic simulation without sufficient support in the form of demographic data for building detailed syringe- and diluent-sharing rules for IDUs.

### 9.4.3   Discussion

The gray bar in Figure 9.3 represents the 19 years (1984–2002) of HIV data used for model training and fitting, and the black bar represents 6 years (2003–2008) of data used for model testing and validation.[1] For each simulation we activated a harm reduction policy in December 2005 (simulation time step 264) and increased the policy participation rate from 30% to 80% in June 2006 (time step 270). Prediction results are presented as the curves marked with squares: pre-2006 results were well above actual 2003–2008 HIV epidemic curves (eg 1047 cases predicted for 2003 compared to 861 actual) and post-2007 results were below the actual number (1782 *versus* 1935).

Taiwanese health authorities initiated an HIV harm reduction policy in December 2005. Despite the low policy participation rate (30%), it exerted a strong positive effect in terms of bringing the HIV epidemic under control by reducing the number of new HIV-positive cases from 3386 to 2924 by the end of 2006. This represents the first decrease in the number of new HIV cases in Taiwan since 1986. A stronger harm reduction policy was activated in June 2006, resulting in a further decrease

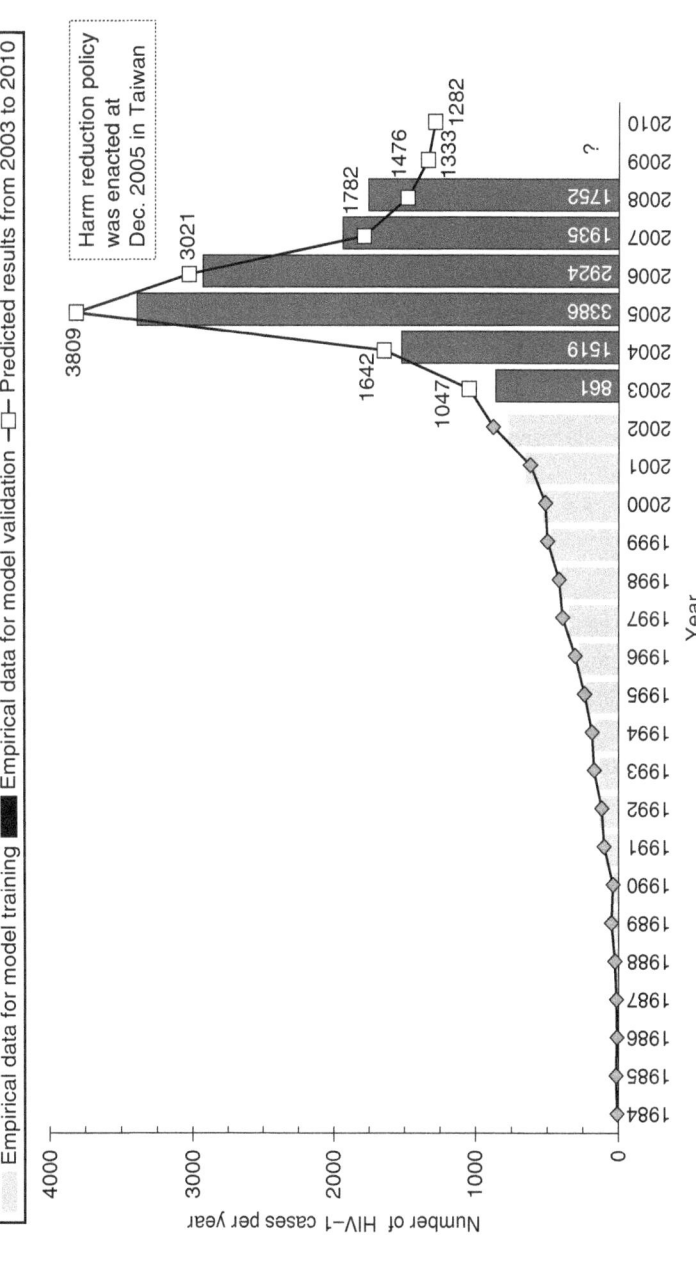

*Figure 9.3* A comparison of actual and predicted[1] HIV epidemic curves from 2003 to 2010 in Taiwan

*Note*: [1]In this prediction simulation, we averaged 1000 independent experiments to obtain the mean value of error in the epidemic parameter space, then chose parameters and named the optimal parameters with minimal mean error. As shown in the figure, the prediction result corresponds to the best one (ie minimal error) among 30 simulations under the optimal parameters. The parameters did not change with time—that is, predictions are only valid for cases with no additional interventions.

in the number of new HIV-positive cases to 1935 by the end of 2007. Our 2002–2010 simulation results also indicate a decreasing trend and suggest that an ongoing harm reduction plan would both lower the number of new HIV-positive individuals and reduce the HIV *reproduction number* from 28 (during 1984–2006) to 1.1 (during 2007–2008).

### 9.4.4   Evaluation results

Participants were 14 graduate students recruited from a 2008 infectious disease informatics course taught as part of Chang Gung University's Advanced Biotechnology Education Program. Students worked in pairs to design simulations and to discuss results. For each of two experiments, students were given a pre-test to determine their understanding of (a) HIV transmission dynamics among IDUs, and (b) harm reduction policies activated by Taiwanese health authorities in December 2005. Participants were also given verbal and written information on simulation goals and a post-test to measure the effects of the simulation activity on learning. Each pair was given a user manual for running simulations. After the end of the experiment we evaluated student knowledge on the HIV epidemic, the role of IDUs in HIV transmission, and harm reduction policies. As predicted, results from a paired sample *t*-test indicated statistically significant improvement in the students' overall understanding of HIV epidemic dynamics among IDUs and the efficacies of various harm reduction policies based on different participation rates (Table 9.2).

## 9.5   Influenza simulation

Up to two billion people may be susceptible to the next high pathogenic influenza virus; the predicted mortality rate will approach 65% (WHO, 2008). According to WHO surveillance reports (WHO, 2007), a novel influenza virus is inevitable, yet it is impossible to predict when and in what form the virus will invade individual countries, or how it will specifically threaten the health of individuals. Taiwanese health authorities have already announced three major public health policies: vaccines, antiviral drugs, and rapid containment operations. As part of this programme, starting in 2006 we participated in a 2-year project managed by the Taiwan CDC to work with sociologists to develop a multi-region influenza simulation for the entire country. Lacking epidemiological data for prior outbreaks, we simulated the transmission dynamics of seasonal influenza and assessed the efficacies of prevention and public health policies to determine the optimal application timing of vaccine and antiviral drug responses.

*Table 9.2*  Statistical results for (a) HIV and (b) Flu simulations pre-tests and post-tests

| Question set | Pre-test score | | Post-test score | | t-test | p-test |
|---|---|---|---|---|---|---|
| | M | SD | M | SD | | |
| *(a) HIV simulation* | | | | | | |
| Set 1. Understanding of HIV epidemic concepts and comparisons of actual and predicted HIV epidemic curves from 2003 to 2010 in Taiwan. | 6.57 | 0.73 | 8.14 | 0.83 | −5.08 | *P<0.001* |
| Set 2. Understanding of harm reduction policies associated with HIV and assessing efficacies according to different participation rates and activation dates. | 6.71 | 1.03 | 8.29 | 0.45 | −5.08 | *P<0.001* |
| *(b) Flu simulation* | | | | | | |
| Set 1. Understand of epidemiology concepts associated with influenza and transmission dynamics of the 1918 influenza pandemic. | 5.63 | 1.15 | 7.77 | 1.26 | −5.89 | *P<0.001* |
| Set 2. Assessing and analysing the prevention effects of five public health policies at low and high regional densities and with three policy activation dates (10/1~10/07, 10/22~10/28, and 11/19~11/25). | 5.13 | 0.62 | 6.68 | 0.9 | −6.86 | *P<0.001* |
| Set 3. Assessing and analyzing the cost-efficacies of five public health policies at low and high regional densities with three policy activation dates (10/1~10/07, 10/22~10/28, and 11/19~11/25). | 5.68 | 0.47 | 6.40 | 0.49 | −5.41 | *P<0.001* |

### 9.5.1  Data collection

We used transportation data to establish a model of daily inter- and intra-regional contact between individuals—specifically, statistics for the average daily movement of railway passengers between counties and cities (Institute of Transportation, Executive Yuan, Republic of China, 2008). Demographic data from the 2006 Social Indicators Report (Directorate General of Budget, Accounting and Statistics, Executive Yuan, Republic of China, 2006) published by the Taiwanese government were used to assign individuals to various locations. These data include statistical distributions of family members per household in each county, numbers of employees in workplaces, and numbers of students in classrooms. We combined data in an effort to achieve an approximate understanding of the overall distribution of the number of persons in each regularly visited activity location. As shown in Table 9.3, most activity locations had fewer than 10; exceptions included movie theatres and classrooms, each with 40 or more.

### 9.5.2  Simulation model

Based on our SARS modelling and simulation experience, we knew that CASMIM is suitable for simulating the transmission dynamics of contagious diseases in well-mixed but not in poorly mixed modern cities. We therefore assigned a separate CASMIM to each county, with model scale determined by the number of counties included in the overall simulation. Each CASMIM model cell represented one real-world activity location (household, classroom, train station, etc), and the number of individuals in each cell was assigned according to the statistical distribution of numbers of observed persons in regularly visited locations. Railway transportation data were used to represent inter-county movement, with each instance representing a pair of social mirror identities

*Table 9.3* Statistical of numbers of persons in regularly visited locations such as households, workplaces and classrooms

| Number of persons in regularly visited locations | Percentage of regularly visited locations |
| --- | --- |
| 1 | 9 |
| 2 | 28 |
| 3 | 14 |
| 4 | 22 |
| 5 | 13 |
| 6 | 5 |
| 7 | 4 |
| 8 | 1 |
| 15 | 1 |
| 25 | 1 |
| 30 | 1 |
| 35 | 1 |
| 40 | 0.3 |
| 45 | 0.3 |
| 50 | 0.3 |

belonging to the same individual but in different counties. Social mirror identities for the majority of individuals stayed within the same county. Since the incubation period for influenza is only 1–3 days, the simulation time unit in this simulation was equivalent to 1 day in the real world.

The epidemiological progress states for influenza shown in Figure 9.4 are the same as those described by Longini *et al* (2005) and used in Stroud *et al*'s influenza simulation system (Stroud *et al*, 2007). Separate epidemiological progress states were implemented for four demographic categories: preschool (younger than 5 years), youth (between 5 and 21 years), adult (between 21 and 65 years), and senior (older than 65 years). Base infection rate (infectivity level) was established as 0.21888 per contact per day for adults and symptomatic seniors, and 0.43680 per contact per day for symptomatic preschoolers and youth. The rate of asymptomatic infectious individuals was equal to one-half the base infection rate (Figures 9.4 and 9.5).

A weak point of our multi-region influenza simulation model was its lack of network topology properties for an epidemic simulation model consisting of multiple poorly mixed cities. Unlike a well-mixed modern city, modellers cannot assume that the interaction and contact networks of individuals distributed among multiple counties have small-world properties. Furthermore, there is a lack of epidemiological data for recent novel influenza pandemics to use for empirical validation. Some epidemiologists have constructed simulations of the 1918–1919 influenza pandemic (Stroud *et al*, 2007), but we believe the network topology structure of modern counties is far different from that observed in 1918. Despite these weaknesses, we used our multi-region influenza model to simulate the transmission dynamics of seasonal influenza and to assess the efficacy of a vaccine policy and related public health policies under different conditions and in different regions.

### 9.5.3 Discussion

We used two assessment indicators—prevention effect and cost-efficacy—to replace previously employed epidemic curves to help epidemiologists and public health experts assess the efficacies of public health policies. The first indicator (Equation 1), *prevention effect*, was used to evaluate the effect of specific public health policies; its value was set at > 1 to produce better prevention effects (for values < 1, the policy actually supports the spread of a disease). By comparing different policies at this level, public health experts can identify the best public health policy. The second indicator (Equation 2), *cost-efficacy*, was used to evaluate the prevention effect per unit cost; it was given a positive

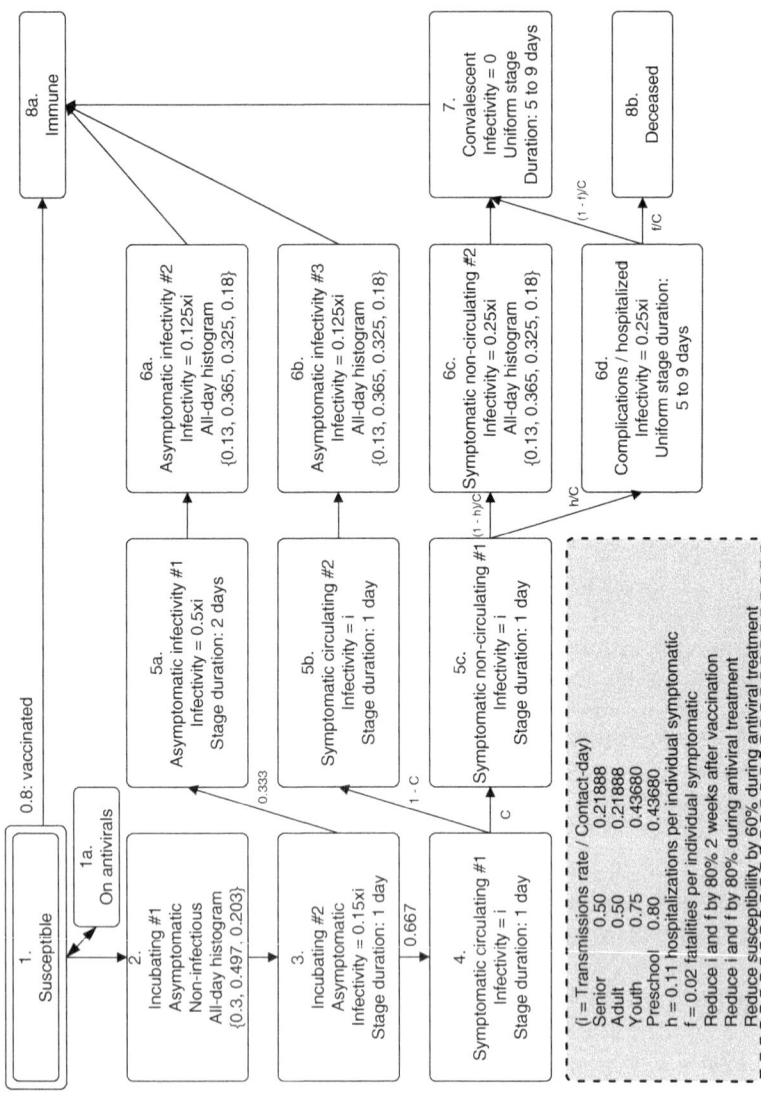

*Figure 9.4* Epidemiological progress states of epidemic influenza disease manifestations for four age categories with no treatment (Longini *et al.*, 2005; Stroud *et al.*, 2007)

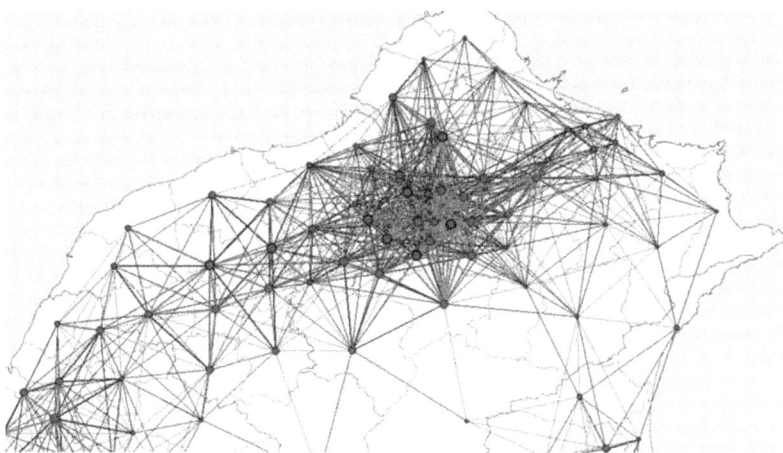

*Figure 9.5* Northern Taiwan commuter network
Each node represents a city or town and each edge represents a commuter connection. Node size reflects the percentage of persons who work and live in the same city. Edge thickness reflects the number of commuters travelling between cities.

value to achieve better prevention effects (when the value = 0, the policy has no preventive effect). Public health experts can use the same benchmark to make decisions for the best timing of public health policies in response to a novel influenza.

Prevention_effect (Policy A)

$$= \frac{\text{Total infected cases without activating any policy}}{\text{Total infected cases with A activated}} \in [0, \infty] \quad (1)$$

Cost_Efficacy (Policy A)

$$= \frac{\substack{\text{Total infected cases with activating any policy} - \\ \text{Total infected cases with A activated}}}{\text{Total consumed resource costs of A}} \quad (2)$$

We used our influenza simulation to compare prevention effects and cost-efficacy for five public health policies, two regional densities (low and high), and three policy application dates (the first at 10/1 ~ 10/07, the fourth at 10/22~ 10/28, and the eighth at 11/19 ~ 11/25). The five public health policies and corresponding objects were (a) give the vaccine to randomly chosen individuals, (b) track and inoculate individuals coming into contact with infected individuals, (c) strongly encourage hand washing and mask-wearing by the general public during the influenza season, (d) enforce home quarantines for infected individuals until they recover and for individuals who have come into contact with them for a minimum of 8 days, and (e) give anti-virus medicine in advance to all individuals. As shown in Table 9.4, the two best public health policies were giving vaccines to randomly chosen individuals and the use of anti-virus medicines; encouraging hand washing and mask-wearing

*Table 9.4* Comparisons of (a) prevention effects and (b) cost-efficacies among five public health policies

| Public health policy | | Activated at the beginning of October | Activated at the end of October | Activated at the end of November |
|---|---|---|---|---|
| *(a) Prevention effects* | | | | |
| Densely populated region | #1 | 40.34 | 10.63 | 3.00 |
| | #2 | 2.16 | 1.98 | 1.62 |
| | #3 | 28.68 | 6.92 | 2.65 |
| | #4 | 1.84 | 1.67 | 1.45 |
| | #5 | 41.55 | 7.38 | 2.64 |
| Sparsely populated region | #1 | 14.79 | 5.60 | 2.05 |
| | #2 | 3.85 | 3.00 | 2.14 |
| | #3 | 10.83 | 5.02 | 3.26 |
| | #4 | 1.86 | 1.80 | 1.46 |
| | #5 | 15.11 | 6.96 | 3.38 |
| *(b) Cost-efficacies* | | | | |
| Densely populated region | #1 | 0.81 | 0.75 | 0.55 |
| | #2 | 0.45 | 0.41 | 0.32 |
| | #3 | 1.39 | 1.23 | 0.90 |
| | #4 | 0.01 | 0.01 | 0.01 |
| | #5 | 0.81 | 0.72 | 0.52 |
| Sparsely populated region | #1 | 0.28 | 0.25 | 0.20 |
| | #2 | 0.22 | 0.20 | 0.16 |
| | #3 | 0.48 | 0.42 | 0.36 |
| | #4 | 0.01 | 0.01 | 0.01 |
| | #5 | 0.28 | 0.26 | 0.21 |

*Note*: #1: Inoculate individuals at random; #2: Locate and inoculate those who have come into contact with infected individuals; #3: Encourage hand washing and mask-wearing by the general public during the flu season; #4: Quarantine infected individuals until complete recovery and home quarantine individuals who have come into contact with them for a minimum of 8 days; #5: Give anti-virus medicine in advance for prevention purposes.

was the third best. All three policies were more effective when activated as early as possible, with little difference in effect between activating the policies in late October and late November. Our main conclusions derived from the simulation results were (a) hand washing and mask-wearing by the general public during the influenza season is the most cost-effective policy, and (b) using anti-virus medicine in advance is more cost-effective than buying and using a mix of vaccines and anti-virus medicines (Table 9.4).

### 9.5.4 Evaluation results

Participants were 22 graduate students recruited from a spring, 2009 data mining course given by the Department of Computer Science and Information Engineering at Chang Gung University. Most of the participants had no previous knowledge of or experience with influenza epidemiology. Students worked in pairs to construct simulations and to discuss results. Each participant pair was asked to conduct three instructional experiments. For each experiment they were given a pre-test to examine their understanding of transmission dynamics of the 1918 influenza pandemic and five public health policies that were established in response to the pandemic, verbal and written information on simulation goals, and a post-test to determine the effects of the simulation on learning. Each pair was given an instructional manual for running multi-region influenza simulations. As shown in Table 9.2, results from a paired-sample *t*-test of evaluation scores indicate statistically significant improvement in the students' overall understanding of 1918 influenza transmission dynamics and public health policies.

## 9.6  Multiple-scale epidemiological dynamics for the geospatial diffusion of directly transmitted infectious diseases

Using high quality epidemiologic data to understand the mechanisms underlying the geographic spread of diseases is central to devising spatially targeted prevention and control strategies, a task requiring comparisons of potential outcomes among control measures. Spatial simulation modelling represents a practical approach to helping policy makers decide among various combinations of control strategies in response to real and potential disease epidemics. In this section we will describe a multi-scale simulation process to support the efforts of students, academic researchers, and policy makers to study the spatial dynamics of epidemics and to observe various control measure scenarios.

## 9.6.1   Data collection

The diffusion of directly transmitted (droplet and air-borne) diseases results from close human contact and population movement. Accordingly, contact structures and commuting routes between homes and workplaces play important roles in spatial dynamics. To determine the role of commuters in disease transmission, we used data from the 2000 Taiwan Census Database to create a link-node network structure in order to simulate complex relationships between cities and towns. Figure 9.5 is an illustration of the commuter network in north Taiwan (the country's economic, cultural, and political centre). It consists of 359 nodes (cities or towns) and more than 120 000 edges (commuter connections between cities). We calculated *contact density* as the number of commuters between cities multiplied by each city's population density.

## 9.6.2   Simulation model

To simulate different contact patterns at different levels, we constructed the four-layer multi-scale model shown in Figure 9.6. To model intra-city contacts and to reflect different contact structures among age groups, we divided the population into children (younger than 15 years), adults (16–64 years), and seniors (older than 65 years). Layer 1 addresses population contact within the same age group, with *Susceptible, Exposed, Infective* and *Removed* (S-E-I-R) statuses used as governing equations to simulate disease transmission. The *Susceptible*-to-*Exposed* transmission process begins with the initial transmission of a very small number of pathogens. During the early part of the *Exposed* stage, pathogens reproduce but remain below a threshold for active transmission to other *Susceptible* individuals. After a certain period in which individuals move from *Exposed* to *Infective* status, the number of pathogens becomes sufficiently large for transmission to other *Susceptible* hosts. Eventually the host enters the *Removed* stage in which it achieves a state of immunity or dies.

   Layer 2 addresses the difference in contact densities between two age groups. Layer 3 addresses regional commuting between population centres. We assumed that children and seniors are immobile, since the bulk of their activities occur close to their homes. In contrast, adults are more likely to move between fixed geographic locations on a daily basis, increasing their likelihood of carrying pathogens between two or more populations. Layer 4 addresses the national commuting network that can be used to simulate daily population movement throughout Taiwan. The link-node network structure is used to determine disease dynamics among cities.

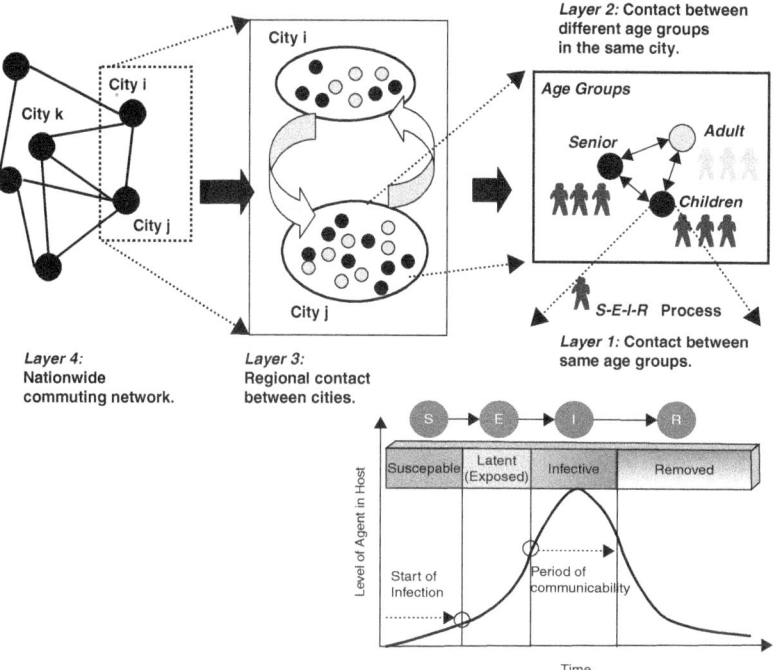

*Figure 9.6*   Multi-scale framework for epidemiologic dynamics simulation

### 9.6.3   Discussion

Developing appropriate prevention and control measures entails making and monitoring the results of multiple rules and decisions made at different points during an epidemic. Conflicts among decision criteria for different strategies are inevitable, and our proposed multi-scale simulation framework can help decision makers test and refine different strategies at different layers. For example, Layer 1 can be used to simulate and evaluate a vaccination policy by changing transmission rates among groups at greater risk of infection (eg children or seniors). This would allow for the testing of social distance measures such as school closures. Layer 2 can be used to evaluate quarantine strategies by changing contact rates among different age groups, Layer 3 can be used to evaluate travel restrictions by changing regional contact rates among cities, and Layer 4 can be used for the same purpose by changing the structure of the commuting network. By analysing multi-scale interactions, decision makers can prepare themselves for making rapid proactive intervention decisions in response to identified outbreak transmission pathways.

Furthermore, our simulation framework can provide additional geospatial insight into epidemiological processes underlying control measures. Spatial orientation and visualization are necessary when monitoring disease progression and generating potential control strategies. We incorporated a geographic information system (GIS) into our multi-scale simulation framework in order to capture spatial variation in disease transmission throughout Taiwan. The GIS supports a visual analysis of the spatial impacts of individual control measures. Combining multi-scale simulations, spatial visualization, and geographic information can clarify spatial and temporal characteristics in support of potential pandemic preparation and control measures.

## 9.7   Conclusion

In this paper we proposed a pre-analysis framework for network-based epidemic simulations for purposes of training students and novice researchers, and gave framework reduction and extension examples in terms of collected geographic and demographic data. Epidemiologists can use this information to support such tasks as analysing spreading situations and outbreak patterns, predicting future transmission dynamics, and assessing the efficacies of public health policies for disease prevention and control, vaccine development, and other efforts to fight epidemics. We also described two sample cases to discuss applications of network-based epidemic simulations. Our experiences in teaching epidemiological modelling and simulations have allowed us to identify three challenges for instructors: choice of a suitable network model, preparation for instruction-based teaching, and evaluating student understanding. Network-based simulations for solving epidemiology issues require more demographic and geographic data support and larger amounts of initial domain knowledge. In other words, most epidemiology issues require collaborations among computer scientists, sociologists, epidemiologists, and policy decision-makers.

### Acknowledgements

This work was supported in part by the Republic of China (ROC) National Science Council (NSC98-2314-B-182-043 and NSC98-2410-H-002-168-MY2), and Chang Gung Memorial Hospital (CMRPD260023). Tzai-Hung Wen also acknowledges administrative support from the Infectious Disease Research and Education Center, Department of Health, Executive Yuan, and National Taiwan University.

# References

Aldrich C (2004). *Simulations and the Future of Learning: An Innovative (and Perhaps Revolutionary) Approach to e-Learning*. Pfeiffer: San Francisco, CA.

Alfonseca M, Martinez-Bravo MT and Torrea JL (2000). Mathematical models for the analysis of Hepatitis B and AIDS epidemics. *Simulation* **74**(4): 219–226.

Axelrod R (1997). Advancing the art of simulation in the social sciences. *Complexity* **3**(2): 16–22.

Barrett CL, Eubank SG and Smith JP (2003). If smallpox strikes Portland. *Sci Am* **292**(3): 42–49.

Bertsche D, Crawford C and Macadam SE (1996). Is simulation better than experience. *McKinsey Quart* **1**(1): 50–58.

Bruner JS and Lufburrow RA (1963). The process of education. *Am J Phys* **31**: 468.

Boccara N and Cheong K (1993). Critical-behavior of a probabilistic-automata network SIS model for the spread of an infectious-disease in a group of moving individuals. *J Phys A-Math Gen* **26**: 3707–3717.

Colpitts BG (2002). Teaching transmission lines: A project of measurement and simulation. *IEEE T Educ* **45**(3): 245–252.

Directorate General of Budget, Accounting and Statistics (2006). *Social indicators*, Executive Yuan, Republic of China.

Ferguson NM *et al* (2005). Strategies for containing an emerging influenza pandemic in Southeast Asia. *Nature* **437**(7056): 209–214.

Gilbert GN and Troitzsch KG (1999). *Simulation for the Social Scientist*. Open University Press: Philadelphia, PA.

Hargrave CP and Kenton JM (2000). Preinstructional simulations: Implications for science classroom teaching. *J Comput Math Sci Teach* **19**(1): 47–58.

Hsieh JL, Huang CY, Sun CT and Chen YMA (2005). Using the CAMIM small-world epidemic model to analyze public health policies. In: *Proceedings of Western Simulation Multiconference on Health Sciences Simulation*. New Orleans, Louisiana, USA, pp 63–69. The Society for Modeling and Simulation International: San Diego, California, USA.

Hsieh JL, Sun CT, Kao GYM and Huang CY (2006). Teaching through simulation: Epidemic dynamics and public health policies. *Simulation* **82**(11): 731–759.

Huang CY, Sun CT, Hsieh JL and Lin H (2004). Simulating SARS: Small-world epidemiological modelling and public health policy assessments. *JASSS* **7**(4), http://jasss.soc.surrey.ac.uk/7/4/2.html.

Huang CY, Sun CT and Lin HC (2005a). Influence of local information on social simulations in small-world network models. *JASSS* **8**(4), http://jasss.soc.surrey.ac.uk/8/4/8.html.

Huang CY, *et al* (2005b). A novel small-world model: Using social mirror identities for epidemic simulations. *Simulation* **81**(10): 671–699.

Institute of Transportation, Executive Yuan, Republic of China (2008). *General profile of respective transportation and communications sectors-RAILWAY*, IOT – Transportation Information-Statistical Trend, http://www.iot.gov.tw/english/ct.asp.

Kao RR, Danon L, Green DM and Kiss IZ (2006). Demographic structure and pathogen dynamics on the network of livestock movements in Great Britain. *P Roy Soc B: Biol Sci* **273**(1597): 1999–2007.

Klein CA, Berlin LS, Kostolansky TJ and Del Palacio JR (2004). *Stock simulation Engine for an Options Trading Game*, Issued on March 23, 2003. United States Patent No. 6709330.

Levy M, Levy H and Solomon S (1995). Microscopic simulation of the stock market: The effect of microscopic diversity. *J Phys I* **5**: 1087–1107.

Liao YH and Sun CT (2001). An educational genetic algorithms learning tool. *IEEE T Educ* **44**(2): 20.

Longini Jr IM *et al* (2005). Containing pandemic influenza at the source. *Science* **309**(5737): 1083–1087.

Moore C and Newman MEJ (2000). Epidemics and percolation in small-world networks. *Phys Rev E* **61**(5): 5678–5682.

Oehme F (2000). Learn by doing: How to include new requirements of research in engineering education. *Eur J Eng Educ* **25**(2): 131–137.

Piaget J (1978). *The Development of Thought: Equilibration of Cognitive Structures*. Viking Press: New York, NY.

Savery JR and Duffy TM 1995. Problem based learning: An instructional model and its constructivist framework. *Educ Technol* **35**(5): 31–38.

Schneeberger A *et al* (2004). Scale-free networks and sexually transmitted diseases: A description of observed patterns of sexual contacts in Britain and Zimbabwe. *Sex Transm Dis* **31**(6): 380–387.

Stroud P *et al* (2007). Spatial dynamics of pandemic influenza in a massive artificial society. *JASSS* **10**(4), http://jasss.soc.surrey.ac.uk/10/4/9.html.

Sumodhee CJ, *et al* (2005). Impact of social behaviors on HIV epidemic: A computer simulation view. In: *Proceedings of International Conference on Computational Intelligence for Modelling, Control and Automation*, Vienna, Austria 2: 550–556. IEEE Computer Society: Los Alamitos, CA, USA.

Wenglinsky H 1998. *Does it Compute? The Relationship Between Educational Technology and Student Achievement in Mathematics*. Educational Testing Service: Princeton, NJ.

World Health Organization (WHO) (2003). *HIV/AIDS in Asia and the Pacific region*. http://www.wpro.who.int/NR/rdonlyres/11ED3283-9821-43BE-9B73-B3444A3DADE6/0/HIV_AIDS_ Asia_Pacific_Region2003.pdf.

WHO (2007). *Ten things you need to know about pandemic influenza*, http://www.who.int/csr/disease/influenza/pandemic10things/en.

WHO (2008). *Confirmed Human Cases of Avian Influenza A (H5N1)*, http://www.who.int/csr/disease/avian_influenza/country/cases_table_2008_09_10/en/index.html.

# 10
## Proposing a Systems Vision of Knowledge Management in Emergency Care

*J. S. Edwards, M. J. Hall and D. Shaw*
Aston University, Birmingham, UK

*This paper makes a case for taking a systems view of knowledge management within health-care provision, concentrating on the emergency care process in the UK National Health Service. It draws upon research in two case-study organizations (a hospital and an ambulance service). The case-study organizations appear to be approaching knowledge (and information) management in a somewhat fragmented way. They are trying to think more holistically, but (perhaps) because of the ways their organizations and their work are structured, they cannot 'see' the whole of the care process. The paper explores the complexity of knowledge management in emergency health care and draws the distinction for knowledge management between managing local and operational knowledge, and global and clinical knowledge.*

### 10.1 Introduction

The government-funded National Health Service (NHS) provides the majority of health care in the UK. It comprises many interacting organizations of different types, such as doctors' surgeries, hospitals and ambulance services. Provision of care to a patient during any particular 'episode' may involve several of these organizations, operating in a form of supply chain, or rather a 'care chain'. Clearly with a number of organizations concerned, there is a danger of fragmentation or compartmentalization in the planning and delivery of patient care.

Reprinted from *Journal of the Operational Research Society*, 56: 180–192, 2005, 'Proposing a Systems Vision of Knowledge Management in Emergency Care', by J. S. Edwards, M. J. Hall and D. Shaw. With kind permission from Operational Research Society Ltd. All rights reserved.

This paper takes as its starting-point the desirability of a systemic and process-based view, not just within a single organization, but across all the organizational units involved in providing a given type of care for a patient. This process integration across different organizations is now very much advocated in other sectors of industry.[1,2] A patient-centred view is important, since the patients' perspective does not always match with those of the health-care professionals, as a survey[3] of 2000 patients in the USA revealed. The need for a patient-centred, process-orientated view has been accepted in some parts of the NHS, for example in the design of care pathways or treatment pathways involving different healthcare professions. However, the care pathways only cover what happens once the appropriate treatment has been determined, and are at a relatively high level. Note that a number of organizations in the UK NHS have taken a more detailed process view within the boundaries of their own organization, for example Leicester Royal Infirmary[4] and St James's Hospital Leeds.[5]

The paper draws upon research in two case-study organizations within the NHS. One is a hospital, and the other an ambulance service. They will be referred to as Hospital and Ambulance throughout this paper to maintain their anonymity. These case studies are used to argue for the importance of taking a systems view of knowledge management (KM) within health-care provision. The case-study organizations appear to be approaching KM in a fragmented way. They are trying to think more widely towards the 'whole', but (perhaps) because of the ways their organizations and their work are structured, they cannot see the whole of the process. This paper helps in taking forward an understanding of where the process boundaries are from a KM perspective in the NHS. There is a particular emphasis in the paper on the actual and potential roles of information and communication technologies (ICT) in this process. This stems from the interests of the two case-study organizations. ICT is also very high on the NHS agenda nationally at the time of writing.[6]

Through the case studies, the paper offers insight and help to understand how a 'systems vision' might improve KM in the NHS. We concentrate exclusively on what we term the 'emergency care' process in the NHS, and on the implications of this 'process' for how the organizations approach KM. The term emergency care is used in an effort to avoid using standard NHS terminology, which in some aspects reinforces a bounded view. Its meaning in this paper is 'a patient urgently and unexpectedly requires advanced medical attention'.

The paper is structured as follows. We begin by reviewing the literature on KM, processes and systems, and their relevance to health care.

This includes consideration of ICT in KM. We go on to describe the research methodology, including the workshop methodology used and the approach to data collection and analysis. Results from the two cases, Hospital and Ambulance, are presented next, followed by analysis and discussion. In this we distinguish two kinds of foci for KM (local and operational knowledge, and global and clinical knowledge). Finally, we offer the limitations of this work, suggestions for future research, and our conclusions.

## 10.2   KM, processes and systems

There is no generally agreed definition of KM to be found in the literature. For the purposes of this paper, we offer the following: 'supporting and achieving the creation, sharing, retention, refinement, and use of knowledge (generally in an organizational context)'. This was used in structuring the workshops and analysing the data collected. Frequently, information is an essential input to a KM activity, especially in an organizational context. Consideration of a KM system (whether ICT-based or not) thus also normally requires consideration of information and its management. However, KM is more than information management, because of the vital additional element of the 'knower'.

Our further discussion in this section concentrates on the role of processes and systems in KM. The perspective taken in this paper is that the notions of systems and processes are complementary to each other. Both imply an holistic view, and the concept of purposeful activity directed towards some form of customer(s) or indeed victim(s). Given the organizational setting of most KM, the potential for a systems view to offer a holistic approach to KM seems clear. However, most reported approaches to KM do not take such an approach. For example, Rubenstein-Montano *et al*[7] also advocate a systems approach to KM in their extensive study, and analyse no fewer than 26 frameworks from the literature. Their conclusion is that none of these KM frameworks meet the systemic requirements fully, in particular the lack of allowance for double-loop learning, as proposed originally by Argyris and Schön.[8]

More specific examples of systems or process thinking in KM may be found, but relatively rarely. For example, Cuthbertson and Farrington[9] use Soft Systems Methodology (SSM) in KM strategy formulation, while Ferrari *et al*[10] discuss using SSM for KM in a Brazilian company. Al-Karaghouli *et al*,[11] on the other hand, use the SSM technique of rich pictures to understand knowledge requirements, but not the rest of SSM.

Senge's[12] work on systems thinking and organizational learning is often cited in the KM literature, but the emphasis in the citations is often more on learning than on systems. Another systems view is seen in the collection of work written from a sociotechnical systems perspective edited by Coakes *et al.*[13]

Given the relative rarity of systems approaches to KM overall, it is not surprising that there are few specific examples of a systems or process approach to KM in health care reported in the literature. We have found three. The first is by Reuthe and Allee,[14] who discuss a team-based approach to providing health care, using an example of 'birthing' (maternity) provision. This is designed as a patient-centred process, with the emphasis on the patient and her history rather than the specific 'episode'. The second is the work by Desouza,[15] who offers a process model for KM in hospitals. Our paper differs from both of these in that it goes beyond the boundaries of a single organization in the health-care process. The most similar to our work is the third paper, by Newell *et al.*[16] This reports a KM project concerning cataract surgery. The project implemented a redesigned process for the steps prior to the surgery itself, which changed the roles of different professional groups. The authors describe their approach as holistic, in that multiple professional groups worked together to design the new system, but the project did not explicitly take a systems approach, as we or Rubenstein-Montano[7] would characterize one.

In view of the paucity of references to KM, systems and health care, we now go on to review the literature on systems in health care and knowledge management in health care separately.

## 10.3   Systems in health care

Beyond the context of KM, the idea of taking a systems view of health-care organizations is not a novel one. Indeed, various parts of the UK NHS have served as examples in the core texts on Soft Systems Methodology. These include community medicine in East Berkshire Health Authority[17,18] and information systems in Huddersfield Royal Infirmary, the Royal Victoria Infirmary and Hexham General hospital, among others.[19] Lehaney and Paul[20] describe and Lehaney *et al*[21] evaluate the use of SSM in the construction of simulation models for a hospital outpatient department. Batalden and Splaine[22] also advocate taking a process view of health-care provision, with an emphasis on what they call the microsystems level. The microsystem is the group of people actually giving care to an individual patient.

## 10.4 KM in health care

The importance of KM has been well recognized in many parts of the health sector. At the most general level, Van Beveren[23] studied the KM needs of a public health-care system in Australia. He concluded that specific models and techniques were needed for KM in the public sector in general, and the health-care sector in particular. The whole of the February 2001 issue of the journal *Topics in Health Information Management* (Volume 21, issue 3) was also devoted to KM. Most of the articles were visions of future issues and possibilities rather than reports of completed projects.

There are also more specific examples. A system that checks drug prescriptions given by hospital doctors in Boston, USA was devised by Davenport and Glaser.[24,25] Like us, Pedersen and Larsen[26] look at inter-organizational KM, but their focus is on decision support, and in administration not treatment.

Within the UK NHS, the changing relationship between clinicians and managers has been a significant issue for many years. Ashburner and Fitzgerald[27] have looked at how these changes affect the management of expertise. The NHS National Electronic Library for Health offers a whole website on KM (http://www.nelh.nhs.uk/knowledge_management/km1/nhs.asp#knowledge, accessed 10 February 2004).

KM practitioners more generally also see health as an important application area. For example, Hansen *et al*[28] included a health-care provider as one of the case studies in their widely cited paper introducing the concept of codification and personalization strategies for KM.

## 10.5 ICT and KM in health care

ICT merits specific consideration because it was the focus of interest in both of our case study organizations. The role of ICT in KM has been the source of much controversy in the literature. A complete range of positions may be found from that of Carter,[29] who sees technology as key to KM, to that of Scarbrough and Swan,[30] who see ICT as a minor issue compared to aspects such as leadership and motivation. Earl[31] gives a good discussion of various different types of KM strategy, and the different relevance of ICT to each of them. Alavi and Leidner[32] review the state-of-the-art of the use of ICT in KM, and discuss future research challenges.

There are many articles about specific ICT systems for KM in health care. For example, Forgionne and Kohli[33] examined the effects of ICT in the form of a management support system on health-care decision-making. Indeed, advanced ICT has been used in health care in many forms for several years, including digital imaging, videoconferencing, results messaging and expert systems.[34] Moreno *et al*[35] report a further use of knowledge-based systems in a hospital. Moseley and Mead[36] also cover expert system-based DSS. There are many other similar examples. A rather different one is the work of Standridge and Steward,[37] who use an expert system to help build a simulation model. This is in marked contrast to the use of SSM for the same purpose mentioned earlier.

We now introduce the methodology used to investigate a systems view of KM. This leads to a discussion of the two case studies.

## 10.6    Research methodology

Data collection on the opinions of NHS staff about KM was based on computer-supported group workshops. One workshop was held for Hospital, and three for Ambulance. (The precise arrangements were the choice of the participating organizations.)

Table 10.1 shows the major stages in the research methodology, from the initial contact with the organization through to analysis of data and feedback of results.

### 10.6.1    Journey making

The methodology used to structure the group workshops is one that was initially called Strategic Options Development and Analysis (SODA)[38] and more recently has been renamed Journey Making, a mnemonic for JOint Understanding, Reflection, NEgotiation of strategY.[39] An example of its prior use in the health sector is that of Roginski,[40] who used SODA (as it then was) in working with senior management in the NHS.

Journey Making was used because it offers groups a methodology through which they can share their individual views/perspectives/ideas of the situation—effectively surfacing the diversity of views and the complexity of the situation. Through *jointly understanding* this complexity, the participants can individually and collectively *reflect on* that complexity to broaden and deepen their awareness of the issues. *Negotiation* is used to explore the legitimacy of the conflicting views and move the group members towards beginning to agree *jointly* what are the critical issues. Through this process, the group begin to identify combinations of actions to tackle the critical issues—essentially building a *strategic* plan of action.

In terms of the practical arrangements of a Journey Making workshop, each participant has access to a laptop computer, which is networked,

*Table 10.1*  Notable stages in the research methodology

| Stage description | Implication for research methodology |
| --- | --- |
| Initiate contact with the client organization | Self-selection of client organization to participate in the research following general invitation |
| Pre-workshop discussion with client organization | To gain insight on the background of KM in the organization and contextual workshop factors effecting the workshop, eg participants, location, culture, etc |
| Design and agreement of workshop agenda (with the client and then the participants) | To address the particular concerns of the client organization, and accounting for contextual factors. A validation of what might be the important factors |
| The workshop | An opportunity to collect data in the form of group built and validated maps, researcher observations, facilitator insights, participant-completed exit questionnaires. Also the directions of the re-modelling of the flexible workshop agenda provided insight to what was/was not important, and why |
| Client de-brief | To gain immediate insight into the client's impression of the topics discussed, concerns for the future, motivation to pursue next steps and reaction to the workshop process. Initial client validation of the data/process/direction |
| Post-workshop data analysis | Analysis of all sources of data to feed into the final report and identify directions for future collaboration |
| Workshop report | To feedback to the participants and organization the key output/decisions from the workshop. Identification/invitation to pursue further work |
| Client/participant feedback on report | Further validation of the key outcomes from the workshop |
| Identification of generic and specific KM themes | Synthesis of data and outcomes from the multiple workshops to inform the development of KM theory, and workshop practice |

and running a brainstorming-type software, Group Explorer. In response to a particular prompt about a situation (eg 'What KM issues face your organization?'), participants type their views into the laptop (these views can be contributed anonymously). Once participants have finished typing, all the views are shown on a large projection screen using Decision Explorer software. The facilitator assists the participants to cluster the views to make the volume of information (typically as many as 80 views) more manageable. Participants have the opportunity to read other participants' views, expand on them, critique them or identify relationships between them. Extensive group discussion about the views, the clusters and relationships between the views then follows. (In the map, a relationship between two views is represented as an arrow linking the views.)

The benefits of a computer-supported approach are numerous[41] and include: providing an environment in which views can be shared anonymously, encouraging a more open sharing of views;[42] more rapid sharing of views through all participants simultaneously sharing ideas;[43] sharing views without being influenced by others, that is, having your thinking being limited by the ideas from others;[44] flexibility in the presentation of the views enabling participants to play with the layout of the views thus freeing their creativity.[45]

### 10.6.2    Workshop agenda

A Journey Making workshop is divided into a series of sessions, referred to as the agenda. An initial (flexible) agenda was agreed for each workshop—primarily to reassure all parties involved. However, the agenda actually emerged during each workshop—in that it was designed by the participants during the workshop. Each emerging item on each agenda was pursued due to the participants' belief that it would help them to achieve the declared aims of the workshop. The aims of both sets of workshops were very similar and included:

1. To understand what knowledge needs to be harnessed by the KM system.
2. To design effective processes to enable the system to harness knowledge, skills and experience.
3. To consider the barriers to staff using the system.
4. To explore what are the metrics against which the system would be evaluated.

### 10.6.3    Research data and the analysis

The primary tangible research output from these workshops were group maps that show the participants' views, and their interrelationships to other views, on a range of issues (see Figure 10.1). The maps are artefacts of the group discussion that are used by the groups to stimulate and structure their systematic consideration of the issues. As such, in this project the content of the maps was provided and validated by the participants. Thus, an initial analysis and validation of the research data was performed by participants during the workshop.

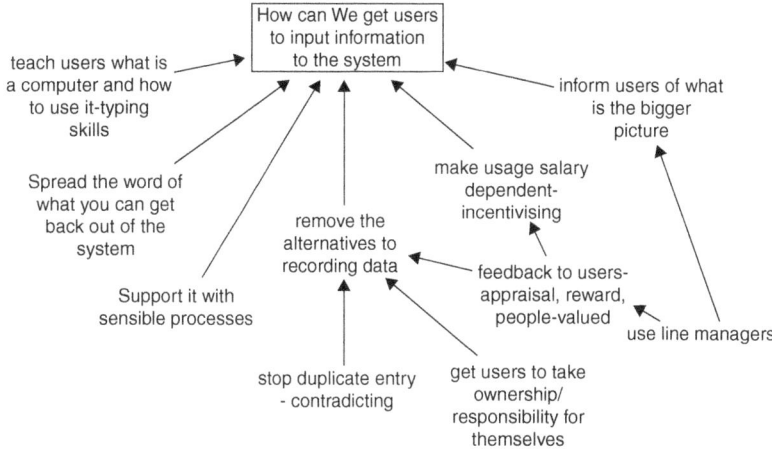

*Figure 10.1*   An extract of a map from Hospital (to illustrate structure)

The initial constructs of the maps were used to inform more in-depth interpretative post-workshop analysis. For example, the maps were analysed to understand as much as possible about critical issues that were identified in the maps by the participants. This analysis, together with copies of the maps, was fed back as a final report to the workshop sponsor and the participants. This served to validate the analysis and act as further validation of the content of the maps. All recipients were invited to respond to the report.

In addition to the maps, other forms of data were collected to triangulate and enrich the findings from the maps, including: researcher observations of the group members and any side conversations that were not captured in the maps; participant feedback on the process, collected through exit questionnaires; and sponsor feedback on the process and the outcome, collected through a post-workshop de-brief. Thus, the validation of the analysis of the group discussions was four-fold: the participants; the sponsor; the researchers; the facilitator.

We include extracts from two maps for background (Figures 10.1 and 10.2). We do not discuss their detail as the focus of this paper is on the overall direction and context of the discussions, although in places we have used specific quotes.

These workshops formed part of a continuing programme of KM research using this approach, the first phase results of which are reported in Edwards *et al.*[46] The Journey Making approach is highly relevant to KM, because KM activities are to a great extent group activities, validated and legitimized by the group context: see, for example,

212

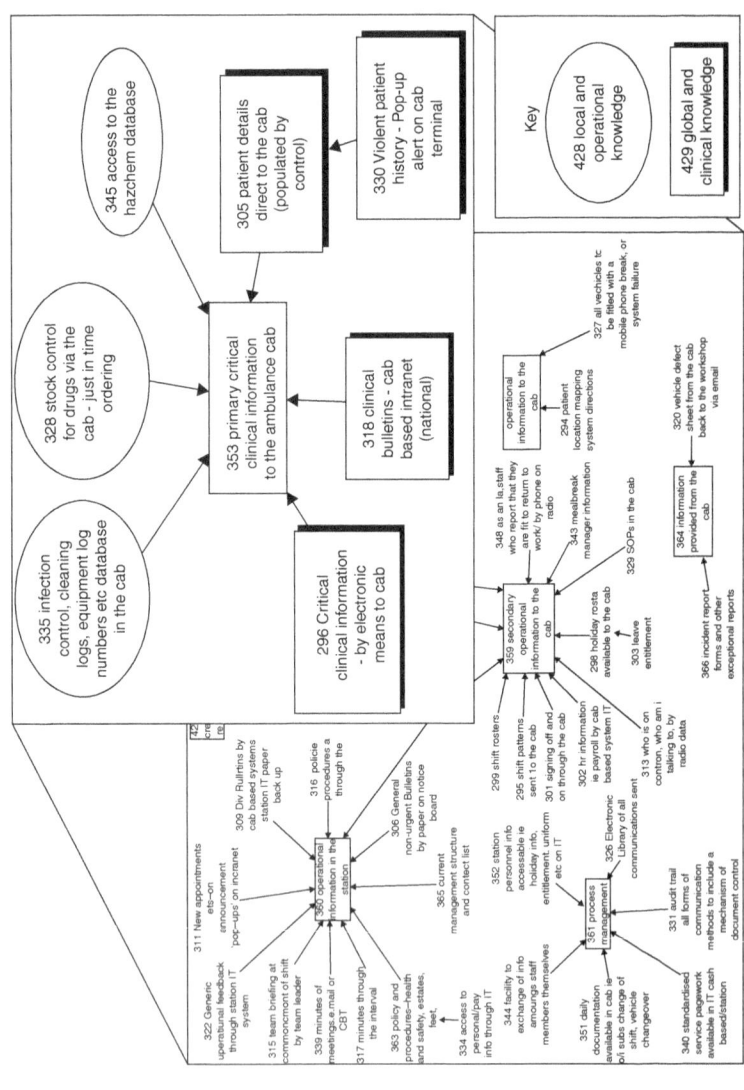

*Figure 10.2*   An extract from a map from Ambulance (to illustrate local and global knowledge)

Scarbrough[47] and Newell *et al.*[16] Note that we have also conducted a workshop for the whole NHS Trust of which Hospital is a part, but this concentrated on management issues, and thus is not described in detail in this paper.

## 10.7 The cases

### 10.7.1 Case 1—Hospital

*The background to the knowledge management system*

The challenges and opportunities posed by new ICT are recognized by all stakeholders in the NHS, particularly managers and doctors as they strive to keep up with the ever growing pace of demand on the service. In Hospital, there is an ICT Committee (exact title omitted to preserve anonymity), which has the remit of overseeing the many ongoing projects and initiatives with an ICT focus. One of these is a local patient records system. The NHS Trust to which Hospital is responsible have been considering funding the development and implementation of their own patient record system to network local general practitioners (GPs), two local hospitals within the Trust and ancillary patient support services, for example, physiotherapists or dietitians. The aim of such a system is to allow faster and more efficient recording and sharing among users of patient information, which is consolidated in one electronic source. Doctors in this workshop called this an Electronic Patient Record, although it should be noted that this is not quite the same as the national NHS initiative with that name.

*Positioning the workshop*

The workshop was convened in order to help scope the needs and requirements of such a local patient record to support the Hospital's Medical Assessment Unit (MAU). Staff in MAU deemed it particularly important for MAU to have an ICT system, as the history accompanying patients arriving at MAU, even though referred by their GP, is 'often extremely sketchy and inaccurate. It mostly consists of a scribbled, illegible note and a list of drugs. We sometimes (seldom) get a printed history.' Preceding the workshop there was also a realization in Hospital's management of the need to change from the existing paper-based system of patient records. Their motivation to change was driven by repeated failures of the paper-based system, for example, missing records, unreadable handwriting and loss of time in transferring records from the GP to the Hospital.

*Those involved in the workshop*

Bringing together medical staff, patient representatives and IT staff within the Hospital, the workshop was therefore an opportunity for a variety of stakeholders to help shape the design of an Electronic Patient Record system. In the event, the dominant group within the workshop were the doctors and consultants: The workshop had been organized by a senior Consultant, and of the nine core participants, six were doctors ranging from Junior to Consultant. Nurses were invited to participate, but none was available to attend because of staffing pressures. Also participating were one member of the Information Systems department in Hospital, and two representatives from the Patients and Carers Association. It is unsurprising, therefore, that the doctors became the dominant group in the workshop. The discussion became largely focused on doctors' clinical information and knowledge needs, and how they might make use of and interact with an Electronic Patient Record system.

*How a KM system might help Hospital*

A key issue facing Hospital is the pressure to admit patients from MAU to the ward (or send them home) within a certain time limit. The same is also true of the Accident and Emergency (A&E) department, with a shorter time limit. For the doctors and consultants in the process, there is particular pressure to reach a correct diagnosis—of patients arriving with no medical history—within that deadline. The process involves doctors making a 'differential diagnosis'—that is, a list of probable conditions and their treatments—during which time they may need to draw upon a range of information and knowledge sources. These include the patients themselves and their observable symptoms, GP records, results of tests, opinions of colleagues, medical databases and published works from respected sources. Sources not immediately to hand have to be accessed separately, and it can be frustrating and time-consuming waiting for paper-based records (eg doctors' records) to be delivered. Doctors are also under pressure to keep up with the ever-growing body of knowledge in medicine, which is becoming increasingly available online: As one doctor said, 'in order to keep up you would have to be reading all day every day.' This means that they have to consult a wide range of sources that are accessed separately in different forms, placing great strain upon their professional judgement. Doctors must decide whether to take the time to access a source that may not return any useful knowledge or information. However, as well as using knowledge and gathering information, the diagnosis also involves recording information, often in (albeit unintentionally) illegible handwriting. The current information system supporting the patient's progress from MAU to ward is therefore perceived by doctors to be unreliable and inefficient: In the words of one participant, 'the trouble with the current system is that there isn't one.'

When the discussion turned to what form their ideal system would take, participants conceived of an integrated Electronic Patient Record system, allowing both the recording of information about the patient (and generation of 'paperwork') and provision of access to all information and knowledge sources needed to make a (differential) diagnosis. This would include links to ICT-systems in GP surgeries, care pathways (eg physiotherapy, social services) and locally or nationally established NHS protocols. There would also be the capability in the system to display exactly what they need, rather than all the information a GP has on the patient, as well as helping them to identify the information they need to know. The system would provide support for decision-making, both in drilling down the differential diagnosis and helping to record the decisions made. As this system would need to be mobile and give access to the Internet, it would necessarily be ICT-based, most probably via a laptop (this was considered a more practical 'diagnosis-centred' solution than another suggestion for the patient to carry a smart card). As one Consultant suggested, 'the computer makes up for us not having a perfect memory.'

*Users interacting with the system*

While the doctors discussed in detail what the system should be able to provide for them, and how they would like to access it, they had a less clear vision of who should be putting information into the system. Indeed, the question provoked a substantial discussion of the perceived barriers to such an ideal system working, for example, limited time for input, whether it is the role of doctors to type up records, cultural inertia in the implementation of new working practices. It was evident that the doctors perceived the benefits of an Electronic Patient Record would make it worthwhile for them to overcome the changes to their working practices. However, their reservations were perhaps more deeply rooted in the realization that, if such a system is to work in the way they would like, then it is not just the responsibility of doctors to be putting information into the system: They are dependent upon other groups—for example, nurses, GP surgeries—also to be inputting information, even though the doctors may be getting more out of the system than they themselves put in.

*Concluding comments*

In this case, the requirements were clearly defined from the perspective of the doctor's needs. The participant from Hospital's IT department was keen to warn against doctors designing their own ideal system, as there were already a number of similar ICT-based initiatives (in areas like delivery of X-ray or test results) already in the pipeline. Furthermore, the patient representatives frequently reminded doctors of a role for the patient in providing information for the decision-making process. While it was clear that the doctors were conceiving first and foremost how the Electronic Patient Record would be of help to them in reaching a diagnosis, they did nevertheless stress the importance of linking the system with other initiatives in the NHS.

Subsequent to the workshop, a pilot system linking various databases using a vortal (virtual portal) interface has been developed and implemented for use in the MAU at Hospital.

### 10.7.2   Case 2—Ambulance

*The background to the knowledge management system*

The need to incorporate new ICT is equally pressing within Ambulance. For example, Ambulance is currently bidding for £12 million funding from central government to introduce new technologies with remote links between Ambulance management, central control, local stations and mobile crews. Ambulance also has a 5-year ICT Strategy overarching several interlinked projects, one of which—the Knowledge and Information Management (KIM) project—is concerned with how information in Ambulance is stored, made available and reported via the Intranet platform. According to the KIM Project Initiation Document, it aims to oversee the 'ongoing development of the Intranet,' together with the implementation of a 'content management system' and an 'enterprise reporting tool,' while promoting the concept of the 'paperless office.'

*Positioning the workshop*

A key problem which the KIM project aims to address is the perception of 'information overload' in the service—of too much 'blanket' sending of information across the organization, and not enough specific targeting of information to different groups. However, the project team is also keen for staff across the service to view knowledge and information needs as something they need to take a proactive part in defining for themselves. The project team had tried other ways of eliciting these needs, for example, through the use of questionnaires, but these had achieved limited participation. Furthermore, the project is determined to promote the Intranet as a tool into which all staff proactively input information, and which is integrated into their normal working practices. It would also be intended to form a tool for knowledge management, not just information management, especially if the normal working base for the ambulance crews became the cab, rather than the ambulance station, as was intended. It was therefore decided to hold participative workshops with a cross-section of groups across the organization.

*Those involved in the workshop*

A series of three, daylong workshops were run on successive days, including a total of 24 participants (six, seven and 11 participants on each day). The intention was to include a cross-section of the entire organization, in terms of:

- the level of the hierarchy, including all tiers from Executive Director to middle management to Ambulance Care Assistant;
- responsibilities, including centrally and locally based staff from patient facing divisions, the control room, fleet management, procurement, unions, and beyond;
- size of station;
- city/rural location of station;
- length of service;
- hospital- and non-hospital-based stations.

Since each participant in a given workshop had a different background, they could perhaps bring a unique perspective of the situation. This cross-section of the organization also aimed to foster a sense of user involvement in the project, and define exactly what the different parties wanted to get out of Ambulance's ICT systems.

*How a KM system might help Ambulance*

This wide cross-section in all three workshops made the outcomes highly eclectic in their representation of knowledge and information needs across the service. Nevertheless, each of the three workshops was similar in tone, and with similar overall views and discussions occurring. The workshop approach had sought to elicit the knowledge and information needs of participants, that is, what knowledge informs their roles, a question which clearly involves knowing where they seek and how they access information. However, as there was a cross section of participants in each workshop, the participants were expressing a broad range of knowledge and information needs, thus giving only a general picture across the service. Discussions also became dominated by the perceived barriers to an ICT Strategy working—indeed there was a pervasive preoccupation with the difficulties of implementing cultural change in the service, which many participants said they had witnessed over the years (it is important to remember that this is an organization with a fairly mature workforce, and where long service is the norm). In the first two workshops, participants were grappling with what they were being required to do, and this is perhaps why the familiar territory of barriers to change gave them a tangible focus.

For the third workshop, the KIM project manager (who had not been participating in the workshops, but observing from a distance) intervened to provide the group with specific direction related to the project's needs. Precise questions posed to this workshop were 'what information should be communicated to you?' and 'how do you want the information communicated to you?' There was clearly an underlying view by the KIM project team that this was about defining the information which they, as managers, should be disseminating. This is also evident in the Project Initiation Document, which defines a set of 'Information Requirements of the Service' explicitly stating that they are 'from the perspective of providing sufficient information to support consistent decision-making and management control throughout the organization.' The information they are talking about here is predominantly that which supports their highly command and control style of managing the organization, for example, the provision of shift and holiday rosters, and the minutes of meetings.

The workshop group was comfortable with this, as it appeared feasible within the time, deciding for themselves that it would be most productive if they concentrated on the requirements of a specific group. They settled on the information requirements of mobile cab-based crews, which was something most participants felt they could contribute to, most having been out 'on the road' at some stage in their career. Their view of this focussed on the local operational needs of the crews—what they need in order to be able to perform their roles effectively. This varied from clinical advice such as 'do not give Ms. ABC adrenaline' to staffing information and traffic details.

The issue was raised of a difference between information, which crews may need to seek or 'pull in' for themselves, and information, which needs to be provided from management. However, the focus was predominantly on information provided from management. As the human resources director at the third workshop pointed out, there is a lot about management 'doing it right', but no clear enunciation of what people believe should be the management's role in the provision of information. Even though each workshop took a different route, the content of discussion in each was nevertheless focused on the requirements of organizational management and control. Non-management participants were also viewing their requirements in terms of what managers should provide to them.

There was some discussion in the workshops about cooperating with other NHS organizations and groups. Participants in the first workshop talked about an ongoing project to share information directly with hospitals via remote terminals in A&E departments. Participants in the first two workshops specifically stressed the desirability of 'electronic patient report forms' and the need for crews to have access to these, and help with making a diagnosis, from a mobile laptop. Also, one participant in the first workshop warned of the danger that KIM might not be able to 'integrate with the NHS.'

*Concluding comments*

In Ambulance, a particular type of requirement is knowledge and information about what people are doing—for managers, what the operational people are doing, and for the operational people, what managers want, that is, the operational knowledge and information requirements. This is knowledge, which is easier to make explicit and thus put in an ICT system. The deeper more tacit knowledge (eg how to deal with a difficult patient) is more difficult to capture and disseminate. Indeed, it was observed that some knowledge, which is at present circulated by word of mouth within an ambulance station, could not be put into an ICT system because of the Data Protection Act. For example, 'beware if you have to collect Mr. XYZ; he is likely to swear and throw things at you'.

## 10.8  Analysis and discussion

First, it is important to note that both organizations are proposing ICT-based solutions to their knowledge and information management challenges, and that essentially these solutions are locally bounded. We concentrate on the local boundedness here; the issue of the extent to which ICT can actually provide such solutions is beyond the scope of this paper. The findings from both cases point to the importance of taking an holistic view of the emergency care process or 'care chain' and the role of KM within it.

Through the cases we can identify six parties with quite different KM needs involved at different stages in the process of providing emergency care: (1) the ambulance crews that first attend to patients, the knowledge needs of which have been explored above; (2) ambulance control that, for example, provides traffic and vehicle management knowledge support to the ambulance crews; (3) GP surgeries that request ambulances for their patients, as well as providing emergency information to, and receiving information from, hospitals; (4) nurses in A&E and MAU; (5) junior doctors in A&E and MAU; and (6) consultants in A&E and MAU. The knowledge needs of the last two parties have been explored above. However, the significant KM differences between junior doctors and consultants are of particular note. For example, a key decision for a junior doctor in A&E or MAU facing a difficult diagnosis or treatment decision in the early hours of the morning is 'should I wake my senior consultant on this one'? A KM system may help here.

At present, the question of KM in the emergency care process has been approached in a fragmented way and is viewed from the narrow perspective of the organization itself. This is not a criticism of the way Ambulance and Hospital are developing their ICT systems and grappling with the importance of KM. In the absence of a coherent view of the process, the organizations inevitably develop solutions in a fragmented way. In both case studies, there is certainly a recognition that there are other players up and down the care chain which it makes sense to cooperate with (eg Hospital talked about exchanging information with GPs, Ambulance talked about sharing information with A&E). However, as we shall go on to argue, as the participants in the chain essentially have an underlying view of information use which is locally bounded, their solutions to knowledge and information management challenges are bound to be local ones.

It is interesting how the cases differed in this respect, but nevertheless are illustrative of the same underlying approach. In the Ambulance case, questions about knowledge needed within the system, and the nature of the information which flows through it, are only viewed from the perspective of Ambulance. Furthermore, there is a preoccupation in the discussion with information provision from management to Ambulance staff, and how an ICT system could be provided to support such a role. Staff generally overlook the importance and nature of what they may need to put onto such as system (which could have no immediate payoff for them), or how they should interact with the wider system. One exception to this was the desire of paramedics to use in-cab ICT to transmit a patient's cardiac rhythm to an A&E doctor to get expert immediate advice on the most appropriate treatment for the patient. Nor in Ambulance is there any widespread realization of knowledge and information which Ambulance staff need to 'pull' in for themselves in order to do their jobs—albeit paramedics are aware of the importance of getting drug dose information for babies. These are perhaps understandable in an organization where the relationship between management and staff is oriented toward command and control-style management, unlike Hospital. Information flow is largely discussed from the perspective of structures for management and control of the organization, hence the remote laptops, which all Ambulance crews are to have, are seen as a management device.

In Hospital, on the other hand, the need for a global Electronic Patient Record system is recognised, although it is approached from the perspective of how consultants can use the system to support their own local operational knowledge needs. Although there is a strong management tier in Hospital, this is very separate from the professional sanctity of the doctors and their application of clinical knowledge. Indeed, the pilot system in Hospital referred to above has been 'programmed and delivered by clinical staff with no input or funding from managers'. In the Hospital workshop, while the focus was on an Electronic Patient Record 'following' patients, the doctors were understandably scoping up its characteristics from the perspective of how they can use a system to gain the information and knowledge required to make a differential diagnosis. This is essentially the application of their professional knowledge, and a judgement for which often they alone will take responsibility. Their predominant perspective is of what they can pull in and use to support them in their decision-making. However, the doctors were rarely talking in terms of how they could contribute to the patient record, but more often talked about such input as someone else's (often the nurse's) responsibility.

The cases therefore point to the importance of distinguishing between what might be called (a) local and operational knowledge and (b) global and clinical knowledge. Note that by knowledge we mean the knowledge which participants themselves have in this process, and information is what the participants interact with. The knowledge needs to be applied to the information (Figure 10.2 illustrates examples of these differences for Ambulance).

### 10.8.1 Local and operational knowledge

This is the knowledge and associated information which various groups involved in the emergency care process—for example, ambulance control staff, paramedics, consultants—need and apply in their jobs. It can be viewed from the individual perspective of how they know what to do and how to act in the operational aspects of their work. For example, in Figure 10.2 we identify 'stock control for drugs via the cab—just in time ordering' and 'infection control, cleaning logs, equipment log numbers, etc. database in cab' as examples of operational knowledge which is only really needed locally by paramedics. For Hospital, examples include 'potentially useful drug interactions' and 'previous cases with similar symptoms' as examples of local, operational knowledge for doctors. Such needs, both for knowledge and supporting information, are by nature local and context-specific and vary enormously from group to group.

### 10.8.2  Global and clinical knowledge

This is the knowledge and associated information which needs to flow along the emergency care process, which managers, doctors, nurses, ambulance staff and other healthcare professionals all play a part in contributing to, and which could perhaps be thought of as more generic to the system. In addition, where it is specific, it is specific to the patient rather than the staff or organization. This might be thought of both as the accumulated clinical knowledge relating to the patient and his/her medical condition, and the perhaps more factual information about the patient such as who they are, where they live, next of kin, etc. (such information may not all need to go on an Electronic Patient Record at all, but some may also be gained directly from the patient where possible).

Thus an Electronic Patient Record should contain the sum total of both information and knowledge, which has accumulated thus far in the patient's journey through the emergency care chain—for example, symptoms diagnosed, treatments already given. This is completely distinct from say, the bodies of knowledge a doctor may need to consult in reaching a diagnosis, or the information that control gives to the ambulance about where to take the patient. The latter example falls into the local, operational category. However, the former illustrates that information and knowledge about a specific patient is not all that needs to travel along the care chain. While traffic information and bed availability might be relatively local matters, the system would also benefit by sharing knowledge about making a diagnosis along the care chain.

Both Ambulance and Hospital see a need for local and operational information and KM, and for global *information* management relating to the specific patient. However, there was no explicit recognition in any of the workshops of the need for any other knowledge to be shared or transferred along the emergency care process.

## 10.9 Limitations of this work

This paper is limited by only two organizations being studied. However, we have had good exposure to these organizations, both through the range of individuals involved in the workshops and through meetings before and after these workshops. We recognize that it is unwise to generalize from a sample of two, but in the absence of any other studies, anecdotal evidence is that both Hospital and Ambulance are typical. The work of Newell *et al*[16] confirms the local boundedness of much NHS thinking about knowledge.

Earlier we identified six parties involved in the emergency care process that may have different KM needs. A wide cross-section of individuals from four of these parties have informed the development of the ideas presented in this paper. In the context of MAU and A&E, where patients only remain for less than 2 days, we conjecture that the knowledge and information needs of the nurses may not be very different from those of the doctors. Noticeable, however, is the lack of any GP surgeries informing our proposal of a systems vision for emergency health-care provision. The contribution of GP surgeries to this vision has been captured from all but the individuals in the GP surgeries. To explain, information is sometimes transferred between both the GP and ambulance crews (if the ambulance crew are responding to an emergency call by a GP) and the GP and A&E/MAU (often in the form of patient up-dates from A&E/MAU to GPs). We are unable to evaluate the implications of this with confidence. It might be that the perspective of the doctors in A&E and MAU (who have most contact with GPs, and most similarity of background to them) satisfactorily represents GPs' current involvement. However, it also might be that the GPs want to take a more active role in emergency health provision, and that additional knowledge or integration into the process would facilitate this. GP surgeries increasingly use other types of health-care worker, too. Further research is necessary, but we believe that a systems vision of emergency care is appropriate whatever the GPs' perspective.

## 10.10 Conclusions

Health care is one of many areas in which ICT-based KM systems are suggested as offering potential benefits. In this research, we have studied the perceptions of some of the potential 'customers' of KM systems relating to emergency health care. These include both those who would be hands-on users of the systems (eg health-care professionals) and their indirect beneficiaries (eg patients). The care of any one patient is likely to involve many different groups of staff across several organizations, for example ambulance crews, nurses and hospital doctors. Previous studies have tended to focus on a single organization and/or on the providers of KM systems rather than their users/beneficiaries.

Our findings are that on the whole the potential users have a good appreciation of the need for better KM locally, and of the need to communicate with other groups involved in emergency care. However, they do not appear to have put these two together to realize the importance of KM systems applying to the whole process: to be global rather than local.

The principal contribution of this paper is therefore to explore the complexity of KM in the emergency care process, and to draw an important distinction between two types and applications of knowledge: local operational knowledge and global clinical knowledge. Viewing emergency care or the care chain as one complete process or system in which many organizations play a part, brings the focus of attention to the information and knowledge which needs to flow through this process. It also illustrates how different organizations and professions both interact with and add to the information as it snowballs with the patient. If we can identify the roles of the various participants, and how they interact with information and knowledge needed in the emergency care process, this will usefully inform the requirements of a process-wide ICT system.

Of course, there is a need for local solutions to address the specific operational knowledge and information needs of the various groups involved in the emergency care process. It is also understandable, given funding and governance structures, that the organizations should be attempting separate local solutions to knowledge and information management challenges. However, the important question for these organizations is how these separate local systems in the process interact with the system carrying the patient information. The Electronic Patient Record cannot be constructed as the domain of the group or organization, but something which they all need to incorporate into their local systems. However, there is a danger that the organizations involved continue to develop different systems that then become incompatible with the systems needed to support process-wide information flow and KM.

Therefore, we are arguing for a different approach to the development of KM systems and their supporting information systems, including an Electronic Patient Record-type system. This is an issue which clearly cannot be solved by Hospital or Ambulance alone. The potential users have a view of knowledge and information, which is locally bound, and stems predominantly from the perspective of how they can use a system to support the application of their own local operational knowledge needs. The balance between local operational knowledge and global clinical knowledge needs to be addressed before an Electronic Patient Record system could properly function. In Hospital, there is an evident willingness to share this 'global view' of the NHS (this was seen both in the doctors' workshop and the management workshop not drawn upon in this paper). However, it is hard for the organizations to do this, given that the process is so fragmentary, and it will require considerable change to make it possible. Considering the issue at Primary Care Trust level may help, but this still does not cover all six interacting parties identified above.

Taking the systems view even more broadly, considerations of KM in emergency care should also not be separated from those relating to non-emergency care in the same organizations. This is an even larger task, and here the needs of other health-care professionals may well diverge more from those of the doctors.

From the KM standpoint, the following questions therefore need to be addressed in relation to any Electronic Patient Record system. In which health-care processes will the Electronic Patient Record be used? Which organizations will need to use it, which groups of staff (professional and other) within them, and when? Which information relates only to local operational knowledge, and which to global clinical knowledge?

Only when these answers are known can the scope of an Electronic Patient Record system—which in principle could range from an all-encompassing national system to one only applying for a single 'episode' within a single hospital—be determined.

KM can then support the design and implementation of any system. Some of the questions that it would be able to address include: What are the user requirements of such a system regarding the input and output of information? How do operational staff use such a system across a variety of situations, for example, attending a patient on the 30th floor of a high-rise building, in an Accident and Emergency department on a chaotic Saturday night, or during a very large-scale local/national emergency?

There are, therefore, many barriers to be overcome in providing better support for emergency health care. This paper helps by arguing for the importance of a systems vision for KM in the NHS. Some of the barriers may be addressed by helping the NHS to view emergency care as a process necessitating the flow of patient-centred information and knowledge, to which all participants have a responsibility to contribute. Other barriers will require organizational, cultural and practical changes to be made, to enable all participants to play a full part in contributing to the ICT systems and use them to their maximum advantage. The relationship between managers, clinical and other NHS staff is an important element in this. It was very different in the two cases we have described. Much of this cultural change will need to focus on the willingness of participants to share their knowledge. However, it is clear that they are at present far from being able to exchange even information in the emergency care process, so it seems a long way away before all participants will be able to share effectively their knowledge along the chain for the ultimate benefit of the patient.

## Acknowledgements

We are grateful for the very helpful comments of two anonymous referees.

## References

1. Fawcett SE and Cooper MB (2001). Process integration for competitive success: benchmarking barriers and bridges. *Benchmarking* **8**: 396–412.
2. Morash EA and Clinton SR (1998). Supply chain integration: customer value through collaborative closeness versus operational excellence. *J Marketing Theory Prac* **6**: 104–120.
3. Minnick A, Young WB and Roberts MJ (1995). 2,000 patients relate their hospital experiences. *Nurs Mngt* **26**: 25–31.
4. Newman K (1994). The single visit clinic: a case study in process re-engineering. *Bus Change Re-eng* **2**: 10–18.
5. Bence V (1995). St James's Hospital and Lucas Engineering Systems: a BPR collaboration. *Bus Change Re-eng* **2**: 30–39.
6. Arnott S (2003). National buying to slash NHS costs. *Computing*, 26 February. http://www.computing.co.uk/news/1139071, last accessed 27 September 2004.
7. Rubenstein-Montano B, *et al* and The Knowledge Management Methodology Team (2001). A systems thinking framework for knowledge management. *Decision Support Syst* **31**: 5–16.
8. Argyris C and Schön DA (1978). *Organizational Learning, A Theory of Action Perspective*. Addison-Wesley: Reading, MA.
9. Cuthbertson C and Farrington J (2002). Methods for knowledge management strategy formulation: a case study. In: Coakes E, Willis D and Clarke S (eds). *Knowledge Management in the SocioTechnical World: The Graffiti Continues*. Springer-Verlag, London, pp 139–152.

10. Ferrari FM, Fares CB and Martinelli DP (2002). The systemic approach of SSM: the case of a Brazilian company. *Syst Prac Action Res* **15**: 51–66.
11. Al-Karaghouli W, Fitzgerald G and Alshawi S (2002). Knowledge requirements systems (KRS): an approach to improving and understanding requirements. In: Coakes E, Willis D and Clarke S (eds). *Knowledge Management in the Sociotechnical World: The Graffiti Continues*. Springer-Verlag, London, pp 170–184.
12. Senge PM (1990). *The Fifth Discipline, The Art and Practice of the Learning Organization*. Doubleday: New York.
13. Coakes E, Willis D and Clarke S (2002). *Knowledge Management in the SocioTechnical World: The Graffiti Continues*. Springer-Verlag: London.
14. Reuthe E and Allee V (1999). Knowledge management: moving the care model from a 'snapshot' to a 'story'. *Health Forum J* **42**: 26–28.
15. Desouza KC (2002). Knowledge management in hospitals: a process oriented view and staged look at managerial issues. *Int J Healthcare Technol Mngt* **4**: 478–497.
16. Newell S et al (2003). 'Best practice' development and transfer in the NHS: the importance of process as well as product knowledge. *Health Services Mngt Res* **16**: 1–12.
17. Checkland P and Scholes J (1990). *Soft Systems Methodology in Action*. John Wiley: Chichester.
18. Checkland P (1999). *Systems Thinking, Systems Practice*. John Wiley: Chichester.
19. Checkland P and Holwell S (1998). *Information, Systems and Information Systems—Making Sense of the Field*. John Wiley: Chichester.
20. Lehaney B and Paul RJ (1996). The use of soft systems methodology in the development of a simulation of out-patient services at Watford General Hospital. *J Opl Res Soc* **47**: 864–870.
21. Lehaney B, Clarke SA and Paul RJ (1999). A case of intervention in an out-patients department. *J Opl Res Soc* **50**: 877–891.
22. Batalden P and Splaine M (2002). What will it take to lead the continual improvement and innovation of health care in the twenty-first century? *Qual Mngt Health Care* **11**: 45–54.
23. Van Beveren J (2003). Does health care for knowledge management? *J Knowledge Mngt* **7**: 90–95.
24. Davenport TH and Glaser J (2002). Just-in-time-delivery comes to knowledge management. *Harvard Bus Rev* **80**: 107–112.
25. Melymuka K (2002). Knowledge management helps cut errors by half. *Computerworld* **36**: 44.
26. Pedersen MK and Larsen MH (2001). Distributed knowledge management based on product state models—the case of decision support in health care administration. *Decision Support Syst* **31**: 139–158.
27. Ashburner L and Fitzgerald L (1996). Beleaguered professionals: clinicians and institutional change in the NHS. In: Scarbrough H (ed). *The Management of Expertise*. Macmillan Press, Basingstoke, pp 190–216.
28. Hansen MT, Nohria N and Tierney T (1999). What's your strategy for managing knowledge? *Harvard Bus Rev* **77**: 106–116.
29. Carter B (2000). The expert's opinion: knowledge management. *J Database Mngt* **11**: 42–43.

30. Scarbrough H and Swan J (2001). Explaining the diffusion of knowledge management: the role of fashion. *Br J Mngt* **12**: 3–12.
31. Earl M (2001). Knowledge management strategies: toward a taxonomy. *J Mngt Inform Syst* **18**: 215–233.
32. Alavi M and Leidner DE (2001). Review: knowledge management and knowledge management systems: conceptual foundations and research issues. *MIS Q* **25**: 107–136.
33. Forgionne GA and Kohli R (1995). Integrated MSS effects: an empirical health care investigation. *Inform Process Mngt* **31**: 879–896.
34. Slipy SM (1995). Boston hospital using seven telemedicine systems within facility. *Health Mngt Technol* **16**: 34.
35. Moreno L et al (2001). Using KADS methodology in a simulation assisted knowledge based system: application to hospital management. *Expert Syst Appl* **20**: 235–249.
36. Moseley L and Mead D (2001). Explaining the low penetration of decision support systems into clinical practice. *Expert Update* **3**: 30–34.
37. Standridge CR and Steward D (2000). Using expert systems for simulation modeling of patient scheduling. *Simulation* **75**: 148–156.
38. Eden C and Ackermann F (1989). Strategic options development and analysis (SODA)—using a computer to help with the management of strategic vision. In: Doukidis GI, Land F and Miller G (eds). *Knowledge-based Management Support Systems*. Ellis Horwood, Chichester, pp 198–207.
39. Eden C and Ackermann F (1998). Making Strategy: The Journey of Strategic Management. Sage: London.
40. Roginski C (1995). Applying SODA in the NHS—a facilitator's story. *OR Insight* **8**: 28–32.
41. Shaw D (2003). Evaluating electronic brainstorms using new techniques to analyse the brainstormed ideas. *J Opl Res Soc* **54**: 692–705.
42. Sosik JJ, Avolio BJ and Kahai SS (1998). Inspiring group creativity—comparing anonymous and identified electronic brainstorming. *Small Group Res* **29**: 3–31.
43. Dennis AR, Haley BJ and Vandenberg RJ (1996). A meta-analysis of effectiveness, efficiency, and participant satisfaction in group support systems. In: DeGross JI, Jarvenpaa SL and Srinivasan A (eds). *Proceedings of the International Conference on Information Systems, Cleveland, Ohio*. Association of Information Systems, Atlanta, Georgia, USA, pp 278–289.
44. Shaw D (2003). Evaluating electronic workshops through analysing the 'brainstormed' ideas. *J Opl Res Soc* **54**: 692–705.
45. Shaw D, Ackermann F and Eden C (2003). Sharing knowledge in group problem structuring. *J Opl Res Soc* **54**: 936–948.
46. Edwards JS, Collier PM and Shaw D (2003). *Management Accounting and Knowledge Management*. CIMA: London.
47. Scarbrough H (1996). Strategic IT in financial services: the social construction of strategic knowledge. In: Scarbrough H (ed). *The Management of Expertise*. Macmillan, Basingstoke, pp 150–173.

# Part VII
# Application of OR within the Wider Healthcare Context

.

# 11

# An Analysis of the Academic Literature on Simulation and Modeling in Health Care

*S. C. Brailsford[1], P. R. Harper[2], B. Patel[1] and M. Pitt[3]*
[1]*University of Southampton, Southampton, UK;* [2]*Cardiff University, Cardiff, UK; and* [3]*Peninsula Medical School, Exeter, UK*

*This article describes a multi-dimensional approach to the classification of the research literature on simulation and modelling in health care. The aim of the study was to analyse the relative frequency of use of a range of operational research modelling approaches in health care, along with the specific domains of application and the level of implementation. Given the vast scale of the health care modelling literature, a novel review methodology was adopted, similar in concept to the approach of stratified sampling. The results provide new insights into the level of activity across many areas of application, highlighting important relationships and pointing to key areas of omission and neglect in the literature. In addition, the approach presented in this article provides a systematic and generic methodology that can be extended to other application domains as well as other types of information source in healthcare modelling.*

## 11.1 Introduction

Undertaking a review of modelling and simulation in health care is without doubt a Herculean task. This is a literature which, having carried out searches on consecutive days using the Web of Knowledge (WoK) bibliographic database (wok.mimas.ac.uk) and the search string *'((healthcare or health care) and (modelling or modeling or simulation))'*, was

Reprinted from *Journal of Simulation*, 3: 130–140, 2009, 'An Analysis of the Academic Literature on Simulation and Modeling in Health care', by S. C. Brailsford, P. R. Harper, B. Patel and M. Pitt. With kind permission from Operational Research Society Ltd. All rights reserved.

found to be expanding at the rate of about 30 articles a day. A search carried out on June 21, 2007 using the Ovid search engine (www.ovid. com) and the same search string resulted in 176320 hits. It is hard to imagine how a single person, research group or academic department could begin to keep up with such a literature.

Nevertheless this is the task that the Research Into Global Healthcare Tool (RIGHT) project team set itself. RIGHT (www.right.org.uk) is a collaborative research venture between six UK universities, funded by the British Engineering and Physical Sciences Research Council. The aim of RIGHT is to assess the feasibility of applying to decision making in health care some of the best-practice modelling and simulation methods that are used to support decision making in other sectors, such as manufacturing industry and defence.

The first phase of the RIGHT project has involved eight extensive literature reviews, of which this is one. Nearly all of these involved massive literatures and therefore an innovative common methodology was devised and developed, in order to reduce the scope of the task to something achievable in the time available. The other review topics are: simulation and modelling in manufacturing industry, simulation and modelling in aerospace, simulation and modelling in defence, management methods (excluding simulation and modelling) in health care, management methods (excluding simulation and modelling) in manufacturing industry, stakeholder analysis and framework development.

The study was concerned only with modelling as understood by an operational researcher, namely a structured approach to understanding (and possibly, but not always, solving) a real-world problem through developing a simplified version of the real system. We were particularly, but not exclusively, interested in applications of simulation. This covered computer-based approaches such as discrete-event simulation, agent-based simulation and system dynamics, as well as role-playing or business-gaming simulations. In a medical context the word 'model' covers a wide range of meanings. Therefore, in order to avoid as far as possible clinical, biochemical, microbiological or pharmacological articles where the word model has a very technical and specialised meaning, we restricted the search criteria to the terms *modelling* and *modeling*.

The aim of undertaking this review, and indeed the other reviews in the RIGHT project, was not merely to produce an academic article. The overall aim of RIGHT is to produce a 'toolkit' of methods and an explanatory framework or user guide that will suggest, for a given type of health-care problem and a given set of available resources at the user's disposal, the most suitable method(s) to use. The RIGHT project is a feasibility study and the toolkit and user guide will be tested on a sample range of exemplar sites (Naseer *et al*, 2009).

## 11.2 The ancestry of health-care modelling reviews

Several review articles over the years have been written on health-care modelling. These have tended to focus either on a specific modelling methodology, such as discrete event simulation (for example, Fone *et al*, 2003) or on the use of modelling for a specific health-care setting, such as clinics (for example, Jun *et al*, 1999).

One of the earliest review articles in this field, and possibly the first comprehensive review of health-care modelling, was by Fries (1976), who compiled a list of 188 articles that the author grouped into 15 categories according to their area of application. These include forecasting demand, appointment systems, ambulance requirements and deployment, and health planning and programme evaluation. The articles were selected only if they used what Fries describes as 'mathematical methods of modelling and solving decision problems that form the core of OR'. This bibliography was later supplemented with an additional 164 articles to make a total of 352 references (Fries, 1979). The review covers more than a dozen mainstream OR journals of that time, up to 1979, as well as referencing chasing as appropriate. The author does not provide details of the full list of journals searched nor the selection criteria, but one imagines that the 352 articles cited represent a large proportion of the body of health-care modelling literature at that time.

Two separate review articles on computer simulation projects were published 1 year later in 1980 by Tunnicliffe Wilson (1980). One article focused on applications to healthcare population problems and the other on health-care facilities. Between them, they covered over 200 articles. A follow-up article by the same author (Wilson, 1981) focussed on implementation issues as the author reported that from the 200 reviewed articles, only 16 studies reported recommendations that had been acted upon.

Towards the end of the 1980s, Smith-Daniels *et al* (1988) reviewed the literature pertaining to acquisition decisions, for example sizing of facilities and facility location, and allocation decisions, for example inpatient admissions scheduling. They covered a number of techniques including simulation, queueing theory, Markov chains and heuristics. A few years later, Klein *et al* (1993) presented a bibliography that included medical decision making and simulation modelling with a focus on planning models.

Jun *et al* (1999) surveyed articles on the application of discrete event simulation modelling to health-care clinics and systems of clinics, for example hospitals, outpatient clinics and emergency departments. A taxonomy of the literature is presented covering published articles over the previous 20 years and categorised under two main themes: patient flow and allocation of resources. No discussion is made on the adopted review methodology and thus it is not possible to ascertain how systematic and wide-ranging this review is.

More recently, Fone *et al* (2003) produced a systematic review of computer simulation modelling in population health and health-care delivery. It is fair to say that this article is the first in health-care modelling to adopt a rigorous systematic review process that is described in detail in the article, and involved the screening of some 2729 references that eventually were reduced to 182 using inclusion criteria. The focus is entirely on discrete event simulation and articles are grouped into four application areas. The authors comment that although the number of modelling articles has grown substantially in recent years, very few report on outcomes of implementation of models and so the value of modelling requires further research. It is of interest to note that nothing appears to have changed over the years since Tunnicliffe Wilson made similar observations in 1981 (Wilson, 1981).

In summary, most of these previous reviews have focussed on simulation (and, in particular, discrete event simulation) or have included a broader range of OR and mathematical methodologies, but have focussed on specific application areas. Furthermore, most fail to describe the review process and presumably represent an exhaustive bibliography of articles from journals that happen to be searched by the review team. Certainly no systematic approach is reported, except that by Fone *et al* (2003). This article therefore fills a gap in the review literature by producing an up-to-date review unrestricted by methodology or application, and based on a systematic heuristic sampling review process covering a vast body of literature.

## 11.3   Review methodology and the RIGHT Information Template (RIT)

Within the 2-year timescale of the RIGHT project (of which the first 4 months was assigned to the literature reviews), it was clearly impossible to carry out anything approaching an exhaustive systematic review of any of these massive literatures. Therefore a heuristic, sampling-based approach was adopted across all eight reviews, using a variety of methods to identify the key articles and the emerging issues. This methodology has more in common with stratified experimental sampling than the kind of exhaustive survey typically attempted in a conventional literature review, for example a Cochrane systematic review (www.cochrane-handbook.org), where the aim is to ensure that *all* articles that meet a clearly defined set of inclusion criteria are read. In order to achieve a consistent approach across all eight reviews, a common template called the RIT was developed. The RIT contains the fields as shown in Table 11.1, which are recorded with fixed categories or free-text as appropriate. For this particular review, some of the fields of the standard RIT were modified slightly, as described at the end of this section. Some of the free-text fields in the RIT, in particular the 'MethodName' and the 'FunctionalArea' fields, were replaced by constrained lists in this study to facilitate quantitative analysis. The choice of specific methods was informed by the findings from the other RIGHT reviews.

This study was far broader in scope than any of the previous healthcare modelling reviews described above. The source literature was mainstream academic journal publications, accessible through three of the most widely used academic electronic databases: JSTOR (www. jstor.org), SCOPUS (www.scopus.com) and ISI WoK (www.wok. mimas. ac.uk). More general web searches using Google showed that the 'grey' literature in this area is equally massive and is worthy of further study in its own right. It will be the subject of a follow-up article later in the project, as arguably some of the most widely implemented work appears

*Table 11.1*  Information items included in the RIT

| Method | Problem | Resources |
|---|---|---|
| 1 M_MethodName | 7P_Country | 12R_Time |
| 2M_Initiator | 8P_Industry | 13R_Information |
| 3M_Purpose | 9P_Layer | 14R_People |
| 4M_ImplementationLevel | 10P_FunctionalAreas | 15R_Others |
| 5M_Strengths | 11P_ProblemsIssues | |
| 6M_Limitations | | |
| *Others* | *Administration* | |
| 16O_AuthorsFactsConclusions | 19A_Deliverable | 22A_Source |
| 17O_ReviewerCritique | 20A_ArticleID | 23A_Channel |
| 18O_FundingSource | 21A_Reference | |

N.B. Information items 19A–23A we captured for RIGHT internal administrative purposes only, to facilitate data storage and data handling across all RIGHT literature reviews.

in the grey literature rather than the academic literature. SCOPUS covers journal publications from more diverse sources than JSTOR, but concentrates on more recent publications. Despite innovations in medical technology, the nature of the problems arising in health-care management has remained remarkably similar over the years. The SCOPUS search was limited to articles published after 1990, but the JSTOR search was unrestricted by date in order to capture the significant but older publications.

The literature review methodology consisted of three stages (Figure 11.1). In stage 1, a very broad set of search terms was used to produce an initial set of articles. The search string was '(health-care OR health care) AND (modelling OR modeling OR simulat*OR (system AND

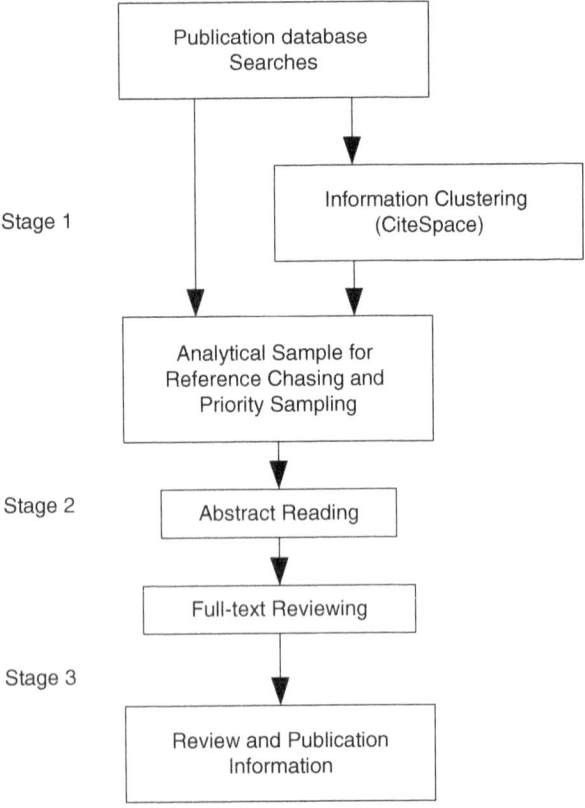

*Figure 11.1*   Stages of the review methodology

dynamic*) OR markov*)', appearing in the title, abstract or keywords. In stage 2, a subset of these articles was selected for abstract review by a combination of 'relevance rating' and reference chasing as described below. Overall, 16% of the stage 1 articles were selected for abstract review, although this varied from 10% to 25% across the three different literature sources. In stage 3, the abstracts of all the stage 2 articles were read and a further down-selection made for inclusion in the final data set. The criteria used at this stage were that the article described a genuine application of modelling or simulation to a health-care problem. Any duplicates were removed at this stage, although there were surprisingly few of these between JSTOR and SCOPUS. The suitability of the stage 3 articles was then verified by full-text reading. In all 22% of the stage 2 articles were judged suitable for final inclusion, resulting in a total data set of 342 articles (119 from SCOPUS, 163 from JSTOR and 60 from WoK). A summary of the search results for stage 1 and sample sizes for stages 2 and 3 is shown in Table 11.2. The three stages required 3 months extensive work on searching, screening and recording required information, with approximately 20% of the time required for stage 1 and 40% each for stages 2 and 3.

JSTOR and SCOPUS both provide 'relevance ratings' and these were used in stage 2 to rank the first 500 articles in both databases for abstract scanning. It was not possible to discover the exact algorithm used to determine this relevance rating, but it was clearly based on the frequency of occurrence of the search terms. Many articles were eliminated at this stage, for example book reviews, abstracts of conference presentations or cost-effectiveness analyses of drug treatments (given we wanted to exclude the clinical, biochemical, microbiological and pharmacological literature). However, WoK does not provide such a ranking and therefore the innovative bibliometric visualisation tool CiteSpace Chen (2004, 2006) was used. Chen (2004, 2006) has demonstrated various uses of citation information and network analysis for the scientific literature. In particular, co-citation networks are a useful analytical method

Table 11.2  Publication counts for the three stages of literature review

|  | JSTOR | SCOPUS | WoK |
| --- | --- | --- | --- |
| Search results (Stage 1) | >2200 | ~5000 | >2500 |
| Selected sample for abstract reviews (Stage 2) | 550 | 500 | 491 |
| Full-text reviews (Stage 3) | 163 | 119 | 60 |

for the task of reference chasing. A co-citation network is a graphical representation of the references cited by a given set of publications enabling key articles that are widely referenced by later authors (ie, highly connected nodes of the network) to be identified. Using Citespace, a network was constructed using the cited references and citation count details from the stage 1 WoK articles, in order to down-select a set of relevant publications for stage 2 review. This set consisted of the 491 most cited references by more than 2500 publications in WoK selected with co-citation network; hence, it was representative of outcome from usual reference-chasing by researchers.

## 11.4   Data collection and recording

For each of the 342 articles in the final data set, the following information was recorded in an Excel worksheet:

1. Methods
2. Initiators
3. Funding source
4. Level of implementation
5. Functional area
6. Layer in the industry
7. Country
8. Databases and processes for literature review
9. Year of publication

The 'MethodName' field from the standard RIT was expanded to allow up to three separate methods (primary, secondary and tertiary) to be recorded for each reviewed article, together with the software used, if stated. A two-level hierarchy was used to classify modelling and simulation methods in this review. For example, the high-level category 'Simulation' had eight sub-categories, including discrete-event, system dynamics, agent-based, distributed and Monte Carlo simulation. For each publication, a main method was assigned to the principal modelling approach employed in the study. A constrained set of method categories was used. Because many studies used more than one method, up to two subsidiary methods could be recorded. Thus, for instance, a study by Lehaney *et al* (1999) that used a Soft Systems (SSM) approach as a means to develop a discrete event simulation model would have two methods recorded, firstly its primary method, Simulation/ Discrete Event Simulation, and secondly, Qualitative/SSM. Of the total

342 articles, 204 used only one method, 113 used two methods and 25 used three methods.

Similarly, data for the field 'FunctionalArea' were recorded at two levels. At the top level, four broad categories were used: stakeholder interest, clinical or organisational processes, patient care delivery planning and research/policy. A more detailed classification of health-care function used the following nine categories:

1. Finance, Policy, Governance, Regulation
2. Public Health, Community service planning
3. Patient behaviour/characteristics
4. Planning, System/resource utilisation
5. Quality management, Performance monitoring or review
6. Risk management, Forecasting
7. Workforce/Staff management
8. Research
9. Other

Up to three of these categories could be recorded: a primary function and up to two other subsidiary functions. Of the total 342 articles, 102 were classified in one function only, 149 were classified in two categories and 91 were classified in three categories.

'Layer' (in the industry) was recorded at three levels: policy or regulation; facilitation or commissioning; and operation. Data for the field 'ImplementationLevel' were rated according to a three-level scale of implementation (see the Results section for further details).

## 11.5 Validation and verification

Systematic review approaches such as the Cochrane review methodology have a formalised structure in which the search strategy is highly prescriptive, and the inclusion and exclusion criteria for articles are precisely defined. A systematic review is (in theory at least) repeatable by other researchers, with identical results apart from the possible inclusion of articles that were unpublished at the time of the original review. The methodology described in this article can be similarly validated and repeated. Moreover, by way of 'reality check', the final list of 342 references was scanned by all four authors (who have, between them, over 50 years experience in the field of health-care modelling) to verify that certain well known, important articles from the literature had in fact been found and that no misclassified articles had been included.

The full data set of references will be made available on the RIGHT website.

## 11.6   Results

### 11.6.1   Date of publication

The publication dates of the selected articles ranged from 1952–2007. However, the vast majority (82%) in our review was published after 1990. By decade, the percentages were: pre-1979: 7.0%; 1980–1989: 10.8%; 1990–1999: 36.3%; 2000–2007: 45.9%.

### 11.6.2   Country of origin

Each article was classified by the country in which the research study was carried out. When analysed by continent, the relative proportions were as follows: North America: 206 (60.2%); Europe: 84 (24.6%); Asia: 31 (9.1%); Africa: 10 (2.9%); Australasia: 6 (1.8%); South and Central America: 1 (0.3%). Four of the articles (1.2%) could not be classified by country. The vast majority of studies (85%), therefore, were undertaken in North America and Europe. Of the North American articles all but seven were conducted in the USA (the rest being Canada) and of the publications based in Europe, 55 of the 84 articles were from the UK. The preponderance of studies based in the US and UK is to a degree explained by the fact that the review was restricted to English language articles. However, it also almost certainly reflects the relatively high levels of health-care OR in these two countries.

### 11.6.3   Method

The majority of publications were found to fall into the categories of statistical analysis, statistical modelling, simulation and qualitative modelling. A smaller but significant number employ mathematical modelling, and very few fall into the remaining three categories, which are therefore aggregated and jointly classified as 'Other'. Interestingly, where qualitative methods are used, they are very often a subsidiary method, whereas when mathematical modelling is used, it almost always forms the primary method. The primary method employed is shown in Figure 11.2 and Table 11.3.

When the more detailed second level of the modelling methodology tree was examined, a very wide range of methods was found in each of the major categories. Table 11.4 shows those methods which were used at least three times.

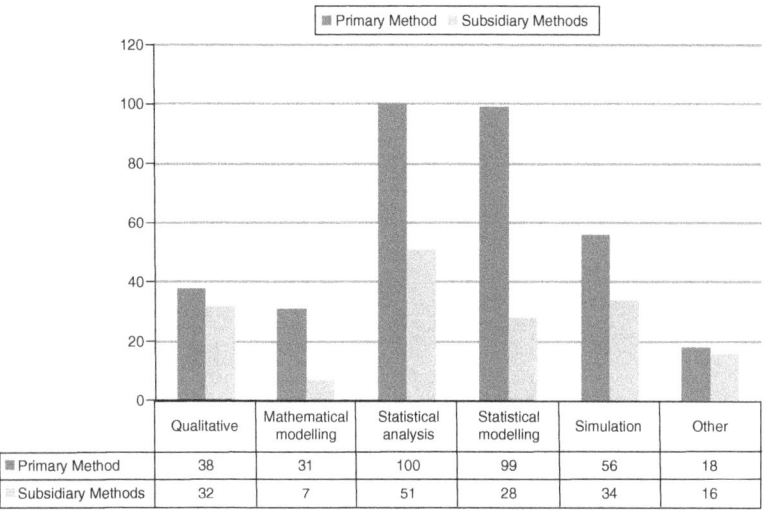

| | Qualitative | Mathematical modelling | Statistical analysis | Statistical modelling | Simulation | Other |
|---|---|---|---|---|---|---|
| ■ Primary Method | 38 | 31 | 100 | 99 | 56 | 18 |
| Subsidiary Methods | 32 | 7 | 51 | 28 | 34 | 16 |

*Figure 11.2* Analysis of method by primary and subsidiary classifications

Perhaps the most striking feature of this breakdown is the relatively low proportion of articles using these most common methods, with more than half of all articles having a primary method not shown in Table 11.4. In all 53% of articles have a primary method that is not observed in more than two articles. This gives an indication of the very wide variety of methods evident in the review. It can be seen that the most common primary method is some form of regression analysis (23% of all articles).

Interestingly, some techniques such as process mapping and Monte Carlo simulation were more commonly used as subsidiary methods. Typically, for instance, Monte Carlo simulation was used for testing or as a method of probabilistic sensitivity analysis for another form of model (eg, a Markov model). Qualitative approaches often formed a precursor to the development of a quantitative model such as a discrete event simulation.

The distribution of methods by year of publication, Figure 11.3, indicates that simulation and qualitative methods in particular are currently increasing in use. In contrast, other methods appear to have a similar uptake to the previous decade with mathematical modelling methods possibly in relative decline. The 'Other' category, for which the majority of articles are first observed post-2000, include spatial/GIS modelling, and system/software related methods such as UML (Unified Modeling

*Table 11.3* Table of association between primary and subsidiary methods

| | | Secondary methods | | | | | |
|---|---|---|---|---|---|---|---|
| | | Qualitative | Mathematical modelling | Statistical analysis | Statistical modelling | Simulation | Other | Total |
| Primary methods | Qualitative | 5 | 0 | 11 | 0 | 3 | 0 | 19 |
| | Mathematical modelling | 2 | 1 | 5 | 4 | 6 | 1 | 19 |
| | Statistical analysis | 6 | 1 | 23 | 6 | 7 | 0 | 43 |
| | Statistical modelling | 6 | 3 | 8 | 11 | 14 | 3 | 45 |
| | Simulation | 12 | 2 | 2 | 5 | 1 | 1 | 23 |
| | Other | 1 | 0 | 2 | 2 | 3 | 6 | 14 |
| | Total | 32 | 7 | 51 | 28 | 34 | 11 | 163 |

*Table 11.4*  Number of articles for each sub-category of method

|  | Primary method | Subsidiary method |
|---|---|---|
| Qualitative modelling | | |
| Cognitive modelling | 3 | 1 |
| Process mapping | 6 | 14 |
| Statistical analysis | | |
| Regression analysis | 77 | 24 |
| Statistical modelling | | |
| Markov models | 19 | 9 |
| Structural equation modelling | 11 | 1 |
| Simulation | | |
| Discrete event simulation | 31 | 6 |
| System dynamics | 6 | 0 |
| Monte Carlo simulation | 4 | 20 |
| Spatial modelling | | |
| Spatial mapping | 5 | 2 |

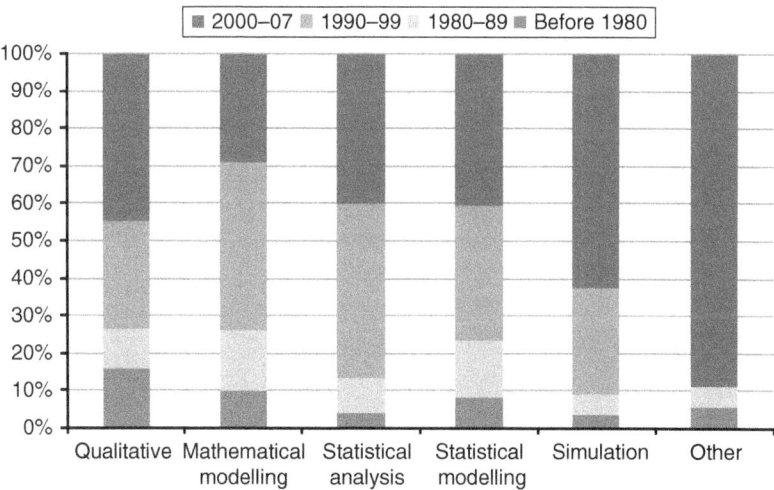

*Figure 11.3*  Analysis of method by year

Language) and IDEF (Integrated Definition Methods) for enterprise modelling and analysis.

### 11.6.4  Funding

The primary source of funding, where reported, is shown in Figure 11.4. Funding sources were classified as commerce (such as consulting or

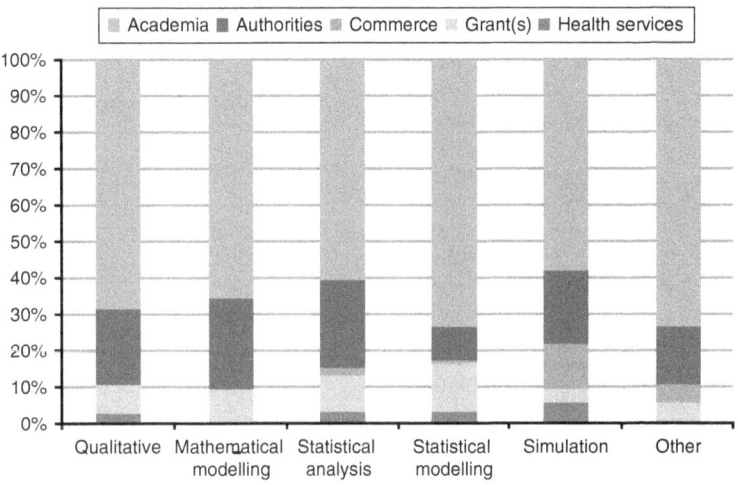

*Figure 11.4*   Primary source of funding by method

commercial firms), academia (no formal Research Council grant/bursary provision), authorities (such as a Government organisation or agency), grants (funding bodies) or health services (such as direct funding from a hospital).

Overall, 60% of published work reported no formal funding, with only 4% funded directly by health services organisations. Notably, commercial funding has been mainly restricted to simulation studies with no examples of qualitative or mathematical modelling. However, in contrast, simulation fares less well with formal grant funding compared with other methods.

### 11.6.5   Functional area

The breakdown of publications by the top-level classification was as follows: stakeholder interest: 38 (11%); clinical and organisational processes and setup: 79 (23%); patient care requirement profiles and delivery planning: 117 (34%); research and policy: 108 (32%). The distribution of articles within the more detailed categories described above is shown in Figure 11.5, broken down by primary function and subsidiary functions. It demonstrates, for example, that planning and system/resource utilisation methods are predominant, and that unlike the other methods, quality management, performance monitoring and review methods are used more commonly as subsidiary methods.

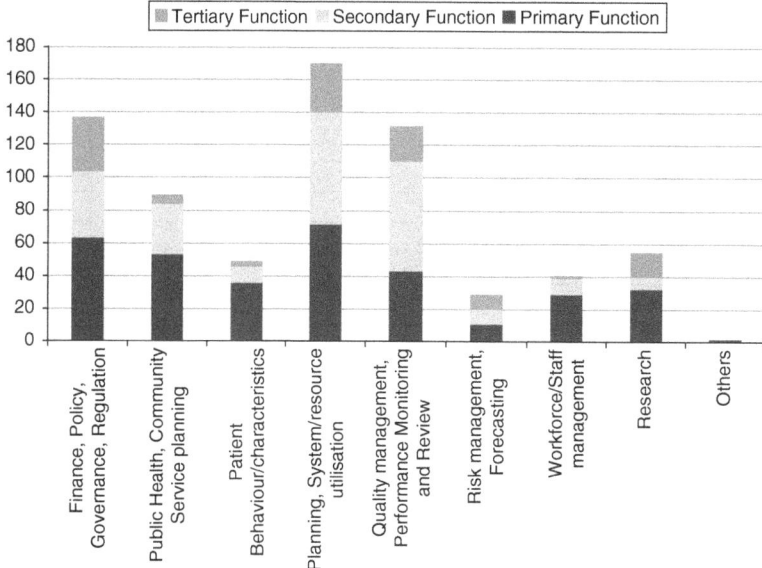

*Figure 11.5* Distribution of function by primary and subsidiary classifications

Figure 11.6 shows the relationships between function and method. Two particular features are that simulation methods are dominant in planning and system/resource utilisation, whereas statistical methods are dominant in finance, policy, governance and regulation. Further, more detailed analysis showed clear tendencies for certain functions to be associated with each other. For example, quality management and performance review was often coupled with planning system and resource allocation.

### 11.6.6 Analysis by level of implementation

A key aspect of any study is the extent to which the model has actually been used in practice for its stated purpose. Each modelling study was rated according to a three-level scale of implementation: 1: Suggested (theoretically proposed by the authors); 2: Conceptualised (discussed with a client organisation); 3: Implemented (actually used in practice). The number of articles rated in each category was Suggested 171 (50%); Conceptualised 153 (44.7%); Implemented 18 (5.3%). Depressingly, these figures emphasise previous findings (Wilson, 1981; Fone *et al*, 2003) that levels of implementation for models in health-care OR are

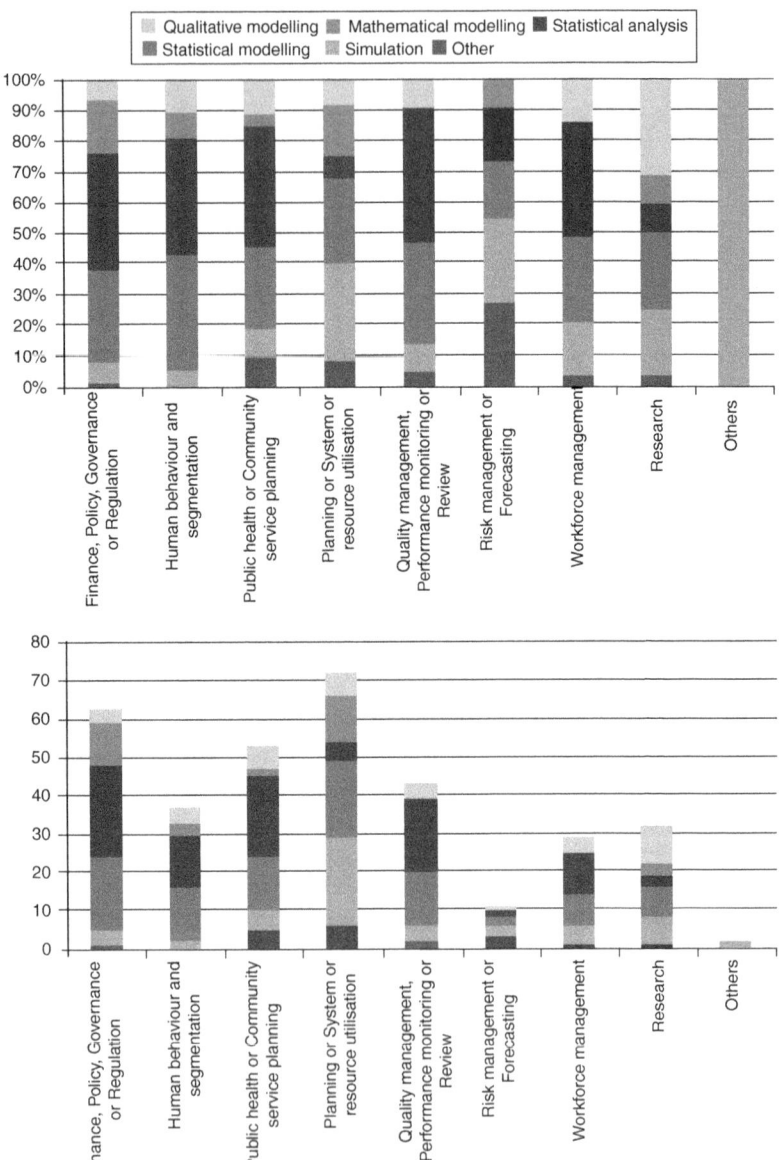

*Figure 11.6* Relationship between function and method

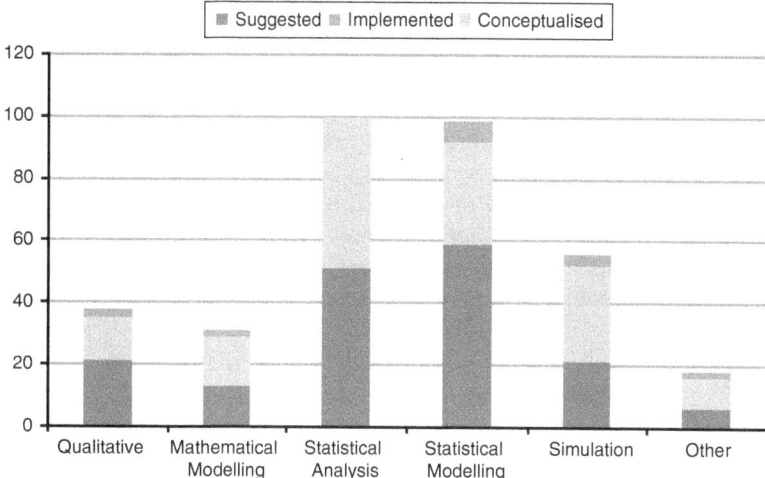

*Figure 11.7* Level of implementation by method

very small indeed and have not improved since the 1980s. A large proportion of modelling studies do, however, reach a conceptualised stage whereby a coherent approach is specified in a practical context with a health-care organisation.

Figure 11.7 shows the levels of implementation for each method. Statistical analysis was always either conceptualised or suggested with no instances of implementation. The proportion of conceptualised to suggested was higher for qualitative and statistical modelling, compared with mathematical modelling and simulation methods.

## 11.7 Discussion

The aim of this review was to quantify and describe current levels of utilisation of modelling and simulation methods in health care, as reported in the mainstream academic literature. Ultimately, as part of the RIGHT project, this information will be used to develop an evidence-based 'model selection toolkit' to assist health-care professionals to choose an appropriate modelling approach to tackle a particular problem in a specific context. However, in a broader context, this study belongs to the family of healthcare modelling reviews described earlier, and extends and develops some of this earlier work.

The findings on publication dates show a steadily increasing rate of publication in this field, with simulation and qualitative (soft) methods in particular rising in popularity. However, straightforward simulation studies are generally less successful in gaining Research Council funding, compared with other more complex methodologies. This is likely to be because Research Councils are generally looking for innovative experimental approaches, rather than standard methodologies with a proven track record. This is understandable, given that their role is to encourage new theoretical developments, but it does support the argument that the academic literature may not be the best place to look for practical applications of simulation. However, we have shown that simulation studies are generally more successful in attracting commercial funding.

In general, when considering funding sources, the academic literature shows a huge contrast with the 'grey' literature, as only 4% of studies were funded by a health service organisation. It is clear that the modelling work that is undoubtedly being undertaken within the health sector by business consultancies or by analysts employed within healthcare organisations does not get written up for publication in academic journals.

The relationships between function and method suggest that certain business functions, such as finance, policy and regulation, are more likely to use statistical methods, arguably because these managers traditionally tend to have a more numerate background and are familiar with these approaches. On the other hand, simulation methods fare better in highly stochastic settings where the visual interface may be more important, such as resource utilisation and planning.

Overall levels of implementation are depressingly low and suggest that little has changed since previous review articles. Taylor *et al* (2009) report similar insights across the simulation modelling field, citing a lack of real-world involvement in published simulation modelling as a great, missed opportunity. Interestingly in our study, the implementation rates for statistical methods were particularly low. This may simply reflect the fact that such methods are very difficult for the lay person to understand, although they are of theoretical interest, so that a disproportionate number of statistical articles may get published in academic journals. This type of article often does not need a 'client' as such, as it may simply involve the application of some statistical method to secondary data derived from the literature. Conversely, qualitative approaches *require* a client as they cannot be used without interacting with human beings in some way. Therefore, it is less surprising that these methods report a comparatively high level of implementation.

When reflecting on the adopted methodology, a particular benefit of the approach was classifying the studies by more than one method that permitted co-associations to be explored. Likewise, there were benefits of allowing multiple functional areas that permitted examination of associations between functions and methods. A particular difficulty, however, was in constructing a viable taxonomy for all the methods. Eight categories were defined for this review but these are clearly open to debate. Having worked through the review process and resulting analyses, this is likely to assist in shaping future search criteria for bibliographic searches.

A key area of specific interest is the field of the so-called 'grey litera-ture'. It seems clear that many references to healthcare modelling exist outside the domain of conventional journal publications. Commercial and promotional literature, website references and unpublished pres-entations, for instance, contain much of interest in this field. The challenge is to find a viable means of accessing and referencing these sources, which by definition are not recorded in conventional biblio-graphic databases. Despite this we believe that 'grey literature' may be centrally important in revealing lessons to be learned from the imple-mentation of models in health care, an area that seems to be sorely absent in most of the research literature reviewed here.

In this review, the scope is limited to the specific area of OR type health-care modelling. This study begins to provide insights into the level of activity across many areas of application. It highlights impor-tant relationships and points to key areas of omission and neglect in the literature. Some of the key findings are summarised below:

- The vast majority of studies were carried out in North America and Europe.
- There is a preponderance of statistical approaches in the literature; however, simulation and qualitative modelling both currently appear to be enjoying a strong period of popularity, relative to earlier decades.
- Qualitative methods are commonly used as a secondary method and often as a subsidiary to simulation.
- Overall, an extraordinarily wide range of methods is revealed in the literature, and many of these methods are highly specific or bespoke to the project in question.
- Simulation methods are prominent in planning and system/resource utilisation.
- Statistical methods are prominent in the areas of finance, policy, governance and regulation.

- In general there are few obvious strong associations and the data are highly varied.
- Startlingly few studies report evidence of implementation, although a relatively large proportion do demonstrate a conceptualised model.

## 11.8   Conclusion

Clearly the literature in health-care simulation and modelling is vast and is expanding at a rapid rate. Moreover, this literature covers a very diverse range of applications with many interacting and overlapping areas. Added to this is the lack of standards and consistency in the use of key terms (for example, the use of the term 'model') between publications. The work of systematically reviewing and classifying the research literature in this area is therefore fraught with difficulties. Despite, and maybe *because* of this, there is great value in developing a viable taxonomy of the documented research. Such a framework provides a potential basis and structure for understanding the field as a whole.

The approach presented in this article provides a systematic and generic methodology that can be extended to review further areas of the literature as well as other types of information sources in health-care modelling and simulation. The field of Health Technology Assessment, for instance, is a fertile area of research in economic modeling, which could yield useful insights into the application of these techniques.

Given the multi-dimensional and relatively complex nature of this literature review, presentation is another important challenge. Here there is a role for visualisation tools (such as that presented by Citespace) to provide user-friendly, accessible means to graphically depict the key relationships in the analysis.

### Acknowledgements

We thank the anonymous referees for their very helpful comments. We are also grateful for the support of the Engineering and Physical Sciences Research Council (EPSRC) under grant EP/E019900/1, and for the support and input from the other members of the RIGHT team.

### References

Chen C (2004). Searching for intellectual turning points: Progressive knowledge domain visualization. *Proceedings of the National Academy of Sciences* **101**(1): pp 5303–5310.

Chen C (2006). CiteSpace II: Detecting and visualizing emerging trends and transient patterns in scientific literature. *J Am Soc Inf Sci Tec* **57**(3): 359–377.

Fone D *et al* (2003). Systematic review of the use and value of computer simulation modelling in population health and health care delivery. *J Public Health Med* **25**(4): 325–335.

Fries BE (1976). Bibliography of operations research in health-care systems. *Opns Res* **24**(5): 801–814.

Fries BE (1979). Bibliography of operations research in health-care systems: An update. *Opns Res* **27**(2): 408–419.

Jun JB, Jacobson SH and Swisher JR (1999). Application of discrete-event simulation in health care clinics: A survey. *J Opl Res Soc* **50**(2): 109–123.

Klein RW, Dittus RS, Roberts SD and Wilson JR (1993).Simulation modeling and health-care decision making. *Med Decis Making* **13**(4): 347.

Lehaney B, Clarke SA and Paul RJ (1999). A case of an intervention in an outpatients department. *J Opl Res Soc* **50**(9): 877–891.

Naseer A, Eldabi T and Young T (2009). RIGHT: A toolkit for selecting healthcare modelling methods. J Simulation, forthcoming.

Smith-Daniels VL, Schweikhart SB and Smith-Daniels DE (1988). Capacity management in health-care services—Review and future-research directions. *Decision Sci* **19**(4): 889–919.

Taylor SJE *et al* (2009). Simulation modelling is 50! Do we need a reality check? *J Opl Res Soc* **60**(S1): S69–S82.

Wilson JCT (1980). A review of population health care problems tackled by computer simulation. *Public Health* **94**: 174–182.

Wilson JCT (1981). Implementation of computer simulation projects in health care. *J Opl Res Soc* **32**(9): 825–832.

# 12

# Applications of Simulation within the Healthcare Context

*K. Katsaliaki[1] and N. Mustafee[2]*
[1] *International Hellenic University, Thessaloniki, Greece*
[2] *Swansea University, Swansea, Wales, UK*

*A large number of studies have applied simulation to a multitude of issues relating to healthcare. These studies have been published in a number of unrelated publishing outlets, which may hamper the widespread reference and use of such resources. In this paper, we analyse existing research in healthcare simulation in order to categorise and synthesise it in a meaningful manner. Hence, the aim of this paper is to conduct a review of the literature pertaining to simulation research within healthcare in order to ascertain its current development. A review of approximately 250 high-quality journal papers published between 1970 and 2007 on healthcare-related simulation research was conducted. The results present a classification of the healthcare publications according to the simulation techniques they employ; the impact of published literature in healthcare simulation; a report on demonstration and implementation of the studies' results; the sources of funding; and the software used. Healthcare planners and researchers will benefit from this study by having ready access to an indicative article collection of simulation techniques applied to healthcare problems that are clustered under meaningful headings. This study facilitates the understanding of the potential of different simulation techniques in solving diverse healthcare problems.*

## 12.1 Introduction

Healthcare needs grow and healthcare services become larger, more complex and costly (Eveborn *et al*, 2006; Wand, 2009). Moreover, the

Reprinted from *Journal of the Operational Research Society*, 62: 1431–1451, 2011, 'Applications of Simulation within the Healthcare Context', by K. Katsaliaki and N. Mustafee. With kind permission from Operational Research Society Ltd. All rights reserved.

intrinsic uncertainty of healthcare demands and outcomes dictates that healthcare policy and management should be based on the evidence of its potential to tackle these stochastic problems. It seems apparent that computer modelling should be valuable in providing evidence and insights in coping with these systems. They can be used to forecast the outcome of a change in strategy or predict and evaluate the implications of the implementation of an alternative policy (Wierzbicki, 2007). The use of modelling in healthcare is not limited to the management of activities necessary to deliver care alone. It is also used for the study of several topics related to healthcare, for example, air pollution, pharmacokinetics and food poisoning. In this paper, we aim at profiling studies that have designed, applied, described, analysed or evaluated healthcare problems with the use of simulation modelling.

Computer simulation is a decision support technique that allows stakeholders to conduct experiments with models that represent real-world systems of interest (Pidd, 2004). It can be used as an alternative to 'learning by doing' or empirical research (Royston, 1999). Furthermore, simulation modelling gives stakeholders the opportunity to participate in model development and, hopefully, gain a deeper understanding of the problems they face. As a result, decision makers and stakeholders can gain a new perspective on the relationships between the given parameters, the level of systems' performance, the cost-effectiveness and its quality, or risk association.

In the field of Operations Management, simulation is recognised as the second most widely used technique after 'Modelling' (Amoako-Gympah and Meredith, 1989; Pannirselvam *et al*, 1999). Thus far, there have been a number of reviews in the literature on the applications of simulation to health. Fone *et al* (2003) have conducted a systematic review of the use and value of computer simulation methods in population health and healthcare. Eldabi *et al* (2007) reviewed the application of a diverse range of simulation techniques in healthcare settings. Brennan and Akehurst (2000) and Barrios *et al* (2008) considered the application of simulation in the economic evaluation of health technologies and health products as well as a proposed method for the evaluation of pharmacoecomonic models (Hay, 2004). Dexter (1999) includes a review of computer simulation and patient appointment systems. A number of reviews have focused on the applications of Discrete-Event Simulation (DES) in healthcare in general (England and Roberts, 1978), and more specifically in health clinics (Jun *et al*, 1999) and healthcare capacity management (Smith-Daniels *et al*, 1988). Hollocks (2006) gives a personal review of the use of Discrete Event Simulation in health among other fields.

However, most reviews limit themselves to either a single application area or/and a single simulation technique. Most of the current reviews lack the breadth of simulation techniques, the width of applications coverage and are published in outlets of different fields (eg medical, OR, health informatics journals, etc), thus potentially hampering the widespread reference and use of such studies.

Hence, the purpose of this review is to fill these gaps and categorise and synthesise academic literature pertaining to the use of computer simulation in health problems (a) over a number of unrelated publishing outlets, (b) with a broader scope of simulation techniques and (c) in a variety of health applications. This would, in turn, help in ascertaining the current development in the field of healthcare simulation.

In light of the above, by sampling publications pertaining to the application of simulation in the healthcare domain, we hope to realise the following objectives: (1) to classify publications according to the simulation methods they employ; (2) to determine the healthcare problems often investigated by these methods and to analyse their trends; (3) to identify the impact of published simulation research in the healthcare context; (4) to monitor results' demonstration and implementation; (5) to identify funding sources for healthcare simulation studies; (6) to identify software associated with the studies and show their frequency of use. In order to achieve these objectives, we have conducted a review of 251 articles published during the period 1970–2007. The main objective of this review is to offer a broad and extensive picture of the role of simulation techniques in healthcare. To the best of our knowledge, objectives (1) and (2) have not been previously investigated in a single study for all four selected simulation techniques in the health sector, and objectives (3) to (6) have not been presented in a published source—with the exception of England and Roberts (1978) who presented similar results for Discrete Event Simulation and System Dynamics over 30 years ago. It is hoped that the findings of our analysis will be beneficial to the community of simulation and health-related academics and practitioners.

The remainder of this paper is structured as follows. The next section ('Simulation modelling') provides a discussion of the different simulation methods selected for this study. The methodology employed for the research is explained under the 'Research methodology' section. The section on 'Research paradigm' categorises the applications of simulation under various simulation techniques and healthcare problems— this fulfils objectives (1) and (2). This is followed by the 'Research impact' section (fulfils objective 3) that identifies some important papers that have been reviewed in our study and measures their impact through a citation-based analysis. The section on 'Results implementation, funding sources and analysis of simulation software' presents statistics pertaining to these variables, and thereby fulfils objectives (4), (5) and (6). The penultimate section presents a 'Discussion' of the findings of this study, and the paper concludes with 'Conclusions and further reflections' that outline the limitations of our approach and reflect on the contribution of this work.

## 12.2 Simulation modelling

The simulation modelling techniques that were found appropriate for the purposes of this study are Monte Carlo Simulation (MCS), Discrete-Event Simulation (DES), System Dynamics (SD) and Agent-Based Simulation (ABS). Journal papers included in this study have been selected based on the criteria that the papers report on the use of one or more of these simulation techniques in the healthcare settings. The choice of simulation techniques was made through interaction with experts in this area but was also backed by the review of Jahangirian *et al* (2009) of simulation in business and manufacturing. The latter identifies the following simulation techniques: DES, SD, ABS, MCS, Intelligent Simulation, Traffic Simulation, Distributed Simulation, Simulation Gaming, Petri-Nets and Virtual Simulation, excluding simulation for physical design. According to this study, the first five techniques were the most commonly presented/used in the selected papers for that review. Initially in our study, we also considered papers that reported on the use of Intelligent Simulation and Parallel & Distributed Simulation. However, these categories were later dropped owing to the fact that only a few relevant papers pertaining to the aforementioned categories were found in our sample study (one or two for each category). Moreover, our choice of simulation techniques is further supported by the study conducted by Fone *et al* (2003), wherein DES, SD and MCS are discussed as popular simulation techniques in healthcare. Those who wish to have an introduction to the aforementioned techniques can refer to Rubinstein (1981) for MCS, Robinson (1994) for DES, and Sterman (2001) for SD. ABS is the most recent of the four simulation methods used since the mid-1990s. A brief description of ABS is provided below.

ABS is a computational technique for modelling the actions and interactions of autonomous individuals (agents) in a network. The objective here is to assess the effects of these agents on the system as a whole (and 'not to' assess the effect of individual agents on the system). ABS is particularly appealing for modelling scenarios in which the consequences on the collective level are not obvious even when the assumptions on the individual level are very simple. This is so because ABS has the capability of generating complex properties emerging from the network of interactions among the agents, although the in-built rules of the individual agents' behaviour are quite simple.

## 12.3   Research methodology

In this paper, we have conducted a review of literature in healthcare simulation. Our review method has been influenced by the systematic literature review approach adopted by Eddama and Coast (2008), wherein (a) databases such as ISI Web of Science® and MedLine® were searched using a combination of search terms, (b) papers were screened by reading article titles and abstracts and in accordance to some inclusion criteria, and (c) the contents of the papers selected in the earlier stage were reviewed. Our literature profiling methodology consists of two stages and is illustrated in Figure 12.1. Stage 1 is the 'Paper Selection' stage and it describes the methodology used for the purpose of selecting papers for inclusion in this study. Stage 2 is the 'Information Capturing' stage and it identifies the information that is captured from papers that have been included in the study; the latter is analysed in the subsequent sections of this paper. Both the stages of our methodology are further described below.

The papers selected for this study were identified from the Web of Science® database The Web of Science® is one of the largest databases of quality academic journals and provides access to bibliographic information pertaining to research articles published from 1970 onwards. It indexes approximately 8500 high impact research journals from all around the world spread across approximately 200 different disciplines. Our aim was to identify publications with the highest credibility and thus we looked only at journal articles having an impact factor (note: only journals with an impact factor are included in the ISI Web of Science® database). We do recognise, however, that other bibliographic databases could have also been looked at. But for the purpose of this research, we decided to include only the Web of Science® database since this study is not a systematic review but is a sample review of publications in healthcare simulation.

The Web of Science® has a user-friendly search engine that assists in the refinement of a search by allowing the user to incorporate specific search conditions. Our search strategy was driven by the simulation methodology used in the sought after papers. To identify articles that

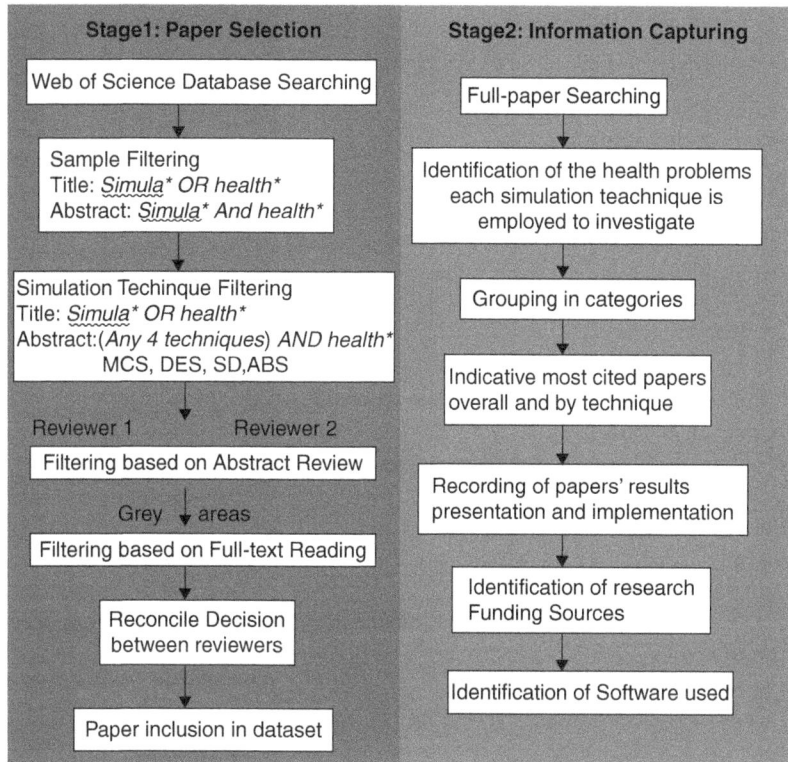

*Figure 12.1*   The literature profiling methodology

would be incorporated in our study's data set, the following criteria were used: inclusion of the words, *'simulat\*'* OR *'health\*'* in the article's title and both of the words/phrases (*'Monte SAME Carlo'* AND *'health\*'*) OR (*'Discrete SAME Event\*'* AND *'health\*'*) OR (*'System\* SAME Dynamics'* AND *'health\*'*) OR (*'Agent SAME Based'* AND *'health\*'*) in the abstract or keywords of the published paper. The SAME operator returns records in which the terms separated by the operator appear in the same sentence. The use of the asterisk, *'\*'* in the Boolean keywords combination, allowed for the inclusion of keyword derivatives in the search options. The search identified only articles and review papers written in the English language from 1970 until 2007 (inclusive). Results from this initial search strategy are shown in the second and third columns of Table 12.1. Sampling returned 251 papers in total.

Table 12.1   Number of identified and selected papers

| Simulation methods | Identified papers | Percentage | Selected papers | Percentage |
|---|---|---|---|---|
| Monte Carlo Simulation | 163 | 64.9 | 139 | 69.15 |
| Discrete-Event Simulation | 51 | 20.3 | 38 | 18.91 |
| System Dynamics | 31 | 12.4 | 17 | 8.46 |
| Agent-Based Simulation | 5 | 2.4 | 2 | 1.00 |
| Multiple Simulation | 0 | 0.0 | 5 | 2.49 |
| Sum | 251 | 100.0 | 201 | 100.00 |

The second step involved the screening of these papers. The two authors independently and critically reviewed all the abstracts of 251 papers' and read the full text when necessary. The appraisal was carried out based on certain inclusion criteria as follows: The selected papers should evidently demonstrate strong relation with the healthcare sector or have an impact on healthcare and use the chosen simulation method to describe, analyse or assess the situation. The paper should include at least one paragraph describing the applied simulation method that was used in the study. Thus, pure physics simulations and human systems simulations did not fulfil the inclusion criteria. The boundaries between health-related papers and non-health-related papers, were not always straightforward. In many papers the impact on human healthcare is provided by a less direct relationship. The reviewers took a flexible approach by including papers in which one could clearly relate the problem described with some kind of health impact. Each of the reviewers assessed all abstracts independently and compared the results were compared. In cases of discrepancies, the full text of the paper was examined and, after discussion between the reviewers, a decision was reached for the paper's inclusion or exclusion. This filtering resulted in a set of 201 relevant papers. The full text papers were collected via online or inter-library loan services.

The second stage concentrated on the content of the 201 papers in order to answer the six objectives of our study as identified in the introductory section. Of the selected papers, MCS seems by far to be (69%) the most applied method dealing with health issues. It is followed by DES and SD. Finally, the method with the least number of papers is ABS—this is not a surprise since it is the most recently developed simulation technique. Table 12.1 (last two columns) lists the results of our screening. The last row of the table ('multiple simulation methods') identifies five papers that use or mention two or more simulation techniques. These ('multiple simulation methods') papers, for simplicity purposes, are described under the research paradigms of the four identified categories as explained in the next section. As this is a sample review, no inferences can be drawn from Table 12.1 as to the impact of each simulation method in healthcare. Nonetheless, we believe that the statistics below provide the readers with some understanding of the research trends in this area.

## 12.4 Research paradigms

The papers that have been included in our review are listed in separate tables [Tables 12.3–12.6]. These tables are presented in the relevant subsections associated with each simulation technique in question. Every paper has a unique identifier beginning with the initials of the simulation method under which it is categorised (MC, DES, SD, ABS) and is suffixed with a numerical value, for example MC1, MC20, etc. When many papers are listed in a row under the same category, the prefix is entered only at the beginning and is omitted from the rest of the papers for brevity (eg MC11, 27, 81). In the tables, these papers are presented in a descending date of publication order, and this, in turn, shows the research effort over these 37 years. Thus, small numbers correspond to the most recent publications and large numbers to the older ones. The Vancouver reference style is followed. Rather than including the references alphabetically at the end of the paper, we consider this scheme of collecting and tabulating all references pertaining to a particular simulation technique together at the end of each section as important because we feel that it improves the readability of the paper. These tables will also serve as a future reference/study list for the reader.

The papers pertaining to the different simulation techniques have been categorised under several general headings/categories. An overview of these categories is presented in Table 12.2 (objective 1). This is followed by a discussion of the categories under each of the four identified simulation techniques (objective 2). Some papers can be categorised under multiple headings and the decision to favour one classification category over the other was based on the relative importance attributed to specific simulation techniques in the discussion part of the paper.

### 12.4.1  Monte Carlo Simulation

MCS is the most predominantly used simulation technique of the four identified techniques. Of the 163 reviewed papers in MCS, we found 142 to be suitable for inclusion in our dataset (Table 12.3).

In the context of healthcare, MCS has generally been used for the following purposes: (a) To assess health risks from exposure to certain

Table 12.2 Categories and number of papers in healthcare simulation per simulation technique

| | |
|---|---|
| *MCS* | **142** |
| (a) Health risk assessment (drug development–dose response, air–water–food–soil contamination) | 60 |
| (b) Prognostic and transmission models of health interventions (disease transmission stages, regression and robustness models) | 18 |
| (c) Cost-benefit analysis and policy evaluation of medical treatment and disease management (population-based screen-and-treat strategy) | 41 |
| (d) Miscellaneous (literature reviews and taxonomies, health surveys and service delivery) | 23 |
| *DES* | **40** |
| (a) Planning of healthcare services (hospitals, A & E departments, Scheduling health staff–patient admissions/appointments–ambulances, bed and equipment capacity, health information systems, organ transplantation, locations of healthcare services and facilities design) | 13 |
| (b) Health economic models (cost of providing healthcare, alternative healthcare interventions, screening strategies, cost-effectiveness of ordering and distribution policies) | 10 |
| (c) Reviews and methodology papers (comparison and evaluation of modelling techniques) | 13 |
| (d) Contagious disease interventions (control the spread of diseases/epidemics, plan emergency clinics) | 4 |
| *SD* | **17** |
| (a) Public health policy evaluation and economic models (harm reduction policies, treating strategies, long-term health impact, disease population dynamics, reconfiguration of health services, health insurance strategies) | 9 |
| (b) Modelling healthcare systems and infrastructure (Unscheduled care, A & E demand pattern, resource deployment, parallel hospital processes, health infrastructure disruptions and disasters) | 4 |
| (c) Training (health policymakers–understanding the dynamics of diseases, students experimentation with pharmacological systems) | 3 |
| (d) Review | 1 |
| *ABS* | 2 |
| (Interactions of cancer hallmarks and therapies, health data confidentiality) | |

elements and determine drug dose-response portions; this is the most popular sub-category with 60 papers in our sample; (b) as the main approach to modelling used in economic evaluations in healthcare interventions when there is a need to increase the number of states in the model to overcome the homogeneity assumptions inherent in

*Table 12.3* MCS papers included in the present study

| S No. | MC paper |
| --- | --- |
| 1 | Piatt JH, Cosgriff M. Monte Carlo simulation of cerebrospinal fluid shunt failure and definition of instability among shunt-treated patients with hydrocephalus. *J. Neurosurg.* 2007 DEC; 107(6): 474–478. |
| 2 | Mannan HR, Kuiman M, Hobbs M. A Markov simulation model for analyzing and forecasting the number of coronary artery revascularization procedures in Western Australia. *Ann. Epidemiol.* 2007 DEC; 17(12): 964–975. |
| 3 | Lee D, Shaddick G. Time-varying coefficient models for the analysis of air pollution and health outcome data. *Biometrics* 2007 DEC; 63(4): 1253–1261. |
| 4 | Fabre MA, Fuseau E, Ficheux H. Selection of dosing regimen with WST11 by Monte Carlo simulations, using PK data collected after single IV administration in healthy subjects and population PK Modelling. *J. Pharm. Sci.* 2007 DEC; 96(12): 3444–3456. |
| 5 | Antonijevic B, Matthys C, Sioen I, Bilau M, Van Camp J, Willems JL, *et al.* Simulated impact of a fish based shift in the population n-3 fatty acids intake on exposure to dioxins and dioxin-like compounds. *Food and Chemical Toxicology* 2007 NOV; 45(11): 2279–2286. |
| 6 | Schadlich PK, Schmidt-Lucke C, Huppertz E, Lehmacher W, Nixdorff U, Stellbrink C, *et al.* Economic evaluation of Enoxaparin for anticoagulation in early Cardioversion of persisting nonvalvular atrial fibrillation: A statutory health insurance perspective from Germany. *American Journal of Cardiovascular Drugs* 2007; 7(3): 199–217. |
| 7 | Huang ES, Zhang Q, Brown SES, Drum ML, Meltzer DO, Chin MH. The cost-effectiveness of improving diabetes care in US Federally qualified community health centers. *Health Serv. Res.* 2007 DEC; 42(6): 2174–2193. |
| 8 | O'Hagan A, Stevenson M, Madan J. Monte Carlo probabilistic sensitivity analysis for patient level simulation models: Efficient estimation of mean and variance using ANOVA. *Health Econ.* 2007 OCT; 16(10): 1009–1023. |
| 9 | Schwenkglenks M, Lippuner K. Simulation-based cost-utility analysis of population screening-based alendronate use in Switzerland. *Osteoporosis Int.* 2007 NOV; 18(11): 1481–1491. |
| 10 | Djohan D, Yu J, Connell D, Christensen E. Health risk assessment of chlorobenzenes in the air of residential houses using probabilistic techniques. *Journal of Toxicology and Environmental Health-Part A-Current Issues* 2007; 70(19): 1594–1603. |
| 11 | Peeler EJ, Murray AG, Thebault A, Brun E, Giovaninni A, Thrush MA. The application of risk analysis in aquatic animal health management. *Prev. Vet. Med.* 2007 SEP 14; 81(1–3): 3–20. |
| 12 | Gerkens S, Nechelput M, Annemans L, Peraux B, Mouchart M, Beguin C, *et al.* A health economic model to assess the cost-effectiveness of PEG IFN alpha-2a and ribavirin in patients with mild chronic hepatitis C. *J. Viral Hepat.* 2007 AUG; 14(8): 523–536. |
| 13 | Straver JM, Janssen AFW, Linnemann AR, van Boekel MAJS, Beumer RR, Zwietering MH. Number of *Salmonella* on chicken breast filet at retail level and its implications for public health risk. *J. Food Prot.* 2007 SEP; 70(9): 2045–2055. |

*(continued)*

262

*Table 12.3* Continued

| S No. | MC paper |
|-------|----------|
| 14 | Vinks AA, van Rossem RN, Mathot RAA, Heijerman HGM, Mouton JW. Pharmacokinetics of aztreonam in healthy subjects and patients with cystic fibrosis and evaluation of dose-exposure relationships using Monte Carlo simulation. *Antimicrob. Agents Chemother.* 2007 SEP; 51(9): 3049–3055. |
| 15 | Gerkens S, Nechelput M, Annemans L, Peraux B, Beguin C, Horsmans Y. A health economic model to assess the cost-effectiveness of pegylated interferon alpha-2a and ribavirin in patients with moderate chronic hepatitis C and persistently normal alanine aminotransferase levels. *Acta Gastroenterol. Belg.* 2007 APR-JUN; 70(2): 177–187. |
| 16 | Santori G, Valente R, Andorno E, Ghirelli R, Valente U. Application of a Bayesian simulation model to a database for split liver transplantation on two adult recipients in the environment of WinBUGS (Bayesian inference Using Gibbs Sampling). *Transplant. Proc.* 2007 JUL–AUG; 39(6): 1918–1920. |
| 17 | Burgess DS, Hall RG. Simulated comparison of the pharmacodynamics of ciprofloxacin and levofloxacin against *Pseudomonas aeruginosa* using pharmacokinetic data from healthy volunteers and 2002 minimum inhibitory concentration data. *Clin. Ther.* 2007 JUL; 29(7): 1421–1427. |
| 18 | Lawson AB, Williams FLR, Liu Y. Some simple tests for spatial effects around putative sources of health risk. *Biometrical Journal* 2007 AUG; 49(4): 493–504. |
| 19 | Bulitta JB, Duffull SB, Kinzig-Schippers M, Holzgrabe U, Stephan U, Drusano GL, *et al.* Systematic comparison of the population pharmacokinetics and pharmacodynamics of piperacillin in cystic fibrosis patients and healthy volunteers. *Antimicrob. Agents Chemother.* 2007 JUL; 51(7): 2497–2507. |
| 20 | Lonati G, Cernuschi S, Giugliano M, Grosso M. Health risk analysis of PCDD. *Chemosphere* 2007 APR; 67(9): S334–S343. |
| 21 | Mara DD, Sleigh PA, Blumenthal UJ, Carr RM. Health risks in wastewater irrigation: Comparing estimates from quantitative microbial risk analyses and epidemiological studies. *Journal of Water and Health* 2007 MAR; 5(1): 39–50. |
| 22 | Sparrow JM. Monte-Carlo simulation of random clustering of endophthalmitis following cataract surgery. *Eye* 2007 FEB; 21(2): 209–213. |
| 23 | Kahn JM, Kramer AA, Rubenfeld GD. Transferring critically ill patients out of hospital improves the standardized mortality ratio—A simulation study. *Chest* 2007 JAN; 131(1): 68–75. |
| 24 | Lamotte M, Annemans L, Kawalec P, Zoellner Y. A multi-country health-economic evaluation of highly concentrated n-3 polyunsaturated fatty acids in the secondary prevention after myocardial infarction. *Herz* 2006 DEC; 31: 74–82. |
| 25 | Roze S, Liens D, Palmer A, Berger W, Tucker D, Renaudin C. A health economic model to determine the long-term costs and clinical outcomes of raising low HDL-cholesterol in the prevention of coronary heart disease. *Curr. Med. Res. Opin.* 2006 DEC; 22(12): 2549–2556. |

(*continued*)

*Table 12.3* Continued

| S No. | MC paper |
|---|---|
| 26 | Mestl HES, Aunan K, Seip HM. Potential health benefit of reducing household solid fuel use in Shanxi province, China. *Sci. Total Environ.* 2006 DEC 15; 372(1): 120–132. |
| 27 | Nieuwenhuijsen M, Paustenbach D, Duarte-Davidson R. New developments in exposure assessment: The impact on the practice of health risk assessment and epidemiological studies. *Environ. Int.* 2006 DEC; 32(8): 996–1009. |
| 28 | Deb P, Munkin MK, Trivedi PK. Private insurance, selection, and health care use: A Bayesian analysis of a Roy-type model. *Journal of Business & Economic Statistics* 2006 OCT; 24(4): 403–415. |
| 29 | Mudra R, Nadler A, Keller E, Niederer P. Analysis of near-infrared spectroscopy and indocyanine green dye dilution with Monte Carlo simulation of light propagation in the adult brain. *J. Biomed. Opt.* 2006 JUL–AUG; 11(4): 044009. |
| 30 | Feveile H, Mikkelsen KL, Hannerz H, Olsen O. Quantifying inequality in health in the absence of a natural reference group. *Sci. Total Environ.* 2006 AUG 15; 367(1): 112–122. |
| 31 | Sprandel KA, Drusano GL, Hecht DW, Rotschafer JC, Danziger LH, Rodvold KA. Population pharmacokinetic Modelling and Monte Carlo simulation of varying doses of intravenous metronidazole. *Diagn. Microbiol. Infect. Dis.* 2006 AUG; 55(4): 303–309. |
| 32 | Kleinschmidt I, Ramkissoon A, Morris N, Mabude Z, Curtis B, Beksinska M. Mapping indicators of sexually transmitted infection services in the South African public health sector. *Tropical Medicine & International Health* 2006 JUL; 11(7): 1047–1057. |
| 33 | Flampouri S, Jiang SB, Sharp GC, Wolfgang J, Patel AA, Choi NC. Estimation of the delivered patient dose in lung IMRT treatment based on deformable registration of 4D-CT data and Monte Carlo simulations. *Phys. Med. Biol.* 2006 JUN 7; 51(11): 2763–2779. |
| 34 | Chien LC, Han BC, Hsu CS, Jiang CB, You HJ, Shieh MJ, *et al.* Analysis of the health risk of exposure to breast milk mercury in infants in Taiwan. *Chemosphere* 2006 JUN; 64(1): 79–85. |
| 35 | Riedel O. Unisex tariffs in health insurance. *Geneva Papers on Risk and Insurance-Issues and Practice* 2006 APR; 31(2): 233–244. |
| 36 | Langenderfer JE, Carpenter JE, Johnson ME, An KN, Hughes RE. A probabilistic model of glenohumeral external rotation strength for healthy normals and rotator cuff tear cases. *Ann. Biomed. Eng.* 2006 MAR; 34(3): 465–476. |
| 37 | Van Howe RS, Kusnier LP. Diagnosis and management of pharyngitis in a pediatric population based on cost-effectiveness and projected health outcomes. *Pediatrics* 2006 MAR; 117(3): 609–619. |
| 38 | Schoen EJ, Colby CJ, To TT. Cost analysis of neonatal circumcision in a large health maintenance organization. *J. Urol.* 2006 MAR; 175(3): 1111–1115. |
| 39 | Veerman JL, Barendregt JJ, Mackenbach JP. The European Common Agricultural Policy on fruits and vegetables: exploring potential health gain from reform. *Eur. J. Public Health* 2006 FEB; 16(1): 31–35. |

(*continued*)

264

*Table 12.3* Continued

| S No. | MC paper |
|---|---|
| 40 | Hincks TK, Aspinall WP, Baxter PJ, Searl A, Sparks RSJ, Woo G. Long term exposure to respirable volcanic ash on Montserrat: a time series simulation. *Bulletin of Volcanology* 2006 JAN; 68(3): 266–284. |
| 41 | Whited JD, Datta SK, Aiello LM, Aiello LP, Cavallerano JD, Conlin PR, *et al.* A modeled economic analysis of a digital teleophthalmology system as used by three federal healthcare agencies for detecting proliferative diabetic retinopathy. *Telemedicine Journal and E-Health* 2005 DEC; 11(6): 641–651. |
| 42 | Gudowska I, Sobolevsky N. Simulation of secondary particle production and absorbed dose to tissue in light ion beams. *Radiat. Prot. Dosimet.* 2005 DEC 20; 116(1–4): 301–306. |
| 43 | Chen Y, Bielajew AF, Litzenberg DW, Moran JM, Becchetti FD. Magnetic confinement of electron and photon radiotherapy dose: A Monte Carlo simulation with a nonuniform longitudinal magnetic field. *Med. Phys.* 2005 DEC; 32(12): 3810–3818. |
| 44 | Postma MJ, Jansema P, Scheijbeler HWKFH, van Genugten MLL. Scenarios on costs and savings of influenza treatment and prevention for Dutch healthy working adults. *Vaccine* 2005 NOV 16; 23(46–47): 5365–5371. |
| 45 | Zhou H, IsamanDJM, Messinger S, Brown MB, Klein R, Brandle M, *et al.* A computer simulation model of diabetes progression, quality of life, and cost. *Diabetes Care* 2005 DEC; 28(12): 2856–2863. |
| 46 | Zarkin GA, Dunlap LJ, Hicks KA, Mamo D. Benefits and costs of methadone treatment: results from a lifetime simulation model. *Health Econ.* 2005 NOV; 14(11): 1133–1150. |
| 47 | Wei HJ, Xing D, Wu GY, Gu HM, Lu FJ, Jin Y, *et al.* Differences in optical properties between healthy and pathological human colon tissues using a Ti: sapphire laser: an in vitro study using the Monte Carlo inversion technique. *J. Biomed. Opt.* 2005 JUL–AUG; 10(4): 044022. |
| 48 | Jackson BR, Thomas A, Carroll KC, Adler FR, Samore MH. Use of strain typing data to estimate bacterial transmission rates in healthcare settings. *Infection Control and Hospital Epidemiology* 2005 JUL; 26(7): 638–645. |
| 49 | Xu M, Garbuz DS, Kuramoto L, Sobolev B. Classifying health-related quality of life outcomes of total hip arthroplasty. *BMC Musculoskeletal Disorders* 2005 SEP 6; 6: 48. |
| 50 | Roze S, Valentine WJ, Zakrzewska KE, Palmer AJ. Health-economic comparison of continuous subcutaneous insulin infusion with multiple daily injection for the treatment of Type 1 diabetes in the UK. *Diabetic Med.* 2005 SEP; 22(9): 1239–1245. |
| 51 | Yang Y, Tao S, Wong PK, Hu JY, Guo M, Cao HY, *et al.* Human exposure and health risk of alpha-, beta-, gamma- and delta-hexachlorocyclohexane in Tianjin, China. *Chemosphere* 2005 AUG; 60(6): 753–761. |
| 52 | Mouton JW, Punt N, Vinks AA. A retrospective analysis using Monte Carlo simulation to evaluate recommended ceftazidime dosing regimens in healthy volunteers, patients with cystic fibrosis, and patients in the intensive care unit. *Clin. Ther.* 2005 JUN; 27(6): 762–772. |

(*continued*)

*Table 12.3* Continued

| S No. | MC paper |
|---|---|
| 53 | Kuti JL, Horowitz S, Nightingale CH, Nicolau DP. Comparison of pharmacodynamic target attainment between healthy subjects and patients for ceftazidime and meropenem. *Pharmacotherapy* 2005 JUL; 25(7): 935–941. |
| 54 | Krueger WA, Bulitta J, Kinzig-Schippers M, Landersdorfer C, Holzgrabe U, Naber KG, *et al.* Evaluation by Monte Carlo simulation of the pharmacokinetics of two doses of meropenem administered intermittently or as a continuous infusion in healthy volunteers. *Antimicrob. Agents Chemother.* 2005 MAY; 49(5): 1881–1889. |
| 55 | Gower SK, McColl S. Development of the PEARLS model and use of Monte Carlo simulation to predict internal exposure to PM2.5 in Toronto. *Risk Analysis* 2005 APR; 25(2): 301–315. |
| 56 | Shih TW, Chou CC, Morley RS. Monte Carlo simulation of animal-product violations incurred by air passengers at an international airport in Taiwan. *Prev. Vet. Med.* 2005 MAY 10; 68(2–4): 115–122. |
| 57 | Russek-Cohen E, Martinez MN, Nevius AB. A SAS/IML program for simulating pharmacokinetic data. *Comput. Methods Programs Biomed.* 2005 APR; 78(1): 39–60. |
| 58 | Shechter SM, Bryce CL, Alagoz O, Kreke JE, Stahl JE, Schaefer AJ, *et al.* A clinically based discrete-event simulation of end-stage liver disease and the organ allocation process. *Medical Decision Making* 2005 MAR–APR; 25(2): 199–209. |
| 59 | Patten SB. An analysis of data from two general health surveys found that increased incidence and duration contributed to elevated prevalence of major depression in persons with chronic medical conditions. *J. Clin. Epidemiol.* 2005 FEB; 58(2): 184–189. |
| 60 | Rolka H, Bracy D, Russel C, Fram D, Ball R. Using simulation to assess the sensitivity and specificity of a signal detection tool for multidimensional public health surveillance data. *Stat. Med.* 2005 FEB 28; 24(4): 551–562. |
| 61 | Holm MV, Gyldmark M, Hansen EH. Pharmacoeconomic assessment of oseltamivir in treating influenza—the case of otherwise healthy Danish adolescents and adults. *Pharmacy World & Science* 2004 DEC; 26(6): 339–345. |
| 62 | Chowdhury S, Husain T, Veitch B, Bose N, Sadiq R. Human health risk assessment of naturally occurring radioactive materials in produced water—A case study. *Hum. Ecol. Risk Assess.* 2004 DEC; 10(6): 1155–1171. |
| 63 | Gagnon YM, Levy AR, Iloeje UH, Briggs AH. Treatment costs in Canada of health conditions resulting from chronic hepatitis B infection. *J. Clin. Epidemiol.* 2004 AUG; 38(S10): S179–86. |
| 64 | Lynd LD, O'Brien BJ. Advances in risk-benefit evaluation using probabilistic simulation methods: an application to the prophylaxis of deep vein thrombosis. *J. Clin. Epidemiol.* 2004 AUG; 57(8): 795–803. |
| 65 | Palmer AJ, Rodby RA. Health economics studies assessing irbesartan use in patients with hypertension, type 2 diabetes, and microalbuminuria. *Kidney Int.* 2004 NOV; 66: S118–S120. |

(*continued*)

*Table 12.3* Continued

| S No. | MC paper |
|---|---|
| 66 | Jochmann M, Leon-Gonzalez R. Estimating the demand for health care with panel data: a semiparametric Bayesian approach. *Health Econ.* 2004 OCT; 13(10): 1003–1014. |
| 67 | Duggan DM. Improved radial dose function estimation using current version MCNP Monte-Carlo simulation: Model 6711 and ISC3500(125) I brachytherapy sources. *Applied Radiation and Isotopes* 2004 DEC; 61(6): 1443–1450. |
| 68 | van Alem AP, Dijkgraaf MGW, Tijssen JGP, Koster RW. Health system costs of out-of-hospital cardiac arrest in relation to time to shock. *Circulation* 2004 OCT 5; 110(14): 1967–1973. |
| 69 | Nuijten MJC. Incorporation of statistical uncertainty in health economic modelling studies using second-order Monte Carlo simulations. *Pharmacoeconomics* 2004; 22(12): 759–769. |
| 70 | Haby MM, Carter R, Mihalopoulos C, Magnus A, Sanderson K, Andrews G, *et al.* Assessing cost-effectiveness—Mental health: introduction to the study and methods. *Aust. N. Z. J. Psychiatry* 2004 AUG; 38(8): 569–578. |
| 71 | Bonate PL, Floret S, Bentzen C. Population pharmacokinetics of APOMINE (TM): A meta-analysis in cancer patients and healthy males. *Br. J. Clin. Pharmacol.* 2004 AUG; 58(2): 142–155. |
| 72 | Ong MK, Glantz SA. Cardiovascular health and economic effects of smoke-free workplaces. *Am. J. Med.* 2004 JUL 1; 117(1): 32–38. |
| 73 | Sonnenberg FA, Burkman RT, Hagerty CG, Speroff L, Speroff T. Costs and net health effects of contraceptive methods. *Contraception* 2004 JUN; 69(6): 447–459. |
| 74 | Borsuk ME. Predictive assessment of fish health and fish kills in the Neuse River Estuary using elicited expert judgment. *Hum. Ecol. Risk Assess.* 2004 APR; 10(2): 415–434. |
| 75 | Stott SL, Irimia D, Karlsson JM. Parametric analysis of intercellular ice propagation during cryosurgery, simulated using Monte Carlo techniques. *Technology in Cancer Research & Treatment* 2004 APR; 3(2): 113–123. |
| 76 | Pouillot R, Beaudeau P, Denis JB, Derouin F, AFSSA Cryptosporidium Study Grp. A quantitative risk assessment of waterborne cryptosporidiosis in France using second-order Monte Carlo simulation. *Risk Analysis* 2004 FEB; 24(1): 1–17. |
| 77 | Cox LA, Popken DA. Quantifying human health risks from virginiamycin used inchickens. *Risk Analysis* 2004 FEB; 24(1): 271–288. |
| 78 | Stuart B, Singhal PK, Magder LS, Zuckerman IH. How robust are health plan quality indicators to data loss? A Monte Carlo simulation study of pediatric asthma treatment. *Health Serv. Res.* 2003 DEC; 38(6): 1547–1561. |
| 79 | Sanhueza PA, Reed GD, Davis WT, Miller TL. An environmental decision-making tool for evaluating ground-level ozone-related health effects. *J. Air Waste Manage. Assoc.* 2003 DEC; 53(12): 1448–1459. |
| 80 | Kuti JL, Dandekar PK, Nightingale CH, Nicolau DP. Use of Monte Carlo simulation to design an optimized pharmacodynamic dosing strategy for meropenem. *J. Clin. Pharmacol.* 2003 OCT; 43(10): 1116–1123. |

(*continued*)

*Table 12.3* Continued

| S No. | MC paper |
|-------|----------|
| 81 | Rushton G. Public health, GIS, and spatial analytic tools. *Annu. Rev. Public Health* 2003; 24: 43–56. |
| 82 | Romeu A, Balasch J, Balda JAR, Barri PN, Daya S, Auray JP, *et al*. Cost-effectiveness of recombinant versus urinary follicle-stimulating hormone in assisted reproduction techniques in the Spanish public health care system. *J. Assist. Reprod. Genet.* 2003 AUG; 20(8): 294–300. |
| 83 | Nichol KL, Mallon KP, Mendelman PM. Cost benefit of influenza vaccination in healthy, working adults: an economic analysis based on the results of a clinical trial of trivalent live attenuated influenza virus vaccine. *Vaccine* 2003 MAY 16; 21(17–18): 2207–2217. |
| 84 | Munkin MK, Trivedi PK. Bayesian analysis of a self-selection model with multiple outcomes using simulation-based estimation: an application to the demand for healthcare. *J. Econ.* 2003 JUN; 114(2): 197–220. |
| 85 | Hahl J, Simell T, Kupila A, Keskinen P, Knip M, Ilonen J, *et al*. A simulation model for estimating direct costs of type 1 diabetes prevention. *Pharmacoeconomics* 2003; 21(5): 295–303. |
| 86 | Carlsson F, Martinsson P. Design techniques for stated preference methods in health economics. *Health Econ.* 2003 APR; 12(4): 281–294. |
| 87 | O'Brien BJ, Goeree R, Blackhouse G, Smieja M, Loeb M. Oseltarnivir for treatment of influenza in healthy adults: Pooled trial evidence and cost-effectiveness model for Canada. *Value in Health* 2003 MAR–APR; 6(2): 116–125. |
| 88 | Chabaud S, Girard P, Nony P, Boissel JP, THERMOS Grp. Clinical trial simulation using therapeutic effect Modelling: Application to ivabradine efficacy in patients with angina pectoris. *Journal of Pharmacokinetics and Pharmacodynamics* 2002 AUG; 29(4): 339–363. |
| 89 | Vichiendilokkul A. Breaking out of the silo: One health system's experience. *American Journal of Health-System Pharmacy* 2002 OCT 15; 59: S15–S17. |
| 90 | Dobrev ID, Andersen ME, Yang RSH. In silico toxicology: Simulating interaction thresholds for human exposure to mixtures of trichloroethylene, tetrachloroethylene, and 1,1,1-trichloroethane. *Environ. Health Perspect.* 2002 OCT; 110(10): 1031–1039. |
| 91 | McCleese DL, LaPuma PT. Using Monte Carlo simulation in life cycle assessment for electric and internal combustion vehicles. *International Journal of Life Cycle Assessment* 2002; 7(4): 230–236. |
| 92 | Nichol KL, Goodman M. Cost effectiveness of influenza vaccination for healthy persons between ages 65 and 74 years. *Vaccine* 2002 MAY 15; 20: S21–S24. |
| 93 | Sadiq R, Husain T, Kar S. Chloroform associated health risk assessment using bootstrapping: A case study for limited drinking water samples. *Water Air and Soil Pollution* 2002 JUL; 138(1-4): 123–140. |
| 94 | Richter A, Hauber B, Simpson K, Mauskopf JA, YinDP. A Monte Carlo simulation for modelling outcomes of AIDS treatment regimens. *Pharmacoeconomics* 2002; 20(4): 215–224. |

(*continued*)

268

*Table 12.3* Continued

| S No. | MC paper |
|---|---|
| 95 | Lee LJH, Chan CC, Chung CW, Ma YC, Wang GS, Wang JD. Health risk assessment on residents exposed to chlorinated hydrocarbons contaminated in groundwater of a hazardous waste site. *Journal of Toxicology and Environmental Health-Part A* 2002 FEB; 65(3–4): 219–235. |
| 96 | Emery S, Ake CF, Navarro AM, Kaplan RM. Simulated effect of tobacco tax variation on Latino health in California. *Am. J. Prev. Med.* 2001 NOV; 21(4): 278–283. |
| 97 | Chan TL, Dong G, Cheung CS, Leung CW, Wong CP, Hung WT. Monte Carlo simulation of nitrogen oxides dispersion from a vehicular exhaust plume and its sensitivity studies. *Atmos. Environ.* 2001 DEC; 35(35): 6117–6127. |
| 98 | Chen Z, Huang GH, Chakma A. Simulation and assessment of subsurface contamination caused by spill and leakage of petroleum products—A multiphase, multicomponent modelling approach. *J Can Pet Technol* 2001 SEP; 40(9): 43–49. |
| 99 | Pereira A. Health and economic consequences of HCV lookback. *Transfusion* 2001 JUN; 41(6): 832–839. |
| 100 | Wilson ND, Price PS, Paustenbach DJ. An event-by-event probabilistic methodology for assessing the health risks of persistent chemicals in fish: A case study at the Palos Verdes Shelf. *Journal of Toxicology and Environmental Health-Part A* 2001 APR 20; 62(8): 595–642. |
| 101 | Nichol KL. Cost-benefit analysis of a strategy to vaccinate healthy working adults against influenza. *Arch. Intern. Med.* 2001 MAR 12; 161(5): 749–759. |
| 102 | Thornburg J, Ensor DS, Rodes CE, Lawless PA, Sparks LE, Mosley RB. Penetration of particles into buildings and associated physical factors. Part I: Model development and computer simulations. *Aerosol Science and Technology* 2001 MAR; 34(3): 284–296. |
| 103 | Warila J, Batterman S, Passino-Reader DR. A probabilistic model for silver bioaccumulation in aquatic systems and assessment of human health risks. *Environmental Toxicology and Chemistry* 2001 FEB; 20(2): 432–441. |
| 104 | Silcocks PBS, Jenner DA, Reza R. Life expectancy as a summary of mortality in a population: statistical considerations and suitability for use by health authorities. *J. Epidemiol. Community Health* 2001 JAN; 55(1): 38–43. |
| 105 | Austin PC, Escobar M, Kopec JA. The use of the Tobit model for analyzing measures of health status. *Quality of Life Research* 2000; 9(8): 901–910. |
| 106 | Ambrose PG, Grasela DM. The use of Monte Carlo simulation to examine pharmacodynamic variance of drugs: fluoroquinolone pharmacodynamics against *Streptococcus pneumoniae*. *Diagn. Microbiol. Infect. Dis.* 2000 NOV; 38(3): 151–157. |
| 107 | Draper D, Fouskakis D. A case study of stochastic optimization in health policy: Problem formulation and preliminary results. *J. Global Optimiz.* 2000 DEC; 18(4): 399–416. |

*(continued)*

*Table 12.3* Continued

| S No. | MC paper |
|-------|----------|
| 108 | Pereira A, Sanz C. A model of the health and economic impact of post-transfusion hepatitis C: application to cost-effectiveness analysis of further expansion of HCV screening protocols. *Transfusion* 2000 OCT; 40(10): 1182–1191. |
| 109 | Scheid DC, Hamm RM, Stevens KW. Cost effectiveness of human immunodeficiency virus postexposure prophylaxis for healthcare workers. *Pharmacoeconomics* 2000 OCT; 18(4): 355–368. |
| 110 | Taibi A, Royle GJ, Speller RD. A Monte Carlo simulation study to investigate the potential of diffraction enhanced breast imaging. *IEEE Trans. Nucl. Sci.* 2000 AUG; 47(4): 1581–1586. |
| 111 | Ostergaard S, Sorensen JT, Kristensen AR. A stochastic model simulating the feeding-health-production complex in a dairy herd. *J. Dairy Sci.* 2000 APR; 83(4): 721–733. |
| 112 | Veugelers PJ, Kim AL, Guernsey JR. Inequalities in health. Analytic approaches based on life expectancy and suitable for small area comparisons. *J. Epidemiol. Community Health* 2000 MAY; 54(5): 375–380. |
| 113 | Gates P, Johansson K, Danell B. 'Quasi-REML' correlation estimates between production and health traits in the presence of selection and confounding: A simulation study. *J. Anim. Sci.* 1999 MAR; 77(3): 558–568. |
| 114 | Boudet C, Zmirou D, Laffond M, Balducci F, Benoit-Guyod JL. Health risk assessment of a modern municipal waste incinerator. *Risk Analysis* 1999 DEC; 19(6): 1215–1222. |
| 115 | Briggs AH, Mooney CZ, Wonderling DE. Constructing confidence intervals for cost-effectiveness ratios: An evaluation of parametric and non-parametric techniques using Monte Carlo simulation. *Stat. Med.* 1999 DEC 15; 18(23): 3245–3262. |
| 116 | Olivieri A, Eisenberg D, Soller J, Eisenberg J, Cooper R, Tchobanoglous G, *et al.* Estimation of pathogen removal in an advanced water treatment facility using Monte Carlo simulation. *Water Science and Technology* 1999; 40(4–5): 223–233. |
| 117 | Zmirou D, Deloraine A, Balducci F, Boudet C, Dechenaux J. Health effects costs of particulate air pollution. *Journal of Occupational and Environmental Medicine* 1999 OCT; 41(10): 847–856. |
| 118 | Jordan D, McEwen SA, Lammerding AM, McNab WB, Wilson JB. A simulation model for studying the role of pre-slaughter factors on the exposure of beef carcasses to human microbial hazards. *Prev. Vet. Med.* 1999 JUN 29; 41(1): 37–54. |
| 119 | Hamed MM. Probabilistic sensitivity analysis of public health risk assessment from contaminated soil. *J. Soil Contam.* 1999 MAY; 8(3): 285–306. |
| 120 | Crijns H, Casparie AF, Hendrikse F. Continuous computer simulation analysis of the cost-effectiveness of screening and treating diabetic retinopathy. *Int. J. Technol. Assess. Health Care* 1999 WIN; 15(1): 198–206. |
| 121 | Sumner W, Truszczynski M, Marek VW. Simulating patients with parallel health state networks. *Journal of the American Medical Informatics Association* 1998: 438–442. |

(*continued*)

270

*Table 12.3* Continued

| S No. | MC paper |
|---|---|
| 122 | Cassin MH, Paoli GM, Lammerding AM. Simulation Modelling for microbial risk assessment. *J. Food Prot.* 1998 NOV; 61(11): 1560–1566. |
| 123 | Jacobson SH, Morrice DJ. A mathematical model for assessing the temporal association between health disorders and medical treatments. *Journal of Statistical Planning and Inference* 1998 AUG 1; 71(1–2): 209–228. |
| 124 | Katsumata PT, Kastenberg WE. On the assessment of the maximally exposed individual at superfund sites using Monte Carlo simulations. *Journal of Environmental Science and Health Part A—Toxic/hazardous Substances & Environmental Engineering* 1998; 33(6): 951–985. |
| 125 | Marseguerra M, Zio E. Contaminant transport in bidimensional porous media via biased Monte Carlo simulation. *Ann. Nucl. Energy* 1998 NOV; 25(16): 1301–1316. |
| 126 | Allan M, Richardson GM. Probability density functions describing 24-hour inhalation rates for use in human health risk assessments. *Hum. Ecol. Risk Assess.* 1998 APR; 4(2): 379–408. |
| 127 | Piver WT, Duval LA, Schreifer JA. Evaluating health risks from groundwater contaminants. *Journal of Environmental Engineering-ASCE* 1998 MAY; 124(5): 475–478. |
| 128 | James AL, Oldenburg CM. Linear and Monte Carlo uncertainty analysis for subsurface contaminant transport simulation. *Water Resour. Res.* 1997 NOV; 33(11): 2495–2508. |
| 129 | Hamed MM. First-order reliability analysis of public health risk assessment. *Risk Analysis* 1997 APR; 17(2): 177–185. |
| 130 | Burmaster DE, Wilson AM. An introduction to second-order random variables in human health risk assessments. *Hum. Ecol. Risk Assess.* 1996 DEC; 2(4): 892–919. |
| 131 | Jeong J, Mauldin PD. Estimating the weighting components of a health quality index. *Biometrical Journal* 1996; 38(7): 779–790. |
| 132 | Lew CS, Mills WB, Wilkinson KJ, Gherini SA. RIVRISK: A model to assess potential human health and ecological risks from chemical and thermal releases into rivers. *Water Air and Soil Pollution* 1996 JUL; 90(1–2): 123–132. |
| 133 | Lipfert FW, Moskowitz PD, Fthenakis VE, Saroff L. Probabilistic assessment of health risks of methylmercury from burning coal. *Neurotoxicology* 1996 SPR; 17(1): 197–211. |
| 134 | Weinberg J. The Impact of Aging upon the Need for Medical Beds—a Monte-Carlo Simulation. *J. Public Health Med.* 1995 SEP; 17(3): 290–296. |
| 135 | Hattis D, Silver K. Human Interindividual Variability—a Major Source of Uncertainty in Assessing Risks for Noncancer Health-Effects. *Risk Analysis* 1994 AUG; 14(4): 421–431. |
| 136 | Smith RL. Use of a Monte-Carlo Simulation for Human Exposure Assessment at the Superfund Site. *Risk Analysis* 1994 AUG; 14(4): 433–439. |
| 137 | Eltahtawy AA, Jackson AJ, Ludden TM. Comparison of Single and Multiple-Dose Pharmacokinetics using Clinical Bioequivalence Data and Monte-Carlo Simulations. *Pharm. Res.* 1994 SEP; 11(9): 1330–1336. |

(*continued*)

*Table 12.3* Continued

| S No. | MC paper |
|-------|----------|
| 138 | Javitt JC, Aiello LP, Chiang YP, Ferris FL, Canner JK, Greenfield S. Preventive Eye Care in People with Diabetes is Cost-Saving to the Federal-Government—Implications for Health-Care Reform. *Diabetes Care* 1994 AUG; 17(8): 909–917. |
| 139 | Chrischilles E, Shireman T, Wallace R. Costs and Health-Effects of Osteoporotic Fractures. *Bone* 1994 JUL–AUG; 15(4): 377–386. |
| 140 | Schulman KA, Mcdonald RC, Lynn LA, Frank I, Christakis NA, Schwartz JS. Screening Surgeons for HIV-Infection—Assessment of a Potential Public-Health Program. *Infection Control and Hospital Epidemiology* 1994 MAR; 15(3): 147–155. |
| 141 | Thompson KM, Burmaster DE, Crouch EAC. Monte-Carlo Techniques for Quantitative Uncertainty Analysis in Public-Health Risk Assessments. *Risk Analysis* 1992 MAR; 12(1): 53–63. |
| 142 | Paustenbach DJ, Meyer DM, Sheehan PJ, Lau V. An Assessment and Quantitative Uncertainty Analysis of the Health Risks to Workers Exposed to Chromium Contaminated Soils. *Toxicol. Ind. Health* 1991 MAY; 7(3): 159–196. |

Markov models and decision trees (Barton *et al*, 2004) (18 papers); (c) to evaluate the cost-effectiveness of competing technologies or health-care strategies that require the description of patient pathways over extended time horizons with 41 papers in this sub-category; and (d) for Miscellaneous taxonomies, literature review and feasibility studies with 23 papers altogether. Each of these four issues will now be looked at in greater depth.

### 12.4.1.1 Health risk assessment

Numerous environmental and occupational studies have shown a link between the measures of public health and intake of contaminants, via different environmental media and exposure routes such as inhalation, skin and ingestion. Twenty-two studies focused on air pollution [MC3, 10, 20, 26, 29, 40, 43, 51, 55, 79, 88, 90, 97, 102, 114, 124, 126, 132, 133, 135, 136, 140], nine on water pollution [MC21, 62, 76, 93, 95, 98, 103, 116, 127], 11 on food poisoning [MC5, 13, 34, 56, 77, 100, 111, 113, 118, 122, 125] and three on soil contamination [MC119, 128, 142]. In such health risk assessments or epidemiological studies, the exact amount of a chemical or contaminant that an individual comes into contact with over a lifetime should ideally be estimated. However, for many obvious reasons this estimation is difficult. Simulation studies can fill in data gaps regarding historical exposures by generating these data using parametric functions, which are critical to improving the power of such studies. MCS is the method most commonly used for classical probabilistic risk assessments that uses mathematical or statistical models to estimate the frequency in which an event will occur. This technique is particularly useful when a large number of algorithms are required to address various multi-pathways of exposure to humans. The use of Monte Carlo analysis has reformed the practice of exposure assessment and has greatly enhanced the quality of the risk characterisation.

Moreover, 15 risk assessment studies focus on drug development and dose-response portion [MC4, 14, 17, 19, 31, 42, 47, 52, 53, 54, 67, 71, 80, 106, 137]. MCS can be used to determine the Probability of Target Attainment of pharmaco-dynamic indices by taking the inherent variation of different populations into account. In MCS, the model parameters are treated as stochastic or random variables, by using a probability density function for example, rather than fixed values. The aim of these studies is to establish a population pharmacokinetic model to study the parameters for the drug being administered through an intravenous escalating dosing regimen in healthy subjects, which could, in turn, be used for design of patient protocols with direct therapeutic benefit and maximal safety. These simulations are dependent on the assumptions in the model, including the types and number of subjects in the pharmacokinetic studies and the data used. Differences in pharmacokinetic parameters (for different patient populations) and/or data can lead to differences in the target attainment rates obtained with these simulations. Studies of these kinds usually derive their data from clinical trials.

### 12.4.1.2   Prognostic and transmission models of health interventions

MCS is extensively used to measure the number and impact of medical interventions for the prevention of disease deterioration or disease transmission. Many intervention procedures with medical treatment show substantial reductions in disease morbidity or mortality. However, their use is expensive and to some extent determined by local practice, with great variation in the rates of these procedures. The optimum level of such procedures may therefore be uncertain, and this uncertainty is a major problem for both clinicians and health service administrators. It is therefore important to have methods that model the requirements for these interventions at the population level by capturing the movement of individuals between different states based on disease and/or procedure history. Such interventions that usually involve patients or disease transmission stages use Markov processes to measure the probabilities of transmission. MCS analysis of the Markov process is the most useful model for this situation, which also allows the enumeration of events as individuals move between states [MC1, 2, 22, 22, 32, 39, 48, 57, 58, 59, 64, 66, 75, 84, 91, 94, 99]. Moreover, there are studies that seek to develop criteria that classify risk factor levels during intervention or treatment outcomes after intervention. In such studies, regression analysis is the most commonly used tool (some others are Bayesian statistics and bootstrapping) that specifies the inclusion criteria or variables. MCS is used in addition to this method to investigate the robustness of these variables or classification criteria [MC49, 74]. Subsequently, in these studies, MCS techniques evaluate the propagation of the variability of input parameters used in regression models by analysing the effects of uncertainty and the intrinsic variability of parameters.

### 12.4.1.3   *Cost-benefit analysis and policy evaluation of medical treatment and disease management programmes*

The above research can easily be adapted or expanded to fit economic data, which evaluate the cost-effectiveness of specific interventions, treatments, tests and health programmes. Certain medical conditions have a profound and growing impact on healthcare resource utilisation. In many circumstances the direct expenditures for screening or treatment (with drugs or other therapy) of these conditions have substantially increased due to the overall ageing of the population. Therefore, research in this field tries to assess the economic value of a population-based screen-and-treat strategy for diseases or medical conditions compared to alternative strategies or no intervention [MC6, 7, 9, 12, 16, 23, 25, 35, 37, 38, 39, 40, 44, 45, 46, 50, 60, 63, 65, 68, 70, 72, 73, 82, 83, 87, 89, 92, 96, 101, 108, 109, 112, 117, 120, 131, 138, 139]. Briefly, a Markov state transition model with different health states is developed to simulate the medical condition fractures or disease states as a function of demographic change and other influences allowing for a wide variety of scenarios regarding planned medication usage, drug efficacy and individual persistence with treatment. The cost-effectiveness of these alternative strategies is evaluated in an MCS-based incremental cost-utility analysis. The main outcome is usually cost per quality-adjusted life year gained. These results provide policymakers with a common metric for comparing diverse technologies and programmes. Model inputs for the simulation models are usually obtained from published literature and surveys, expert interviews and clinical trials and studies.

## 12.4.1.4  Miscellaneous

There are a number of MCS studies emerging from our search strategy that form smaller categories or do not clearly fall within a distinguished category. These studies are literature review studies and taxonomies of various statistical methods, including Monte Carlo simulation, which can be useful decision tools pertaining to a particular health problem and usually pertinent to risk assessment [MC11, 27, 81]. Other studies focus on the development of new methods, for example, probabilistic public health risk assessment/treatments or improvement of an existing modelling method or comparison between different methods in the form of feasibility studies [MC8, 18, 30, 36, 60, 69, 78, 86, 105, 110, 115, 121, 123, 129, 130, 141, 142] (16 papers). Finally, there are MCS studies about health surveys and service delivery examination, including, for example, the determinants of health and measures of health status, the quality of hospital care and the impact of demographic change on the need for hospital resources [MC23, 104, 107, 134].

## 12.4.1.5  Discrete-Event Simulation

This is the second most popular category in our study with 40 papers overall after screening (Table 12.4). It is said that DES can create significantly more insight than MCS in areas such as health economics (Eldabi et al, 2000). Applications of DES in health have been clustered under the following headings: (a) planning of healthcare services described in 13 papers in our search; (b) health economic models that are presented in 10 papers; (c) seven review and six methodology papers; and (d) contagious disease interventions presented in four papers.

An extensive taxonomy of DES studies in healthcare over the past 20 years is presented in Jun et al (1999) and Fone et al (2003). The study conducted by Fone et al (2003) is a systematic review from 1980 to 1999. Our DES categories bring some similarities to those identified by Fone et al (costs of illness and economic evaluation, hospital scheduling and organisation, infection and communicable disease, screening and miscellaneous). The work carried out by Jun et al (1999) is a survey, specifically, on the applications of DES to healthcare clinics over the 1980s up to 1997. The categories identified by Jun et al (patient scheduling and admissions, patient flow schemes, and staff scheduling on patient flow and work flow, allocation of resources when sizing and planning beds, rooms, and staff personnel) also bear resemblance to our sub-categories in 'Planning healthcare services', as the latter study is focused on a specific area of DES and is more analytic. We now discuss each of our DES categories according to the number of publications identified in each cluster in a descending order.

*Table 12.4*   DES papers included in the present study

| S No. | DES paper |
|---|---|
| 1 | Scherrer CR, Griffin PM, Swann JL. Public health sealant delivery programs: Optimal delivery and the cost of practice acts. *Medical Decision Making* 2007 NOV–DEC; 27(6): 762–771. |
| 2 | Duguay C, Chetouane F. Modelling and improving emergency department systems using discrete event simulation. *Simulation—Transactions of the Society for Modelling and Simulation International* 2007 APR; 83(4): 311–320. |
| 3 | Ward A, Bozkaya D, Fleischmann J, Dubois D, Sabatowski R, Caro JJ. Modelling the economic and health consequences of managing chronic osteoarthritis pain with opioids in Germany: comparison of extended-release oxycodone and OROS hydromorphone. *Curr. Med. Res. Opin.* 2007 OCT; 23(10): 2333–2345. |
| 4 | Hollingworth W, Spackman DE. Emerging methods in economic Modelling of imaging costs and outcomes: A short report on discrete event simulation. *Acad. Radiol.* 2007 APR; 14(4): 406–410. |
| 5 | Cooper K, Brailsford SC, Davies R. Choice of modelling technique for evaluating health care interventions. *J. Oper. Res. Soc.* 2007 FEB; 58(2): 168–176. |
| 6 | Vasilakis C, Sobolev BG, Kuramoto L, Levy AR. A simulation study of scheduling clinic appointments in surgical care: individual versus pooled lists. *J. Oper. Res. Soc.* 2007 FEB; 58(2): 202–211. |
| 7 | Katsaliaki K, Brailsford SC. Using simulation to improve the blood supply chain. *J. Oper. Res. Soc.* 2007 FEB; 58(2): 219–227. |
| 8 | Ceglowski R, Churilov L, Wasserthiel J. Combining Data Mining and Discrete Event Simulation for a value-added view of a hospital emergency department. *J. Oper. Res. Soc.* 2007 FEB; 58(2): 246–254. |
| 9 | Eldabi T, Paul RJ, Young T. Simulation modelling in healthcare: reviewing legacies and investigating futures. *J. Oper. Res. Soc.* 2007 FEB; 58(2): 262–270. |
| 10 | Brennan A, Chick SE, Davies R. A taxonomy of model structures for economic evaluation of health technologies. *Health Econ.* 2006 DEC; 15(12): 1295–1310. |
| 11 | Aaby K, Herrmann JW, Jordan CS, Treadwell M, Wood K. Montgomery Countys Public Health Service uses operations research to plan emergency mass dispensing and vaccination clinics. *Interfaces* 2006 NOV–DEC; 36(6): 569–579. |
| 12 | Hollocks BW. Forty years of discrete-event simulation—a personal reflection. *J. Oper. Res. Soc.* 2006 DEC; 57(12): 1383–1399. |
| 13 | Caro JJ, Guo S, Ward A, Chalil S, Malik F, Leyva F. Modelling the economic and health consequences of cardiac resynchronization therapy in the UK. *Curr. Med. Res. Opin.* 2006 JUN; 22(6): 1171–1179. |
| 14 | Caro J, Ward A, Moller J. Modelling the health benefits and economic implications of implanting dual-chamber vs. single-chamber ventricular pacemakers in the UK. *Europace* 2006 JUN; 8(6): 449–455. |

(*continued*)

*Table 12.4* Continued

| S No. | DES paper |
|-------|-----------|
| 15 | Heeg BMS, Buskens E, Knapp M, van Aalst G, Dries PJT, de Haan L, *et al.* Modelling the treated course of schizophrenia: Development of a discrete event simulation model. *Pharmacoeconomics* 2005; 23: 17–33. |
| 16 | Willis BH, Barton P, Pearmain P, Bryan S, Hyde C. Cervical screening programmes: canautomation help? Evidence from systematic reviews, an economic analysis and a simulation modelling exercise applied to the UK. *Health Technol.Assess.* 2005 MAR; 9(13): 1–207, iii. |
| 17 | Shechter SM, Bryce CL, Alagoz O, Kreke JE, Stahl JE, Schaefer AJ, *et al.* A clinically based discrete-event simulation of end-stage liver disease and the organ allocation process. *Medical Decision Making* 2005 MAR–APR; 25(2): 199–209. |
| 18 | Harper PR, Shahani AK, Gallagher JE, Bowie C. Planning health services with explicit geographical considerations: a stochastic location-allocation approach. *Omega-International Journal of Management Science* 2005 APR; 33(2): 141–152. |
| 19 | Rauner MS, Brailsford SC, Flessa S. Use of discrete-event simulation to evaluate strategies for the prevention of mother-to-child transmission of HIV in developing countries. *J. Oper. Res. Soc.* 2005 FEB; 56(2): 222–233. |
| 20 | Connelly LG, Bair AE. Discrete event simulation of emergency department activity: A platform for system-level operations research. *Acad. Emerg. Med.* 2004 NOV; 11(11): 1177–1185. |
| 21 | Stahl JE, Rattner D, Wiklund R, Lester J, Beinfeld M, Gazelle GS. Reorganizing the system of care surrounding laparoscopic surgery: A cost-effectiveness analysis using discrete-event simulation. *Medical Decision Making* 2004 SEP-OCT; 24(5): 461–471. |
| 22 | Karnon J. Alternative decision modelling techniques for the evaluation of health care technologies: Markov processes versus discrete event simulation. *Health Econ.* 2003 OCT; 12(10): 837–848. |
| 23 | Vieira IT, Harper PR, Shahani AK, de Senna V. Mother-to-child transmission of HIV: a simulation-based approach for the evaluation of intervention strategies. *J. Oper. Res. Soc.* 2003 JUL; 54(7): 713–722. |
| 24 | Ingolfsson A, Erkut E, Budge S. Simulation of single start station for Edmonton EMS. *J. Oper. Res. Soc.* 2003 JUL; 54(7): 736–746. |
| 25 | Brailsford S, Schmidt B. Towards incorporating human behaviour in models of health care systems: An approach using discrete event simulation. *Eur. J. Oper. Res.* 2003 OCT 1; 150(1): 19–31. |
| 26 | Hupert N, Mushlin AL, Callahan MA. Modelling the public health response to bioterrorism: Using discrete event simulation to design antibiotic distribution centers. *Medical Decision Making* 2002 SEP–OCT; 22(5): S17–S25. |
| 27 | Davies R, Roderick P, Canning C, Brailsford S. The evaluation of screening policies for diabetic retinopathy using simulation. *Diabetic Med.* 2002 SEP; 19(9): 762–770. |
| 28 | Swisher JR, Jacobson SH, Jun JB, Balci O. Modelling and analyzing a physician clinic environment using discrete-event simulation. *Comput. Oper. Res.* 2001 FEB; 28(2): 105–125. |

(*continued*)

*Table 12.4* Continued

| S No. | DES paper |
| --- | --- |
| 29 | Moreno L, Aguilar RM, Martin CA, Pineiro JD, Estevez JI, Sigut JF, *et al.* Patient-centered simulation to aid decision-making in hospital management. *Simulation* 2000 MAY; 74(5): 290–304. |
| 30 | Groothuis S, van Merode GG. Discrete event simulation in the health policy and management program. *Methods Inf. Med.* 2000 DEC; 39(4–5): 339–342. |
| 31 | Eldabi T, Paul RJ, Taylor SJE. Simulating economic factors in adjuvant breast cancer treatment. *J. Oper. Res. Soc.* 2000 APR; 51(4): 465–475. |
| 32 | Jun JB, Jacobson SH, Swisher JR. Application of discrete-event simulation in health care clinics: A survey. *J. Oper. Res. Soc.* 1999 FEB; 50(2): 109–123. |
| 33 | Davies R, Roderick P. Planning resources for renal services throughout UK using simulation. *Eur. J. Oper.Res.* 1998 MAR 1; 105(2): 285–295. |
| 34 | Hart WM, Espinosa C, Rovira J. A simulation model of the cost of the incidence of IDDM in Spain. *Diabetologia* 1997 MAR; 40(3): 311–318. |
| 35 | Dittus RS, Klein RW, DeBrota DJ, Dame MA, Fitzgerald JF. Medical resident work schedules: Design and evaluation by simulation Modelling. *Management Science* 1996 JUN; 42(6): 891–906. |
| 36 | Davies R, Canning C. Discrete event simulation to evaluate screening for diabetic eye disease. *Simulation* 1996 APR; 66(4): 209–216. |
| 37 | Steward D, Standridge CR. A veterinary practice simulator based on the integration of expert system and process Modelling. *Simulation* 1996 MAR; 66(3): 143–159. |
| 38 | Davies HTO, Davies R. Simulating Health Systems—Modelling Problems and Software Solutions. *Eur. J. Oper. Res.* 1995 NOV 16; 87(1): 35–44. |
| 39 | Davies R, Davies HTO. Modelling Patient Flows and Resource Provision in Health Systems. *Omega-International Journal of Management Science* 1994 MAR; 22(2): 123–131. |
| 40 | Irvine SR, Levary RR. A Discrete-Event Simulation of the Mcdonnell Douglas Health Information-Systems Online Executive. *Comput. Oper. Res.* 1988; 15(6): 535–549. |

### 12.4.1.6 *Planning of healthcare services and health interventions*

DES allows decision makers to effectively assess the efficiency of existing healthcare delivery systems such as hospitals [DES29], to improve system performance or design and to plan new ones in a risk-free and costless environment by investigating the complex relationships among the different model variables (ie rate of arrivals, time spent in the system, etc) and overcoming bottlenecks. The scope of evaluation can be micro in scale, for example by examining resource needs in terms of scheduling staff and measuring bed and equipment capacity at individual clinics, or macro in proportion (healthcare policy for the entire population). DES allows the decision makers to gather insights and obtain approximate results of the differing but competing policies that may be implemented in the future. Moreover, since DES allows the creation of dynamic population-based models, wherein each entity in the simulation represents an individual, the results could indicate the number of people who may be affected by the adoption of a particular strategy.

Some of the applications of DES therefore relate to managing patient admissions and staff scheduling, for example DES studies that compared the 'individual surgeons' strategy with the 'pooled lists' strategy for scheduling outpatient clinical appointments in surgical care [DES6]; designed a new house staff work schedule [DES35] and ambulance schedules [DES24]. They also relate to identifying areas of improvement of service through possible reorganisation of existing resources, for example; reorganisation of surgical and anaesthesia care surrounding laparoscopic surgery [DES21]; experimenting with real-time health information system to reduce response time [DES40]; evaluating operating policies in clinical environments [DES28] and allocation policies for liver transplantation [DES17]; forecasting the impact of changing demand for treatment of irreversible renal failure [DES33] and planning for the geographical locations of new healthcare services taking into account the demographics of the population and the location of the patients who need the services [DES18]. Furthermore, DES is well-suited to tackle problems in A&E departments, where resources are scarce and patients arrive at irregular times [DES2], and effectively combine Total Quality Management strategies [DES24] and data mining [DES8] for better results. Moreover, DES applications relate to estimating performance measures impacting facilities design and planning of veterinary practice [DES37]. As large majorities of the population depend on edible products or by-products from livestock, the health of livestock has a significant effect on public health.

### 12.4.1.7   Health economic models

Health economic models evaluate the health implications and the economic costs of providing healthcare to the population at large. They usually do so by comparing alternative healthcare interventions aiming to maximise welfare through optimal utilisation of the allocated public health funds. With respect to health economic models, the use of DES has been reported for evaluating, among others, the cost of providing dental care to children [DES1]; for comparing methods of managing chronic osteoarthritis pain [DES3]; for modelling the treated course of schizophrenia so as to estimate the long-term costs and effects of new interventions [DES15]; for evaluating the cost effectiveness of screening strategies for diabetic retinopathy by varying the screening method and interval [DES27, 36] and of introducing a range of automated image analysis systems for cervical screening programmes [DES16]; and for estimating the cost-effectiveness and the direct healthcare costs pertaining to insulin-dependent diabetes mellitus [DES34]. The use of DES health economic models have also been reported for the economic evaluation of pacemakers. For example, DES was used for modelling the health benefits and economic implications of implanting dual-chamber *versus* single-chamber ventricular pacemakers in the UK [DES14] and of implanting a Cardiac Resynchronization device of Therapy for reducing heart failure as opposed to Optimum Pharmacologic Therapy that does not require a pacemaker [DES13]. DES was also used to improve the National Blood Service supply chain by investigating different blood ordering and distribution policies [DES7].

### 12.4.1.8   Review and methodology papers

Our research methodology identified a number of review papers in the healthcare literature. Some of these papers compared modelling techniques used in healthcare, such as DES, Markov and semi-Markov chain models, queuing models and deterministic models (in the context of patient flow models [DES39] and economic evaluations of healthcare technologies [DES22]) and presented taxonomies of modelling structures [DES5, 10, 32]. Other papers present a personal reflection of DES [DES12] and outline a vision of the future use of simulation in healthcare [DES9]. They all found DES to be particularly suitable for estimating cost and health benefits of dynamic population-based models with individual attributes and patient care systems with scarce resources.

In our search, five methodology papers were identified. They deal with various issues such as the use of patient-chart-driven computer simulation to advance A&E system [DES20]; the use of DES as one emerging modelling technique for supporting decision making in randomized clinical trials of breast cancer [DES31], for modelling patient behaviour when screening for diabetic retinopathy [DES25] and for evaluating imaging technologies [DES4]. Moreover, DES has been acknowledged as a well-suited methodology for modelling health systems [DES38] and a valuable training tool for students who learnt to analyse and design efficiently work-flow processes in healthcare [DES30].

### 12.4.1.9   Contagious disease interventions

DES applications in this category usually relate to proposing ways to suppress the spread of HIV in developing countries [DES19, 23], and to the public response to control the outbreak of contagious diseases that may be caused by natural occurrence [DES11] or an act of terrorism [DES26]. These DES models are developed to plan emergency clinics and distribution centres for mass-dispensing and vaccination.

### 12.4.1.10   System Dynamics

SD can assist the design of healthcare policies by examining how the fundamental structure might influence the progressive behaviour of a system. It takes into consideration factors such as the time variation of both the tangible elements, such as waiting times and healthcare costs, as well as intangible elements, such as patient anxiety and the effects of various pressures on purchasing decisions (Taylor and Lane, 1998).

Seventeen studies are counted under this technique. The papers pertaining to SD have been categorised under the following headings: (a) public health policy evaluation and economic models, represented in nine papers in our search; (b) modelling healthcare systems and infrastructure disruption (four papers); (c) use of SD as a training tool (three papers); and (d) one review paper of SD for modelling public health matters of disease epidemiology and healthcare capacity [SD6]. The first three categories are described below in the same order as above. The papers are listed in Table 12.5.

### 12.4.1.11   Public health policy evaluation and economic models

SD has been applied for the evaluation of several public health policies. With regard to communicable diseases, SD models were developed to estimate the effect of harm reduction policies for HIV/AIDS and tuberculosis (such as 'needle-sharing and injection-frequency among drug users and multi-drug resistant tuberculosis control [SD2]) and to assess economic consequences of testing and treating pregnant women for HIV virus with different regimens to avoid prenatal transmission [SD16]. Moreover, SD was used in several studies to evaluate the long-term health impact of smoking by comparing policies such as increasing cigarette excise taxes, raising the legal smoking age to 21 [SD4] and introducing tobacco harm reduction policies [SD8, 9, 11]. They suggested that a large tax increase would have the largest and most immediate effect on smoking prevalence. Control over the cigarette content would bring a net gain in population health, although 'healthier' cigarettes make smoking more attractive and increase tobacco consumption. SD has also been used by health planners to gain a better understanding of diabetes population dynamics [SD7]; to model the feedback effects of reconfiguring health services [SD10] by shifting towards the primary

*Table 12.5* SD papers included in the present study

| S No. | SD paper |
|---|---|
| 1 | Arboleda CA, Abraham DM, Lubitz R. Simulation as a tool to assess the vulnerability of the operation of a health care facility. *J. Perform. Constr. Facil.* 2007 JUL–AUG; 21(4): 302–312. |
| 2 | Atun RA, Lebcir RM, Mckee M, Habicht J, Coker RJ. Impact of joined-up HIV harm reduction and multidrug resistant tuberculosis control programmes in Estonia: System dynamics simulation model. *Health Policy* 2007 MAY; 81(2–3): 207–217. |
| 3 | Hsieh JL, Sun CT, Kao GYM, Huang CY. Teaching through simulation: Epidemic dynamics and public health policies. *Simulation—Transactions of the Society for Modelling and Simulation International* 2006 NOV; 82(11): 731–759. |
| 4 | Ahmad S, Billimek J. Limiting youth access to tobacco: Comparing the long-term health impacts of increasing cigarette excise taxes and raising the legal smoking age to 21 in the United States. *Health Policy* 2007 MAR; 80(3): 378–391. |
| 5 | Min HSJ, Beyeler W, Brown T, Son YJ, Jones AT. Toward Modelling and simulation of critical national infrastructure interdependencies. *IIE Transactions* 2007 JAN; 39(1): 57–71. |
| 6 | Homer JB, Hirsch GB. System dynamics Modelling for public health: Background and opportunities. *Am. J. Public Health* 2006 MAR; 96(3): 452–458. |
| 7 | Jones AP, Homer JB, Murphy DL, Essien JDK, Milstein B, Seville DA. Understanding diabetes population dynamics through simulation Modelling and experimentation. *Am. J. Public Health* 2006 MAR; 96(3): 488–494. |
| 8 | Ahmad S. Closing the youth access gap: The projected health benefits and cost savings of a national policy to raise the legal smoking age to 21 in the United States. *Health Policy* 2005 DEC; 75(1): 74–84. |
| 9 | Ahmad S, Billimek J. Estimating the health impacts of tobacco harm reduction policies: A simulation Modelling approach. *Risk Analysis* 2005 AUG; 25(4): 801–812. |
| 10 | Taylor K, Dangerfield B. Modelling the feedback effects of reconfiguring health services. *J. Oper. Res. Soc.* 2005 JUN; 56(6): 659–675. |
| 11 | Tengs TO, Ahmad S, Moore R, Gage E. Federal policy mandating safer cigarettes: A hypothetical simulation of the anticipated population health gains or losses. *Journal of Policy Analysis and Management* 2004 FAL; 23(4): 857–872. |
| 12 | Brailsford SC, Lattimer VA, Tarnaras P, Turnbull JC. Emergency and on-demand health care: modelling a large complex system. *J. Oper. Res. Soc.* 2004 JAN; 55(1): 34–42. |
| 13 | Charles BG, Duffull SB. Pharmacokinetic software for the health sciences—Choosing the right package for teaching purposes. *Clin. Pharmacokinet.* 2001; 40(6): 395–403. |
| 14 | Thatcher ME, Clemons EK. Managing the costs of informational privacy: Pure bundling as a strategy on the individual health insurance market. *J. Manage. Inf. Syst.* 2000 FAL; 17(2): 29–57. |

(*continued*)

*Table 12.5* Continued

| S No. | SD paper |
| --- | --- |
| 15 | Lane DC, Monefeldt C, Rosenhead JV. Looking in the wrong place for healthcare improvements: A system dynamics study of an accident and emergency department. *J. Oper. Res. Soc.* 2000 MAY; 51(5): 518–531. |
| 16 | Anderson JG, Anderson MM. HIV screening and treatment of pregnant women and their newborns: Asimulation-based analysis. *Simulation* 1998 OCT; 71(4): 276–284. |
| 17 | Navarro JDS, Alvarez JAT, Ortega FP, Casado MPS, Polo MP. A Dynamo Application of Microcomputer-Based Simulation in Health-Sciences Teaching. 1993: 30(5): 425–436 |

level and bringing services 'closer to home'; to investigate the impact of privacy legislation in the individual health insurance market and the social costs that are borne when applicants do not divulge private information about their medical conditions [SD14].

### 12.4.1.12   Modelling healthcare systems and infrastructure disruptions

A healthcare system consists of many individual sub-parts that interact with each other, for example the national health system (NHS) consists of vast numbers of GP clinics, walk-in centres, hospitals, tertiary care centres, A&E, IT infrastructure, NHS supply chains, etc. SD allows modelling of several sub-parts of these complex healthcare systems, such as a city's delivery of emergency and on-demand, unscheduled care [SD12], an A&E dynamics of demand pattern, resource deployment and parallel hospital processes [SD15]. In this regard, SD also has the potential to simulate multiple, independent key elements of an infrastructure. Innovative modelling and analysis framework based on SD could study the entire system of physical and economic infrastructures, and specifically of healthcare facilities, and propose public responses to infrastructure disruptions [SD5] and disasters [SD1], as well as to reduce the devastating health effects of such phenomena by modelling into a unified whole the relief effort of evacuations, provision of temporary shelters, restoration of electricity and communication lines, etc.

### 12.4.1.13   Training

SD has also been used as a tool for training health policymakers. It can facilitate the understanding of the dynamics of an epidemic such as SARS [SD3] and explore the applicable combinations of prevention or suppression strategies. Moreover, SD provides an opportunity in some educational environments such as in health sciences by allowing students to experiment in the classroom with the use of professional tools. SD software together with calculator-simulators has been used for teaching pharmacokinetics [SD13], and pharmacological system dynamics models have also been developed for the same purpose [SD17].

### 12.4.1.14 Agent-Based Simulation

Applications of ABS in the healthcare sector are not yet widespread but it has been used to study problems such as the spread of epidemics (Bagni *et al*, 2002). The research methodology that we have followed in our review has identified only two papers that have used ABS. The papers are listed in Table 12.6.

One study reported an ABS model called *CancerSIM*, which allows researchers to study the dynamics and interactions of cancer hallmarks and possible therapies [ABS1]. The other study [ABS2] used software agents to preserve individual health data confidentiality in micro-scale geographical analyses and showed that by limiting the accuracy of geocodes for the purposes of privacy protection, the ability to identify areas of high disease risk is degraded.

The five papers that report on several simulation techniques (refer to Table 12.1) have been included in the MCS and the DES category for the sake of simplicity. Three papers report both on MCS and DES and were described under the 'Prognostic and transmission models of health interventions' [MC48, 58] and the 'Cost-benefit analysis and policy evaluation of medical treatment and disease management programs' [MC65] headings of MCS. Moreover, there are two papers that were described under the 'Review papers' heading of DES. A review paper [DES9] that refers simultaneously to DES, SD and MCS and a taxonomy paper [DES10] that refers to DES and SD among other operational research techniques.

*Table 12.6* ABS papers included in the present study

| S No. | ABS paper |
| --- | --- |
| 1 | Abbott RG, Forrest S, Pienta KJ. Simulating the hallmarks of Cancer. *Artif. Life* 2006 FAL; 12(4): 617–634. |
| 2 | Boulos MNK, Cai Q, Padget JA, Rushton G. Using software agents to preserve individual health data confidentiality in micro-scale geographical analyses. *J. Biomed. Inform.* 2006 APR; 39(2): 160–170. |

## 12.5   Research impact

In this section, we present the citation statistics of a few highly cited papers in the field of healthcare simulation (objective 3) (Table 12.7). The table shows the total citations and the average article citations as a means of identifying the impact of these publications. The list is sorted (and therefore publications for inclusion in Table 12.7 are selected) based on the total citation count. However, the authors recognise that the average citation is also a very useful measure as it eliminates the discrepancies caused by the number of years passed since publication. It is generally expected that review papers have more citations than research papers. It is therefore surprising that none of the papers included in the list are review papers. Even more surprising is the fact that all papers use the MCS technique as their main method of analysis. Many of the papers in Table 12.7 present cost-effectiveness analyses of specific healthcare applications or disease prevention methods, including the first paper that was published in the journal *Bone* in 1994.

It should be noted here that a good number of journals in Table 12.7 are either medical or health-related journals. It is widely accepted that medical journals generally have citations that are much higher compared to the OR journals, from which it might be concluded that impact is not incomparable between them. A more stratified representation would shed more light. However, this was out of the main scope of this study.

## 12.6   Results implementation, funding sources and analysis of simulation software

In this section, we examine the evidence of results presentation, implementation (objective 4), funding (objective 5) and software usage (objective 6) from among those papers that were selected for inclusion in this study after screening.

Of the 201 papers, 184 (91%) present results and have a separate, typically large section supported with tables and graphs to give a full analysis and explanation to the readers. There are seven MCS papers, eight DES, three SDS and one ABS paper, which do not present results. Of these, the majority are review and methodology papers. There are only five papers that fall in other categories (health risk assessment; health economic model; planning of healthcare services) and do not demonstrate results in a numerical format in the way described above. Yet, implementation of research results is hardly mentioned in these publications, with only

*Table 12.7*  Publications with high number of citations

| Total citations | Average Citations | Publication |
|---|---|---|
| 166 | 11.07 | 1. Chrischilles E, Shireman T, Wallace R. Costs and Health-Effects of Osteoporotic Fractures. *Bone* 1994 JUL–AUG; 15(4): 377–386. |
| 134 | 8.93 | 2. Javitt JC, Aiello LP, Chiang YP, Ferris FL, Canner JK, Greenfield S. Preventive Eye Care in People with Diabetes is Cost-Saving to the Federal-Government—Implications for Health-Care Reform. *Diabetes Care* 1994 AUG; 17(8): 909–917. |
| 102 | 6 | 3. Thompson KM, Burmaster DE, Crouch EAC. Monte-Carlo Techniques for Quantitative Uncertainty Analysis in Public-Health Risk Assessments. *Risk Analysis* 1992 MAR; 12(1): 53–63. |
| 76 | 9.5 | 4. Nichol KL. Cost-benefit analysis of a strategy to vaccinate healthy working adults against influenza. *Arch. Intern. Med.* 2001 MAR 12; 161(5): 749–759. |
| 67 | 8.38 | 5. Ambrose PG, Grasela DM. The use of Monte Carlo simulation to examine pharmacodynamic variance of drugs: fluoroquinolone pharmacodynamics against *Streptococcus pneumoniae*. *Diagn. Microbiol. Infect. Dis.* 2000 NOV; 38(3): 151–157. |
| 46 | 2.56 | 6. Nieuwenhuijsen M, Paustenbach D, Duarte-Davidson R. New developments in exposure assessment: The impact on the practice of health risk assessment and epidemiological studies. *Environ. Int.* 2006 DEC; 32(8): 996–1009. |
| 42 | 2.8 | 7. Hattis D, Silver K. Human Interindividual Variability—a Major Source of Uncertainty in Assessing Risks for Noncancer Health-Effects. *Risk Analysis* 1994 AUG; 14(4): 421–431. |
| 35 | 3.5 | 8. Briggs AH, Mooney CZ, Wonderling DE. Constructing confidence intervals for cost-effectiveness ratios: An evaluation of parametric and non-parametric techniques using Monte Carlo simulation. *Stat. Med.* 1999 DEC 15; 18(23): 3245–3262. |

a few papers (11 out of 201, 5.4%) reporting on the implementation of results to the stakeholder organisations, in which the case studies were based. Six are reported in the MCS category, four in DES and one in SD. However, this is not to say that the case-oriented simulation studies that have not implemented their results have gone astray. Neither should it be implied that their impact is only academic and does not reflect the real world. Looking further at the issue, one may realise that healthcare simulation studies generally have a long gestation period before they reach the ultimate decision makers in a comprehensive format. These decision makers need to decide among a plethora of similar studies, taking into consideration various other factors, and come to a conclusion of turning a specific recommendation from a study into a policy applicable in health organisations and settings. Subsequently, it is unlikely that implementation will be part of the paper. Moreover, researchers are eager to publish once they have the first results in hand and only very occasionally will they wait until the impact of their method is shown in the real world in order to incorporate it into their paper.

Perhaps a better measure of the interest in the research being conducted in the healthcare simulation studies is the funding process. Of the 201 studies, 87 (43%) have received full or partial funding. Of the 163 identified MCS studies, around 39% mention their project's funding source, 48% of the DES papers, 65% of the SD papers and 100% of the ABS papers (two papers) report a funding source. Many of these papers refer to various sources of funding. Table 12.8 illustrates some of these sources. As can be seen from the table, health departments and national foundations are the major sources of funding, closely followed by pharmaceutical companies. Other governmental departments and national institutions also fund healthcare studies. Funds for research are also derived from internal University funding and research council grants.

From our sampled list of papers, we find that funding seems to be consistent throughout the years. This suggests that there is no identified trend that more funding is provided for healthcare research over the last years or vice versa.

Finally, we conclude by presenting some statistics on simulation software/programming languages that were used to support model development in the selected studies. It is important to mention that, from our sample of 201 selected papers, only 83 papers acknowledge the software or programming language that was used to develop the model. This data is presented in Table 12.9 (MCS software), Table 12.10 (DES software) and Table 12.11 (SD software), respectively. With regard to MCS (Table 12.9), @Risk and Crystal Ball were among the most popular software,

*Table 12.8* Research funding sources

| Funding source | No. of papers | Percentage |
|---|---|---|
| Department of Health | 13 | 12.7 |
| National Foundations/Centres | 13 | 12.7 |
| Pharmaceutical Companies | 12 | 11.8 |
| Other Governmental Departments | 11 | 10.8 |
| National Institutes for Health-related Research | 11 | 10.8 |
| Universities/Colleges | 9 | 8.8 |
| National Research Council | 9 | 8.8 |
| Health/environment Research Agencies | 6 | 5.9 |
| European Research Programs | 4 | 3.9 |
| Non-Pharmaceutical Companies | 3 | 2.9 |
| Private Foundations | 3 | 2.9 |
| Funding Organisations for Academic Research | 3 | 2.9 |
| National Health Services | 3 | 2.9 |
| Health Authorities | 2 | 2.0 |
| **Sum** | **102** | **100.0** |

*Table 12.9* Monte Carlo Simulation software

| MCS software | No. of papers | Percentage |
|---|---|---|
| @Risk | 10 | 23.3 |
| Crystal Ball | 10 | 23.3 |
| Excel | 3 | 7.0 |
| SimHerd | 2 | 4.7 |
| NONMEM | 2 | 4.7 |
| Matlab | 2 | 4.7 |
| WinBUGS | 2 | 4.7 |
| RIVRISK, SimTools, Mathematica®, GENMM.exe, ITOUGH, DATA 3.5 for Healthcare, BASIC, Stata, Hexalog, Java, C11, SAS | 1 | 2.3 |
| **Sum** | **43** | **100.0** |

followed by Excel. Numerous other software and programs have also been used, some of them specific to health or other applications.

The process of building DES models involves some form of software. The software can either be a high-level programming language or a Commercial, Off-The-Shelf (COTS) simulation package. DES software Arena is the most popular in this sample review, followed by the programming language Borland Delphi and COTS package Simul8 (Table 12.10).

*Table 12.10*   Discrete Event Simulation software

| DES Software | No. of papers | Percentage |
|---|---|---|
| Arena | 6 | 20.7 |
| Borland Delphi (Programming Language) | 5 | 17.2 |
| Simul8 | 3 | 10.3 |
| PASCAL (Programming Language) | 2 | 6.9 |
| AutoMod | 2 | 6.9 |
| SIGMA | 2 | 6.9 |
| Extend, SIMAN, ServiceModel (Promodel), @Risk and Excel, SLAMSYSTEM software, C Program, Visual Basic (Programming Languages), MODSIM, INSIGHT, Visual Simulation Environment (Orca Computer) simulation language, Statecharts | 1 | 3.4 |
| Sum | 29 | 100.0 |

*Table 12.11*   System Dynamics Simulation software

| SD Simulation software | No. of papers | Percentage |
|---|---|---|
| Vensim | 5 | 50.0 |
| STELLA | 4 | 40.0 |
| DYNAMO | 1 | 10.0 |
| Sum | 10 | 100.0 |

As for SD, the use of only few types of software is reported. Vensim is first in the list, closely followed by STELLA. DYNAMO comes last (Table 12.11).

Finally, one of the two ABS papers reported the use of the programming language C++ to create *CancerSIM*.

In general, the rapid growth in simulation software technology has created numerous new application opportunities, including more sophisticated implementations, as well as combining simulation and other methods for complex models and processes. Trends from our data analysis suggest that, in the most recent years, COTS packages have taken the lead over one-off models that are coded using programming languages. This is explained by the fact that COTS simulation packages are rapidly evolving through inclusion of more advanced features (eg 3-D graphics, parallel processor support, etc).

## 12.7  Discussion

The field of healthcare simulation has evolved significantly over the past 30 years. A great number of health problems have been approached with simulation techniques, which have offered greater precision with regard to resource allocations, evaluations between health strategies and risk assessments. In this review paper reflecting on 37 years of healthcare simulation, we see some trends that apply to the discipline as a whole.

Looking first at the statistics of our sampled papers, we could derive the conclusion that the proportion of papers published in the field has drastically increased, with more than three-quarters published after 2000. Annual paper contributions amounted from one paper in 1988 to 36 in 2007. It is, however, surprising that the oldest paper in our data set is from 1988 as our search strategy concentrated on identifying healthcare simulation papers published from 1970 onwards. One reason for this is possibly that the number of journals indexed by ISI WoS has swelled with the rising popularity of the Internet and the availability of electronic bibliographical information (this may not have been the case during 1970s–1980s). Furthermore, it is arguable that although simulation has been applied to manufacturing, defence, supply chains etc., for a long time, its application in the healthcare context is comparatively new. Figure 12.2 illustrates the historical trends of the healthcare modelling papers for each simulation technique (the only exception is ABS which has only two papers). The ascending lines show the increasing number of published papers in the field especially after the mid-1990s for all three simulation methods. This is in line with the clear increase in simulation usage in the general service sector from the 1990s onwards (Robinson, 2005). Year-to-date figures suggest that this gradual upward trend will continue. It is apparent that during the last 4 years the published papers in this field have drastically increased. A reason might be the possible increase of funding in recent years (Murphy and Topel, 2003).

Simulation as a technique in health problems is used both as the main methodology of the research and as a supportive method to evaluate the robustness of other methods in different papers. MCS seems to be the most popular simulation technique in health studies, and the majority of papers fall within the health risk assessment category. In this category studies pertaining to air and water pollution, food poisoning and soil contamination are leading in terms of published papers, and drug development and dose-response portion studies follow. Cost-benefit analyses health studies with the use of MCS are also popular. They assess the economic value of population-based screen-and-treat

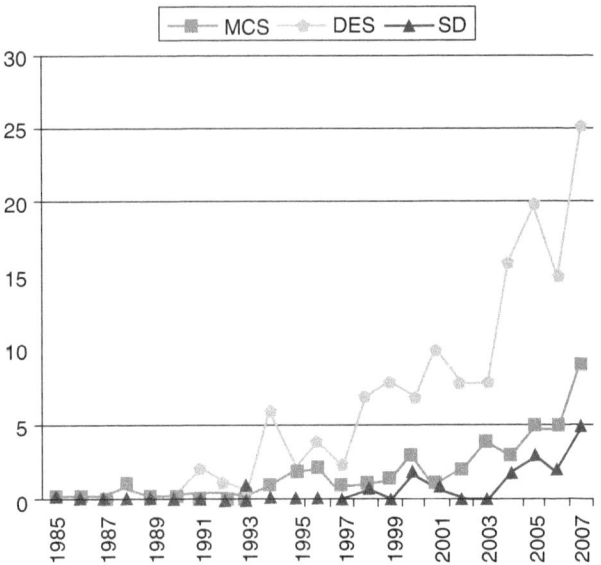

*Figure 12.2*   Number of papers per simulation techniques over the years

alternative strategies for diseases and medical conditions. Some of these studies hold the first positions in terms of research impact and are found to have the maximum average number of citations in our dataset. Moreover, it is particularly noticeable that of the 142 MCS papers, none were published in an OR journal (as defined by the Association of Business School-ABS list). One reason for this may be that MCS is extensively used by health professionals/academics who wish to publish in health-related outlets, or that OR academics have lost interest in the use of MCS and have focused in the use of other simulation techniques to tackle health problems. Nevertheless, several of the MCS papers identified in our study would fit the aim and scope of OR journals. For example MC7, 8, 9, 23, 25, 26, 2, 30, 32, 38 and many more.

In the analysis of the research paradigms categories, it is obvious that some overlap exists among the health applications examined by simulation technique. A very apparent example is that all simulation techniques deal with screening strategies and cost-benefit analysis of medical interventions. Assuming that the categorisation of papers was made according to the health problem tackled and regardless of the simulation technique employed, the papers of cost-benefit analysis would be at about the same level of the health risk assessment category.

However, many researchers will agree that, although the application area is the same, the extent, the level and the detail at which this is examined differs according to the technique employed. SD takes a holistic approach and thus the health problem or situation is looked at from a more global level to a greater extent. Consequently, this technique is appropriate for facilitating health policy making at the macro-level. DES and ABS examine the health problems in more detail (micro-level), taking into account the properties of individual entities, yet this restricts the extent of the system that can be modelled. Therefore, decisions can usually be reached with the use of DES and ABS only at the operational level. Monte Carlo simulation incorporates the random sampling element at aggregated level, which makes modelling of population-based diseases easy to handle. When the individual aspect is important then DES is more appropriate. Moreover, DES and SD are more suitable for modelling problems in which the time element plays a significant role, such as utilisation of health services' resources and bed/equipment capacity management. Nonetheless, looking at the categories presented in this study, one can see that health risk assessment is pertinent to MCS modelling; planning of health services is most of the times handled with the DES models (and less with SD); and training of health students and managers is prevalent in the SD approach. Unfortunately, we could not make a distinct category for ABS since the sample was so small. Moreover, a year-by-year analysis of the number of papers in each research paradigm showed that there are no chroni gaps in the identified categories, and for that reason published research in these general fields are continuous.

Relatively few of the published healthcare simulation articles reported significant effects that simulation had on the healthcare system being studied. This may imply that, although authors document the model, the issues they model and the model results, there are few real implementation results to report. England and Roberts (1978) implied that the reasons behind this are either inadequate models that cannot quantify the impact of the human factor, or the diversity of authority in healthcare facilities, which thwarts the simplicity of a single administrative decision to change the system. The latter problem lies mostly in the political sphere. However, governmental bodies and other national or local council/agency fund a considerable number of studies (43% in our review).

In terms of the modelling approach, it seems that the use of COTS packages is quite widespread, although many models are still being developed in high-level programming languages that usually have larger capabilities in accommodating complex behaviours of the system modelled. Yet, the ease of use that is offered by COTS simulation packages allows those who are not computer programmers to develop valid simulation models. This gives the opportunity to a number of people, including some stakeholders of the systems under question to engage in modelling and quantify their problems and the impact of alternative actions. However, in this way, limitations to the models are posed not only by the data availability and the computer operating cost but also by the imagination and capabilities of the modeller and the software. Simulation software costs can be high, yet since the mid-1990s, a number of low cost COTS packages have come to the market. The latter have certainly widened access to simulation (Robinson, 2005).

It is widely accepted that one of the most important results of computer simulation in healthcare, as well as in other sectors, is the increased understanding of the systems being modelled, which results from constructing the models. We hope that in the future it will become more imperative that healthcare modellers seek close ties and cooperation with healthcare administrators to ensure utilisation and implementation of the worthwhile models that are developed. However, the exact same anticipation was expressed some 30 years ago (England and Roberts, 1978).

As stated by Robinson (2005), simulation techniques have all followed separate paths in both research and practice until now. A closer integration among simulation techniques conjoined with advances in computing and inclusion of the World Wide Web could lead to the development of better designed models with faster execution times, high level of graphics and, most importantly, enhanced user interaction. Such an advance will be in line with the requirements of the new computer literate generation of users.

## 12.8   Conclusions and further reflections

This is a sample review of healthcare simulation studies, which aims at identifying healthcare problems that are modelled using four popular simulation techniques, namely MCS, DES, SD and ABS. The specific selection criteria of articles that were reviewed here may have left out a number of noble publications in the field (eg articles that do not mention health in their title topic but refer to health problems with more specific terms such as hospitals, patients, etc; articles that did not appear in journals indexed by ISI Web of Knowledge®). The implications of this are that there may be an unintentional bias introduced by the specific keywords search and by ISI WoS membership, which leaves out newer journals that have not yet met the 'duration of service' required by the ISI WoS and journals where editorial boards do not wish their journal to have an impact factor. These factors may therefore not be taken into account when basing quality on impact factors. However, the debate as to whether this is right or wrong is outside the scope of this article. We merely wish to provide an analysis of literature within the scope of journals with impact factors and therefore provide some reflection as to the 'health' of healthcare simulation within a potentially metric-driven world. We hope that this study gives an indication of the pulse of research being conducted in the healthcare simulation field, although generalisation of the results may not hold.

Future research could involve a systematic review of the field including all relevant journals from various academic databases and investigate the relationships between impact factor and non-impact factor journals. This approach could more accurately map the discipline and provide us with statistics of interesting variables similar to the ones presented here and with additional ones, such as popular journals, productive institutions and frequently published authors. Future research could also broaden the scope of our literature review by profiling health-related research with the use of other OR/MS techniques.

For the benefit of healthcare and simulation audience, this paper provides an overview of research published in various journals from across different subject areas in health. This research is likely to help authors, reviewers and editors to better understand the potential of different simulation techniques for solving diverse healthcare problems and can also assist upcoming researchers in developing an appreciation of this research area and the various issues considered worthy of research and publication. Furthermore, we hope that healthcare planners, management engineers, as well as researchers will benefit from this study, by having ready access to an up-to-date, indicative collection of articles describing these applications. Finally, our study is likely to stimulate researchers to explore other research areas by undertaking comparative/cross-journal studies.

## Acknowledgements

One of the authors was employed as a research fellow in Warwick Business School while working on this paper, and wishes to thank the School for supporting this research. We also thank Dr Simon J. E. Taylor for his comments, which have improved the paper.

# References

Amoako-Gympah K and Meredith JR (1989). The operations management research agenda: An update. *J Opns Mngt* **8**: 250–262.

Bagni R, Berchi R and Cariello P (2002). A comparison of simulation models applied to epidemics. *JASSS* **5**(3).

Barrios JMR, Serrano D and Monleon T *et al* (2008). Discrete-event simulation models in the economic evaluation of health technologies and health products. *Gac Sanit* **22**: 151–161.

Barton P, Bryan S and Robinson S (2004). Modelling in the economic evaluation of health care: selecting the appropriate approach. *J Health Serv Res Pol* **9**: 110–118.

Brennan A and Akehurst R (2000). Modeling in health economic evaluation: What is its place? What is its value? *Pharmacoeconomics* **17**: 445–459.

Dexter F (1999). Design of appointment systems for preanesthesia evaluation clinics to minimize patient waiting times: A review of computer simulation and patient survey studies. *Anesth Analg* **89**: 925–931.

Eddama O and Coast J (2008). A systematic review of the use of economic evaluation in local decision-making. *Health Policy* **86**:129–141.

Eldabi T, Paul RJ and Taylor SJE (2000). Simulating economic factors in adjuvant breast cancer treatment. *J Opl Res Soc* **51**: 465–475.

Eldabi T, Paul RJ and Young T (2007). Simulation modelling in healthcare: Reviewing legacies and investigating futures. *J Opl Res Soc* **58**: 262–270.

England W and Roberts S (1978). Applications of computer simulation in health care. In: Highland HJ, Hull LG and Neilsen NR (eds). *Proceedings of the 1978 Winter Simulation Conference*. Institute of Electrical and Electronics Engineers: Miami Beach; Florida; USA, 4–6 December, pp 665–676.

Eveborn P, Flisberg P and Rannqvist M (2006). LAPS-CARE—an operational system for staff planning of home care. *Eur J Opl Res* **171**: 962–976.

Fone D *et al* (2003). Systematic review of the use and value of computer simulation modelling in population health and health care delivery. *J Public Health* **25**: 325–335.

Hay JW (2004). Evaluation and review of pharmacoeconomic models. *Informa Pharma Sci* **5**: 1867–1880.

Hollocks BW (2006). Forty years of discrete-event simulation—A personal reflection. *J Opl Res Soc* **57**: 1383–1399.

Jahangirian M, Eldabi T, Naseer A, Stergioulas LK and Young T (2009). Simulation in manufacturing and business: A review. *Eur J Opl Res* **203**: 1–13.

Jun J, Jacobson S and Swisher J (1999). Application of discrete-event simulation in health care clinics: A survey. *J Opl Res Soc* **50**: 109–123.

Murphy KM and Topel R (2003). The economic value of medical research. In: *Measuring the Gains from Medical Research: An Economic Approachc*. University of Chicago Press: Chicago, pp 41–73.

Pannirselvam GP, Ferguson LA, Ash RC and Siferd SP (1999). Operations management research: An update for the 1990s. *J Opns Mngt* **18**: 95–112.

Pidd M (2004). *Systems Modelling: Theory and Practice*. John Wiley & Sons: Chichester, England.

Robinson S (1994). *Successful Simulation: A Practical Approach to Simulation Projects*. McGraw-Hill Companies: Maidenhead, England.

Robinson S (2005). Discrete-event simulation: From the pioneers to the present, what next? *J Opl Res Soc* **56**: 619–629.

Royston P (1999). The use of fractional polynomials to model continuous risk variables in epidemiology. *Int J Epidemiol* **28**: 964–974.

Rubinstein RY (1981). *Simulation and the Monte Carlo Method*. John Wiley & Sons, Inc.: New York, NY, USA.

Smith-Daniels VL, Schweikhart SB and Smith-Daniels DE (1988). Capacity management in health care services: Review and future research directions. *Decis Sci* **19**: 889–918.

Sterman JD (2001). System dynamics modelling. *Calif Mngt Rev* **43**: 8.

Taylor K and Lane D (1998). Simulation applied to health services: Opportunities for applying the system dynamics approach. *J Health Serv Res Policy* **3**: 226–232.

Wand Z (2009). The convergence of health care expenditure in the US states. *Health Econ* **18**: 55–70.

Wierzbicki AP (2007). Modelling as a way of organising knowledge. *Eur J Opl Res* **176**: 610–635.

# 13

## System Dynamics Applications to European Healthcare Issues

*B. C. Dangerfield*
*University of Salford, Salford, UK*

*Taking a European perspective, a review is made of some system dynamics models which address health care issues. Suggestions are made for the types of role which these models should take, bearing in mind the strategic orientation of system dynamics modelling. Examples are described of qualitative models where influence diagrams are the main analytical tool. Quantitative system dynamics models have a contribution to make in epidemiological studies and have been used to analyse the AIDS epidemic. A detailed example of one aspect of model formulation is given. This concerns the AIDS incubation time distribution and shows how real-world complications arising from virological staging and treatment effects are handled in a model of AIDS spread.*

### 13.1 Introduction

As a component of the public sector, health care looms large. All European governments provide the great bulk of health care through the public purse and in the UK this means an estimated budget of £45 billion for 1998 (or approximately 6% of GDP)[1] and employment for around one million people.

The health service in the UK has, over the past ten years, undergone something of a transformation in operation. It has witnessed the introduction of the 'internal market' and the distinction between 'purchasers' of health care, mainly in primary care, and 'providers', such as hospitals and medical specialities. Funding problems have been endemic: an ageing

Reprinted from *Journal of the Operational Research Society*, 50: 345–353, 1999, 'System Dynamics Applications to European Healthcare Issues', by B. C. Dangerfield.

population and the costs of modern health technology have served to bring into sharp focus the political issue of the extent to which general tax rates ought to be raised to finance the burgeoning health budget.

In this climate there is a pressing need for tools of assessment and evaluation for both strategic and tactical issues. Operational Research and statistical techniques have a long track record of use in health care settings, pertinent examples being in out-patient appointment systems and departmental facilities management.[2-5] Yet OR techniques, despite their track record of success in health problems, have primarily addressed tactical and operational matters. With system dynamics there exists a modelling methodology which is suited to handling strategic policy matters and it is the purpose of this paper to provide illustrations of just what can be achieved in this regard within a health care framework.

The paper is organised as follows. A review is made of possible roles which system dynamics models can take with special reference to health care matters. Following this, coverage is given to qualitative (influence diagram) approaches in three health applications: community care, short-stay psychiatric patients and the waiting list phenomenon. Finally, a more detailed account is provided on one facet of a quantitative system dynamics model in the field of epidemiology, namely the formulation of the incubation distribution within the author's model of the spread of AIDS.

What follows is not claimed to be a comprehensive review of health care modelling. For a start its geographic focus is solely the UK and Europe. However, given this context, an attempt has been made to collect all the health-related references arising in the mainstream constituency of system dynamics literature. The purpose of the paper is to review current work but also to stimulate the system dynamics community into becoming more involved in what is a topical feature of most societies, often with a large budget commitment: health care is always in the public eye.

## 13.2   Roles for system dynamics models in health care

Projects for which system dynamics is most properly utilised adopt a vista congruent with the methodology; a vista appropriate to a strategic orientation. This is synonymous with examining aggregate flows of people and resources in the region, hospital or whatever. Therefore studies which inherently involve patient flows and money flows at a strategic level of aggregation are obvious candidates for a system dynamics framework to the analysis. Three examples in this category are the studies by Wolstenholme on community care planning,[6,7] by Coyle on management of a hospital for short-term psychiatric patients[8] and by van Ackere on hospital waiting lists.[9] All are discussed in more detail below in the context of qualitative modelling. This has been done in the light of the strengths offered by all of them at the qualitative level.

There are two main purposes for developing system dynamics models in the health care context and these thoughts may go some way towards the formulation of a research agenda.

## 13.3   The model as a tool of persuasion

There is a role for model-based persuasion at the national or regional level. In a climate characterised by lack of understanding a model can be used to fill a vacuum. Scenarios generated by a model can act as a catalyst to insightful thinking. Examples might be:

(i) an input into the debate on the most appropriate interval for breast cancer screening together with the age groups to be screened.

(ii) the timing of a vaccination offensive against whooping cough, a childhood disease characterised by cycles of infection amongst those children who have missed the usual immunisation offered during their first twelve months of life or for whom the protection was not effective.

(iii) supporting a case for an enhanced or initial budget to deal with or counteract the consequences of a specific trend or likely eventuality. For instance, provision of needle exchanges to combat the spread of AIDS amongst i.v. drug users and their partners, or money to provide better sex education amongst 14–18 y olds.

An example where a fully developed system dynamics model has been used to persuade is that documented by Bronkhurst *et al.*[10] Their model addresses the supply and demand for the dental health care system in the Netherlands. Demand represents a variety of demographic, pathological, psychological, sociological and economic processes, whereas supply concerns the availability of dentists, dental hygienists and associated factors which affect their productivity. The team have been working on this study for over a decade and, for good reasons, have moved from a simple model containing just 20 state variables (levels) to one of 440 state variables.

In order to gain acceptance of the model with their clients (a committee of representatives of those groups most active in the field of dental health care) the researchers engaged in a reconstruction of the detailed model with them. This activity, which they call 'quasi' participatory model construction, took a large investment in time but had the benefit of convincing the clients that, at least partially, it was their model. In fact, little fundamental change occurred in the model as a result of this exercise, but the clients would then hopefully be less resistant to assimilation of the insights gained from the study.

### 13.3.1 The model as a frame for evaluation of tactical studies

The second main purpose for a system dynamics model would be in offering a bigger picture within which tactical initiatives could be better evaluated. It is no use spending time and money devising a new system for bed management on a geriatric ward if part of the problem is basically that patients have nowhere to go, (see the review of Wolstenholme's work below). The hospital management might feel that 'something must be done' about the problem but unless they are prepared to widen the boundary of their mental model they are merely fire-fighting: tackling the symptoms and not the cause.

OR studies at the tactical level have, in many cases, been highly successful. But what is occasionally lacking is some consideration of context. Without this, it is possible to initiate a tactical study, which apparently is a great success, only to find that in a year's time the contextual situation has changed which renders all the excellent operational research work ineffective. It is here that a system dynamics model could prove its value. Elevating the boundary of a model, to a point where it encompasses all the dynamic influences necessary to comprehend the totality, is the normal *modus operandi* of system dynamics.

There are rare instances of studies where both operational and (later) highly aggregated models are separately employed. One such instance concerns personnel planning in the Dutch health care system. The purpose of the study was to shed light on issues surrounding the future provision of rheumatologists.[11] The team employed discrete event simulation techniques to build a group decision support system at the tactical level and, once acceptance and justification at this level was achieved with the clients, then moved on to develop a system dynamics model for national planning. In other words a bottom-up approach was adopted.

It is worth noting that this is the exact opposite of what can occur when system dynamics models are deployed. Having demonstrated the benefits of policy changes at the strategic level, there is often then a need, working with the clients, to operationalise the sub-structure which would implement the chosen policy.[12] In other words a top-down approach is employed.

## 13.4   Qualitative methods

At the qualitative level system dynamics provides a focus for structuring an issue and also as a vehicle for subsequent debate. Although the first two decades of system dynamics practice saw the emergence of influence (causal-loop) diagrams, it was not until the early 1980s[13] that a case was made for employing such diagrammatic tools as a sole tool in systemic investigations. The traditional view that a system dynamics study should, *ipso facto*, lead to a formal model being simulated on a computer ignored the fact that system dynamics already possessed, in the influence diagram tool, a ready means of illustrating the often devious effects of circular causality. The modelling community needed alerting to a latent potential within their midst. Today there is less of a tendency to overlook the utility of influence diagrams.[14] Indeed, at least one book has appeared illustrating the ways in which systems thinking, using only qualitative influence diagrams, can help in structuring thinking and debate in management.[15]

### 13.4.1   Community care

Within the health sphere Wolstenholme[6,7] has demonstrated the power of qualitative modelling. His study concerned an evaluation of the potential consequences of government legislation in 1993 which caused a transfer of responsibility for community care of the elderly to local government Personal Social Services Directorates which had a cash limited budget imposed upon them. Prior to this date purchase of community care was the responsibility of the Department of Social Security. The intention behind the change was that public funds could be saved if the flow of patients into community care was slowed down.

Figure 13.1 portrays the most important message arising out of this study, although other issues arose too. The reader is referred elsewhere for these.[6] The inner (negative) feedback loop is the intended consequence: as the funds available diminish, social services will not accept any more discharges from hospital care. Previously, hospital consultants had unfettered discretion to discharge patients according to their clinical judgement.

The outer loop in figure 13.1 demonstrates an unintended consequence. Hospitals have a limit of available beds and this limit is not easily changed. With discharges limited by funding, so admissions to

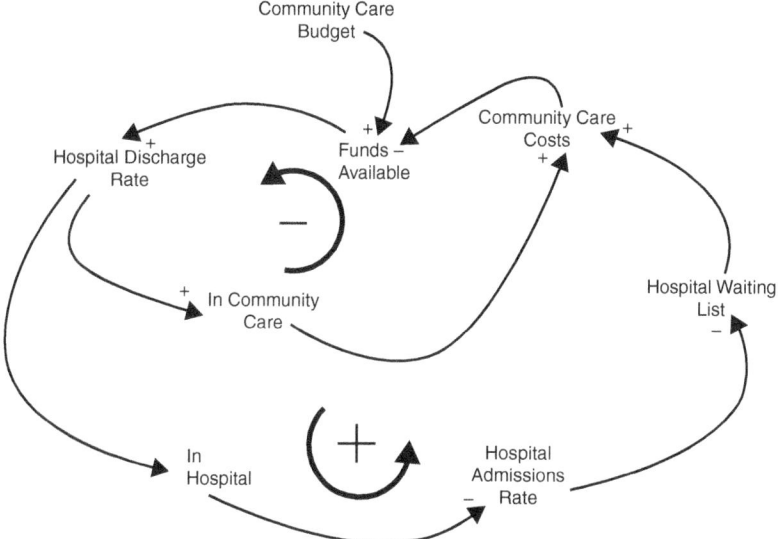

*Figure 13.1* Main feedback loops emerging from the case study in community care (due to Wolstenholme)

hospital are inevitably restricted and waiting lists of elderly people will rise. These cases waiting for admission are still in the community and are still, therefore, a drain on the community care budget. There is thus a re-inforcing effect of strain on the social services cash-limited budget and they will be even more reluctant to accept fresh discharges of the elderly from hospital. The positive (outer) loop clearly shows the key to it all: community care costs arise not just from those who have been discharged from hospital but also from those waiting to be admitted.

Further detailed enhancements of the ideas represented are described elsewhere.[16] These enhancements include the construction of a formal computer model which covers all the states present in community care (nursing homes, residential homes and domiciliary care) together with a management flight simulator, allowing the model to be used in an interactive gaming mode.

A principal outcome of Wolstenholme's study is to expose how unintended effects can cause the hospital waiting list to increase. Perhaps not surprisingly other authors have also explored the waiting list phenomenon using systems thinking ideas, although the reader should be aware that it is a well-researched issue in health care studies using other approaches.[17,18]

### 13.4.2   Short-stay psychiatric patients

An early study by Coyle[8] considered the problem of short-stay psychiatric patients. As part of the construction of his diagrammatic model he
sets out three types of influence link: a physical flow, controls applied
by system managers and, finally, behavioural responses. The latter are
behavioural forces upon which managers have only indirect control. A
prime example here, and in the context of the chosen patient grouping,
is the effect that the duration and method of treatment seems to have
on the delay before a patient recycles for further treatment and, indeed,
whether recycling takes place at all.

The influence diagram shown as Figure 13.2 is adapted from figure 13.4
from Coyle.[8] Loop 1 is the managerial loop. Here the admission rate
has, of necessity, to be reduced as the hospital nears capacity: essentially
the admission rate has to be regulated such that the hospital is accept-
ably full. Loop 2 is the patient loop: as the waiting time for admission
increases this will, in turn, increase the fraction of patients who recycle
in the system and reduce the recycling delay (not shown). Loop 2 is
positive and its activation following a lengthening of the waiting list is
an unwelcome eventuality for hospital managers.

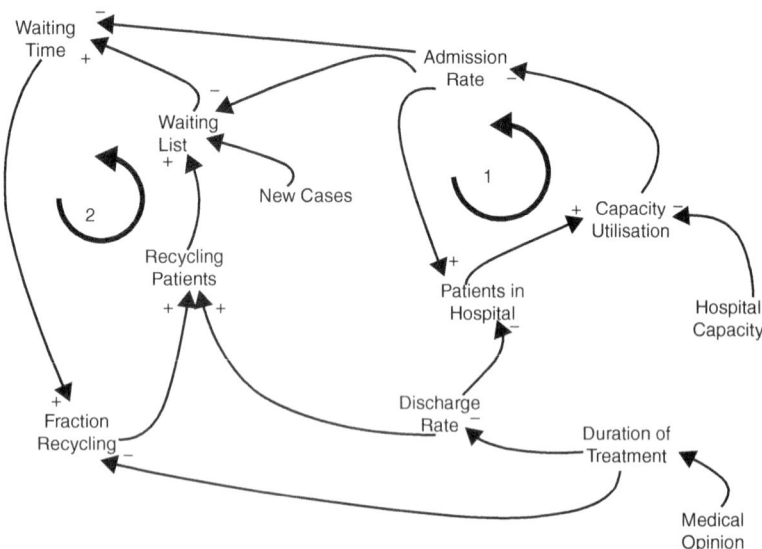

*Figure 13.2*  Influence diagram showing the two main loops involved in the
management of short-term psychiatric patients (due to Coyle)

An interesting parallel can be drawn here with Wolstenholme's model in Figure 13.1. In the former case we have a critical variable 'community care costs' which it is desirous to contain. It certainly cannot exceed the cash limited budget. This cost variable is increased by the costs of new hospital patients discharged into community care, but also, and this is unanticipated, by the extra numbers on the waiting list who cannot get into hospital.

In Coyle's model the equivalent critical variable is the 'waiting list'. It is increased by new cases but also by recycling patients. This is the unanticipated phenomenon here and it is set in train by actions of the system managers, firstly through an increase in the waiting time and, in addition, by the duration (and quality) of treatment afforded to hospital cases. For new cases, the shorter this duration is, in general, the greater the propensity for a patient to recycle. But patients admitted after a long waiting time will often be in a worse condition than had they received prompt admission and so the duration of treatment is necessarily lengthened. This amplifies the initial problem: fewer people can be admitted and the waiting time gets even longer.

The purpose of Coyle's model is nothing more than to open up a debate, at the system level, on how to better manage the situation. He suggests two improvements which are embodied in two further (negative) controlling loops—shown as loops 3 and 4 in Figure 13.3. Loop 3 reflects the notion that admissions might be governed by the waiting time, the idea behind this being that the hospital must find a bed for anyone who has waited more than an agreed period. In this eventuality, loop 1 would have to be set aside as a means of controlling admissions.

In order to be able to achieve the benefits of loop 3 the hospital would, of necessity, be required to discharge patients to make room. So we see that loop 4 would be brought into play. It is suggested that perhaps quarterly meetings might be set in train which bring together GPs, hospital doctors and administrators in an effort to decide how to balance out the effects of loops 1, 3 and 4 in Figure 13.3. Furthermore, these meetings should be furnished with regularly collected local statistics on waiting lists, eschewing national and occasional data. Unless some attempt is made to co-ordinate the actions of the main system players, the system will underperform considerably. Rarely will the systemic effects of individual interest groups be consonant with effective overall performance.

A further interesting insight which emerges from this study concerns measurement of average treatment duration (length of stay). As shown, this is influenced by medical opinion but opinion perhaps which is not

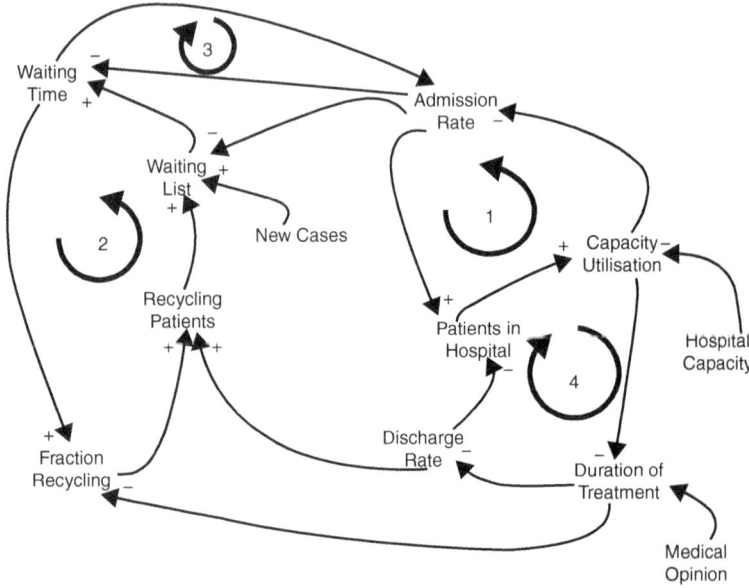

*Figure 13.3*   Enhanced influence diagram introducing two new controlling loops in the management of short-term psychiatric patients (due to Coyle)

informed by the most relevant information. Life cycle monitoring of patients is called for and this is an exceedingly difficult task to perform adequately. Doctors need to be made aware that a simple comparison of a patient's condition at two displaced points in time (admission and discharge) ignores factors like the waiting time previously suffered by that patient. An appreciation is required that a patient's condition is, only in part, determined by the way the clinician manages the treatment. System dependent influences will also be confounding the situation.

### 13.4.3   Waiting lists in the context of public and private health care

A final example of qualitative system dynamics models in health care is due to van Ackere and Smith,[9] whose work is set at the national level, is not predicated upon any particular patient group or medical condition, and explores the trade-off between NHS and private medical care.

As mentioned above, examination of the waiting list is central to this research also and it is interesting to contrast its role in each of the three studies reviewed. In Wolstenholme's analysis, he reveals the problem of an escalating waiting list which emerges as a result of the implementation of a national policy change on a totally unconnected aspect. Coyle's work positions the waiting list as a crucial variable in the model and he demonstrates, for a specific patient group, how admissions policies and treatment duration can, in fact, conspire to affect the waiting list adversely in the guise of recycling patients. Van Ackere's model, on the other hand, makes the waiting list the *raison d'être* for her study reflecting general concerns reviewed elsewhere.[19] She considers the policy issue of government directly funding initiatives to tackle lengthy waiting lists. Leakage to the private health sector, as allowed for in this model, could have been grafted onto Coyle's model too, where it would impact mainly on the variable dealing with the fraction of patients recycled.

The fundamental hypothesis in van Ackere's model is that the attractiveness of private sector health care grows as waiting lists for NHS care increase. This effect is portrayed in the influence diagram shown as Figure 13.4. To this diagram van Ackere adds in a pressure for resources loop (not shown), which represents a possible government policy response when the waiting lists become really excessive. Simulating this

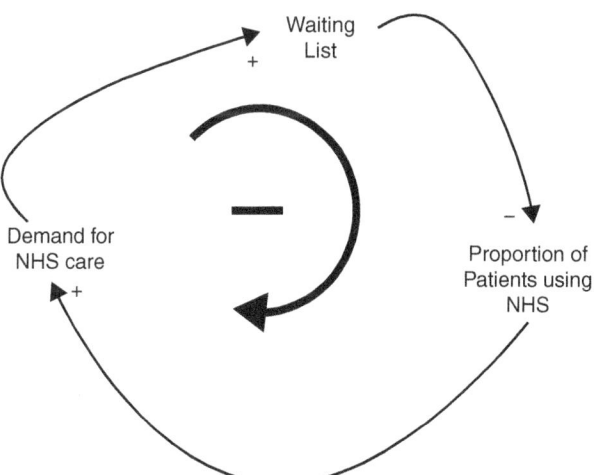

*Figure 13.4* Simplified influence diagram showing how the waiting list can regulate demand (due to van Ackere)

eventuality reveals temporary resource injections designed to reduce or clear NHS waiting lists will create the response that more people are attracted to the NHS and the problem reappears.

An influence diagram is a useful means of portraying, in broad-brush form, the major components of system influences and, by implication, the chosen model boundary. In appraising the suitability of a model it is important not to lose sight of the wood for the trees. We should firstly be concerned to assess if anything has been omitted which might crucially affect the system, rather than become bogged down with an appraisal of the veracity of what is extant, an important task though that undoubtedly is.

Suppose, for instance, we extend van Ackere's initial model to include the activities of consultants who undertake private health care work in addition to their NHS contracts. The model boundary is therefore enlarged and the resulting influence diagram may look as depicted in Figure 13.5. Including a major resource, consultants' time, within the model creates a positive loop. Now, an increase in the waiting list may be reinforced, rather than regulated, by the presence of private sector health care.

Obviously the extent to which, in reality, the additional positive loop operates is open to debate, but it serves to underline the mind-expanding aspect of model conceptualisation in applying system dynamics. Clearly

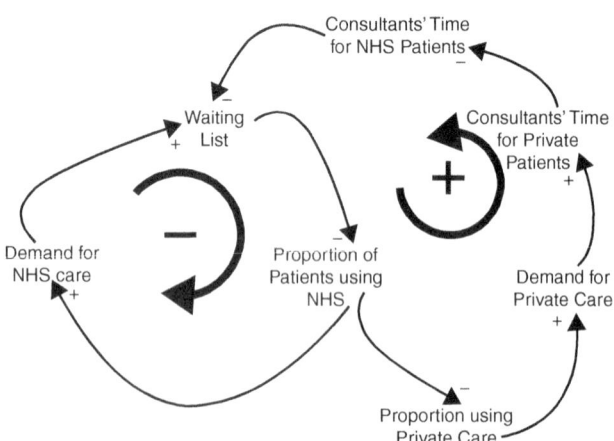

*Figure 13.5*   Enhanced influence diagram showing a wider view of the causes and effects of the waiting list phenomenon

there are consultants who work for both the NHS and private practice and, within limits, there are only so many hours in a working week for them to function effectively. Were they to devote more attention to private patients it may mean that more of their NHS duties are delegated to clinicians below the rank of consultant, which in turn may make for a higher fraction of recycling patients as alluded to by Coyle.

On the other hand, if NHS consultants were prevented from taking on private sector work the effect of the positive loop would not arise, but the alternative of private health care may not be as attractive should that sector not be able to offer sufficient consultants' time. It might exhibit the same phenomenon as evident in the NHS unless the private sector can recruit enough consultants to keep pace with demand.

There is no doubt that the activities of consultant clinicians are an important consideration at the interface between private and state sector health care. Developing influence diagrams in stages can therefore be seen as a means of propelling the qualitative strategic debate forward or, alternatively, showing up gaps in knowledge which may require further investigation (or detailed statistical analysis) to enable a formal quantitative model to be structured and parameterised.

## 13.5   Quantitative models in epidemiology

Given the mathematical principles which underly system dynamics simulations, it is hardly surprising that it is particularly appropriate for modelling the epidemiology of infectious diseases. Indeed, in systems terms, the coupled positive and negative feedback loops (with a dominance switch at a certain point in time), as they describe any infectious epidemic, are exactly equivalent to the same system structure used for modelling diffusion of a new technology or the introduction of a new product into a consumer market.

Furthermore, the presence of delay functions, so routinely used in many system dynamics models, means that the methodology can be offered as having the potential for more transparent analysis of the spread of infectious diseases characterised by long incubation periods than the corresponding mathematical methods. There is a lot of current interest in such diseases, stemming initially from analysis of the AIDS pandemic (discussed in more detail below) but, in the UK particularly, arising from the epidemic of bovine spongiform encephalopathy (BSE) in cattle and a possible consequent epidemic of new-variant Creutzfeldt–Jakob Disease (nvCJD) in humans. BSE arose, almost certainly, out of feeding ruminant-derived protein to cattle in the early

1980s, whilst nvCJD is now widely thought to have originated in the consumption of infected meat by the individuals affected. BSE has an incubation period averaging five years whilst that for nvCJD could be as long as ten years.

The developing interest in epidemiological modelling generally is well-covered in the literature within the past ten years and insofar as it applies to infectious diseases of humans.[20,21] The latter reference is a reasonably recent account of research in this field of mathematical modelling. The work associated with the author is the only item covered which uses the methodology of system dynamics, but it is interesting to note that Jacquez *et al*, researchers from mainstream epidemiology and located in North America, recently published a paper[22] where they described an AIDS-spread model formulated in STELLA. The AIDS model with which the author is associated had included all the complications in the Jacquez model some years earlier.[23] Only two other European references of applying system dynamics to AIDS modelling have been uncovered,[24,25] although its adoption for modelling infectious diseases in general was prophesied by an eminent mathematical epidemiologist in the 1970s.[26]

The author's work in AIDS modelling using system dynamics has progressed from the first phase which saw the development of a transmission model to allow better understanding of the dynamics of the epidemic and to specify data collection needs.[27] As new knowledge emerged from the worldwide research effort on AIDS, particularly of a virological and sociological nature, this was duly reflected in changes in model structure. The second phase involved fitting the model's basic structure to time-series data on reported AIDS cases, whilst the third (and current) phase concerns the costs of and consequences for resources employed in the UKs fight against AIDS.

Fitting the model to data enabled projections of future incidence to be offered and estimates made of relevant parameter values.[28,29] Moreover, fitting a system dynamics model to real-world data is one example of model optimisation, a subject which is being given increasing attention in the field.[30,31] The heuristic search employed for optimisation in the AIDS modelling work is described in detail elsewhere.[32]

Within the framework and context of this paper, it is impossible to fully describe all aspects of the system dynamics models of AIDS spread with which the author has been associated, although a number of references have been given. Rather one example has been selected where the system dynamics formulation has reaffirmed the power of the methodology to embrace real-world complications in a more transparent manner than is allowed by conventional mathematical approaches.

### 13.5.1 AIDS incubation period

The time lapse between HIV infection and subsequent diagnosis with AIDS is a crucial component of any model used in AIDS epidemiology. Estimates of its form and parameters have been offered in a number of studies. Two things are clear: the average incubation duration is of the order of ten years and this average duration has lengthened relatively recently arising from the effects of treatment now routinely offered to anyone diagnosed HIV-positive.

In a system dynamics model the use of one of the DELAY functions would be an appropriate choice for handling the incubation distribution. These functions offer a series of exponential delays from first-order upwards. They generate a family of Erlang distributions,[33] a first-order delay yielding an Erlang type 1 distribution which is equivalent to the negative exponential. Because these distributions can be represented in linked integro-differential equation form, they can overcome the problem faced by the mathematician who has to produce models involving both calendar time and biological time. When a crucial parameter of the distribution (the mean) is also varying with calendar time arising from treatment effects, mathematical models become a lot less tractable.

In earlier studies of AIDS spread, mathematicians suggested that the Weibull would be appropriate for the distribution of incubation time, possibly arising from its widespread use in survival studies. Mathematical epidemiologists need to work with the distribution's hazard function $h(x)$ which is such that $h(x)\,dx$ is the probability that an event occurs in $(x, x + dx)$ given that it has not occurred yet. In the case of the Weibull, the hazard is linearly increasing for a shape parameter $m = 2$ and totally flat for a shape parameter $m = 1$. Either of these cases makes the Weibull an easier function to handle mathematically. However, with data accumulated over the years it has become apparent that distributions of the gamma form are more appropriate since the hazard of AIDS is now known to increase but then flatten after eight years post-serocon-version.[34] An Erlang distribution is merely a gamma distribution with an integer shape coefficient and exhibits (for type 2 and above) a hazard function which increases at a decreasing rate, see Figure 13.6.

In some ways it is fortunate that the Erlang distribution has been shown to be appropriate because it is not possible to render other distributions into integro-differential equation format. If some other distribution needs to be used then the system dynamics model would have to be decomposed into, say, quarterly cohorts of infectives and the chosen distribution's density function employed to propel each cohort

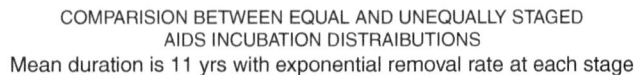

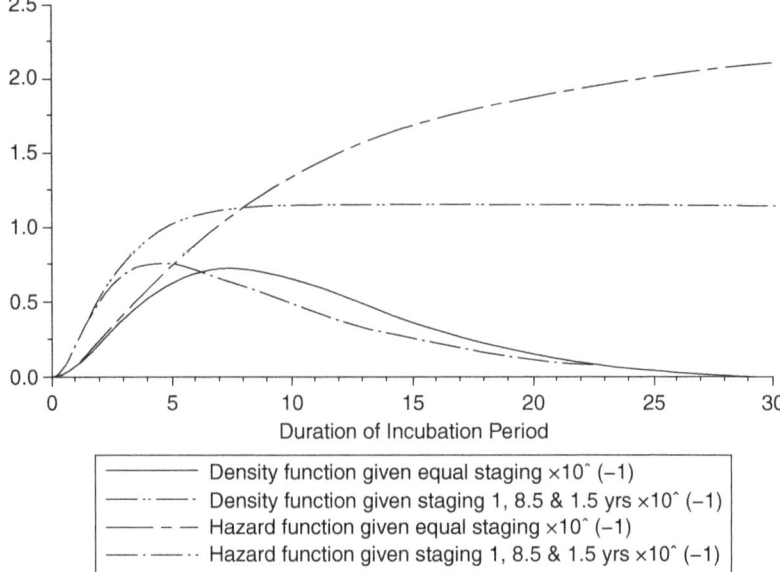

*Figure 13.6* Comparison between density and hazard functions for a three stage distribution with stages equal (Erlang type 3) and unequal: mean is 11 y in each case

through to AIDS. This would make for a much larger model and non-trivial formulation problems. These problems are not insuperable as has been demonstrated in a model used to recover the form and parameters of the AIDS incubation distribution from data of AIDS incidence in blood transfusion cases in the USA.[35]

### 13.5.2   Viral pathogenesis: two peaks in viral load

A further modelling complication arises from knowledge about the viral pathogenesis of HIV. Quite early on in AIDS research, virologists were able to confirm that, around the time of seroconversion in the host, there was a substantial peak in viræmia (measure of viral load). This fell to almost negligible amounts as the immune system responded and the patient would then exhibit an asymptomatic period of, may be, eight years or longer duration. Eventually, however, the immune system would be progressively overcome and the patient would become quite ill, with levels of viræmia increasing towards another peak consistent with a condition permitting a diagnosis of AIDS-Related Complex (ARC) and, ultimately, AIDS itself. Figure 13.7 gives a representation of this profile. Relative to the long asymptomatic period, the early and late stages are of quite short duration.

Now if this knowledge is faithfully incorporated into a model, and assuming that levels of viræmia are equivalent to levels of infectiousness, then the incubation distribution needs to be disaggregated so that the HIV-infecteds at each stage of biological time can be assigned different probabilities of transmission to a susceptible. These probabilities will reflect the high-low-high profile of assumed infectiousness.

This means that use of a DELAY3 function is not possible assuming as it does that each cascaded component first order delay is of equal duration. Of necessity, therefore, a series of level divided by life formulations were adopted with the life representing the average sojourn time in the previous stage. Figure 13.6 shows the resulting density and hazard functions for this incubation distribution which assumes exponential removal from each stage and average residence times of 1, 8.5 and 1.5 years respectively. It is interesting to note that with this unequal staging the hazard of AIDS flattens off at around eight years post-seroconversion in line with the results of recent research referred to above.[34]

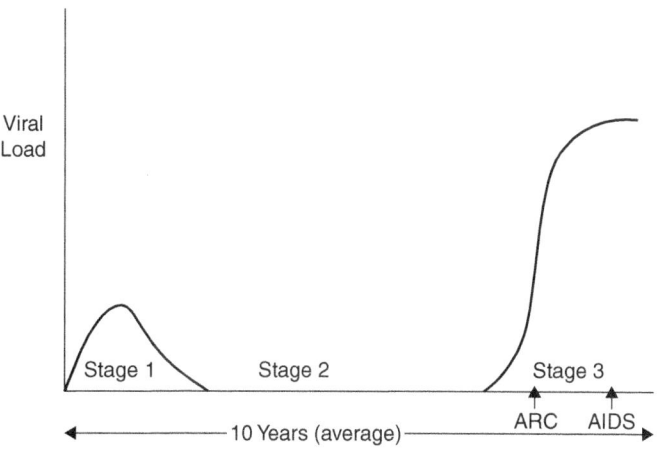

*Figure 13.7*  Two peaks of viral load during the AIDS incubation period

### 13.5.3   Treatment effects

Finally, consideration is given to treatment effects on the incubation distribution. There have been phases of pre-AIDS treatment offered to seropositives. The early zidovudine therapy, despite initial optimism, was eventually shown not to be effective in delaying progression to AIDS. Primary prophylaxis for *Pneumocystis carinii pneumonia,* however, has met with considerable success in reducing the extent of this particular condition as an AIDS-defining illness. The most spectacular success, however, has occurred since mid-1996 with the introduction of triple-combination antiretroviral therapy, a trio of retrovirals which the patient is required to take on a regular basis and indefinitely. Provided the regime is faithfully adhered to, this seems to virtually clear virions (infectious virus particles) from plasma; indeed, the reduction occurs within the first two weeks following the initiation of treatment.

In order to re-structure that part of the model handling the incubation period, it was necessary to introduce the state of being on treatment following initial infection. Figure 13.8 shows the revised arrangement. A fit of this model to AIDS incidence in Greater London, using data to end-1995, reveals that the average sojourn time in the state 'on-treatment' is 11.1 y as opposed to 9.4 y in the asymptomatic phase for those not on treatment.

Notice that both routes involve cases passing through the final phase of HIV pathogenesis. This, much shorter, period is characterised by patients having rapidly increasing viral loads and equally rapidly declining CD4 lymphocyte counts (a measure of the health of the immune

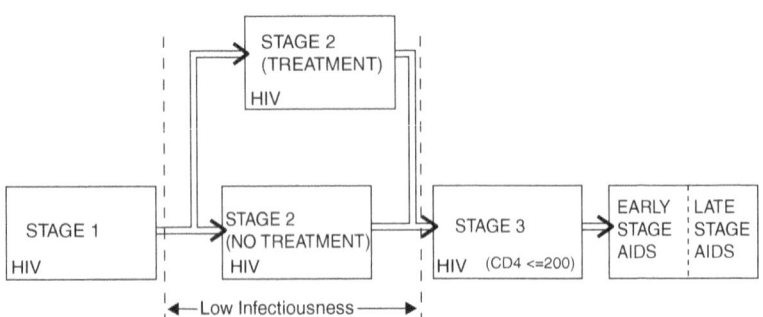

*Figure 13.8* Schematic flow diagram showing staging of the incubation distribution and the incorporation of pre-AIDS treatment

system). If HIV in an infected person eventually overcomes the ability of the combination of antiretrovirals to clear it from the host's system then the outcome, in that person passing through the final stage (advanced HIV disease), will be no different to an untreated patient passing through the same stage. It is just that an untreated case will reach this stage more quickly.

## 13.6 Conclusions

This overview of system dynamics based modelling of health care issues has shown that, at least on this side of the Atlantic, the literature is not vast, certainly as compared to studies modelling organisational and managerial issues. However, new work is in the process of publication[36] and it is proposed to have a special issue of the *System Dynamics Review* devoted to health and health care dynamics appearing within the next twelve months. This future contribution to the literature will, however, embrace a geographical perspective much wider than just Europe, the focus of the current paper.

There is a clear potential for system dynamics to be employed in support of health care policy and, as the millenium approaches, health care is a subject not far off the top of the European political agenda. Moreover, readers from the health care (rather than modelling) community will have learned of the variety of issues which are capable of being addressed. If some fresh coalitions can now be forged between health care professionals and the system dynamics community, then this paper will have proved its worth.

## Acknowledgement

The research reported on HIV and AIDS has profited from insights gained in participating in the EU Concerted Action 'Multinational Scenario Analysis Concerning Epidemiological, Social and Economic Impacts of HIV/AIDS on Society' (BMH1-CT-941723).

## References

1. Office of Health Economics (1997). *Compendium of Health Statistics,* 10th Edn, (Table 2.1: 1998 estimates), Office of Health Economics, UK.
2. Bailey NTJ (1952). A study of queues and appointment systems in hospital out-patient departments. *JR Statist Soc* **14**: 185–199.
3. Brahimi M and Worthington DJ (1991). Queueing models for out-patient appointment systems—a case study. *J Opl Res Soc* **42**: 746–766.

4. Moores B and Sissouras AA (1975). The optimum number of beds in an emergency care unit. *Omega* **4**: 59–65.
5. Harris RA (1986). Hospital bed requirements planning. *Eur J Opl Res* **25**: 121–126.
6. Wolstenholme EF (1993). A case study in community care using systems thinking. *J Opl Res Soc* **44**: 925–934.
7. Wolstenholme EF (1995). Organisational re-engineering using systems modelling: rediscovering the physics of the health service. *IMA J Med Biol* **12**: 283–296.
8. Coyle RG (1984). A systems approach to the management of a hospital for short-term patients. *Socio-Econ Plan Sci* **18**: 219–226.
9. van Ackere A and Smith P (1997). Making static models dynamic: the case of the National Health Service. Technical Paper 9, Centre for Health Economics, University of York, UK.
10. Bronkhorst EM, Wiersma T and Truin GJ (1990). Using complex system dynamics models: an example concerning the Dutch dental health care system. In: Andersen DF, Richardson GP and Sterman JD (eds). *Proceedings of the 1990 International System Dynamics Conference—Volume 1.* System Dynamics Society: Cambridge, Massachusetts, pp 155–163.
11. Postma MJ, Smits MT, Terpstra S and Takkenberg CATh (1992). Personnel planning in health care: an example in the field of rheumatology. In: Vennix JAM, Faber J, Scheper WJ and Takkenberg CATh (eds). *Proceedings of the 1992 International System Dynamics Conference.* System Dynamics Society: Cambridge, Massachusetts, pp 515–524.
12. Morecroft JDW (1984). Strategy support models. *Strut Mgmt J* **5**: 215–229.
13. Wolstenholme EF and Coyle RG (1983). The development of system dynamics as a methodology for system description and qualitative analysis. *J Opl Res Soc* **34**: 569–581.
14. Wolstenholme EF (1999). Qualitative versus quantitative modelling: the evolving balance. *J Opl Res Soc* **50**: 422–429.
15. Balle M (1994). *Managing with Systems Thinking.* McGraw-Hill: Maidenhead.
16. Wolstenholme EF and Crook J (1997). A management flight simulator for community care. In: Cropper S and Forte P (eds). *Enhancing Health Services Management: the Role of Decision Support Systems.* Open University Press: Buckingham, 217–244.
17. Ellis BW (1991). Factors influencing waiting lists and cost of surgical treatment. *Annals of the Roy Coll of Surg of Engl* **73**: 74–77.
18. Worthington DJ (1987). Queueing models for hospital waiting lists. *J Opl Res Soc* **38**: 413–422.
19. Frankel S and West R (eds) (1993). *Rationing and Rationality in the NHS: the Persistence of Waiting Lists.* Macmillan: Basingstoke.
20. Anderson RM and May RM (1991). *Infectious Diseases of Humans.* OUP: Oxford.
21. Isham V and Medley G (eds). *Models for Infectious Human Diseases: Their Structure and Relation to Data.* CUP: Cambridge.
22. Jacquez JA, Koopman JS, Simon CP and Longini IM (1994). Role of the primary infection in epidemics of HIV infection in gay cohorts. *J AIDS* **7**: 1169–1184.
23. Dangerfield BC and Roberts CA (1989). A role for system dynamics in modelling the spread of AIDS. *Trans Inst Msmt Ctrl* **11**: 187–195.

24. Dijkgraaf MGW, van Griensven GJP and Geurts JLA (1988). Interactive simulation as a tool in the decision-making process to prevent HIV incidence among homosexual men in the Netherlands: a proposal. In: Jager JC and Ruitenberg EJ (eds). *Statistical Analysis and Mathematical Modelling of AIDS.* OUP: Oxford, pp 112–122.
25. Lagergren M (1992). A family of models for analysis and evaluation of strategies for preventing AIDS. In: Jager JC and Ruitenberg EJ (eds). *AIDS Impact Assessment: Modelling and Scenario Analysis.* Elsevier: Amsterdam, 117–145.
26. Bailey NTJ (1977). *Mathematics, Statistics and Systems for Health.* Wiley: Chichester.
27. Roberts CA and Dangerfield BC (1990). Modelling the epidemiological consequences of HIV infection and AIDS: a contribution from operational research. *J Opl Res Soc* **41**: 273–289.
28. Dangerfield BC and Roberts CA (1994). Fitting a model of the spread of AIDS to data from five European countries. In: Dangerfield BC and Roberts CA (eds). *O.R. Work in HIV/AIDS*, 2nd edn. Operational Research Society: Birmingham, 7–13.
29. Dangerfield BC and Roberts CA (1996). Relating a transmission model of AIDS spread to data: some international comparisons. In: Isham V and Medley G (eds). *Models for Infectious Human Diseases: Their Structure and Relation to Data.* CUP: Cambridge, 473–476.
30. Wolstenholme EF (1990). *System Enquiry.* Wiley: Chichester.
31. Coyle RG (1996). *System Dynamics Modelling: a Practical Approach.* Chapman & Hall: London.
32. Dangerfield BC and Roberts CA (1996). An overview of strategy and tactics in system dynamics optimisation. *J Opl Res Soc* **47**: 405–423.
33. Hamilton MS (1980). Estimating lengths and orders of delays in system dynamics models. In: Randers J (ed). *Elements of the System Dynamics Method.* MIT Press: Cambridge, Massachusetts, pp 162–183.
34. De Angelis D, Gilks WR and Day NE (1998). Bayesian projection of the acquired immune deficiency syndrome epidemic. *Appl Statist* **47**: 447–448.
35. Roberts CA and Dangerfield BC (1991). System dynamics and statistics: recovering the AIDS incubation time distribution from right-censored data. In: Saeed K, Andersen D and Machuca J (eds). *Proceedings of the 1991 International System Dynamics Conference.* System Dynamics Society: Cambridge, Massachusetts, pp 504–514.
36. Taylor KS and Lane DC (1998). Simulation applied to health services: some experiences so far and opportunities for applying the system dynamics approach. *J of Health Services Res and Policy* **3**: 226–232.

# 14
## One Hundred Years of Operational Research in Health—UK 1948–2048*

G. Royston
*Department of Health, UK*

*This paper presents a personal view, drawing on some 30 years of working in this area, of past, present and future contributions of operational research (OR) in health in the UK. It considers developments in health and care and in OR contributions to these at local and national level since the creation of the National Health Service 60 years ago; likely future developments in health and care; and associated priorities for preparing now for OR to make a major impact on health and care in the next 40 years. The aim is to stimulate reflective thinking and promote anticipatory action among health OR practitioners of the future.*

### 14.1 Introduction

Readers may already have—correctly—judged the title of this paper as hubristic. Or perhaps—charitably—as an outline model. Either way, a more realistic heading would be 'Some brief observations on the development of health and care and on some associated contributions of Operational Research (OR) in the UK (mostly England) from 1948 to the present day (although much of the past is skipped over) and the outlook from now until 2048 (but it's necessarily pretty vague about the future)'.

This is a practitioner's perspective, a selective view not a systematic review, but it does draw on around 30 years of personal experience in the area, on literature in various shades of white and grey, and on views

---

*This paper is based on a keynote talk given by the author at the OR 50 Conference in York in September 2008.

recently sought from a range of prominent UK health analysts (see Acknowledgements).

It is driven by concern with three questions about the past, present and future impact of OR in health:

*Yesterday* – What have been areas of health or health care where OR analysts have had a significant impact? How have we achieved this?

*Tomorrow* – What are coming challenges for health or health care where OR analysts should seek to make a significant impact? How could we best contribute?

*Today* – What lessons should OR analysts working in health take from the past to help make a bigger impact in the future? What should we do today to prepare the path?

The paper falls into three main sections corresponding to the above three issues.

## 14.2 Yesterday: 1948–2007—birth and development

### 14.2.1 Development of the National Health Service

1948 was a seminal year for health care in the UK; it saw, on 5 July, the birth of the National Health Service (NHS).

Since then, activity, workforce and expenditure in the NHS have increased dramatically. For example when the NHS started there were about three million inpatient cases a year, now there are annually about 14 million episodes of such treatment. (This is not—see later—because people have become less healthy!) Six decades ago there were around 5000 hospital consultants working in the NHS, now there are some 35 000. NHS spend has risen from £447 *million* in 1949/1950 to £114 *billion* in 2007/2008; even after adjusting for inflation that is still about a tenfold increase.

There have been many changes in the organization, delivery and funding of care; even just in the last decade—new structures such as Strategic Health Authorities, Primary Care Trusts and Foundation Trusts; new agencies such as the National Institute of Health and Clinical Excellence, the National Patient Safety Agency and the Health Protection Agency; new care pathways and settings such as NHS Treatment Centres, NHS Walk-in Centres and NHS Direct; new transactional processes such as payment by results and health and social service resource pooling; and new modes of patient engagement such as choose and book and expert patient programmes.

Although many challenges remain, for example in variations and inequalities in treatment and access with people in lower socioeconomic groups at a particular disadvantage—for instance hip replacements are lower among these groups despite higher need (Dixon *et al*, 2004), many aspects of NHS care have hugely improved. A wide range of procedures that were unknown when the NHS began, such as joint replacement, organ transplants or computerized tomography, are now common-place—for example there have now been well over 5000 UK heart transplants. More conditions can be treated effectively, and more people can be operated on safely—especially the very young and the very old: the record age for a UK hip replacement currently stands at 101! And access is faster—for example, a decade ago it was not uncommon to wait for over 12 months for an operation in hospital or over 12 hours for treatment in an Accident & Emergency (A&E) department, now hardly any people wait over 6 months for an operation or over 4 hours for treatment in A&E (Department of Health, 2007).

There have also been some significant measures to improve public health; in particular there has been a dramatic decline in cigarette smoking—from 65% in 1948 to 23% today for men (Office of National Statistics, 2006)—and vaccination has almost eliminated several child-hood infectious diseases such as polio—the last natural case of which in the UK was in 1982. Although inequalities in health status persist with sizeable variations across the country—notably the north-south divide—and between different population groups—poverty and poor health tend to go together (Marmot and Wilkinson, 2005)—there have been major improvements in the health of the UK population as a whole. Mortality rates from infections, from cancers and from circulatory and respiratory illnesses have fallen considerably, for example in the last decade there has been an 18% decline in mortality rates from cancer and a 44% decline from heart disease and stroke (Department of Health, 2008a) and life expectancy has risen from 65 for men and 70 for women in 1948 to 77 for men and 82 for women today (Office of National Statistics, 2008)—an unprecedented rise of around 2 years every decade.

Figure 14.1 shows some milestones in health care and its management 1948–2007, drawn from a comprehensive source (www.nhshistory.net and www.nhs.uk, accessed July 2008). The top section relates to organi-zational and service areas, the middle section to public health and the bottom section to surgical and other clinical milestones.

### 14.2.2   Development of OR

1948 was also a seminal year for OR, as in April the fore-runner of the OR Society, the OR Club, was inaugurated. Since then OR in the UK has developed with an expansion of UK OR into nationalized industries, civil

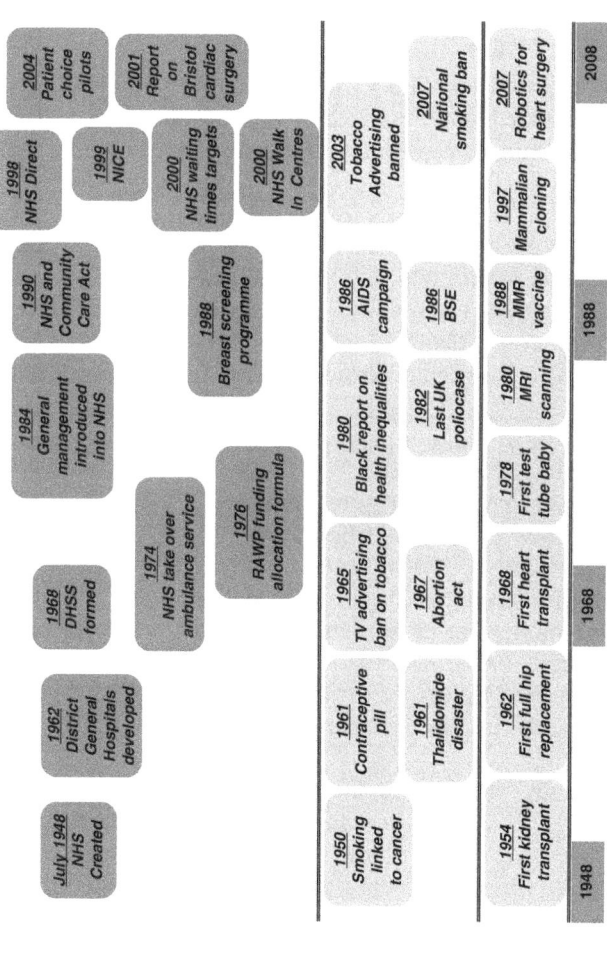

*Figure 14.1* Some UK milestones in health care and health care management 1948–2007

government and the corporate sector, with OR Society membership rising from about 100 in 1955 to 3000 in 1975, a strength that it has maintained since. Since 1975, UK OR has adapted to a changing economy, shrinking in industry but expanding in the service and public sectors—for example, civil Government Operational Research Service staff numbers have risen from about 100 to around 400 over the last two decades (Turner, 2007).

### 14.2.3   OR in health

Explicit UK health OR applications date from the 1950s, with two papers by Norman Bailey being notable early examples (Bailey, 1952a, 1957). There have of course been some significant contributions from UK OR in health over the intervening years.

As noted in the introduction, this paper does not attempt to provide a comprehensive overview, for which readers should refer to other publications (eg Brandeau *et al*, 2004), but the sustained contribution of UK OR in health since the 1950s can be illustrated by taking one small but important area—waiting in outpatient and accident and emergency departments. OR work in this field has been published in every decade, for example

- a study of queues and appointment systems in hospital outpatient departments (Bailey, 1952b);
- design of an appointment system (Jackson, 1964);
- an application of queuing theory to a congestion problem in an outpatient clinic (Keller and Laughhunn, 1973);
- investigating outpatient departments (O'Keefe, 1985);
- queueing models for outpatient appointment systems (Brahimi and Worthington, 1991);

and continues to this day for example

- using queuing theory to analyze the Government's 4h completion time target in A&E (Mayhew and Smith, 2008).

More generally UK health OR practitioners have contributed on a world-wide front, with contributions evident from landmark compilations such as:

- *'Patients, Hospitals and Operational Research'* (Luck *et al*, 1971).
- *'Operational Research Applied to Health Services'* (Boldy, 1981).
- *'Enhancing Health Services Management'* (Cropper and Forte, 1997).
- *'Health Operations Management'* (Vissers and Beech, 2005).

UK OR practitioners are active contributors to the European Working Group on OR Applied to Health Services, established in 1975, as a glance at their published proceedings for example *Operational Research for Health Policy: Making Better Decisions* (Brailsford and Harper, 2007a) or website (www.management.soton.ac.uk/ORAHS) will show.

### 14.2.4  National and local UK applications of health OR

There are wide ranging recent national UK applications of health OR. For instance, examples from the work of OR analysts in the Department of Health include:

Policies and strategies

- setting targets for waiting times;
- creation of NHS Direct;
- strategic framework for supporting self care;
- blood safety and vCJD risk strategy;
- chlamydia screening strategy;
- preparedness for a flu pandemic;
- vaccination programmes;
- emergency incident counter measures.

Implementation and delivery

- peak load capacity planning (hospitals, walk-in centres, NHS Direct);
- reducing waiting times (elective care and emergency care);
- improving stroke services (ASSET analytical toolkit);
- introducing total booking systems;
- estimating future demand for and supply of doctors;
- NHS pay deal costing;
- expenditure forecasts for services (children, mental health, patient safety etc).

Monitoring and evaluation

- developing performance ratings for hospitals;
- evaluating hospital improvement programmes;
- assessing the Expert Patient programme;
- understanding NHS financial deficits.

Recent, mainly local, UK applications are exemplified in special issues of both *JORS* (Davies and Bensley, 2005; Brailsford and Harper, 2007b) and of *Health Care Management Science* (Baker *et al*, 2008) such as (respectively):

- forecasting costs of long-term care at local authority level;
- assessing demand for nurses in intensive care units;
- planning regional oral surgery services across London;
- operational design of a NHS walk-in centre;
- design of an integrated musculoskeletal service;
- involving public and patients in improving services.

- cancer staging and treatment;
- ambulance dispatch and location;
- scheduling surgical clinics;
- blood supply;
- monitoring surgical infection;
- hospital and community care for older patients.

- gauging future demand for social care for older people;
- strategic commissioning for example, for diabetes care;
- managing care of elderly patients in emergency departments;
- optimizing inventory of hospital supplies;
- evaluating outcomes in patient-centred health monitoring services.

UK health OR has a good reputation among its professional peers with a recent Research Council Review (EPSRC, 2004) concluding: *'Unique selling points of significant strength within the British OR agenda are soft OR and applications in healthcare'*.

### 14.2.5   Some concerns about health OR in the UK

The number and organization of health OR analysts in England have had their ups and downs. There are some structural strengths: a number of university groups have been working in health OR/management science (MS) since the 1950s and 1960s and of course play a key role both in research and in training in health OR; several management consultancies have people with skills in health OR/MS (although often not explicitly badged as such); the Department of Health (DHSS as was) set up an OR group in the early 1970s (it had around 15 health OR analysts in the 1980s, and it now has more than twice that number, working with economists and statisticians in multidisciplinary teams embedded in policy and delivery commands); a national clinical OR unit was established in 1983 and recently celebrated its 25th anniversary; an OR Society UK health and care study/special interest group has been in existence since at least the early 1970s and there have been more specialized such groups from time to time such as the AIDS study group (Dangerfield and Roberts, 1994) and there are new health modelling networks notably MASHnet.

However, there are also some structural weaknesses. Only a few of the national health agencies—notably NICE and the NHS Blood and Transplant Service—appear to make extensive use of the services of OR analysts. In the 1980's, as many as nine of the then 14 NHS Regional Health Authorities (RHAs) had OR groups; but the RHAs were abolished in the mid-1990s and their modern counterparts (Strategic Health Authorities) do not have a recognizable OR function. And at hospital level the situation is neatly summarized in an editorial in the BMJ (Buhaug, 2002), which concluded that *'Compared with many other organisations, hospitals have been slow in adopting operational research as a means to improve their performance. Applications are scattered and the results not always used, even if they are relevant and reliable. The implication is that, so far, hospitals have largely failed to use one of the most potent methods currently available for improving the performance of complex organisations'*.

A specific concern is that UK health OR does not appear very visible to managers or clinicians. (This is not, of course, a problem unique to health; many fashionable approaches in management generally—for example lean thinking, theory of constraints, system and process mapping—do not recognize their debt to OR. What they often do, however, is get straight to the point; which may hold a lesson for us.) Although there has been a large growth in publication of papers on health topics in OR/MS journals such as *JORS* or *Health Care Management Science*, there is vastly lower exposure of OR in the literature that managers and clinicians read such as the *Health Service Journal* or the *British Medical Journal (BMJ)*. (Some of the recent few exceptions include *BMJ* papers by Young *et al*, 2004 and by Gallivan *et al*, 2002.) Table 14.1 illustrates this using a search (Google Scholar, July 2008) on *operational* (or *operations*) *research*. (An analogous search on *management science* scored somewhat higher in 'all publications' but no better—indeed worse—in '*BMJ* group publications only'.)

Other disciplines have higher visibility, for example while in 2007 OR got just nine mentions in *British Medical Journal* group publications, a similar search (Google Scholar, July 2008) for mentions of health services research, economics, and statistics found respectively, 105, 183 and 966 mentions. Other disciplines do however share concerns about perceptions and use—a paper on the impact of health services research (Dash *et al*, 2003) noted that *'researchers are frustrated that their work is not used more widely'* while *'NHS managers see little of relevance in the research available to them and see health services research as poor value for money'* and *'policy makers are concerned about the timeliness of research!'*

*Table 14.1*   OR publications in health have grown considerably, but not in the literature that managers and clinicians read

| Year [Search using Google Scholar, July 2008] | In all publications [Search on operational (or operations) research + health] | In BMJ group publications only [Search on operational (or operations) research] |
|---|---|---|
| 1975 | 114 | 0 |
| 1985 | 126 | 0 |
| 1990 | 146 | 0 |
| 2000 | 681 | 4 |
| 2005 | 1260 | 5 |
| 2007 | 1720 | 9 |

There are also—probably related—issues about lack of implementation of modelling work. For example, a 1981 review (Wilson, 1981) of 200 simulation projects in health care found that only 16 reported successful implementation and a 2003 review (Fone *et al*, 2003) found 182 papers on simulation in health (1980–1999), but so few reported on implementation (in itself a revealing and worrying sign!) that their *'value could not be assessed'*.

The requirements for user engagement and support and for effective implementation of OR in health, as in other areas, form a long chain. OR needs to be: available, visible, relevant, affordable, comprehensible, convincing, practical and timely. A weak link anywhere can lead to failure of the whole implementation chain.

If OR is to be part of 'mainstreaming' modelling and evidence-based management in health care then working harder on implementation must be a key requirement. Recent papers (Harper and Pitt, 2004; Proudlove *et al*, 2007; Eldabi *et al*, 2007) have considered these issues further.

However, important as this is, it is not the whole picture. Although one indicator of success in health OR is the implementation of published OR work, another is the impact of OR on health service developments, much of which may never reach the academic journals. OR *has* made some major contributions to UK health care since 1948. For example, the selection of milestones in UK health care policy and management was influenced by personal knowledge that many had benefited from, and in some instances were driven by, work of OR analysts. See Figure 14.2. (These examples relate to the largely organizational and service changes shown in the top section of Figure 14.1, there would be further examples in the public health or clinical arenas.)

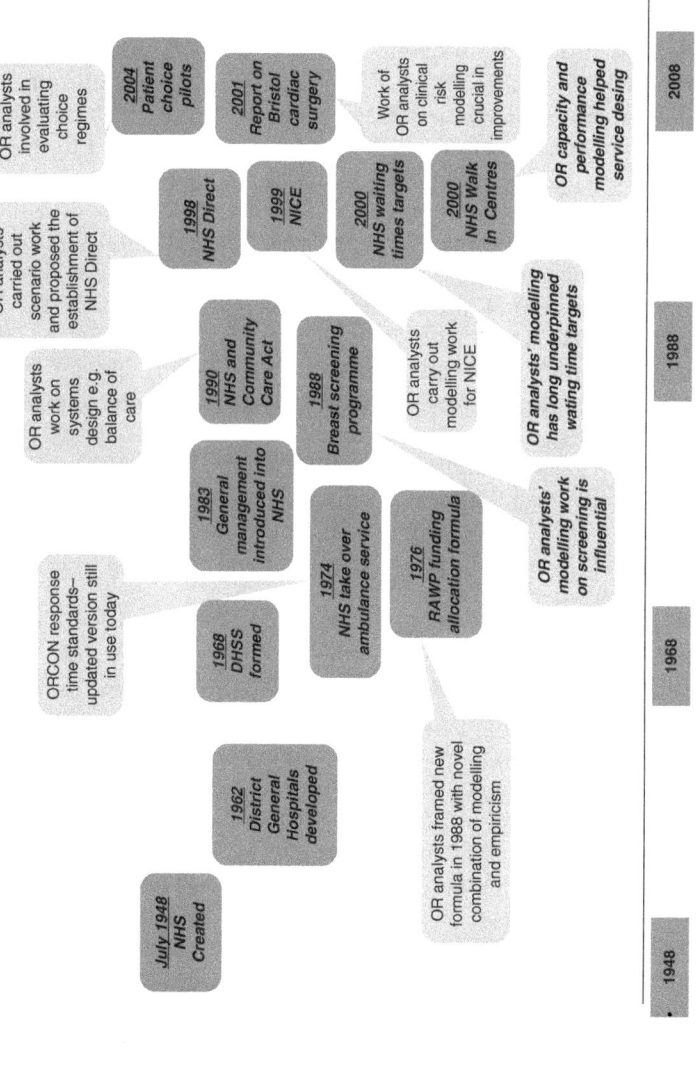

*Figure 14.2* OR has contributed to a number of milestones in UK health care policy and management

## 14.3   Tomorrow: 2009–2048—challenges of change

### 14.3.1   Health and care futures

Health care is likely to continue as a major UK growth area. Medical advance continues to expand what is possible, an ageing population increases what is required, and a more prosperous society increases what is affordable and expected. The proportion of UK GDP spent on health care has risen steadily from about 3% when the NHS was created, to about 6% in 1990, and to about 9% today. For most countries health care spend increases with (indeed faster than) GDP and, barring perhaps long lasting economic recession, UK health spend is expected to rise to around 12% of GDP by 2020 (Wanless, 2002).

Moves will continue to reform the NHS to strengthen patient choice and voice, to encourage more diverse, efficient and innovative provision, and to ensure a high quality, safe, fair and value for money health system. Recent White Papers–*Choosing Health* (Department of Health, 2004), *Our Health, Our Care, Our Say* (Department of Health, 2006), *High Quality Care for All* (Department of Health, 2008b)—map out the envisaged path. We should for example see more care safely and cost-effectively delivered 'upstream'—in or closer to home, aided by advances in telecare and a better integration between health and social care, better chronic disease management—with more risk profiling for anticipatory, preventative, care and more support for 'expert patients' and self care, and a greater emphasis on promoting health and well-being across the whole population.

There remains much scope for improvement in efficiency and productivity; for example, in surgery there are still huge national and local variations in rates of procedures, in length of hospital stay and in use of day cases, which is a focus of the work of the NHS Institute for Innovation and Improvement (www.productivity.nhs.uk, accessed October 2008). Improvements will need to be supported by modern—indeed transformational—information and communication technology and by good financial management, both of which have proved a challenge for the NHS. And changes in patterns and pathways of care can involve major system redesign and will not be problem free—for example, on the one hand specialization requiring more tertiary care and on the other a shift to providing more care in a community setting puts strain on the traditional model of care centred on the acute district general hospital.

Looking further ahead, there are many possible health futures. (This is now quite an active research area eg Government Office for Science,

2007; Kendall, 2001; Dargie, 2000; Royston, 1998; Harrison and Prentice, 1996; Nicholson *et al*, 1995). We need to watch for trends—the 'white sails' we can clearly see coming over the horizon—eg an ageing population, obesity, telecare—and also be ready for discontinuities or 'black swans' (Taleb, 2007)—think of AIDS, viagra or avian flu. Our uncertainty about the future increases with time, although the track record in health crystal ball gazing is sometimes not too bad. For example, 10 years ago a 'technology calendar' (Smith, 1998) suggested that full medical records would be stored on smart cards by 2000 (achieved in 2002 in Taiwan) and that the whole human DNA base sequence would be determined by 2005 (achieved earlier—in 2001!). And there are growing signs in favour of the BT calendar predictions of robots being used extensively for routine hospital tasks (2012). Time will tell in regard to other forecasts such as an individual's genome forming part of their medical record (2015) and extension of average human life span to 100 years (2020).

So we need to scan a range of major external factors influencing health and care: demography, lifestyle, public expectations, technology, information, workforce and global factors (economic, environmental, epidemiological etc). These will affect both the demand and supply of health care as the simple system view in Figure 14.3 illustrates.

Their combined effect on the health and care system is likely to be profound. For example:

- An ageing baby boomer population will put increasing pressure on both demand for and supply of NHS care.
- Our lifestyles are offsetting the gains made in public and personal health care.
- The public will expect far more from public services, tailored to their individual needs.
- Medical technology – genomics, robotics, nanotechnology – holds out the prospect of a new era in personalized care.
- Information will become ever more accessible, with ubiquitous connectivity.
- The workforce is likely to become increasingly diverse, and depend more on women and immigrants.
- Neither health not health care will escape impact from turbulence in the global economy.
- Climate change is expected to increasingly impact on health and care.
- Security of world food and water supply is also emerging as a key issue.

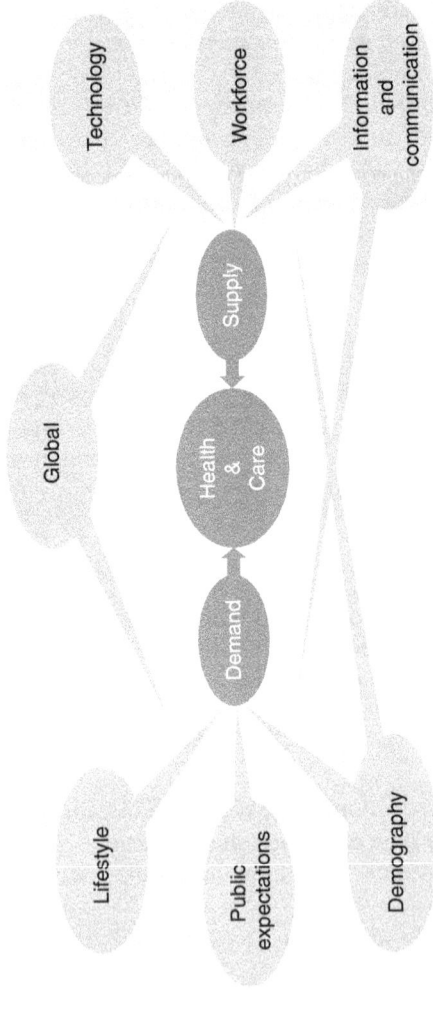

*Figure 14.3*  A simple system view of external factors impacting on future health and care

- Emerging diseases can come from abroad, but the UK is also highly susceptible to home grown diseases.

### 14.3.2   OR to meet the challenges of change—back to the future?

How can OR meet these future challenges of change? We do have a significant contribution to offer on many specific challenges, drawing on a range of methodologies (See Table 14.2 for an illustration).

Some more detailed thoughts on this were given in an earlier paper (Royston, 1998) and will not be repeated here; this paper will focus on some of the more generic factors that are likely to determine an effective response.

We should remember some wise words from the past—looking back again to our starting year of 1948 when Blackett's war-time principles for effective OR were published (Blackett, 1948) which included:

*Collaborative* 'An OR section should be an integral part of a command and should work in the closest collaboration with the various departments at the command'

*Grounded* 'All members of an OR section should spend part of their time at operational stations in close touch with the personnel actually on the job'

*Table 14.2*   OR can help meet the future challenges of change in health and health care

| Challenges (eg) | OR contribution (eg) | Analytical tools (eg) |
| --- | --- | --- |
| *Aging 'Baby Boomer' Generation:* Ensuring provision for older people is more joined up—hospital and social care working together | Helping understand and manage the interface between health and social care | 'Whole system' mapping and modelling |
| *Rising expectations:* Changing services to allow care to be tailored to individual needs—more choice and responsiveness | Helping to set, implement and monitor standards for customer service | Waiting time and capacity modelling |
| *Changing lifestyles:* Promoting healthy lifestyles—shifting care upstream from treatment to prevention | Exploring balance and timing of impact for treatment and prevention options | System dynamics modelling, decision analysis |

*Pathfinding* 'An OR section which contents itself with the routine production of statistical reports and narratives will be of very limited value'

and also looking back to 1974, with Tomlinson's principles (Tomlinson, 1998) including:

*Catholic* – OR should not be hide bound in techniques but should be wide ranging in the problems it addresses and the methods it is prepared to use

*Balanced* – the programme of the OR group should be balanced between long and short projects, tactical and strategic work and between old and new work

*Catalytic* – OR is an agent of change within the organisation

It's *not* rocket science—technical advance is important but this is not one of the greatest challenges facing OR in health—or indeed many other areas. In health, as elsewhere, we are generally dealing with complex adaptive human activity systems (Plsek and Greenhalgh, 2001) where 'softer' contextual factors play a crucial role. Table 14.3, from an *INFORMS* survey of OR practice (Abdel-Malek *et al*, 1999) makes the point clear.

There are many possible futures for health OR depending on its impact and its visibility (See Figure 14.4).

*Table 14.3*   Factors affecting success or failure of OR applications

| Factors supporting project success | Factors leading to project failure |
|---|---|
| • Management support/involvement | • Too technical/abstract approach |
| • User support/involvement | • Customer not sold on the project |
| • Understanding true spirit of request | • Poor problem definition/planning |
| • Verifiable and useful results | • Lack of professional competence |
| • Economic benefits/business results | • Over budget, not timely |
| • Timeliness | • Poor communication |
| • Well organized/communicated/ presented | |

*Source*: Abdel-Malek *et al*, 1999.

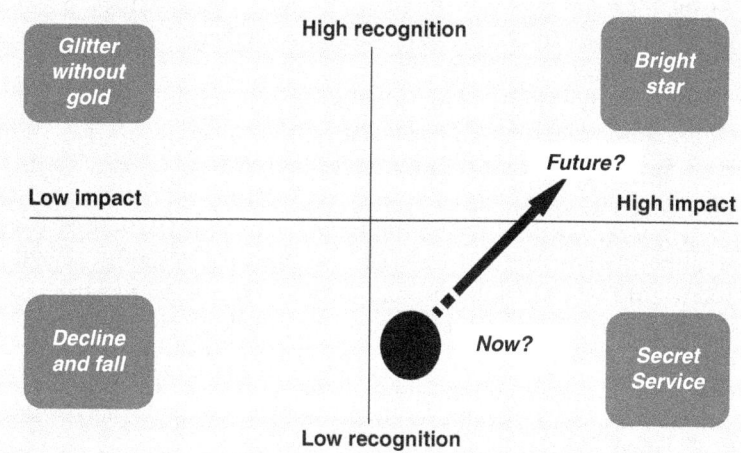

*Figure 14.4* There are many possible futures for health OR—depending on its impact and its visibility

If we want to move successfully forward we will need to prepare the path, which is the subject of the next section.

## 14.4   Today: 2008—preparing the path

What do we need to do *today* so health OR is equipped to make a strong contribution *tomorrow*? Five suggested key areas for investment are:

- *Focusing on the key emerging challenges* for the UK health and care system at local, national and global levels—so we work on the right problems at the right time.
- *Equipping ourselves to help tackle them*—so we have the right skills, positioned in the right places.
- *Gaining powerful champions* who own the problems—so we work with the right people who can embed solutions in their organization.
- *Making success plainly visible* to and recognized by our stakeholders— so we get the right messages to the right audiences.
- *Understanding better what we need to do*—this list is not exhaustive!

What might be important ingredients for these?

Firstly, for *focusing on key emerging challenges* we can draw on our spectrum of methods to scan for and to assess challenges on the horizon (See Figure 14.5.)

We can also develop and use intelligence such as the emerging 'hot' topics for health managers. For instance, the categories for the Health Service Journal awards are quite revealing—this year features: managing long-term care, data-driven service improvement, world class commissioning, patient safety, improving care with technology, social marketing, patient centred care, clinical service redesign, innovation, workforce development, improving patient access and reducing health inequalities. In many of these areas policy makers, managers and clinicians will be looking for (to borrow a term from the former NHS Modernisation Agency) 'high impact changes'—how they can get the best out of necessarily limited resources—surely a challenge with which OR can assist.

Secondly, to *equip ourselves to help tackle the key challenges* we need to build strength in key problem solving areas. Surveys across OR generally (Fildes and Ranyard, 1997), across civil government (Turner, 2007) and of OR analysts in the Department of Health have all shown that it is not the more esoteric methods but the fundamental skills—notably problem structuring, spreadsheet modelling, basic statistics, consulting, project management and presentation—that are generally most valued and used by OR practitioners. Those involved in training health OR practitioners of the future are, of course, key to building firm

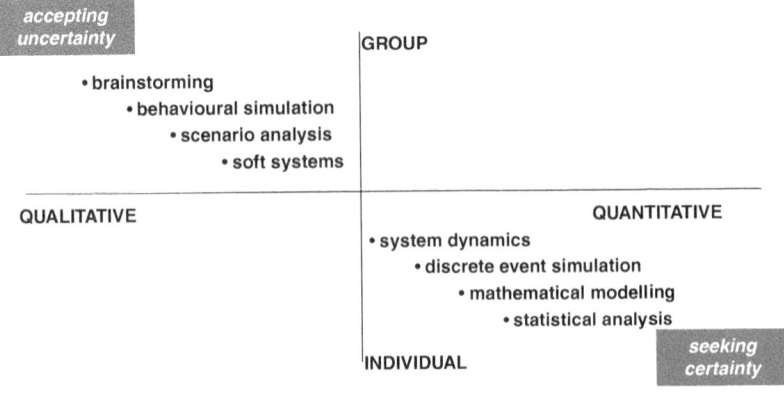

*Figure 14.5* We have a spectrum of methods to scan for and assess challenges on the horizon

foundations in these areas. (Like the construction and use of a samurai sword, developing fundamental OR skills, honed to a fine edge and wielded effectively, is not as simple as it might appear; perhaps we need more of an apprenticeship type approach to training OR analysts.)

Equally we need to develop a networked presence at all levels to allow both tactical and strategic work. To (just once) go back to before 1948—in fact, back over 300 years—we might note the words of Sir Isaac Newton:

> *'If, instead of sending the observations of able seamen to able mathematicians on land, the land would send able mathematicians to sea, it would signify much more to the improvement of navigation and to the safety of men's lives and estates on that element.'* (Sir Isaac Newton, 1694).

In a more devolved and decentralized care system effective OR requires a strong grass root presence in patient groups, primary care trusts, and hospitals, as well as in regional strategic health authorities, in national bodies (NICE, NHS Institute for Health Care Improvement, National Patient Safety Agency, Health Care Commission etc) and in the Department of Health. There should also be an opportunity for OR to play a role in the work of the recently announced Academic Health Science Centres (Department of Health, 2008b).

Thirdly, to *gain powerful champions* we need to focus on adding crucial value for key problem owners, which entails understanding their business, appreciating their environment, focusing on their needs and offering something distinctive. For the latter, we need to remember that OR analysts' value to any business depends on being able to work closely with clients to help with a number of thorny problem areas such as understanding how systems work, clarifying complex and messy problems, coping with uncertainty and risk, and creating, developing and appraising options for change. In short, remembering the characterization of OR as the *science of better*. (Which suggests incidentally that we might usefully develop closer links with the current movement on '*the science of improvement*' in health! (Berwick, 2008).)

Fourthly, to *make our success plainly visible* and recognized by our stakeholders we need to publish and publicize in the right way to the right audiences in the right places. Recalling Table 14.1, it is noteworthy that Bailey's 1952 paper on queues and hospital appointment systems in the analytical literature was accompanied by a publication in the medical literature (Welch and Bailey, 1952). Such parallel or twin publication could usefully be much more common practice. (A paper covering some

334

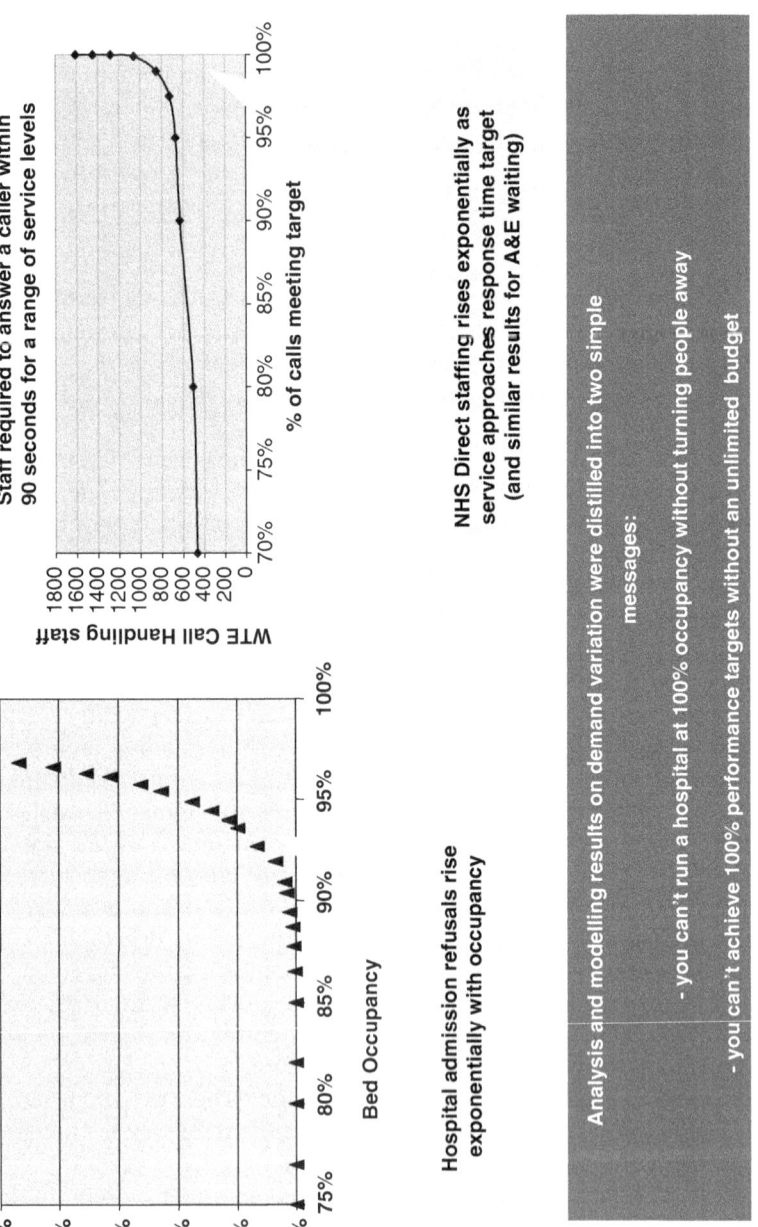

*Figure 14.6* Look for simple but powerful generic messages that will stick in users' minds

of the arguments of this paper is also to be published in the *British Journal of Health Care Management* (Pitt *et al*, 2009).)

Of course making success visible requires successes, so as noted earlier, health OR needs to pay much more attention to implementation issues—both in designing projects for impact and evaluating the impact they actually have. Again a twin approach–seeking to get more published OR work showing a follow through to implementation and to get more OR work focused on tackling policy and delivery 'milestone' issues, and publishing it—should bear fruit.

There is a second aspect to being 'plainly' visible—clarity and force of message. So a further contribution to both visibility and implementation would come from OR looking for simple but powerful *generic messages* that will stick in users' minds. (There is also incidentally a—related—case for making more use of *generic models* see, eg, Fletcher *et al*, 2007). For example, modelling results by Department of Health and other analysts on peak load demand variation (Department of Health, 1997; Bagust *et al*, 1999; Royston *et al*, 2003) had greater impact with policy makers when they were distilled into two simple messages 'you can't run a hospital at 100% occupancy without turning people away' and 'you can't achieve 100% performance targets without an unlimited budget' (See Figure 14.6). Similar views about the importance of simple models and clear messages have been expressed in the context of using OR modelling to improve patient flows (Proudlove *et al*, 2007). We should search for other types of simple but powerful generic messages from OR/MS for health care policy and management, such as on feedback effects in systems (see, eg, Taylor and Dangerfield, 2005).

Fifthly, to *understand better what we need to do*, we must continuously seek to learn about how to enhance our impact. For example, it is hoped that MASHnet will be able to follow up its pilot survey on the three questions posed at the beginning of this paper.

## 14.5  Conclusion

This paper has considered developments in health and care and in OR contributions to these at local and national level since the creation of the NHS 60 years ago; likely future developments in health and care; and associated priorities for preparing now for OR to make a major impact on health and care in the next 40 years.

What that future holds must fall somewhere between a 'white sails' and a 'black swan' dominated scenario (a grey mist?). But the future is not to be discovered but to be created. The foundations for successful

OR and MS in health in the coming decades will be formed through historical reflection, innovative thinking and anticipatory action among today's—and tomorrow's—practitioners.

## Acknowledgements

The preparation of this paper was informed by some very helpful responses from MASHnet members and others on the 'three questions' posed at the start. My thanks are due to Adrian Bagust, Roger Beech, Tom Bowen, Sally Brailsford, Chris Brasted, Alan Brennan, Steve Burnell, Thierry Chaussaulet, Ruth Davies, David Fone, Nick Gaunt, Jeff Griffiths, David Meechan, Peter Millard, Mike Pidd, Martin Pitt, Martin Utley, David Worthington, and particularly to David Bensley for coordinating the MASHnet pilot survey. Responsibility for the use or misuse of their contributions is, of course, mine.

## References

Abdel-Malek L, Wolf C, Johnson F and Spencer III T (1999). OR practice: Survey results and reflections of practising INFORMS members. *J Opl Res Soc* **50**: 994–1003.

Bagust A, Place M and Posnett JW (1999). Dynamics of bed use in accommodating emergency admissions: Stochastic simulation model. *BMJ* **319**: 155–158.

Bailey NT (1952). Operational research in medicine. *OR Qtly* **3**: 24–30.

Bailey NT (1952). A study of queues and appointment systems in hospital outpatient departments. *J R Stat Soc* **14**: 185–199.

Bailey NT (1957). Operational research in hospital planning and design. *OR Qtly* **8**: 149–157.

Baker RD, Chaussalet TJ and Utley M (eds) (2008). Special issue on IMA conference. *Health Care Mngt Sci* **11**: 87–213.

Berwick D (2008). The science of improvement. *JAMA* **299**: 1182–1184.

Blackett PMS (1948). Scientists at the operational level. *Advancement of Science* **5**: 30–38.

Boldy D (ed) (1981). *Operational Research Applied to Health Services*. Palgrave Macmillan: Basingstoke, UK.

Brahimi M and Worthington DJ (1991). Queueing models for outpatient appointment systems—A case study. *J Opl Res Soc* **42**: 733–746.

Brailsford S and Harper P (2007). Operational research for health policy: Making better decisions. *Proceedings of the 31st Annual Conference of the European Working Group of Operational Research Applied to Health Services*. Peter Lang: Oxford, UK.

Brailsford S and Harper P (eds) (2007b). Special issue: Operational research in health. *J Opl Res Soc* **58**: 141–270.

Brandeau ML, Sainfort F and Pierskalla WP (eds) (2004). *Operations Research and Health Care: A Handbook of Methods and Applications*. Springer: Berlin.

Buhaug T (2002). Long waiting lists in hospitals. *BMJ* **324**: 252–253.

Cropper S and Forte P (eds) (1997). *Enhancing Health Services Management*. Open University Press: Buckingham.

Dangerfield B and Roberts C (eds) (1994). *OR Work in HIV/AIDS*, 2nd edn. OR Society: Birmingham.

Dargie C (2000). Policy futures for UK health. *Foresight* **2**(4): 401–409.

Dash P, Gowman N and Traynor M (2003). Increasing the impact of health services research. *BMJ* **327**: 1339–1341.

Davies R and Bensley D (eds) (2005). Special issue: Meeting health challenges with OR. *J Opl Res Soc* **56**: 123–233.

Department of Health (1997). The use of simulation modelling to examine the local balance between elective and non-elective demands for treatment. Appendix by Economics and Operational Research Division. *DH Executive Letter EL(97) 42*.

Department of Health (2004). *Choosing Health*. Department of Health: London.

Department of Health (2006). *Our Health, Our Care, Our Say*. Department of Health: London.

Department of Health (2007). *Annual Report*. Department of Health: London.

Department of Health (2008a). *Mortality Target Monitoring Update for 2007*. Department of Health: London.

Department of Health (2008b). *High Quality Care for All*. Department of Health: London.

Dixon T, Shaw M, Ebrahim S and Dieppe P (2004). Trends in hip and knee joint replacement: Socioeconomic inequalities and projections of need. *Ann Rheum Dis* **63**: 825–830.

Eldabi T, Paul RJ and Young T (2007). Simulation modelling in healthcare: Reviewing legacies and investigating futures. *J Opl Res Soc* **58**: 262–270.

EPSRC, ESRC and OR Society (2004). *Review of Research Status of OR in the UK*.

Fildes R and Ranyard J (1997). Success and survival of operational research groups–A review. *J Opl Res Soc* **48**: 336–360.

Fletcher A, Halsall D, Huxham S and Worthington D (2007). The DH accident and emergency department model: A national generic model used locally. *J Opl Res Soc* **58**: 1554–1562.

Fone D, Hollinghurst S, Temple M, Round A, Lester N, Weightman A, Roberts K, Coyle E, Bevan G and Palmer S (2003). Systematic review of the use and value of computer simulation modelling in population health and health care delivery. *J Public Health Med* **25**: 325–335.

Gallivan S, Utley M, Treasure T and Valencia O (2002). Booked inpatient admission and hospital capacity: Mathematical modelling study. *BMJ* **324**: 280–282.

Government Office for Science (2007). *Tacking Obesities: Future Choices*. Department of Innovation Universities and Skills, London.

Harper PR and Pitt MA (2004). On the challenges of healthcare modelling and a proposed project life cycle for successful implementation. *J Opl Res Soc* **55**: 657–661.

Harrison A and Prentice S (1996). *Acute Futures*. Kings Fund: London.

Jackson RRP (1964). Design of an appointments system. *OR Qtly* **15**:219–224.

Keller TF and Laughhunn. An application of queuing theory to a congestion problem in an outpatient clinic. *Decision Sci* **4**: 379–394.

Kendall L (2001). *The Future Patient*. Institute for Public Policy Research, London.

Luck GM, Luckman J, Smith BW and Stringer J (1971). *Patients, Hospitals, and Operational Research*. Tavistock: London.

Marmot M and Wilkinson RG (eds) (2005). *Social Determinants of Health*. 2nd edn. Oxford University Press: Oxford.

Mayhew L and Smith D (2008). Using queuing theory to analyse the Government's 4h completion time target in accident and emergency departments. *Health Care Mngt Sci* **11**: 11–21.

Nicholson D, Hadridge P and Royston G (1995). Some practical hints for newcomers to health futures. *Futures* **27**(9/10): 1059–1065.

Office for National Statistics (2006). *General Household Survey*. Office for National Statistics: London.

Office for National Statistics (2008). *Interim Life Tables 2005–2007*. Office for National Statistics: London.

O'Keefe RM (1985). Investigating outpatient departments: Implementable policies and qualitative approaches. *J Opl Res Soc* **36**: 705–712.

Pitt M, Bensley S, Royston G and Stein K (2009). The potential for operational research. *Br J Health Care Mngt* **15**: 346–351.

Plsek PE and Greenhalgh T (2001). The challenge of complexity in health care. *BMJ* **323**: 625–628.

Proudlove NC, Black S and Fletcher A (2007). OR and the challenge to improve the NHS: Modelling for insight and improvement in in-patient flows. *J Opl Res Soc* **58**: 145–158.

Royston G (1998). Shifting the balance of health care into the 21st century. *European J Opl Res* **105**: 267–276.

Royston G, Halsall J, Halsall D and Braithwaite C (2003). Operational research for informed innovation: NHS Direct as a case study in the design, implementation and evaluation of a new public service. *J Opl Res Soc* **54**: 1022–1028.

Smith R (ed) (1998). Imagining futures for the NHS. *BMJ* **317**: 3–4.

Taleb NN (2007). *The Black Swan*. Allen Lane: London.

Taylor K and Dangerfield B (2005). Modelling the feedback effects of reconfiguring health services. *J Opl Res Soc* **56**: 659–675.

Tomlinson R (1998). The six principles for effective OR—Their relevance in the 90s (from Presidential Address to OR Society in 1974). *J Opl Res Soc* **49**: 403–407.

Turner H (2007). Government operational research service: Civil OR in UK central government. *J Opl Res Soc* **58**: 1–15.

Vissers J and Beech R (eds) (2005). *Health Operations Management*. Routledge: London.

Welch JD and Bailey NT (1952). Appointment systems in hospital outpatient departments. *Lancet* **1**: 1105–1108.

Wanless D (2002). *Securing Our Future Health: Taking A Long-Term View*. HM Treasury: London.

Wilson JCT (1981). Implementation of computer simulation projects in health care. *J Opl Res Soc* **32**: 825–832.

Young T, Brailsford S, Connell C, Davies R, Harper P and Klein JH (2004). Using industrial processes to improve patient care. *BMJ* **328**: 162–164.

# Index

Printed and bound by CPI Group (UK) Ltd, Croydon, CR0 4YY